Data Mining
A TUTORIAL-BASED PRIMER

Richard J. Roiger
Minnesota State University, Mankato

Michael W. Geatz
Information Acumen Corporation

Addison
Wesley

Boston San Francisco New York
London Toronto Sydney Tokyo Singapore Madrid
Mexico City Munich Paris Cape Town Hong Kong Montreal

Senior Acquisitions Editor	Maite Suarez-Rivas
Executive Editor	Susan Hartman Sullivan
Executive Marketing Manager	Michael Hirsch
Associate Managing Editor	Patty Mahtani
Production Supervisor	Marilyn Lloyd
Project Management	Keith Henry/Dartmouth Publishing, Inc.
Composition and Art	Dartmouth Publishing, Inc.
Text Design	Dartmouth Publishing, Inc.
Cover Design	Joyce Cosentino Wells
Design Manager	Gina Hagen Kolenda
Prepress and Manufacturing	Caroline Fell

Access the latest information about Addison-Wesley titles from our World Wide Web site: http://www.aw.com/cs

Library of Congress Cataloging-in-Publication Data

Roiger, Richard
    Data mining : a tutorial-based primer / Richard J. Roiger, Michael W. Geatz.
      p. cm.
    Includes bibliographical references and index.
    ISBN 0-201-74128-8
      1. Data mining. I. Geatz, Michael. II. Title.

QA76.9.D343 R65 2003
006.3—dc21   2002026262

 **Preface**

Data mining is the process of finding useful patterns in data. The objective of data mining is to use discovered patterns to help explain current behavior or to predict future outcomes. Several aspects of the data mining process can be studied. These include:

- Data gathering and storage

- Data selection and preparation

- Model building and testing

- Interpreting and validating results

- Model application

A single book cannot concentrate on all areas of the data mining process. Although we furnish some detail about all aspects of data mining and knowledge discovery, our primary focus is centered on *model building and testing*, as well as on *interpreting and validating results*.

To help you better understand the data mining process, we provide a Microsoft Excel-based data mining tool that enables you to experimentally build and test data mining models. The Intelligent Data Analyzer (iDA), a product of Information Acumen Corporation, provides support for the business or technical analyst by offering a visual learning environment, an integrated tool set, and data mining process support. Although we recommend the provided software, you may choose to supplement this software or use an alternative software package. The parts of the text directly tied to the accompanying software are Chapters 4, 9, and Section 10 of Chapter 5.

Objectives

We wrote the text to facilitate the following student learning goals:

- Understand what data mining is and how data mining can be employed to solve real problems.

- Recognize whether a data mining solution is a feasible alternative for a specific problem.

- Step through the knowledge discovery process and write a report about the results of a data mining session.

- Apply basic statistical and nonstatistical techniques to evaluate the results of a data mining session.

- Recognize several data mining strategies and know when each strategy is appropriate.

- Develop a comprehensive understanding of how several data mining techniques build models to solve problems.

- Develop a general awareness about the structure of a data warehouse and how a data warehouse can be used to enhance business opportunities.

- Understand what on-line analytical processing (OLAP) is and how it can be applied to analyze data.

- Know that expert systems represent general models that emulate human actions.

- Know how to use a goal tree to help design a rule-based system.

- Recognize that intelligent agents are computer programs able to assist us with everyday tasks.

- Understand the types of problems that can be solved by combining an expert systems problem-solving approach and a data mining strategy.

- Know how to apply the software that accompanies this text to solve real problems.

Intended Audience

We developed most of the material for this book while teaching a one-semester introductory data mining course open to undergraduate students majoring or minoring in business or computer science. Our course also includes a unit on rule-based expert systems and intelligent agents. In writing this text, we directed our attention toward three groups of individuals:

- **Educators** who wish to teach a unit, workshop, or entire course on data mining and intelligent systems.

- **Students** who want to learn about data mining and desire hands-on experience with a data mining tool.

- **Business professionals** who need to understand how data mining and intelligent systems can be applied to help solve their business problems.

Chapter Features

We take the approach that model building is both an art and a science best understood from the perspective of learning by doing. Our view is supported by several features found within the pages of the text. The following is a partial list of these features.

- **Simple, detailed examples.** We remove much of the mystery surrounding data mining by presenting simple, detailed examples of how the various data mining techniques build their models. Because of its tutorial nature, the text is appropriate as a self-study guide as well as a college-level textbook for a course about data mining and knowledge discovery.

- **Overall tutorial style.** Selected sections in Chapters 4, 5, 6, 7, 9, and 10 offer easy to follow, step-by-step tutorials for performing data analysis.

- **Data mining sessions.** Data mining sessions allow students to work through the steps of the data mining process with the provided software. Each session is specially highlighted for easy differentiation from regular text.

- **Datasets for data mining.** A variety of datasets from business, medicine, and science are ready for data mining.

- **Aside boxes.** Aside boxes introduce the datasets for data mining and emphasize important information.

- **Web sites for data mining.** Links to several Web sites containing interesting datasets are provided.

- **Data analysis tools.** Several useful data analysis tools found within Excel are illustrated. These tools include Excel's *LINEST function* for performing linear regression analysis and *pivot tables* for summarizing and analyzing data.

- **Key term definitions.** Each chapter introduces several key terms. A list of definitions for these terms is provided at the end of each chapter.

- **End-of-chapter exercises.** The end-of-chapter exercises reinforce the techniques and concepts found within each chapter. The exercises are grouped into one of three categories—review questions, data mining questions, and computational questions. Exercises appropriate for a laboratory setting are starred.

  - *Review questions* ask basic questions about the concepts and content found within each chapter. The questions are designed to help determine if the reader understands the major points conveyed in each chapter.
  - *Data mining questions* require the reader to use one or several data mining tools to perform data mining sessions.
  - *Computational questions* have a mathematical flavor in that they require the reader to perform one or several calculations. Many of the computational questions are appropriate for challenging the more advanced student.

Chapter Content

The ordering of the chapters and the division of the book into separate parts is based on several years of experience in teaching courses on data mining and expert systems. *Part I introduces material that is fundamental to understanding the data mining process.* The presentation is informal and easy to follow. Basic data mining concepts, strategies, and techniques are introduced. Students learn about the types of problems that can be solved with data mining and become proficient with the software that accompanies the text. Several real-world examples of successful data mining applications are described.

Once the basic concepts are understood, *Part II formalizes data mining problem-solving by introducing the knowledge discovery in databases (KDD) process model.* The KDD process model is the application of the scientific method to data mining. The fact that data preprocessing is fundamental to successful data mining is emphasized. Special attention is placed on the role of the data warehouse and on data mining evaluation techniques.

Part III details several advanced data mining methods. Topics of current interest such as neural network learning, time-series analysis, logistic regression, and Web-based data mining are described. A tutorial on using the iDA neural network software is provided.

Although data mining is an appropriate solution method for many applications, there are times when this approach is not feasible. Fortunately, when data mining is not a viable choice, other options for creating useful decision-making models may be available. *Part IV examines rule-based systems and intelligent agents as alternative methods for building models to aid in the decision-making process.* Particular attention is directed toward combining these techniques with data mining to solve complex problems.

A brief description of the contents found within each chapter of the text follows.

Part I: Data Mining Fundamentals

- **Chapter 1** offers an overview of all aspects of the data mining process. Special emphasis is placed on helping the student determine when data mining is an appropriate problem-solving strategy.

- **Chapter 2** presents a synopsis of several common data mining strategies and techniques. Basic methods for evaluating the outcome of a data mining session are described.

- **Chapter 3** details a decision tree algorithm, the *apriori* algorithm for producing association rules, the K-Means algorithm for unsupervised clustering, and two genetic learning techniques. Tools are provided to help determine which data mining techniques should be used to solve specific problems.

- **Chapter 4** presents a tutorial introduction to the iDA software suite of data mining tools. A general methodology for performing supervised learning and unsupervised clustering is described.

Part II: Tools for Knowledge Discovery

- **Chapter 5** introduces the KDD process model as a formal methodology for solving problems with data mining. A simplified adaptation of this model is used to solve two data mining problems.

- **Chapter 6** offers a gentle introduction to data warehouse design and OLAP. A tutorial on using Excel pivot tables for data analysis is included.

- **Chapter 7** describes formal statistical and nonstatistical methods for evaluating the outcome of a data mining session. Instructions for using Excel to compute attribute correlations and display scatterplot diagrams are provided.

Part III: Advanced Data Mining Techniques

- **Chapter 8** presents two popular neural network models. A detailed explanation of neural network training is offered for the more technically inclined reader.

- **Chapter 9** offers a tutorial on applying the iDA neural network building tools to solve data mining problems. A method for using supervised learning to evaluate the results of an unsupervised neural network clustering is described.

- **Chapter 10** details several statistical techniques, including linear and logistic regression, Bayes classifier, and three unsupervised data mining methods. Instructions for using Excel's LINEST function to perform linear regression are provided.

- **Chapter 11** introduces techniques for performing time-series analysis, Web-based mining, and textual data mining. Bagging and boosting are described as methods for improving model performance.

Part IV: Intelligent Systems

The chapters of Part IV as well as appendices C, D and E are stored as Adobe PDF files on the CD that accompanies the text. To read these files you will need to have Adobe Acrobat Reader installed on you computer. To download a free copy of Adobe Acrobat Reader, visit the Web site *www.adobe.com*.

- **Chapter 12** provides an introduction to artificial intelligence and rule-based systems. A general methodology for using goal trees to build rule-based systems is described.

- **Chapter 13** reveals sources of uncertainty in rule-based systems. Fuzzy logic and Bayesian reasoning are described as methods for reasoning about uncertain information.

- **Chapter 14** introduces intelligent agents as computer programs able to assist us with everyday tasks. A model for combining intelligent agents, data mining, and expert systems to solve difficult problems is described.

Text Supplements

Each copy of this book comes with the iDA software suite of data mining tools as well as several datasets ready for data mining. Additional supplements are designed specifically for the course instructor. The following is a brief description of these supplements.

The iDA Software Package

Experiential learning is required to develop the skills required of a data mining expert. The iDA software is designed to give students this needed hands-on experience with the data mining process. The iDA software is used in several chapters to illustrate many important data mining concepts. Chapters 4, 5, 7, 9, 10, 11, and 13 have several end-of-chapter exercises designed for the iDA software.

iDA consists of a preprocessor, a report generator, and three data mining tools—ESX for supervised learning and unsupervised clustering, a neural network tool for creating supervised backpropagation models and unsupervised self-organizing maps, and a production rule generator. As iDA is an Excel add-on, the user interface is Microsoft Excel. We chose iDA because of its flexibility and ease of use.

The iDA Dataset Package

Several datasets are included with the iDA software. The datasets come from three general application areas—business, medicine and health, and science. All datasets are in Excel format and are ready to use.

Datasets can be described along several dimensions, including the number of data instances; the number of attributes; the amount of missing or noisy data; whether data attributes are clearly defined; whether the data is categorical, numeric, or a combination of both data types; whether well-defined classes exist in the data; whether a time element is implicit in the data; whether the input attributes can differentiate between known classes contained in the data; and whether input attributes are correlated. As these factors affect the way data mining is performed, the iDA datasets were chosen to provide variety among these dimensions. The datasets also serve several general purposes. Specifically, the datasets

- Provide the beginning student with experimental data to experience the data mining process without requiring the student to deal with data preprocessing issues.

- Show the wide range of problem areas and problem types appropriate for data mining solution.

- Explain data mining outcomes.

- Illustrate the knowledge discovery process.

- Recognize that experimentation with several data mining techniques may be necessary to create a best model for a specific dataset.

The following is a short description of the datasets that are part of the iDA software package. The description includes a short statement about one or more characteristics of each dataset.

Business Applications

The Credit Card Promotion Dataset. This is a hypothetical dataset containing information about credit card holders who have accepted or rejected various promotional offerings. The dataset is used to illustrate many of the data mining techniques discussed in the text.

The Credit Card Screening Dataset. This file contains data about individuals who have applied for a credit card. The output attribute indicates whether each individual's credit card application was accepted or rejected. The input attributes have been changed to meaningless symbols to protect confidentiality of the data.

The Deer Hunters Dataset. This dataset holds information about deer hunters who are either willing or unwilling to spend more for their next hunting trip. Several irrelevant input attributes are present in the data.

The Stock Index Dataset. The data is a time-series representation of average weekly closing prices for the Nasdaq and the Dow Jones Industrial Average.

Medicine and Health

The Cardiology Patient Dataset. This dataset holds medical information about two groups of individuals. Members of the first group have suffered one or more heart attacks. Members of the second group have not experienced a heart attack. The dataset contains a nice mix of categorical and numeric attributes.

The Spine Clinic Dataset. This dataset contains medical information about individuals who have had lower back surgery. Some of these folks have returned to work while others have not. A clear definition of the mean of each attribute is not given. The dataset contains both numeric and categorical data.

Science

The Gamma Ray Burst Dataset. This dataset contains recorded information about individual gamma-ray bursts. Gamma ray bursts are brief gamma ray flashes whose origins are outside our solar system. The bursts were observed by the Burst And Transient Source Experiment (BATSE) aboard NASA's Compton Gamma Ray Observatory between April 1991 and March 1993. Although astronomers agree that classes of gamma ray bursts exists, they do not agree on a specific class structure.

The Landsat Image Dataset. The dataset contains pixels representing a digitized satellite image of a portion of the earth's surface. Each instance has been classified into one of 15 categories. Because of the large number of individual classes, classification accuracy is affected by model-specific parameter settings.

The Temperature Dataset. This dataset offers the normal average January minimum temperature in degrees Fahrenheit for 56 U.S. cities. City latitude and longitude values are also provided. All attributes are numeric.

Miscellaneous

The Titanic Dataset. This dataset contains 2201 instances. Each instance describes attributes of an individual passenger or crew member aboard the Titanic. The output attribute indicates whether the passenger or crew member survived.

Instructor Supplements

The following supplements are provided to help the instructor organize lectures and write examinations.

- **PowerPoint slides.** Each figure and table in the text is part of a PowerPoint presentation.

- **Test questions.** Several test questions are provided for each chapter.

- **Answers to selected exercises.** Answers are given for most of the end-of-chapter exercises.

- **Lesson planner.** The lesson planner contains ideas for lecture format and points for discussion. The planner also provides suggestions for using selected end-of-chapter exercises in a laboratory setting.

Please note that these supplements are available to qualified instructors only. Contact your Addison-Wesley sales representative or an send e-mail to Computing@aw.com for access to this material.

Suggested Course Outlines

For the reader interested in the most basic understanding about the benefits and limitations of data mining, we suggest the study of Chapters 1, 2, 5, and 6. For a hands-on opportunity, include Chapter 4.

Parts I, II, and III of the text provide material for an introductory course in data mining and knowledge discovery. By including the material in Part IV, the text may also be used for a combined data mining/expert systems course that places emphasis on data mining and knowledge discovery. The prerequisite knowledge required for someone using this text is minimal. A basic understanding of spreadsheet operations, elementary statistics, and fundamental algebra is helpful.

Chapter 1 provides the essential framework for Chapters 2 through 14. Chapter 2 offers the necessary background information for Chapters 3 through 11. If you wish to provide students with an immediate hands-on learning experience, Chapter 4 can be covered after Chapter 1 is completed. Once Chapters 2 and 3 have been studied, most of the material in Chapters 4 through 7 and 10 through 12 may be covered in any order. Chapter 9 should follow Chapter 8, and Chapters 13 and 14 should follow Chapter 12.

The text is appropriate for the undergraduate MIS or computer science student. It can also provide tutorial assistance for the graduate student who desires a working knowledge of data mining and knowledge discovery. We believe that most of the text can be covered in a single semester. Here are some options for structuring a course.

A Basic Data Mining Course for Undergraduate MIS Majors or Minors

Cover Chapters 1 through 6 in detail. However, Sections 3.3 and 3.4 of Chapter 3 may be omitted or lightly covered. Spend enough time on Chapter 4 for students to feel comfortable working with the iDA software tools.

If your students lack a course in basic statistics, Chapter 7 can be excluded or lightly covered. If Chapter 7 is skipped, spend additional time on the material in Section 2.5 (evaluating performance). Students with at least one business statistics course should be able to handle the material in Chapter 7.

Cover Chapter 8 but make Section 8.5 an optional section. Spend considerable time in Chapter 9, which shows students how to use the iDA neural net software tools.

Chapter 10 is optional. Students with some statistics in their background will find linear and logistic regression as well as Bayes classifier to be of interest. For Chapter 11, all students need some exposure to time-series analysis as well as Web-based and textual data mining. Section 11.4 is optional. As time permits, spend a day or two talking about rule-based systems (Chapter 12).

An Undergraduate MIS Course about Intelligent Systems That Emphasizes Data Mining

Follow the data mining course plan for the MIS undergraduate. Cover all material in Chapters 12 through 14. Omit the previously mentioned optional sections to make time for the added material. If time permits, supplement Chapters 12 through 14 by giving students hands-on experience with a simple rule-based expert system building tool.

A Basic Data Mining Course for Undergraduate Computer Science Majors or Minors

Cover Chapters 1 through 5 in detail. Spend a day or two on the material in Chapter 6 to provide students with a basic understanding of data warehouse design. Cover most of the material in Chapters 7 through 11. If time is an issue, you may wish to limit your coverage of Sections 10.4, 10.5, and 11.4. Spend any extra time covering material in Chapter 12.

For a more intense course, the material on Decision Tree Attribute Selection (Appendix C) and Statistics for Performance Evaluation (Appendix D) can be covered as part of the regular course. You may wish to have students experiment with one or more of the public domain data mining tools downloadable at *www.kdnuggets.com*.

An Undergraduate Computer Science Course about Intelligent Systems That Emphasizes Data Mining

Follow the data mining course plan for the computer science undergraduate. In addition, cover the material in Chapters 12 through 14. If time is an issue, you may wish to cover only those sections of Chapters 10 and 11 that are of special interest. One plan is to cover sections 10.1, 10.2, and one subsection of 10.4.

If time permits, you can supplement Chapters 12 through 14 by giving students hands-on experience with a rule-based expert system building tool. You may also wish to have students experiment with one or more of the public domain data mining tools downloadable at *www.kdnuggets.com*.

A Data Mining Short Course

The undergraduate or graduate student interested in quickly developing a working knowledge of data mining should devote time to Chapters 1, 2, 4, and 5. A working knowledge of neural networks can be obtained through the study of Chapter 8 (Sections 8.1 through 8.4) and Chapter 9.

 # Acknowledgments

Many individuals helped make this book a reality. We are indebted to David Haglin and Jon Hakkila for posing critical questions on data mining performance evaluation. We are also indebted to these individuals for preprocessing several of the datasets that accompany the book. We are very grateful to Yifan Tang and Suzy for helping critique the chapters of the text. We wish to thank all of the undergraduate business and computer science students who worked with prepublished versions of our text. A special thanks goes to Information Acumen's programming team consisting of Russ Huguley, Jin Feng, and Karl Gunderson.

We also would like to thank our production coordinator Keith Henry and offer a special thanks to all of the people at Addison-Wesley for their commitment to excellence in book publishing. We are deeply indebted to our editor Maite Suarez-Rivas. Finally, we are grateful to the following reviewers of our book and found their constructive comments to be particularly helpful during revisions of the manuscript:

Ananth Grama *Purdue University*

John Keane *Department of Computation, UMIST—UK*

Selwyn Piramuthu *Decision and Information Sciences, University of Florida*

Mary Ann Robbert *Bentley College*

Lynne Stokes *Southern Methodist University*

Stuart A. Varden *Pace University*

Contents

★★ *Part IV (Chapters 12, 13, and 14) are available on the CD that accompanies this book.*

Appendixes

⋆⋆ *Appendices C, D, and E are available on the CD that accompanies this book.*

PART I

Data Mining Fundamentals

Chapter 1

Data Mining: A First View

Chapter Objectives

▶ Define data mining and understand how data mining can be used to solve problems.

▶ Understand that computers are best at learning concept definitions.

▶ Know when data mining should be considered as a possible problem-solving strategy.

▶ Understand that expert systems and data mining use different means to accomplish similar goals.

▶ Understand that supervised learning builds models by forming concept definitions from data containing predefined classes.

▶ Understand that unsupervised clustering builds models from data without the aid of predefined classes.

▶ Recognize that classification models are able to classify new data of unknown origin.

▶ Realize that data mining has been successfully applied to solve problems in several domains.

This chapter offers an introduction to the fascinating world of data mining and knowledge discovery. You will learn about the basics of data mining and how data mining has been applied to solve real-world problems. In Section 1.1 we provide a definition of data mining. Section 1.2 discusses how computers are best at learning concept definitions and how concept definitions can be transformed into useful patterns. Section 1.3 offers guidance in understanding the types of problems that may be appropriate for data mining. In Section 1.4 we introduce expert systems and explain how expert systems build models by extracting problem-solving knowledge from one or more human experts. In Section 1.5 we offer a simple process model for data mining. Section 1.6 explores why using a simple table search may not be an appropriate data mining strategy. In Section 1.7 we detail several data mining applications. We conclude this chapter, as well as all chapters in this book, with a short summary, key term definitions, and a set of exercises. Let's get started!

1.1   Data Mining: A Definition

We define **data mining** as the process of employing one or more computer learning techniques to automatically analyze and extract knowledge from data contained within a database. The purpose of a data mining session is to identify trends and patterns in data. Ray Kurzwell, "the father of voice-recognition software" and designer of the Kurzwell keyboard, recently stated that 98% of all human learning is "pattern recognition."

The knowledge gained from a data mining session is given as a model or generalization of the data. Several data mining techniques exist. However, all data mining methods use **induction-based learning.** Induction-based learning is the process of forming general concept definitions by observing specific examples of concepts to be learned. Here are three examples of knowledge gained through the process of induction-based learning:

- Did you ever wonder why so many televised golf tournaments are sponsored by online brokerage firms such as Charles Schwab and TD Waterhouse? A primary reason is that over 70% of all online investors are males over the age of 40 who play golf. In addition, 60% of all stock investors are golfers.

- Does it make sense for a music company to advertise rap music in magazines for senior citizens? It does when you learn that senior citizens often purchase rap music for their teenage grandchildren.

- Did you know that credit card companies can often suspect a stolen credit card, even if the card holder is unaware of the theft? Many credit card companies store a generalized model of your credit card purchasing habits. The model alerts the credit card company of a possible stolen card as soon as someone attempts a transaction that does not fit your general purchasing profile.

These three examples make it easy for us to see why data mining is fast becoming a preferred technique for extracting useful knowledge from data. Later in this chapter and throughout the text you will see additional examples of how data mining has been applied to solve real-world problems.

Knowledge Discovery in Databases (KDD) is a term frequently used interchangeably with data mining. Technically, KDD is the application of the scientific method to data mining. In addition to performing data mining, a typical KDD process model includes a methodology for extracting and preparing data as well as making decisions about actions to be taken once data mining has taken place. When a particular application involves the analysis of large volumes of data stored in several locations, data extraction and preparation become the most time-consuming parts of the discovery process. As data mining has become a popular name for the broader term, we do not concern ourselves with clearly discriminating between data mining and KDD. However, we do recognize the distinction and have devoted Chapter 5 to detailing the steps of two popular KDD process models.

1.2   What Can Computers Learn?

As the definition implies, data mining is about learning. Learning is a complex process. Four levels of learning can be differentiated (Merril and Tennyson, 1977):

- **Facts.** A fact is a simple statement of truth.

- **Concepts.** A concept is a set of objects, symbols, or events grouped together because they share certain characteristics.

- **Procedures.** A procedure is a step-by-step course of action to achieve a goal. We use procedures in our everyday functioning as well as in the solution of difficult problems.

- **Principles.** Principles represent the highest level of learning. Principles are general truths or laws that are basic to other truths.

Computers are good at learning concepts. Concepts are the output of a data mining session. The data mining tool dictates the form of learned concepts. Common concept structures include trees, rules, networks, and mathematical equations. Tree structures and production rules are easy for humans to interpret and understand. Networks and mathematical equations are black-box concept structures in that the knowledge they contain is not easily understood. We will examine these and other data mining structures throughout the text. First, we take a look at three common concept views.

Three Concept Views

Concepts can be viewed from different perspectives. An understanding of each view will help you categorize the data mining techniques discussed in this text. Let's take a moment to define and illustrate each view.

The **classical view** attests that all concepts have definite defining properties. These properties determine if an individual item is an example of a particular concept. The classical view definition of a concept is crisp and leaves no room for misinterpretation. This view supports all examples of a particular concept as being equally representative of the concept. Here is a rule that employs a classical view definition of a good credit risk for an unsecured loan:

> **IF** *Annual Income* >= 30,000
> & *Years at Current Position* >=5
> & *Owns Home* = True
> **THEN** *Good Credit Risk* = True

The classical view states that all three rule conditions must be met for the applicant to be considered a good credit risk.

The probabilistic and exemplar views are similar in that neither requires concept representations to have defining properties. The **probabilistic view** holds that concepts are represented by properties that are probable of concept members. The assumption is that people store and recall concepts as generalizations created from individual exemplar (instance) observations. A probabilistic view definition of a good credit risk might look like this:

- The mean annual income for individuals who consistently make loan payments on time is $30,000.

- Most individuals who are good credit risks have been working for the same company for at least five years.

- The majority of good credit risks own their own home.

This definition offers general guidelines about the characteristics representative of a good credit risk. Unlike the classical view definition, this definition cannot be directly applied to achieve an answer about whether a specific person should be given an unsecured loan. However, the definition can be used to help with the decision-making process. The probabilistic view may also associate a probability of membership with a specific classification. For example, a homeowner with an annual income of $27,000 employed at the same position for four years might be classified as a good credit risk with a probability of 0.85.

The **exemplar view** states that a given instance is determined to be an example of a particular concept if the instance is similar enough to a set of one or more known examples of the concept. The view attests that people store and recall likely concept exemplars that are then used to classify new instances. Consider the loan applicant described in the previous paragraph. The applicant would be classified as a good credit risk if the applicant were similar enough to one or more of the stored instances representing good credit risk candidates. Here is a possible list of exemplars considered to be good credit risks:

- Exemplar #1:
    Annual Income = 32,000
    Number of Years at Current Position = 6
    Homeowner

- Exemplar #2:
    Annual Income = 52,000
    Number of Years at Current Position = 16
    Renter

- Exemplar #3:
    Annual Income = 28,000
    Number of Years at Current Position = 12
    Homeowner

As with the probabilistic view, the exemplar view can associate a probability of concept membership with each classification.

As we have seen, concepts can be studied from at least three points of view. In addition, concept definitions can be formed in several ways. Supervised learning is probably the best understood concept learning method and the most widely used technique for data mining. We introduce supervised learning in the next section.

Supervised Learning

When we are young, we use induction to form basic concept definitions. We see instances of concepts representing animals, plants, building structures, and the like. We hear the labels given to individual instances and choose what we believe to be the defining concept features (attributes) and form our own classification models. Later, we use the models we have developed to help us identify objects of similar structure.

The name for this type of learning is induction-based supervised concept learning or just **supervised learning.**

The purpose of supervised learning is two-fold. First, we use supervised learning to build classification models from sets of data containing examples and nonexamples of the concepts to be learned. Each example or nonexample is known as an **instance** of data. Second, once a classification model has been constructed, the model is used to determine the classification of newly presented instances of unknown origin. It is worth noting that, although model creation is inductive, applying the model to classify new instances of unknown origin is a deductive process.

To more clearly illustrate the idea of supervised learning, consider the hypothetical dataset shown in Table 1.1. The dataset is very small and is relevant for illustrative purposes only. The table data is displayed in **attribute-value format** where the first row shows names for the attributes whose values are contained in the table. The attributes *sore throat, fever, swollen glands, congestion*, and *headache* are possible symptoms experienced by individuals who have a particular affliction (a *strep throat*, a *cold*, or an *allergy*). These attributes are known as **input attributes** and are used to create a model to represent the data. *Diagnosis* is the attribute whose value we wish to predict. *Diagnosis* is known as the class or **output attribute.**

Starting with the second row of the table, each remaining row is an **instance** of data. An individual row shows the symptoms and affliction of a single patient. For example, the patient with ID = 1 has a sore throat, fever, swollen glands, congestion, and a headache. The patient has been diagnosed as having strep throat.

Table 1.1 ● **Hypothetical Training Data for Disease Diagnosis**

Patient ID#	Sore Throat	Fever	Swollen Glands	Congestion	Headache	Diagnosis
1	Yes	Yes	Yes	Yes	Yes	Strep throat
2	No	No	No	Yes	Yes	Allergy
3	Yes	Yes	No	Yes	No	Cold
4	Yes	No	Yes	No	No	Strep throat
5	No	Yes	No	Yes	No	Cold
6	No	No	No	Yes	No	Allergy
7	No	No	Yes	No	No	Strep throat
8	Yes	No	No	Yes	Yes	Allergy
9	No	Yes	No	Yes	Yes	Cold
10	Yes	Yes	No	Yes	Yes	Cold

Suppose we wish to develop a generalized model to represent the data shown in Table 1.1. Even though this dataset is small, it would be difficult for us to develop a general representation unless we knew something about the relative importance of the individual attributes and possible relationships among the attributes. Fortunately, an appropriate supervised learning algorithm can do the work for us.

Supervised Learning: A Decision Tree Example

We presented the data in Table 1.1 to C4.5 (Quinlan, 1993), a supervised learning program that generalizes a set of input instances by building a decision tree. A **decision tree** is a simple structure where nonterminal nodes represent tests on one or more attributes and terminal nodes reflect decision outcomes. Decision trees have several advantages in that they are easy for us to understand, can be transformed into rules, and have been shown to work well experimentally. A supervised algorithm for creating a decision tree will be detailed in Chapter 3.

Figure 1.1 shows the decision tree created from the data in Table 1.1. The decision tree generalizes the table data. Specifically,

---

Figure 1.1 ● **A decision tree for the data in Table 1.1**

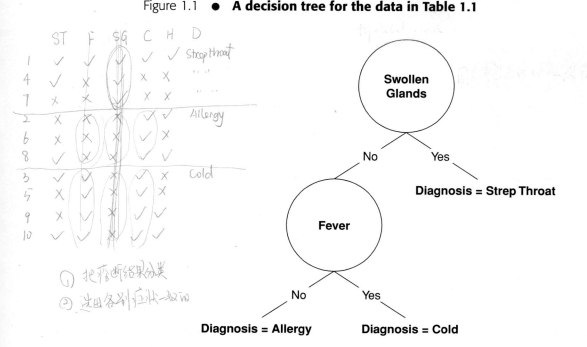

- If a patient has swollen glands, the diagnosis is strep throat.

- If a patient does not have swollen glands and has a fever, the diagnosis is a cold.

- If a patient does not have swollen glands and does not have a fever, the diagnosis is an allergy.

The decision tree tells us that we can accurately diagnose a patient in this dataset by concerning ourselves only with whether the patient has swollen glands and a fever. The attributes *sore throat, congestion,* and *headache* do not play a role in determining a diagnosis. As we can see, the decision tree has generalized the data and provided us with a summary of those attributes and attribute relationships important for an accurate diagnosis.

The instances used to create the decision tree model are known as **training data.** At this point, the training instances are the only instances known to be correctly classified by the model. However, our model is useful to the extent that it can correctly classify new instances whose classification is not known. To determine how well the model is able to be of general use we test the accuracy of the model using a **test set.** The instances of the test set have a known classification. Therefore we can compare the test set instance classifications determined by the model with the correct classification values. Test set classification correctness gives us some indication about the future performance of the model.

Let's use the decision tree to classify the first two instances shown in Table 1.2.

- Since the patient with ID = 11 has a value of *Yes* for *swollen glands,* we follow the right link from the root node of the decision tree. The right link leads to a terminal node, indicating the patient has strep throat.

- The patient with ID = 12 has a value of *No* for *swollen glands.* We follow the left link and check the value of the attribute *fever.* Since *fever* equals *Yes,* we diagnose the patient with a cold.

Table 1.2 ● **Data Instances with an Unknown Classification**

Patient ID#	Sore Throat	Fever	Swollen Glands	Congestion	Headache	Diagnosis
11	No	No	Yes	Yes	Yes	?
12	Yes	Yes	No	No	Yes	?
13	No	No	No	No	Yes	?

We can translate any decision tree into a set of **production rules.** Production rules are rules of the form:

> **IF** *antecedent conditions*
> **THEN** *consequent conditions*

The antecedent conditions detail values or value ranges for one or more input attributes. The consequent conditions specify the values or value ranges for the output attributes. The technique for mapping a decision tree to a set of production rules is simple. A rule is created by starting at the root node and following one path of the tree to a leaf node. The antecedent of a rule is given by the attribute value combinations seen along the path. The consequent of the corresponding rule is the value at the leaf node. Here are the three production rules for the decision tree shown in Fig. 1.1:

1. **IF** *Swollen Glands = Yes*
   THEN *Diagnosis = Strep Throat*

2. **IF** *Swollen Glands = No & Fever = Yes*
   THEN *Diagnosis = Cold*

3. **IF** *Swollen Glands = No & Fever = No*
   THEN *Diagnosis = Allergy*

Let's use the production rules to classify the table instance with patient ID = 13. Because *swollen glands* equals *No*, we pass over the first rule. Likewise, because *fever* equals *No*, the second rule does not apply. Finally, both antecedent conditions for the third rule are satisfied. Therefore we are able to apply the third rule and diagnose the patient as having an allergy.

Unsupervised Clustering

Unlike supervised learning, **unsupervised clustering** builds models from data without predefined classes. Data instances are grouped together based on a similarity scheme defined by the clustering system. With the help of one or several evaluation techniques, it is up to us to decide the meaning of the formed clusters.

To further distinguish between supervised learning and unsupervised clustering, consider the hypothetical data in Table 1.3. The table provides a sampling of information about five customers maintaining a brokerage account with Acme Investors Incorporated. The attributes *customer ID, sex, age, favorite recreation,* and *income* are self-explanatory. *Account type* indicates whether the account is held by a single person

Table 1.3 ● **Acme Investors Incorporated**

Customer ID	Account Type	Margin Account	Transaction Method	Trades/Month	Sex	Age	Favorite Recreation	Annual Income
1005	Joint	No	Online	12.5	F	30–39	Tennis	40–59K
1013	Custodial	No	Broker	0.5	F	50–59	Skiing	80–99K
1245	Joint	No	Online	3.6	M	20–29	Golf	20–39K
2110	Individual	Yes	Broker	22.3	M	30–39	Fishing	40–59K
1001	Individual	Yes	Online	5.0	M	40–49	Golf	60–79K

(individual account), two or more persons (joint account), or by a person or institution under a safe-keeping agreement on behalf of one or more individuals (custodial account). *Transaction method* tells us whether the purchase and sale of stock is made online or through a broker. *Trades/month* indicates the average number of stock transactions per month. Finally, if the account is a *margin account,* the customer is allowed to borrow cash from the investment firm to purchase new securities.

Suppose we wish to use data mining together with the brokerage data to gain insight about possible patterns in the database. In so doing, we might ask the following four questions:

1. Can I develop a general profile of an online investor? If so, what characteristics distinguish online investors from investors that use a broker?

2. Can I determine if a new customer who does not initially open a margin account is likely to do so in the future?

3. Can I build a model able to accurately predict the average number of trades per month for a new investor?

4. What characteristics differentiate female and male investors?

Each question is a candidate for supervised data mining because each question clearly offers an attribute whose values represent a set of predefined output classes. For question 1, the output attribute is *transaction method.* The output attribute for question 2 is *margin account.* The output attribute for question 3 is given as *trades/month,* and the output attribute for question 4 is *sex.* The answers to each of these questions can be used to develop advertising campaigns for new customers as well as marketing strategies for existing customers.

Alternatively, we can ask one or more general questions about the data. Here are two candidate questions for unsupervised clustering:

1. What attribute similarities group customers of Acme Investors together?

2. What differences in attribute values segment the customer database?

Many unsupervised clustering systems require us to provide an initial best estimate about the total number of clusters in the data. Other clustering systems use an algorithm in an attempt to determine a best number of clusters. In either case a clustering system will attempt to group instances into clusters of significant interest. Let's assume that we have presented the Acme Investors data to an unsupervised clustering model and three clusters were formed. Here is a representative rule from each cluster:

IF *Margin Account* = *Yes & Age* = 20–29 & *Annual Income* = 40–59K
THEN *Cluster* = 1
{accuracy = 0.80, coverage = 0.50}

IF *Account Type* = *Custodial & Favorite Recreation* = *Skiing*
& *Annual Income* = 80–90K
THEN *Cluster* = 2
{accuracy = 0.95, coverage = 0.35}

IF *Account Type* = *Joint & Trades/Month* > 5
& *Transaction Method* = *Online*
THEN *Cluster* = 3
{accuracy = 0.82, coverage = 0.65}

Decimal values for rule accuracy and coverage are stated after the consequent condition for each rule. These values give important information about rule confidence and rule significance. The rule for cluster 1 shows an accuracy of 0.80. Stated another way, the rule will be erroneous in 20% of the cases where the antecedent conditions have been met. The cluster 1 rule coverage score indicates that 50% of all instances in the cluster satisfy the antecedent conditions of the rule.

The rule for cluster 1 is not a surprise, as we expect younger investors with a reasonable income to take a less conservative approach to investing. In addition, the rule for cluster 3 is not likely to be a new discovery. However, the rule for cluster 2 could be unexpected and therefore useful. The Acme Investors Corporation might take advantage of this knowledge by investing some of their advertising money in ski magazines with the ads promoting custodial accounts for children and/or grandchildren.

The simple examples above help illustrate the basic concepts surrounding supervised learning and unsupervised clustering. The more difficult tasks such as defining a suitable problem to solve, preparing the data, choosing a data mining strategy, and evaluating performance are topics addressed in the remaining chapters of the text. The next section offers guidelines to help us determine when data mining is an appropriate problem-solving strategy.

1.3   Is Data Mining Appropriate for My Problem?

Making decisions about whether to use data mining as a problem-solving strategy for a particular problem is a difficult task. As a starting point, we offer four general questions to consider:

1. Can we clearly define the problem?

2. Does potentially meaningful data exist?

3. Does the data contain hidden knowledge or is the data factual and useful for reporting purposes only?

4. Will the cost of processing the data be less than the likely increase in profit seen by applying any potential knowledge gained from the data mining project?

The first two questions as well as the fourth cannot be addressed properly in a few sentences. The tools to help us answer these questions for a particular problem are provided throughout the chapters of this text. However, you can gain insight on how to answer the third question with a few simple examples. We begin by differentiating between four types of knowledge.

Data Mining or Data Query?

Four general types of knowledge can be defined to help us determine when data mining should be considered.

- **Shallow knowledge** is factual in nature. Shallow knowledge can be easily stored and manipulated in a database. Database query languages such as SQL are excellent tools for extracting shallow knowledge from data.

- **Multidimensional knowledge** is also factual. However, in this case data is stored in a multidimensional format. On-line Analytical Processing (OLAP) tools are used on multidimensional data.

- **Hidden knowledge** represents patterns or regularities in data that cannot be easily found using a database query language such as SQL. However, data mining algorithms can find such patterns with ease.

- **Deep knowledge** is knowledge stored in a database that can only be found if we are given some direction about what we are looking for. Current data mining tools are not able to locate deep knowledge.

Database query languages and OLAP tools are very good at finding and reporting information within a database when we know exactly what we are looking for. Database queries can easily be written to extract the following information:

- A list of all Acme Department Store customers who used a credit card to buy a gas grill.

- A list of all employees over the age of 40 who have averaged five or fewer sick days per year.

- A list of all patients who have had at least one heart attack and whose blood cholesterol is below 200.

- A list of all credit card holders who used their credit card to purchase more than $300 in groceries during the month of January.

The output of these queries could very well provide valuable information to help make future decisions. Data mining takes us one step further in that it provides us with potentially useful information even when we only have a vague idea about what we are looking for. What is even more exciting is that data mining gives us the ability to find answers to questions we never thought about asking!

Here are a few simple examples of what data mining can do:

- Develop a general profile for credit card customers who take advantage of promotions offered with their credit card billing

- Differentiate individuals who are poor credit risks from those who are likely to make their loan payments on time

- Classify faint objects found within sky image data

- Determine when a patient is likely to return to work after major back surgery

Database query may be able to help us with the above examples, but our chances of success are slim. With data mining, if the data contains information of potential value, we are likely to succeed in our efforts. The next section offers a specific example to help make the distinction between data mining and data query clear.

Data Mining vs. Data Query: An Example

Let's take a look at a specific example to help us determine when data mining is an appropriate problem-solving strategy. Once again, consider the hypothetical data in Table 1.1. As mentioned earlier, this data contains information about individual patients, their symptoms, and a corresponding affliction. As the dataset is small, it seems almost trivial to consider examining the individual instances for patterns. If you like, use your imagination to envision a much larger dataset with thousands of records and several additional attributes.

As a first step, we can state a general **hypothesis** about what we hope to find in the dataset. A hypothesis is an educated guess about what we believe to be true for some or all of the data. For our dataset we might state a general hypothesis as

> *One or more of the attributes in the dataset are relevant in accurately differentiating between individuals who have strep throat, a cold, or an allergic reaction.*

Suppose that through personal experience we have some additional insight indicating that swollen glands are paramount in predicting strep throat. Therefore we state a second hypothesis as

> *Swollen glands are necessary and sufficient for strep throat.*

We pose two table queries to test this hypothesis:

1. List all patients with *Diagnosis = Strep Throat* and *Swollen Glands = No.*

2. List all patients with *Diagnosis = Cold* or *Diagnosis = Allergy* and *Swollen Glands = Yes.*

The result of the first query is an empty table. Therefore we conclude that swollen glands are a necessary condition for strep throat. That is, all patients with strep throat also have swollen glands. The result of the second query is also an empty table. This tells us that any patient who does not have strep throat does not have swollen glands. Combining the results of the two queries we conclude that swollen glands are a necessary and sufficient condition for strep throat. We form the general rule:

IF *Swollen Glands = Yes*
THEN *Diagnosis = Strep Throat*

Our next step is to determine a rule or set of rules to differentiate patients with colds from patients with allergies. Once again we form a hypothesis about what we believe to be true and test the hypothesis by performing one or more table queries. The process we are describing is sometimes referred to as **manual data mining.** We pose queries and maintain control of the search for patterns in data. We will be effective to the extent that we already almost know what we are looking for. If the dataset is small, and if we have a wealth of knowledge about the attributes and the attribute relationships in the data, this approach is appropriate. However, under conditions other than these, our chances of success are limited.

1.4 Expert Systems or Data Mining?

There are times when a data mining or data query approach to problem solving is not feasible. An obvious scenario is any situation where quality data is lacking. When data mining is not a viable choice, other options may be available that allow us to build useful decision-making models. One possibility is to locate one or more human beings who are able to find solutions to the problems we are interested in solving.

Individuals who have the ability to solve problems in one or more difficult problem domains are often referred to as **experts** in their field. Examples include medical doctors who are able to quickly diagnose disease, business executives who are able to make timely decisions, and counselors who are good at helping us with our personal problems. Experts learn their skills by way of education and experience. Experience over a period of several years helps experts develop skills that enable them to solve problems quickly and efficiently.

Computer scientists develop computer programs called **expert systems** that can emulate the problem-solving skills of human experts in specific problem domains. The word **emulate** means to "act like." To emulate a human expert with a computer program means that the program must solve problems using methods similar to those employed by the expert. As we are far from understanding the workings of the human brain, these programs concentrate on emulating the knowledge of human experts rather than their methods of applying knowledge to specific problem situations. Because human experts often use rules to describe what they know, most expert systems incorporate rules as a main medium for storing knowledge.

Figure 1.2 uses our hypothetical domain for disease diagnosis to compare the problem-solving methodologies of data mining and expert systems. The data mining approach uses the data in Table 1.1 together with a data mining tool to create a rule for

Figure 1.2   ●   **Data mining vs. expert systems**

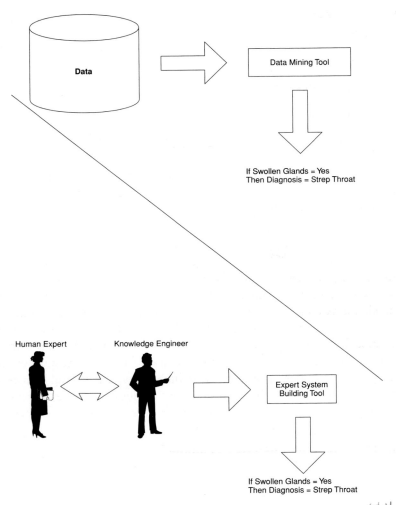

diagnosing strep throat. In contrast, the expert systems approach employs human beings rather than data. The process involves at least two individuals—an expert and a knowledge engineer. A **knowledge engineer** is a person trained to interact with an expert in order to capture their knowledge. Once captured, the knowledge engineer uses one or more automated tools to create a computer model of the new knowledge. For the example shown in Fig. 1.2, the human expert is likely a medical doctor. Notice the model describing the knowledge extracted from the human expert is identical to the model built with the data mining process. In Part IV of your text you will see how expert systems and data mining can be collectively applied to solve difficult problems.

1.5   A Simple Data Mining Process Model

In a broad sense, we can define data mining as a four-step process. To perform a data mining session we:

1. Assemble a collection of data to analyze

2. Present these data to a data mining software program

3. Interpret the results

4. Apply the results to a new problem or situation

Figure 1.3 offers a pictorial diagram of a simple data mining process model that incorporates this four-step approach. We will use Fig. 1.3 to help us describe each step of the data mining process.

Assembling the Data

Data mining requires access to data. The data may be represented as volumes of records in several database files or the data may contain only a few hundred records in a single file. A common misconception is that in order to build an effective model a data mining algorithm must be presented with thousands or millions of instances. In fact, most data mining tools work best with a few hundred or a few thousand pertinent records. Therefore once a problem has been defined, a first step in the data mining process is to extract or assemble a relevant subset of data for processing. Many

Figure 1.3   ●   **A simple data mining process model**

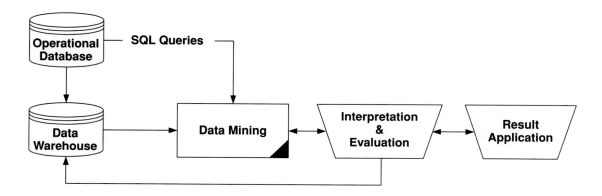

times this first step requires a great amount of human time and effort. There are are three common ways to access data for data mining:

1. Data can be accessed from a data warehouse.
2. Data can be accessed from a relational database.
3. Data can be accessed from a flat file or spreadsheet.

The Data Warehouse

A common scenario for data assembly shows data originating in one or more operational databases. **Operational databases** are transaction-based and frequently designed using the relational database model. An operational database fixed on the relational model will contain several normalized tables. The tables have been normalized to reduce redundancy and promote quick access to individual records. For example, a specific customer might have data appearing in several relational tables where each table views the customer from a different perspective.

Figure 1.3 shows data being transferred from the operational environment to a **data warehouse.** The data warehouse is a historical database designed for decision support rather than transaction processing (Kimball et al., 1998). Thus only data useful for decision support is extracted from the operational environment and entered into the warehouse database. Data transfer from the operational database to the warehouse is an ongoing process usually accomplished on a daily basis after the close of the regular business day. Before each data item enters the warehouse, the item is time-stamped, transformed as necessary, and checked for errors. The transfer process can be complex, especially when several operational databases are involved. Once entered, the records in the data warehouse become read-only and are subject to change only under special conditions.

A data warehouse stores all data relating to the same subject (such as a customer) in the same table. This distinguishes the data warehouse from an operational database, which stores information so as to optimize transaction processing. Because the data warehouse is subject-oriented rather than transaction-oriented, the data will contain redundancies. It is the redundancy stored in a data warehouse that is used by data mining algorithms to develop patterns representing discovered knowledge. Chapter 6 discusses the data warehouse, the relational database model, and on-line analytical processing in more detail. As Chapter 6 is self-contained, it can be read any time you wish to learn more about these topics.

Relational Databases and Flat Files

Figure 1.3 shows that if a data warehouse does not exist, you can make use of a database query language such as SQL to write one or more queries to create a table suitable for data mining. Whether data is being extracted for mining from the data warehouse or the data extraction is via a query language, you will probably need a utility program to convert extracted data to the format required by the chosen data mining tool. Finally, if a database structure to store the data has not been designed, and the amount of collected data is minimal, the data will likely be stored in a flat file or spreadsheet. Table 1.1 is representative of a flat-file format appropriate for many data mining tools.

Mining the Data

Figure 1.3 shows that the next phase of the data mining process is to mine the data. However, prior to giving the data to a data mining tool, we have several choices to make.

1.   Should learning be supervised or unsupervised?

2.   Which instances in the assembled data will be used for building the model and which instances will test the model?

3.   Which attributes will be selected from the list of available attributes?

4.   Data mining tools require the user to specify one or more learning parameters. What parameter settings should be used to build a model to best represent the data?

In Chapter 5, we will provide you with several tools to help you answer each of these questions.

Interpreting the Results

Result interpretation requires us to examine the output of our data mining tool to determine if what has been discovered is both useful and interesting. Figure 1.3 shows that if the results are less than optimal we can repeat the data mining step using new attributes and/or instances. Alternatively, we may decide to return to the data warehouse and repeat the data extraction process. Chapters 2 and 7 examine several techniques to help us make decisions about whether a specific model is useful.

Result Application

Our ultimate goal is to apply what has been discovered to new situations. Suppose through the process of a data mining market analysis we find that product X is almost always purchased with product Y. A classic example of this is the discovery that an unusually high percentage of people who purchase baby diapers on Thursday also purchase beer. An initial surprise reaction to this finding makes sense when we realize that couples with a young baby at home are not likely to go out on Friday or Saturday night but instead prefer to enjoy the weekend by relaxing at home. A market analyst can take advantage of this finding by making beer an obvious display item for customers buying diapers. In Section 1.7 we offer several examples of how data mining has been successfully applied.

1.6 Why Not Simple Search?

Data mining is used to build generalized models to represent unstructured data. For classification problems we might consider an alternative approach. Specifically,

- Create a classification table containing all data items whose classification is known.

- For each new instance we wish to classify:

  - Compute a score representing the similarity of each table item to the new instance
  - Give the new instance the same classification as the table item to which it is most similar
  - Add the newly classified instance to the table of known instances

This approach is called the **nearest neighbor classification** method. As we can see, the approach stores instances rather than a generalized model of the data. There are at least three problems with this approach. First, computation times will be a problem when the classification table contains thousands or millions of records. Second, the approach has no way of differentiating between relevant and irrelevant attributes. Third, we have no way to tell whether any of the chosen attributes are able to differentiate the classes contained in the data.

The first problem is prohibitive when we compare this approach to that of building a generalized classification model such as a decision tree. To illustrate the second problem, we once again turn to the hypothetical data found in Table 1.1. As this table contains instances whose classification is known, the nearest neighbor algorithm can use the table data to classify the new instance defined with the following attribute values:

Patient ID = 14

Sore Throat = *Yes*

Fever = *No*

Swollen Glands = *No*

Congestion = *No*

Headache = *No*

When the attributes are numerical, simple Euclidean distance can be used to measure instance similarity. However, as the attributes shown in Table 1.1 are categorical, we will have to define our own measure of similarity. To measure the similarity of each table item with this instance we can simply count attribute-value matches. Upon doing so, we have one match with patients 1 and 9, two matches with patients 2, 5 and 10, and three matches with patients 3, 6, 7 and 8. Finally, we have four matches with patient 4.

Because the new instance shows a best match with patient 4, the nearest neighbor approach informs us that the patient has a case of strep throat. However, applying the decision tree shown in Fig. 1.1 to the new instance tells us that the correct patient diagnosis is allergy. Assuming that the instances in the training data used to build the decision tree accurately represent the population in general, we see that the nearest neighbor classifier has incorrectly diagnosed the patient. In addition, if strep throat is indeed an incorrect diagnosis, adding the new instance to the nearest neighbor classification table will continue to propagate classification error.

A variation of this approach known as a **k-nearest neighbor classifier** classifies a new instance with the most common class of its k-nearest neighbors. This variation helps ward off the possibility of a single atypical training instance incorrectly classifying new instances. However, the important issue is that neither approach has a way to determine relevant attributes and will likely produce a high classification error rate when presented with instances containing a wealth of irrelevant attributes. Also, contrary to our intuition, a dataset having several independent attributes will show distances between any two instances as being almost equal. This is true even if we are processing hundreds of thousands of records!

Despite its shortcomings, the nearest neighbor approach can be successfully applied if attribute preprocessing is able to determine a best set of relevant attributes. Also, computation times can be reduced by comparing instances to be classified with a subset of typical instances taken from each class represented in the data. Finally, even though the nearest neighbor approach does not provide us with a generalization of the data, a general description of each class can be obtained by examining sets of most typical class instances.

1.7   Data Mining Applications

To help you gain further insight into the types of problems appropriate for a data mining solution, we list several examples about how data mining has been successfully applied to real-world problems. We then offer a detailed look at a specific data mining application area.

Example Applications

Here is a short list of examples showing how data mining has been applied to real-world problems. You can find a wealth of additional information about data mining applications, companies, jobs, public domain and commercial software, as well as seminars and short courses by visiting the Web site www.kdnuggets.com.

1. **Fraud Detection**

   - AT&T uses a system developed via data mining to detect fraudulent international calls (Brachman et al., 1996).

   - The FALCON fraud assessment system developed by HNC Inc. is used to signal possibly fraudulent credit card transactions (Brachman et al., 1996).

   - The Financial Crimes Enforcement Network AI System (FAIS) uses several technologies, including data mining, to identify possible money laundering activity within large cash transactions (Senator et al., 1995).

   - The Aspect (Advanced Security for Personal Communications) European research group has employed unsupervised clustering to detect fraud in mobile phone networks. For each user, the system stores a user history as well as a usage profile. Fraudulent behavior is suspected with marked differences between current usage and user history.

2. **Health Care**

   - Mitchell (1997) describes several prototypical uses of data mining, including an example system able to predict women at high risk of requiring an emergency C-section.

   - Merck-Medco Managed Care, a pharmaceutical insurance and prescription mail-order unit of Merck, uses data mining to help uncover less expensive but equally effective drug treatments for certain types of patients (McCarthy, 1997).

3. **Business and Finance**

   - Risk management applications use data mining to help determine insurance rates, manage investment portfolios, and differentiate between companies and/or individuals who are good and poor credit risks. In a *Wall Street Journal* article titled "Looking for Patterns," Lisa Granstein (1999) describes how Farmer's Group, Inc. used data mining to discover a scenario where someone who owns a sports car is not a higher accident risk. The conditions for the scenario require the sports car to be a second car and the family car to be a station wagon or a sedan.

- Bank of America uses data mining to detect which customers are using which Bank of America products so they can offer the right mix of products and services to better meet customer needs (McCarthy, 1997).

- US West Communications, a Denver-based communications provider servicing 25 million customers, uses data mining and data warehousing to determine customer trends and needs based on characteristics such as family size, median family member age, and location. The results of the data mining project have been used to sign up new customers and draw increased business from new subscribers (McCarthy, 1997).

- Twentieth Century Fox analyzes box office receipts to determine which actors, plots, and films will be well received in various marketing regions. Extracted information is also used to decide which film trailers to show.

4. Scientific Applications

- Gamma ray bursts are brief gamma ray flashes that originate outside of our solar system. More than 1000 such events have been recorded. A widely held belief in the scientific community was that there were two classes of gamma ray bursts. Mukherjee et al. (1998) used statistical cluster analysis to discover a third gamma ray burst class.

- Fayyad et al. (1996) describes several scientific applications, including sky image analysis, locating volcanoes on the planet Venus, and earthquake detection.

5. Sports and Gaming

- Brian James, assistant coach of the Toronto Raptors professional basketball team, uses Advanced Scout, a data mining/warehousing tool developed by IBM especially for the NBA to create favorable player matchups and help call the best plays (Baltazar, 2000).

- The gaming industry has incorporated historical models of customer gambling trends to determine how much an individual customer should be spending (losing) while visiting their favorite casino.

Customer Intrinsic Value

A customer's *intrinsic value* is the customer's expected value based on the historical value of similar customers (Manganaris, 2000). Data mining has been used to build models for predicting intrinsic value. Once a customer's intrinsic value is determined, an appropriate marketing strategy can be applied. Let's assume value is measured in terms of average dollars spent per month by the customer. This being the case, the idea is to build a model able to predict what an individual customer is likely to spend in any given month. The amount spent by the customer is then compared to the customer's intrinsic value to determine if the customer is spending more or less than individuals with similar characteristics.

To focus on a specific example, suppose a credit card company is concerned about a decline in new customer retention rates as well as negative changes in new customer card usage habits. In an attempt to overcome their concern, the company has hired a data mining consulting firm. The data mining specialists use data about established credit card holders to build a historical model for predicting customer spending and card usage habits. Possible attributes of importance include customer age, income range, demographic location, average monthly balance, and number of credit purchases per month, to name a few.

Once built, the model is applied to predict intrinsic value for the population of new customers. Figure 1.4 offers a diagram showing intrinsic value on the *vertical* axis and actual customer value on the *horizontal* axis. We can use this figure to help us understand three possibilities for each new customer.

Figure 1.4   •   **Intrinsic vs. actual customer value**

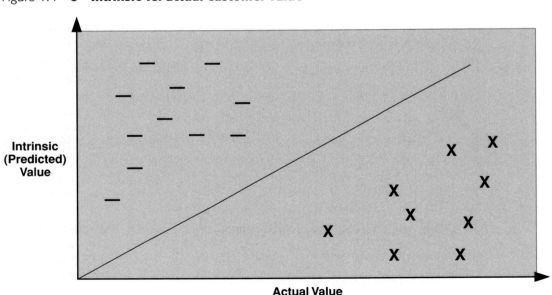

1. **A new customer's intrinsic value is in line with their current value.** These are the customers falling on or close to the diagonal line shown in Fig. 1.4. This group of individuals will likely benefit most from a mildly aggressive marketing strategy aimed at increasing card usage.

2. **A new customer's intrinsic value is greater than their actual value.** This group of customers is shown in Fig. 1.4 as the region above the diagonal. These individuals are likely to eventually quit using their credit card unless an aggressive marketing strategy is deployed.

3. **A new customer's intrinsic value is less than their actual value.** This is seen in Fig. 1.4 as the region below the diagonal. Customers in the lowest-right portion of this region show the largest discrepancy between intrinsic and actual value. A nonaggressive marketing strategy offering intermittent rewards for continued card use may be appropriate for these individuals.

This example illustrates how data mining can be applied to profile strategies for increasing cutomer retention rates and future value. As with all data mining problems, successful application of intrinsic modeling lies in our ability to acquire quality data as well as in our willingness to devote time and effort to the model building process.

1.8   Chapter Summary

Data mining is an induction-based learning strategy that builds models to identify hidden patterns in data. A model created by a data mining algorithm is a conceptual generalization of the data. The generalization may be in the form of a tree, a network, an equation, or a set of rules. Data query can help us find answers to questions we ask about information stored in data. Data mining differs from data query in that data mining gives us the ability to find answers to questions we never thought about asking. Expert systems use human knowledge rather than data to build models for decision making. When quality data is not available, an expert systems approach to problem solving may be a viable alternative.

Data mining is a multistep process that requires accessing and preparing data for a data mining algorithm, mining the data, analyzing results, and taking appropriate action. The data to be accessed can be stored in one or more operational databases, a data warehouse, or a flat file. Data is mined using supervised learning or unsupervised clustering. The most common type of data mining is supervised. With supervised learning, instances whose classification is known are used by the data mining tool to build a general model representing the data. The created model is then employed to determine the classification of new, previously unclassified instances. With unsupervised clustering, predefined classes do not exist. Instead, data instances are grouped together based on a similarity scheme defined by the clustering model.

Data mining has been successfully applied to problems across several disciplines. In the next chapters you will learn more about the steps of the data mining process. You will learn about different data mining algorithms, as well as several techniques to help you determine when to apply data mining to your problems. A common theme we hope to convey throughout this book is that data mining is about model building and not about magic. Human nature requires that we generalize and categorize the world around us. For this reason, model building is a natural process that can be fun and very rewarding!

1.9   Key Terms

Attribute–value format. A table format where the first row of the table contains attribute names. Each row of the table after the first contains a data instance whose attribute values are given in the columns of the table.

Classical view. The view that all concepts have definite defining properties.

Concept. A set of objects, symbols, or events grouped together because they share certain characteristics.

Data mining. The process of employing one or more computer learning techniques to automatically analyze and extract knowledge from data.

Data warehouse. A historical database designed for decision support rather than transaction processing.

Decision tree. A tree structure where nonterminal nodes represent tests on one or more attributes and terminal nodes reflect decision outcomes.

Deep knowledge. Knowledge stored in a database that can only be found if we are given some direction about what we are looking for.

Emulate. To act like.

Exemplar view. The view that people store and recall likely concept exemplars that are used to classify unknown instances.

Expert. A person skilled at solving difficult problems in a limited domain.

Expert system. A computer program that emulates the behavior of a human expert.

Fact. A simple statement of truth.

Hidden knowledge. Patterns or regularities in data that cannot be easily found using database query. However, data mining algorithms can find such patterns with ease.

Hypothesis. An educated guess about what we believe will be the outcome of an experiment.

Induction–based learning. The process of forming a general concept definition by observing specific examples of the concept to be learned.

Input attribute. An attribute used by a data mining algorithm to help create a model of the data. An input attribute is sometimes referred to as an independent variable.

Instance. An example or nonexample of a concept.

K–nearest neighbor classifier. A variation of nearest neighbor classification where a new instance is classified with the most common class of its k-nearest neighbors.

Knowledge Discovery in Databases (KDD). The application of the scientific method to data mining.

Knowledge engineer. A person trained to interact with an expert in order to capture their knowledge.

Manual data mining. The process of posing database queries in an attempt to find hidden patterns in data.

Multidimensional knowledge. Factual knowledge stored in a multidimensional format.

Nearest neighbor classification. An unknown instance is classified by searching the training data for the instance closest in distance to the unknown instance.

Operational database. A database designed for processing the day to day transactions of a company.

Output attribute. With supervised learning, the attribute whose output is to be predicted.

Principle. A general law or truth based on other simpler truths.

Probabilistic view. The view that people store and recall concepts as generalizations created by observation.

Procedure. A step-by-step course of action that is designed to achieve a specific goal.

Production rule. A rule of the form: IF antecedent conditions THEN consequent conditions.

Shallow knowledge. Factual knowledge stored in a database.

Supervised learning. The process of building classification models using data instances of known origin.

Test set. Data instances used to test models built with supervised learning.

Training data. Data instances used to create supervised learning models.

Unsupervised clustering. A data mining method that builds models from data without predefined classes.

1.10 Exercises

Review Questions

28-29 1.   Differentiate between the following terms:

    a.   data warehouse and operational database

    b.   training data and test data

    c.   input attribute and output attribute

    d.   shallow knowledge and hidden knowledge

    e.   exemplar view and probabilistic view

    f.   probabilistic view and classical view

    g.   supervised learning and unsupervised clustering

    h.   intrinsic value and actual value

2.   For each of the following problem scenarios, decide if a solution would best be addressed with supervised learning, unsupervised clustering, or database query. As appropriate, state any initial hypotheses you would like to test. If you decide that supervised learning or unsupervised clustering is the best answer, list several input attributes you believe to be relevant for solving the problem.

    a.   What characteristics differentiate people who have had back surgery and have returned to work from those who have had back surgery and have not returned to their jobs?

    b.   A major automotive manufacturer recently initiated a tire recall for one of their top-selling vehicles. The automotive company blames the tires for the unusually high accident rate seen with their top-seller. The company producing the tires claims the high accident rate only occurs when their tires are on the vehicle in question. Who is to blame?

    c.   When customers visit my Web site, what products are they most likely to buy together?

    d.   What percent of my employees miss one or more days of work per month?

    e.   What relationships can I find between an individual's height, weight, age, and favorite spectator sport?

3.   Medical doctors are experts at disease diagnosis and surgery. Explain how medical doctors use induction to help develop their skills.

4.   Go to the Web site www.kdnuggets.com.

    a.   Locate articles about how data mining has been applied to solve real-world problems.

b. Follow the DATASETS link and scroll the UCI KDD Database Repository for interesting datasets.

5. You are to develop a concept definition for *a good student*.

   a. What attributes would you use in your definition?

   b. Give a definition of a good student from a classical point of view.

   c. Define a good student from a probabilistic point of view.

   d. State the definition from an exemplar point of view.

6. What happens when you try to build a decision tree for the data in Table 1.1 without employing the attributes *Swollen Glands* and *Fever*?

Chapter 2

Data Mining: A Closer Look

Chapter Objectives

▶ Determine an appropriate data mining strategy for a specific problem.

▶ Know about several data mining techniques and how each technique builds a generalized model to represent data.

▶ Understand how a confusion matrix is used to help evaluate supervised learner models.

▶ Understand basic techniques for evaluating supervised learner models with numeric output.

▶ Know how measuring lift can be used to compare the performance of several competing supervised learner models.

▶ Understand basic techniques for evaluating unsupervised learner models.

Although the field of data mining is in a continual state of change, a few basic strategies have remained constant. In Section 2.1 we define five fundamental data mining strategies and give examples of problems appropriate for each strategy. Whereas a data mining strategy outlines an approach for problem solution, a data mining technique applies a strategy. In Sections 2.2 through 2.4 we introduce several data mining techniques with the help of a hypothetical database containing customer information about credit card promotions. Section 2.2 is dedicated to supervised learning techniques. In Section 2.3 we present an overview of association rules, leaving a more detailed discussion for Chapter 3. In Section 2.4 we discuss unsupervised clustering. As you saw in Chapter 1, evaluation is a fundamental step in the data mining process. Section 2.5 provides a few basic tools to help you better understand the evaluation process.

2.1   Data Mining Strategies

As you learned in Chapter 1, **data mining strategies** can be broadly classified as either supervised or unsupervised. Supervised learning builds models by using input attributes to predict output attribute values. Many supervised data mining algorithms only permit a single output attribute. Other supervised learning tools allow us to specify one or several output attributes. Output attributes are also known as **dependent variables** as their outcome depends on the values of one or more input attributes. Input attributes are referred to as **independent variables.** When learning is unsupervised, an output attribute does not exist. Therefore all attributes used for model building are independent variables.

Supervised learning strategies can be further labeled according to whether output attributes are discrete or categorical, as well as by whether models are designed to determine a current condition or predict future outcome. In this section we examine three supervised learning strategies, take a closer look at unsupervised clustering, and introduce a strategy for discovering associations among retail items sold in catalogs and stores. Figure 2.1 shows the five data mining strategies we will discuss.

Classification

Classification is probably the best understood of all data mining strategies. Classification tasks have three common characteristics:

- Learning is supervised.

- The dependent variable is categorical.

Figure 2.1 • **A hierarchy of data mining strategies**

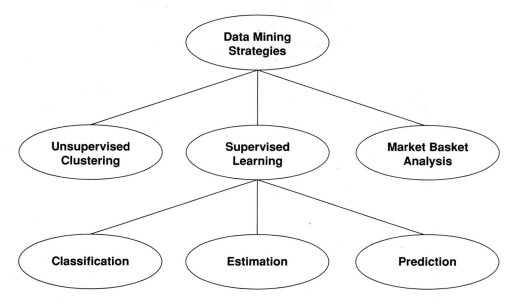

- The emphasis is on building models able to assign new instances to one of a set of well-defined classes.

Some example classification tasks include the following:

- Determine those characteristics that differentiate individuals who have suffered a heart attack from those who have not.
- Develop a profile of a "successful" person.
- Determine if a credit card purchase is fraudulent.
- Classify a car loan applicant as a good or a poor credit risk.
- Develop a profile to differentiate female and male stroke victims.

Notice that each example deals with current rather than future behavior. For example, we want the car loan application model to determine whether an applicant is a good credit risk at this time rather than in some future time period. Prediction models are designed to answer questions about future behavior. Prediction models are discussed later in this section.

Estimation

Like classification, the purpose of an **estimation** model is to determine a value for an unknown output attribute. However, unlike classification, the output attribute(s) for an estimation problem are numeric rather than categorical. Here are four examples of estimation tasks:

- Estimate the number of minutes before a thunderstorm will reach a given location.
- Estimate the salary of an individual who owns a sports car.
- Estimate the likelihood that a credit card has been stolen.
- Estimate the length of a gamma-ray burst.

Most supervised data mining techniques are able to solve classification or estimation problems, but not both. If our data mining tool supports one strategy but not the other, we can usually adapt a problem for solution by either strategy. To illustrate, suppose the output attribute for the original training data in the stolen credit card example above is numeric. Let's also assume the output values range between 0 and 1, with 1 being a most likely case for a stolen card. We can make discrete categories for the output attribute values by replacing scores ranging between 0.0 and 0.3 with the value *unlikely*, scores between 0.3 and 0.7 with *likely*, and scores greater than 0.7 with *highly likely*. In this case the transformation between numeric values and discrete categories is straightforward. Cases such as attempting to make monetary amounts discrete present more of a challenge.

Prediction

It is not easy to differentiate prediction from classification or estimation. However, unlike a classification or estimation model, the purpose of a predictive model is to determine future outcome rather than current behavior. The output attribute(s) of a predictive model can be categorical or numeric. Here are several examples of tasks appropriate for predictive data mining:

- Predict the total number of touchdowns an NFL running back will score during the 2002 NFL season.

- Determine whether a credit card customer is likely to take advantage of a special offer made available with their credit card billing.

- Predict next week's closing price for the Dow Jones Industrial Average.

- Forecast which telephone subscribers are likely to change providers during the next three months.

Most supervised data mining techniques appropriate for classification or estimation problems can also build predictive models. Actually, it is the nature of the data that determines whether a model is suitable for classification, estimation, or prediction. To show this, let's consider a real medical dataset with 303 instances. One hundred thirty-eight instances hold information about patients who have a heart condition. The dataset is summarized in the description box titled *The Cardiology Patient Dataset*.

The attributes and possible attribute values associated with this dataset are shown in Table 2.1. Two forms of the dataset exist. One dataset consists of all numeric attributes. The second dataset has categorical conversions for seven of the original numeric attributes. The table column labeled *Mixed Values* shows the value *Numeric* for attributes that were not converted to a categorical equivalent. For example, the values for attribute *Age* are identical for both datasets. However, the attribute *Fasting Blood Sugar*

The Cardiology Patient Dataset

The cardiology patient dataset is part of the dataset package that comes with your iDA software. The original data was gathered by Dr. Robert Detrano at the VA Medical Center in Long Beach, California. The dataset consists of 303 instances. One hundred thirty-eight of the instances hold information about patients with heart disease. The original dataset contains 13 numeric attributes and a fourteenth attribute indicating whether the patient has a heart condition. The dataset was later modified by Dr. John Gennari. He changed seven of the numerical attributes to categorical equivalents for the pur-pose of testing data mining tools able to classify datasets with mixed data types. The Microsoft Excel file names for the datasets are CardiologyNumerical.xls and CardiologyCategorical.xls, respectively. This dataset is interesting because it represents real patient data and has been used extensively for testing various data mining techniques. We can use this data together with one or more data mining techniques to help us develop profiles for differentiating individuals with heart disease from those without known heart conditions.

Table 2.1 ● **Cardiology Patient Data**

Attribute Name	Mixed Values	Numeric Values	Comments
Age	Numeric	Numeric	Age in years
Sex	Male, Female	1, 0	Patient gender
Chest Pain Type	Angina, Abnormal Angina, NoTang, Asymptomatic	1–4	NoTang = Nonanginal pain
Blood Pressure	Numeric	Numeric	Resting blood pressure upon hospital admission
Cholesterol	Numeric	Numeric	Serum cholesterol
Fasting Blood Sugar < 120	True, False	1, 0	Is fasting blood sugar less than 120?
Resting ECG	Normal, Abnormal, Hyp	0, 1, 2	Hyp = Left ventricular hypertrophy
Maximum Heart Rate	Numeric	Numeric	Maximum heart rate achieved
Induced Angina?	True, False	1, 0	Does the patient experience angina as a result of exercise?
Old Peak	Numeric	Numeric	ST depression induced by exercise relative to rest
Slope	Up, flat, down	1–3	Slope of the peak exercise ST segment
Number Colored Vessels	0, 1, 2, 3	0, 1, 2, 3	Number of major vessels colored by fluoroscopy
Thal	Normal fix, rev	3, 6, 7	Normal, fixed defect, reversible defect
Concept Class	Healthy, Sick	1, 0	Angiographic disease status

Table 2.2 • **Most and Least Typical Instances from the Cardiology Domain**

Attribute Name	Most Typical Healthy Class	Least Typical Healthy Class	Most Typical Sick Class	Least Typical Sick Class
Age	52	63	60	62
Sex	Male	Male	Male	Female
Chest Pain Type	NoTang	Angina	Asymptomatic	Asymptomatic
Blood Pressure	138	145	125	160
Cholesterol	223	233	258	164
Fasting Blood Sugar < 120	False	True	False	False
Resting ECG	Normal	Hyp	Hyp	Hyp
Maximum Heart Rate	169	150	141	145
Induced Angina?	False	False	True	False
Old Peak	0	2.3	2.8	6.2
Slope	Up	Down	Flat	Down
Number of Colored Vessels	0	0	1	3
Thal	Normal	Fix	Rev	Rev

<120 has values *True* or *False* in the converted dataset and values 1 and 0 in the original data.

Table 2.2 lists four instances from the mixed form of the dataset. Two of the instances represent the most typical exemplars from each respective class. The remaining two instances are atypical class members. Some differences between the most typical healthy and the most typical sick patient are easily anticipated. This is the case with typical healthy and sick class values for *Resting ECG* and *Induced Angina*. Surprisingly, we do not see expected differences in cholesterol and blood pressure readings between healthy and sick individuals.

Here are two rules generated for this data by a production rule generator. *Concept class* is specified as the output attribute:

IF *169 <= Maximum Heart Rate <= 202*
THEN *Concept Class = Healthy*
　　　Rule accuracy: 85.07%
　　　Rule coverage: 34.55%

IF *Thal = Rev & Chest Pain Type = Asymptomatic*
THEN *Concept Class = Sick*
      Rule accuracy: 91.14%
      Rule coverage: 52.17%

For the first rule the rule accuracy tells us that if a patient has a maximum heart rate between 169 and 202, we will be correct more than 85 times out of 100 in identifying the patient as healthy. Rule coverage reveals that over 34 percent of all healthy patients have a maximum heart rate in the specified range. When we combine this knowledge with the maximum heart rate values shown in Table 2.2, we are able to conclude that healthy patients are likely to have higher maximum heart rate values.

Is this first rule appropriate for classification or prediction? If the rule is predictive, we can use the rule to warn healthy folks with the statement:

WARNING 1: Have your maximum heart rate checked on a regular basis. If your maximum heart rate is low, you may be at risk of having a heart attack!

If the rule is appropriate for classification but not prediction, the scenario reads:

WARNING 2: If you have a heart attack, expect your maximum heart rate to decrease.

In any case, we cannot imply the stronger statement:

WARNING 3: A low maximum heart rate will cause you to have a heart attack!

That is, with data mining we can state relationships between attributes but we cannot say whether the relationships imply causality. Therefore entering an exercise program to increase maximum heart rate may or may not be a good idea.

The question still remains as to whether either of the first two warnings are correct. This question is not easily answered. A data mining specialist can develop models to generate rules such as those just given. Beyond this, the specialist must have access to additional information—in this case a medical expert—before determining how to use discovered knowledge.

Unsupervised Clustering

With unsupervised clustering we are without a dependent variable to guide the learning process. Rather, the learning program builds a knowledge structure by using some measure of cluster quality to group instances into two or more classes. A primary goal of an unsupervised clustering strategy is to discover concept structures in data. Common uses of unsupervised clustering include:

- Determine if meaningful relationships in the form of concepts can be found in the data
- Evaluate the likely performance of a supervised learner model
- Determine a best set of input attributes for supervised learning
- Detect outliers

You saw an obvious use of unsupervised clustering in Chapter 1 when we showed how clustering was applied to the Acme Investors database to find interesting relationships in the form of concept classes in the data. However, it is not unusual to use unsupervised clustering as an evaluation tool for supervised learning.

To illustrate this idea, let's suppose we have built a supervised learner model using the heart patient data with output attribute *Concept Class*. To evaluate the supervised model, we present the training instances to an unsupervised clustering system. The attribute *Concept Class* is flagged as unused. Next, we examine the output of the unsupervised model to determine if the instances from each concept class (*Healthy* and *Sick*) naturally cluster together. If the instances from the individual classes do not cluster together, we may conclude that the attributes are unable to distinguish healthy patients from those with a heart condition. This being the case, the supervised model is likely to perform poorly. One solution is to revisit the attribute and instance choices used to create the supervised model. In fact, choosing a best set of attributes for a supervised learner model can be implemented by repeatedly applying unsupervised clustering with alternative attribute choices. In this way, those attributes best able to differentiate the classes known to be present in the data can be determined. Unfortunately, even with a small number of attribute choices, the application of this technique can be computationally unmanageable.

Unsupervised clustering can also help detect any atypical instances present in the data. Atypical instances are referred to as **outliers.** Outliers can be of great importance and should be identified whenever possible. Statistical mining applications frequently remove outliers. With data mining, the outliers might be just those instances we are trying to identify. For example, an application that checks credit card purchases would likely identify an outlier as a positive instance of credit card fraud. One way to find outliers is to perform an unsupervised clustering and examine those instances that do not group naturally with the other instances.

Market Basket Analysis

The purpose of **market basket analysis** is to find interesting relationships among retail products. The results of a market basket analysis help retailers design promotions, arrange shelf or catalog items, and develop cross-marketing strategies. Association rule algorithms are often used to apply a market basket analysis to a set of data. Association rules are briefly described later in this chapter and are presented in detail in Chapter 3.

2.2   Supervised Data Mining Techniques

A **data mining technique** is used to apply a data mining strategy to a set of data. A specific data mining technique is defined by an algorithm and an associated knowledge structure such as a tree or a set of rules. In Chapter 1 we introduced decision trees as the most studied of all supervised data mining techniques. Here we present several additional supervised data mining methods. Our goal is to help you develop a basic understanding of the similarities and differences between the various data mining techniques.

The Credit Card Promotion Database

We will use the fictitious data summarized in the description box titled *The Credit Card Promotion Database* and displayed in Table 2.3 to help explain the data mining methods

---

The Credit Card Promotion Database

Credit card companies often include promotional offerings with their monthly credit card billings. The offers provide the credit card customer with an opportunity to purchase items such as luggage, magazines, or jewelry. Credit card companies sponsoring new promotions frequently send bills to individuals without a current card balance hoping that some of these individuals will take advantage of one or more of the promotional offerings. From the perspective of predictive data mining, given the right data, we may be able to find relationships that provide insight about the characteristics of individuals likely to take advantage of future promotions. In doing so, we can divide the pool of zero-balance card holders into two classes. One class will be those persons likely to take advantage of a new credit card promotion. These individuals should be sent a zero-balance billing containing the promotional information. The second class will consist of persons not likely to make a promotional purchase. These individuals should not be sent a zero-balance monthly statement. The end result is a savings in the form of decreased postage, paper, and processing costs for the credit card company.

The credit card promotion database shown in Table 2.3 has fictitious data about 15 individuals holding credit cards with the Acme Credit Card Company. The data contains information obtained about customers through their initial credit card application as well as data about whether these individuals have accepted various promotional offerings sponsored by the credit card company. Although the dataset is small, it serves well for purposes of illustration. We employ this dataset for descriptive purposes throughout the text. ∎

presented here. The table shows data extracted from a database containing information collected on individuals who hold credit cards issued by the Acme Credit Card Company. The first row of Table 2.3 contains the attribute names for each column of data. The first column gives the salary range for an individual credit card holder. Values in columns two through four tell us which card holders have taken advantage of specified promotions sent with their monthly credit card bill. Column five tells us whether an individual has credit card insurance. Column six gives the gender of the card holder, and column seven offers the card holder's age. The first card holder shown in the table has a yearly salary between $40,000 and $50,000, is a 45-year-old male, has purchased one or several magazines advertised with one of his credit card bills, did not take advantage of any other credit card promotions, and does not have credit card insurance. Several attributes likely to be relevant for data mining purposes are not included in the table. Some of these attributes are promotion dates, dollar amounts for purchases, average monthly credit card balance, and marital status. Let's turn our attention to the data mining techniques to see what they can find in the credit card promotion database.

Production Rules

In Chapter 1 you saw that any decision tree can be translated into a set of production rules. However, we do not need an initial tree structure to generate production rules. **RuleMaker,** the production rule generator that comes with your iDA software, uses ratios together with mathematical set theory operations to create rules from spreadsheet data. Earlier in this chapter you saw two rules generated by RuleMaker for the heart patient dataset. Let's apply RuleMaker to the credit card promotion data.

For our experiment we will assume the Acme Credit Card Company has authorized a new life insurance promotion similar to the previous promotion specified in Table 2.3. The promotion material will be sent as part of the credit card billing for all card holders with a non-zero balance. We will use data mining to help us send billings to a select group of individuals who do not have a current credit card balance but are likely to take advantage of the promotion.

Our problem calls for supervised data mining using *life insurance promotion* as the output attribute. Our goal is to develop a profile for individuals likely to take advantage of a life insurance promotion advertised along with their next credit card statement. Here is a possible hypothesis:

> *A combination of one or more of the dataset attributes differentiate between Acme Credit Card Company card holders who have taken advantage of a life insurance promotion and those card holders who have chosen not to participate in the promotional offer.*

Table 2.3 • **The Credit Card Promotion Database**

Income Range ($)	Magazine Promotion	Watch Promotion	Life Insurance Promotion	Credit Card Insurance	Sex	Age
40–50K	Yes	No	No	No	Male	45
30–40K	Yes	Yes	Yes	No	Female	40
40–50K	No	No	No	No	Male	42
30–40K	Yes	Yes	Yes	Yes	Male	43
50–60K	Yes	No	Yes	No	Female	38
20–30K	No	No	No	No	Female	55
30–40K	Yes	No	Yes	Yes	Male	35
20–30K	No	Yes	No	No	Male	27
30–40K	Yes	No	No	No	Male	43
30–40K	Yes	Yes	Yes	No	Female	41
40–50K	No	Yes	Yes	No	Female	43
20–30K	No	Yes	Yes	No	Male	29
50–60K	Yes	Yes	Yes	No	Female	39
40–50K	No	Yes	No	No	Male	55
20–30K	No	No	Yes	Yes	Female	19

The hypothesis is stated in terms of current rather than predicted behavior. However, the nature of the created rules will tell us whether we can use the rules for classification or prediction.

When presented with these data, the iDA rule generator offered several rules of interest. Here are four such rules:

1. **IF** *Sex = Female & 19 <= Age <= 43*
   THEN *Life Insurance Promotion = Yes*
      Rule Accuracy: 100.00%
      Rule Coverage: 66.67%

2. **IF** *Sex = Male & Income Range = 40–50K*
   THEN *Life Insurance Promotion = No*
      Rule Accuracy: 100.00%
      Rule Coverage: 50.00%

3. **IF** *Credit Card Insurance = Yes*
   THEN *Life Insurance Promotion = Yes*
       Rule Accuracy: 100.00%
       Rule Coverage: 33.33%

4. **IF** *Income Range = 30–40K & Watch Promotion = Yes*
   THEN *Life Insurance Promotion = Yes*
       Rule Accuracy: 100.00%
       Rule Coverage: 33.33%

The first rule tells us that we should send a credit card bill containing the promotion to all females between the ages of 19 and 43. Although the coverage for this rule is 66.67%, it would be too optimistic to assume that two-thirds of all females in the specified age range will take advantage of the promotion. The second rule indicates that males who make between $40,000 and $50,000 a year are not good candidates for the insurance promotion. The 100.00% accuracy tells us that our sample does not contain a single male within the $40,000 to $50,000 income range who took advantage of the previous life insurance promotion.

The first and second rules are particularly helpful as neither rule contains an antecedent condition involving a previous promotion. The rule preconditions are based purely on information obtained at the time of initial application. As credit card insurance is always initially offered upon a card approval, the third rule is also useful. However, the fourth rule will not be applicable to new card holders who have not had a chance to take advantage of a previous promotion. For new card holders we should consider the first three rules as predictive and the fourth rule as effective for classification but not predictive purposes.

Neural Networks

A **neural network** is a set of interconnected nodes designed to imitate the functioning of the human brain. As the human brain contains billions of neurons and a typical neural network has fewer than one hundred nodes, the comparison is somewhat superficial. However, neural networks have been successfully applied to problems across several disciplines and for this reason are quite popular in the data mining community.

Neural networks come in many shapes and forms and can be constructed for supervised learning as well as unsupervised clustering. In all cases the values input into a neural network must be numeric. The feed-forward network is a popular supervised learner model. Figure 2.2 shows a fully connected feed-forward neural network consisting of three layers. The network is fully connected, as the nodes at one layer are connected to all nodes at the next layer. In addition, each network node connection

Figure 2.2 ● **A multilayer fully connected neural network**

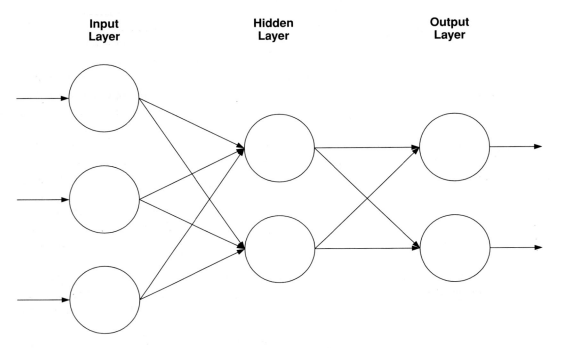

has an associated weight (not shown in the diagram). Notice that nodes within the same layer of the network architecture are not connected to one another.

With a feed-forward network the input attribute values for an individual instance enter at the input layer and pass directly through the output layer of the network structure. The output layer may contain one or several nodes. The output layer of the network shown in Fig. 2.2 contains two nodes. Therefore the output of the neural network will be an ordered pair of values.

Neural networks operate in two phases. The first phase is called the learning phase. During network learning, the input values associated with each instance enter the network at the input layer. One input layer node exists for each input attribute contained in the data. The neural network uses the input values together with the network connection weights to compute the output for each instance. Recall that the output may be one or several values. The output for each instance is compared with the desired network output. Any error between the desired and computed output is propagated back through the network by changing connection-weight values. Training terminates after a certain number of iterations or when the network converges to a predetermined minimum error rate. During the second phase of operation, the network weights are fixed and the network is used to compute output values for new instances.

Your iDA software suite of tools contains a feed-forward neural network for supervised learning as well as a neural network for unsupervised clustering. We applied the supervised network model to the credit card promotion data to test the aforementioned hypothesis. Once again, *life insurance promotion* was designated as the output attribute. Because we wanted to construct a predictive model, the input attributes were limited to *income range, credit card insurance, sex,* and *age.* Therefore the network architecture contained four input nodes and one output node. For our experiment we chose five hidden-layer nodes. Because neural networks cannot accept categorical data, we transformed categorical attribute values by replacing *yes* and *no* with 1 and 0 respectively, *male* and *female* with 1 and 0, and income range values with the lower end of each range score.

Computed and actual (desired) values for the output attribute *life insurance promotion* are shown in Table 2.4. Notice that in most cases, a computed output value is within 0.03 of the actual value. To use the trained network to classify a new unknown instance, the attribute values for the unknown instance are passed through the network and an output score is obtained. If the computed output value is closer to 0, we predict the instance to be an unlikely candidate for the life insurance promotion. A value closer to 1 shows the unknown instance as a good candidate for accepting the life insurance promotion.

A major shortcoming of the neural network approach is a lack of explanation about what has been learned. Converting categorical data to numerical values can also be a challenge. Chapter 8 details two common neural network learning techniques. In Chapter 9 you will learn how to use your iDA neural network software package.

Statistical Regression

Statistical regression is a supervised learning technique that generalizes a set of numeric data by creating a mathematical equation relating one or more input attributes to a single numeric output attribute. A **linear regression** model is characterized by an output attribute whose value is determined by a linear sum of weighted input attribute values. Here is a linear regression equation for the data in Table 2.3:

life insurance promotion = 0.5909 (credit card insurance) − 0.5455 (sex) + 0.7727

Notice that *life insurance promotion* is the attribute whose value is to be determined by a linear combination of attributes *credit card insurance* and *sex.* As with the neural

---

Table 2.4   ●   **Neural Network Training: Actual and Computed Output**

Instance Number	Life Insurance Promotion	Computed Output
1	0	0.024
2	1	0.998
3	0	0.023
4	1	0.986
5	1	0.999
6	0	0.050
7	1	0.999
8	0	0.262
9	0	0.060
10	1	0.997
11	1	0.999
12	1	0.776
13	1	0.999
14	0	0.023
15	1	0.999

---

network model, we transformed all categorical data by replacing *yes* and *no* with 1 and 0, *male* and *female* with 1 and 0, and income range values with the lower end of each range score.

To illustrate the use of the equation, suppose we wish to determine if a female who does not have credit card insurance is a likely candidate for the life insurance promotion. Using the equation, we have:

$$life\ insurance\ promotion \quad = 0.5909(0) - 0.5455(0) + 0.7727$$
$$= 0.7727$$

Because the value 0.7727 is close to 1.0, we conclude that the individual is likely to take advantage of the promotional offer.

Although regression can be nonlinear, the most popular use of regression is for linear modeling. Linear regression is appropriate provided the data can be accurately modeled with a straight line function. Excel has built-in functions for performing several statistical operations, including linear regression. In Chapter 10 we will show you how to use Excel's LINEST function to create linear regression models.

2.3   Association Rules

As the name implies, **association rule** mining techniques are used to discover interesting associations between attributes contained in a database. Unlike traditional production rules, association rules can have one or several output attributes. Also, an output attribute for one rule can be an input attribute for another rule. Association rules are a popular technique for market basket analysis because all possible combinations of potentially interesting product groupings can be explored. For this reason a limited number of attributes are able to generate hundreds of association rules.

We applied the *apriori* association rule algorithm described by Agrawal et al. (1993) to the data in Table 2.3. The algorithm examines baskets of items and generates rules for those baskets containing a minimum number of items. The *apriori* algorithm does not process numerical data. Therefore, before application of the algorithm, we transformed the attribute *age* to the set of discrete categories: *over15, over20, over30, over40,* and *over50.* To illustrate, an individual with *age* = *over40* is between the ages of 40 and 49 inclusive. Once again, we limited the choice of attributes to *income range, credit card insurance, sex,* and *age.* Here is a list of three association rules generated by the *apriori* algorithm for the data in Table 2.3.

1.   **IF** *Sex = Female & Age = over40 & Credit Card Insurance = No*
     THEN *Life Insurance Promotion = Yes*

2.   **IF** *Sex = Male & Age =over40 & Credit Card Insurance = No*
     THEN *Life Insurance Promotion = No*

3.   **IF** *Sex = Female & Age = over40* (40-49)
     THEN *Credit Card Insurance = No & Life Insurance Promotion = Yes*

Each of these three rules has an accuracy of 100% and covers exactly 20% of all data instances. For rule 3, the 20% rule coverage tells us that one in every five individuals is a female over the age of 40 who does not have credit card insurance and has life insurance obtained through the life insurance promotional offer. Notice that in rule 3 *credit card insurance* and *life insurance promotion* are both output attributes.

A problem with association rules is that along with potentially interesting rules, we are likely to see several rules of little value. In Chapter 3 we will explore this issue in more detail when we describe the *apriori* algorithm. The next section continues our discussion by exploring unsupervised clustering techniques.

2.4   Clustering Techniques

Several unsupervised clustering techniques can be identified. One common technique is to apply some measure of similarity to divide instances into disjoint partitions. The partitions are generalized by computing a group mean for each cluster or by listing a most typical subset of instances from each cluster. In Chapter 3 we will examine an unsupervised algorithm that partitions data in this way. A second approach is to partition data in a hierarchical fashion where each level of the hierarchy is a generalization of the data at some level of abstraction. One of the unsupervised clustering models that comes with your iDA software tool is a hierarchical clustering system.

We applied the iDA unsupervised clustering model to the data in Table 2.3. Our choice for input attributes was again limited to *income range, credit card insurance, sex,* and *age.* We set the *life insurance promotion* attribute to "display only," meaning that although the attribute is not used by the clustering system, it will appear as part of the summary statistics. As learning is unsupervised, our hypothesis needs to change. Here is a possible hypothesis that is consistent with our theme of determining likely candidates for the life insurance promotion:

> *By applying unsupervised clustering to the instances of the Acme Credit Card Company database, we will find a subset of input attributes that differentiate card holders who have taken advantage of the life insurance promotion from those cardholders who have not accepted the promotional offer.*

As you can see, we are using unsupervised clustering to find a best set of input attributes for differentiating current customers who have taken advantage of the special promotion from those who have not. Once we determine a best set of input attributes, we can use the attributes to develop a supervised model for predicting future outcomes.

To test the hypothesis, we applied unsupervised clustering to the data several times until we found a set of input attributes that resulted in clusters which differentiate the two classes. The results of one such clustering are displayed in Fig. 2.3. The figure indicates that three clusters were formed. As you can see, the three individuals represented in cluster 1 did not take advantage of the life insurance promotion. Two of the individuals in cluster 2 took advantage of the promotion and three did not. Finally, all seven individuals in cluster 3 purchased the life insurance promotion. Here is a production rule generated by RuleMaker for the third cluster shown in Fig. 2.3:

IF *Sex = Female & 43 >= Age >= 35 & Credit Card Insurance = No*
THEN *Class = 3*
        Rule Accuracy: 100.00%
        Rule Coverage: 66.67%

Figure 2.3 • **An unsupervised clustering of the credit card database**

Cluster 1

Instances: 3
Sex:　　Male => 3
　　　　Female => 0
Age:　　43.3
Credit Card Insurance:　　Yes => 0
　　　　　　　　　　　　　　No => 3

Life Insurance Promotion:　　Yes => 0
　　　　　　　　　　　　　　　No => 3

Cluster 2

Instances: 5
Sex:　　Male => 3
　　　　Female => 2
Age:　　37.0
Credit Card Insurance:　　Yes => 1
　　　　　　　　　　　　　　No => 4
Life Insurance Promotion:　　Yes => 2
　　　　　　　　　　　　　　　No => 3

Cluster 3

Instances: 7
Sex:　　Male => 2
　　　　Female => 5
Age:　　39.9
Credit Card Insurance:　　Yes => 2
　　　　　　　　　　　　　　No => 5
Life Insurance Promotion:　　Yes => 7
　　　　　　　　　　　　　　　No => 0

It is clear that two of the three clusters differentiate individuals who took advantage of the promotion from those who did not. This result offers positive evidence that the attributes used for the clustering are viable choices for building a predictive supervised learner model. In Chapter 4 we will detail unsupervised hierarchical clustering when we investigate the ESX data mining model. In the next section we lay the foundation for evaluating the performance of supervised and unsupervised learner models.

2.5   Evaluating Performance

Performance evaluation is probably the most critical of all the steps in the data mining process. In this section we offer a common sense approach to evaluating supervised and unsupervised learner models. In later chapters we will concentrate on more formal evaluation techniques. As a starting point, we pose three general questions:

1. Will the benefits received from a data mining project more than offset the cost of the data mining process?

2. How do we interpret the results of a data mining session?

3. Can we use the results of a data mining process with confidence?

All three questions are difficult to answer. However, the first is more of a challenge because several factors come into play. Here is a minimal list of considerations for the first question:

1. Is there knowledge about projects similar to the proposed project? What are the success rates and costs of projects similar to the planned project?

2. What is the current form of the data to be analyzed? Does the data exist or will it have to be collected? When a wealth of data exists and is not in a form amenable for data mining, the greatest project cost will fall under the category of data preparation. In fact, a larger question may be whether to develop a data warehouse for future data mining projects.

3. Who will be responsible for the data mining project? How many current employees will be involved? Will outside consultants be hired?

4. Is the necessary software currently available? If not, will the software be purchased or developed? If purchased or developed, how will the software be integrated into the current system?

As you can see, any answer to the first question requires knowledge about the business model, the current state of available data, and current resources. Therefore we will turn our attention to providing evaluation tools for questions 2 and 3. We first consider the evaluation of supervised learner models.

Evaluating Supervised Learner Models

Supervised learner models are designed to classify, estimate, and/or predict future outcome. For some applications the desire is to build models showing consistently high predictive accuracy. The following three applications focus on classification correctness:

- Develop a model to accept or reject credit card applicants
- Develop a model to accept or reject home mortgage applicants
- Develop a model to decide whether or not to drill for oil

Classification correctness is best calculated by presenting previously unseen data in the form of a test set to the model being evaluated. Test set model accuracy can be summarized in a table known as a **confusion matrix.** To illustrate, let's suppose we have three possible classes: C_1, C_2, and C_3. A generic confusion matrix for the three-class case is shown in Table 2.5.

Values along the main diagonal give the total number of correct classifications for each class. For example, a value of 15 for C_{11} means that 15 class C_1 test set instances were correctly classified. Values other than those on the main diagonal represent classification errors. To illustrate, suppose C_{12} has the value 4. This means that four class C_1 instances were incorrectly classified as belonging to class C_2. The following three rules may be helpful in analyzing the information in a confusion matrix:

- **Rule 1.** Values along the main diagonal represent correct classifications. For the matrix in Table 2.5, the value C_{11} represents the total number of class C_1 instances correctly classified by the model. A similar statement can be made for the values C_{22} and C_{33}.

- **Rule 2.** Values in row C_i represent those instances that belong to class C_i. For example, with $i = 2$, the instances associated with cells C_{21}, C_{22}, and C_{23} are all actually members of C_2. To find the total number of C_2 instances incorrectly classified as members of another class, we compute the sum of C_{21} and C_{23}.

- **Rule 3.** Values found in column C_i indicate those instances that have been classified as members of C_i. With $i = 2$, the instances associated with cells C_{12}, C_{22}, and C_{32} have been classified as members of class C_2. To find the total number of instances incorrectly classified as members of class C_2, we compute the sum of C_{12} and C_{32}.

Table 2.5 • **A Three-Class Confusion Matrix**

Computed Decision

	C_1	C_2	C_3
C_1	C_{11}	C_{12}	C_{13}
C_2	C_{21}	C_{22}	C_{23}
C_3	C_{31}	C_{32}	C_{33}

We can use the summary data displayed in a confusion matrix to compute model accuracy. To determine the accuracy of a model we sum the values found on the main diagonal and divide this sum by the total number of test set instances. For example, if we apply a model to a test set of 100 instances and the values along the main diagonal of the resultant confusion matrix sum to 70, the test set accuracy of the model is 0.70 or 70%. As model accuracy is often given as an error rate, we can compute model error rate by subtracting the model accuracy value from 1.0. For our example, the corresponding error rate is 0.30.

Two-Class Error Analysis

The three applications listed at the beginning of this section represent two-class problems. For example, a credit card application is either accepted or rejected. We can use a simple two-class confusion matrix to help us analyze each of these applications.

Consider the confusion matrix displayed in Table 2.6. Cells showing *True Accept* and *True Reject* represent correctly classified test set instances. For the first and second applications presented in the previous section, the cell with *False Accept* denotes accepted applicants that should have been rejected. The cell with *False Reject* designates rejected applicants that should have been accepted. A similar analogy can be made for the third application. Let's use the confusion matrices shown in Table 2.7 to examine the first application in more detail.

Assume the confusion matrices shown in Table 2.7 represent the test set error rates of two supervised learner models built for the credit card application problem. The confusion matrices show that each model displays an error rate of 10%. As the error rates are identical, which model is better? To answer the question we must compare the average cost of credit card payment default to the average potential

---

Table 2.6   •   **A Simple Confusion Matrix**

	Computed Accept	**Computed Reject**
Accept	True Accept	False Reject
Reject	False Accept	True Reject

Table 2.7 • **Two Confusion Matrices Each Showing a 10% Error Rate**

Model A	Computed Accept	Computed Reject	Model B	Computed Accept	Computed Reject
Accept	600	25	Accept	600	75
Reject	75	300	Reject	25	300

loss in profit realized by rejecting individuals who are good approval candidates. Given that credit card purchases are unsecured, the cost of accepting credit card customers likely to default is more of a concern. In this case we should choose Model B because the confusion matrices tell us that this model is less likely to erroneously offer a credit card to an individual likely to default. Does the same reasoning apply for the home mortgage application? How about the application where the question is whether to drill for oil? As you can see, although test set error rate is a useful measure for model evaluation, other factors such as costs incurred for false inclusion as well as losses resulting from false omission must be considered.

Evaluating Numeric Output

A confusion matrix is of little use for evaluating supervised learner models offering numeric output. In addition, the concept of classification correctness takes on a new meaning with numeric output models because instances cannot be directly categorized into one of several possible output classes. However, several useful measures of model accuracy have been defined for supervised models having numeric output. The most common numeric accuracy measures are mean absolute error and mean squared error.

The **mean absolute error** for a set of test data is computed by finding the average absolute difference between computed and desired outcome values. In a similar manner, the **mean squared error** is the average squared difference between computed and desired outcome. It is obvious that for a best test set accuracy we wish to obtain the smallest possible value for each measure. Finally, the **root mean squared error (rms)** is simply the square root of a mean squared error value. *Rms* is frequently used as a measure of test set accuracy with feed-forward neural networks.

Comparing Models by Measuring Lift

Marketing applications that focus on response rates from mass mailings are less concerned with test set classification error and more interested in building models able to extract bias samples from large populations. The hope is to select samples that will show higher response rates than the rates seen within the general population. Supervised learner models designed for extracting bias samples from a general population are often evaluated by a measure that comes directly from marketing known as **lift.** An example illustrates the idea.

Let's consider an expanded version of the credit card promotion database. Suppose the Acme Credit Card Company is about to launch a new promotional offer with next month's credit card statement. The company has determined that for a typical month, approximately 100,000 credit card holders show a zero balance on their credit card. The company has also determined that an average of 1% of all card holders take advantage of promotional offers included with their card billings. Based on this information, approximately 1000 of the 100,000 zero-balance card holders are likely to accept the new promotional offer. As zero-balance card holders do not require a monthly billing statement, the problem is to send a zero-balance billing to exactly those customers who will accept the new promotion.

We can employ the concept of lift to help us choose a best solution. Lift measures the change in percent concentration of a desired class, C_i, taken from a biased sample relative to the concentration of C_i within the entire population. We can formulate lift using conditional probabilities. Specifically,

$$Lift = \frac{P(C_i \mid Sample)}{P(C_i \mid Population)}$$

where $P(C_i \mid Sample)$ is the portion of instances contained in class C_i relative to the biased sample population and $P(C_i \mid Population)$ is the fraction of class C_i instances relative to the entire population. For our problem, C_i is the class of all zero-balance customers who, given the opportunity, will take advantage of the promotional offer.

Figure 2.4 offers a graphical representation of the credit card promotion problem. The graph is sometimes called a **lift chart.** The horizontal axis shows the percent of the total population sampled and the vertical axis represents the number of likely respondents. The graph displays model performance as a function of sample size. The straight line represents the general population. This line tells us that if we randomly select 20% of the population for the mailing, we can expect a response from 200 of the 1000 likely respondents Likewise, selecting 100% of the population will give us all respondents. The curved line shows the lift achieved by employing

Figure 2.4 • **Targeted vs. mass mailing**

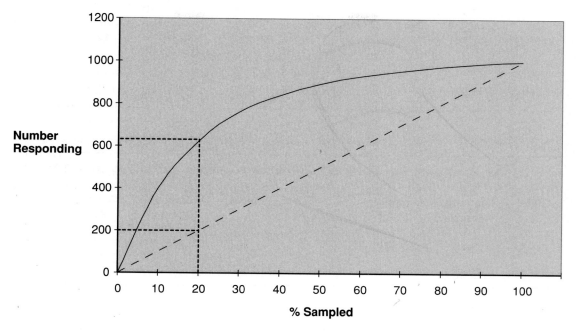

models of varying sample sizes. For example, using the model built with 20% of the population, we can expect a response from 625 of the 20,000 sampled individuals. By examining the graph, you can see that an ideal model will show the greatest lift with the smallest sample size. This is represented in Fig. 2.4 as the upper-left portion of the graph. Although Fig. 2.4 is useful, the confusion matrix also offers us an explanation about how lift can be incorporated to solve problems.

Table 2.8 shows two confusion matrices to help us understand the credit card promotion problem from the perspective of lift. The confusion matrix showing *No Model* tells us that all zero-balance customers are sent a billing statement with the promotional offer. By definition, the lift for this scenario is 1.0 because the sample and the population are identical. The lift for the matrix showing *Ideal Model* is 100 (100%/1%) because the biased sample contains only positive instances.

Consider the confusion matrices for the two models shown in Table 2.9. The lift for model X is computed as:

$$Lift(\text{model X}) = \frac{540 / 24000}{1000 / 100000}$$

Table 2.8   ●   **Two Confusion Matrices: No Model and an Ideal Model**

No Model	Computed Accept	Computed Reject		Ideal Model	Computed Accept	Computed Reject
Accept	1,000	0		Accept	1,000	0
Reject	99,000	0		Reject	0	99,000

Table 2.9   ●   **Two Confusion Matrices for Alternative Models with Lift Equal to 2.25**

Model X	Computed Accept	Computed Reject		Model Y	Computed Accept	Computed Reject
Accept	540	460		Accept	450	550
Reject	23,460	75,540		Reject	19,550	79,450

which evaluates to 2.25. The lift for model Y is computed as:

$$Lift(\text{model Y}) = \frac{450 \ / \ 20000}{1000 \ / \ 100000}$$

which also evaluates to 2.25. As was the case with the previous example, to answer the question about which is a better model we must have additional information about the relative costs of false negative and false positive selections. For our example, model Y is a better choice if the cost savings in mailing fees (4000 fewer mailings) more than offset the loss in profits incurred from fewer sales (90 fewer sales).

Unsupervised Model Evaluation

Evaluating unsupervised data mining is, in general, a more difficult task than supervised evaluation. This is true because the goals of an unsupervised data mining session are frequently not as clear as the goals for supervised learning. Here we will introduce a general technique that employs supervised learning to evaluate an unsupervised clustering and leave a more detailed discussion of unsupervised evaluation for later chapters.

All unsupervised clustering techniques compute some measure of cluster quality. A common technique is to calculate the summation of squared error differences between the instances of each cluster and their corresponding cluster center. Smaller values for sums of squared error differences indicate clusters of higher quality. However, for a detailed evaluation of unsupervised clustering, it is supervised learning that comes to the rescue. The technique is as follows:

1. Perform an unsupervised clustering. Designate each cluster as a class and assign each cluster an arbitrary name. For example, if the clustering technique outputs three clusters, the clusters could be given the class names C_1, C_2, and C_3.

2. Choose a random sample of instances from each of the classes formed as a result of the instance clustering. Each class should be represented in the random sample in the same ratio as it is represented in the entire dataset. The percentage of total instances to sample can vary, but a good initial choice is two-thirds of all instances.

3. Build a supervised learner model with class name as the output attribute using the randomly sampled instances as training data. Employ the remaining instances to test the supervised model for classification correctness.

This evaluation method has at least two advantages. First, the unsupervised clustering can be viewed as a structure supported by a supervised learner model. For example, the results of a clustering created by an unsupervised algorithm can be seen as a decision tree or a rule-based structure. A second advantage of the supervised evaluation is that test set classification correctness scores can provide additional insight into the quality of the formed clusters.

Finally, a common misconception in the business world is that data mining can be accomplished simply by choosing the right tool, turning it loose on some data, and waiting for answers to problems. This approach is doomed to failure. Machines are still machines. It is the analysis of results provided by the human element that ultimately dictates the success or failure of a data mining project. A formal KDD process model such as the one described in Chapter 5 will help provide more complete answers to the questions posed at the beginning of this section.

2.6 Chapter Summary

Data mining strategies include classification, estimation, prediction, unsupervised clustering, and market basket analysis. Classification and estimation strategies are similar in that each strategy is employed to build models able to generalize current outcome.

However, the output of a classification strategy is categorical, whereas the output of an estimation strategy is numeric. A predictive strategy differs from a classification or estimation strategy in that it is used to design models for predicting future outcome rather than current behavior. Unsupervised clustering strategies are employed to discover hidden concept structures in data as well as to locate atypical data instances. The purpose of market basket analysis is to find interesting relationships among retail products. Discovered relationships can be used to design promotions, arrange shelf or catalog items, or develop cross-marketing strategies.

A data mining technique applies a data mining strategy to a set of data. Data mining techniques are defined by an algorithm and a knowledge structure. Common features that distinguish the various techniques are whether learning is supervised or unsupervised and whether their output is categorical or numeric. Familiar supervised data mining techniques include decision tree methods, production rule generators, neural networks, and statistical methods. Association rules are a favorite technique for marketing applications. Clustering techniques employ some measure of similarity to group instances into disjoint partitions. Clustering methods are frequently used to help determine a best set of input attributes for building supervised learner models.

Performance evaluation is probably the most critical of all the steps in the data mining process. Supervised model evaluation is often performed using a training/test set scenario. Supervised models with numeric output can be evaluated by computing average absolute or average squared error differences between computed and desired outcome. Marketing applications that focus on mass mailings are interested in developing models for increasing response rates to promotions. A marketing application measures the goodness of a model by its ability to lift response rate thresholds to levels well above those achieved by naïve (mass) mailing strategies. Unsupervised models support some measure of cluster quality that can be used for evaluative purposes. Supervised learning can also be employed to evaluate the quality of the clusters formed by an unsupervised model.

2.7   Key Terms

Association rule. A production rule whose consequent may contain multiple conditions and attribute relationships. An output attribute in one association rule can be an input attribute in another rule.

Classification. A supervised learning strategy where the output attribute is categorical. The emphasis is on building models able to assign new instances to one of a set of well-defined classes.

Confusion matrix. A matrix used to summarize the results of a supervised classification. Entries along the main diagonal represent the total number of correct classifications. Entries other than those on the main diagonal represent classification errors.

Data mining strategy. An outline of an approach for problem solution.

Data mining technique. One or more algorithms together with an associated knowledge structure.

Dependent variable. A variable whose value is determined by a combination of one or more independent variables.

Estimation. A supervised learning strategy where the output attribute is numeric. Emphasis is on determining current rather than future outcome.

Independent variable. An input attribute used for building supervised or unsupervised learner models.

Lift. The probability of class C_i given a sample taken from population P divided by the probability of C_i given the entire population P.

Lift chart. A graph that displays the performance of a data mining model as a function of sample size.

Linear regression. A supervised learning technique that generalizes numeric data as a linear equation. The equation defines the value of an output attribute as a linear sum of weighted input attribute values.

Market basket analysis. A data mining strategy that attempts to find interesting relationships among retail products.

Mean absolute error. For a set of training or test set instances, the mean absolute error is the average absolute difference between classifier predicted output and actual output.

Mean squared error. For a set of training or test set instances, the mean squared error is the average of the sum of squared differences between classifier predicted output and actual output.

Neural network. A set of interconnected nodes designed to imitate the functioning of the human brain.

Outliers. Atypical data instances.

Prediction. A supervised learning strategy designed to determine future outcome.

Root mean squared error. The square root of the mean squared error.

RuleMaker. A supervised learner model for generating production rules from data.

Statistical regression. A supervised learning technique that generalizes numerical data as a mathematical equation. The equation defines the value of an output attribute as a sum of weighted input attribute values.

2.8 Exercises

Review Questions

1. Differentiate between the following terms:

   a. data mining technique and data mining strategy

   b. dependent variable and independent variable

2. Can a data mining strategy be applied with more than one data mining technique? Can a data mining technique be used for more than one strategy? Explain your answers.

3. State whether each scenario is a classification, estimation, or prediction problem.

   a. Determine a freshman's likely first-year grade point average from the student's combined Scholastic Aptitude Test (SAT) score, high school class standing, and the total number of high school science and mathematics credits.

   b. Develop a model to determine if an individual is a good candidate for a home mortgage loan.

   c. Create a model able to determine if a publicly traded company is likely to split its stock in the near future.

   d. Develop a profile of an individual who has received three or more traffic violations in the past year.

   e. Construct a model to characterize a person who frequently visits an online auction site and makes an average of at least one online purchase per month.

4. For each task listed in question 3:

   a. Choose a best data mining technique. Explain why the technique is a good choice.

   b. Choose one technique that would be a poor choice. Explain why the technique is a poor choice.

   c. Develop a list of candidate attributes for each problem.

5. Several data mining techniques were presented in this chapter. If an explanation of what has been learned is of major importance, which data mining techniques would you consider? Which of the presented techniques do not explain what they discover?

6. Suppose you have used data mining to develop two alternative models designed to accept or reject home mortgage applications. Both models show an 85% test set classification correctness. The majority of errors made by model A are *false accepts* whereas the majority of errors made by model B are *false rejects*. Which model should you choose? Justify your answer.

7. Suppose you have used data mining to develop two alternative models designed to decide whether or not to drill for oil. Both models show an 85% test set classification correctness. The majority of errors made by model A are *false accepts* whereas the majority of errors made by model B are *false rejects*. Which model should you choose? Justify your answer.

8. Explain how unsupervised clustering can be used to evaluate the likely success of a supervised learner model.

9. Explain how supervised learning can be used to help evaluate the results of an unsupervised clustering.

Data Mining Questions

1. Draw a sketch of the feed-forward neural network applied to the credit card promotion database in the section titled Neural Networks.

2. Do you own a credit card? If so, log your card usage for the next month. Place information about each purchase in an Excel spreadsheet. Keep track of the date of purchase, the purchase amount, the city and state where the purchase was made, and a general purchase category (gasoline, groceries, clothing, etc.). In addition, keep track of any other information you believe to be important that would also be available to your credit card company. In Chapter 9 you will use a neural network to build a profile of your credit card purchasing habits. Once built, the model can be applied to new purchases to determine the likelihood that the purchases have been made by you or by someone else.

Computational Questions

1. Consider the following three-class confusion matrix. The matrix shows the classification results of a supervised model that uses previous voting records to determine the political party affiliation (Republican, Democrat, or Independent) of members of the United States Senate.

Computed Decision

	Rep	Dem	Ind
Rep	42	2	1
Dem	5	40	3
Ind	0	3	4

a. What percent of the instances were correctly classified?

b. According to the confusion matrix, how many Democrats are in the Senate? How many Republicans? How many Independents?

c. How many Republicans were classified as belonging to the Democratic Party?

d. How many Independents were classified as Republicans?

2. Suppose we have two classes each with 100 instances. The instances in one class contain information about individuals who currently have credit card insurance. The instances in the second class include information about individuals who have at least one credit card but are without credit card insurance. Use the following rule to answer the questions below:

IF *Life Insurance = Yes & Income > $50K*
THEN *Credit Card Insurance = Yes*
  Rule Accuracy = 80%
  Rule Coverage = 40%

a. How many individuals represented by the instances in the class of credit card insurance holders have life insurance and make more than $50,000 per year?

b. How many instances representing individuals who do not have credit card insurance have life insurance and make more than $50,000 per year?

3. Consider the confusion matrices shown below.

a. Compute the lift for Model X.

b. Compute the lift for Model Y.

Model X	Computed Accept	Computed Reject	Model Y	Computed Accept	Computed Reject
Accept	46	54	Accept	45	55
Reject	2,245	7,655	Reject	1,955	7,945

4. A certain mailing list consists of P names. Suppose a model has been built to determine a select group of individuals from the list who will receive a special flyer. As a second option, the flyer can be sent to all individuals on the list. Use the notation given in the confusion matrix below to show that the *lift* for choosing the model over sending the flyer to the entire population can be computed with the equation:

$$Lift = \frac{C_{11}P}{(C_{11} + C_{12})(C_{11} + C_{21})}$$

Send Flyer?	Computed Send	Computed Don't Send
Send	C_{11}	C_{12}
Don't Send	C_{21}	C_{22}

Chapter 3

Basic Data Mining Techniques

Chapter Objectives

▶ Understand an algorithm for constructing decision trees.

▶ Know an efficient technique for generating association rules.

▶ Understand how support and confidence are used to determine the value of an association rule.

▶ Understand how the K–Means algorithm is used to partition instances containing numeric data into disjoint clusters.

▶ Understand how genetic algorithms perform supervised learning and unsupervised clustering.

▶ Know how to choose a data mining technique for a specific problem.

This chapter offers a tutorial of several common data mining techniques. We chose to detail these methods here so the reader not requiring an in-depth study of the techniques presented later in the text can see how data mining algorithms build models to generalize data. In Section 3.1 we focus on supervised learning by presenting a standard algorithm for creating decision trees. In Section 3.2 we demonstrate an efficient technique for generating association rules. The focal point of Section 3.3 is unsupervised clustering and the K-Means algorithm. Section 3.4 shows you how genetic algorithms can perform supervised learning and unsupervised clustering. We conclude this chapter with a brief discussion about things to consider when choosing a data mining technique.

3.1   Decision Trees

Decision trees are a popular structure for supervised learning. Countless articles have been written about successful applications of decision tree models to real-world problems. We introduced the C4.5 decision tree model in Chapter 1. In this section we take a closer look at the algorithm used by C4.5 for building decision trees. We then apply this algorithm to the credit card promotion database described in Chapter 2.

An Algorithm for Building Decision Trees

Decision trees are constructed using only those attributes best able to differentiate the concepts to be learned. A decision tree is built by initially selecting a subset of instances from a training set. This subset is then used by the algorithm to construct a decision tree. The remaining training set instances test the accuracy of the constructed tree. If the decision tree classifies the instances correctly, the procedure terminates. If an instance is incorrectly classified, the instance is added to the selected subset of training instances and a new tree is constructed. This process continues until a tree that correctly classifies all nonselected instances is created or the decision tree is built from the entire training set. We offer a simplified version of the algorithm that employs the entire set of training instances to build a decision tree. The steps of the algorithm are as follows:

1.   Let T be the set of training instances.

2.   Choose an attribute that best differentiates the instances contained in T.

3.   Create a tree node whose value is the chosen attribute. Create child links from this node where each link represents a unique value for the chosen attribute. Use the child link values to further subdivide the instances into subclasses.

4. For each subclass created in step 3:

   a. If the instances in the subclass satisfy predefined criteria or if the set of remaining attribute choices for this path of the tree is null, specify the classification for new instances following this decision path.

   b. If the subclass does not satisfy the predefined criteria and there is at least one attribute to further subdivide the path of the tree, let *T* be the current set of subclass instances and return to step 2.

Before we show you how to apply the algorithm to a set of data, a word about attribute selection (step 2 of the algorithm) is in order. The attribute choices made when building a decision tree determine the size of the constructed tree. A main goal is to minimize the number of tree levels and tree nodes, thereby maximizing data generalization. C4.5 uses a measure taken from *information theory* to help with the attribute selection process. The basic idea is that for any choice point in the tree, C4.5 selects the attribute that splits the data so as to show the largest amount of gain in information. To show this, suppose we have *n* possible outcomes (classes). The information conveyed by any of these outcomes can be measured in bits as $-\log_2(1/n)$. For example, with $n = 4$, we have $-\log_2(1/4) = 2$. That is, it takes two bits to represent four possible outcomes (00, 01, 10, and 11). Stated another way, two bits uniquely identify four classes. Suppose attribute A is chosen for the next data split, and the split results in an average of two classes for each new branch of the tree. Because of this, each tree branch will require an average of $-\log_2(1/2) = 1$ bit to represent two possible outcomes. Therefore choosing attribute A results in an information gain of one bit. At each choice point in the tree C4.5 computes a *gain ratio* based on this idea for all available attributes. The attribute with the largest value for this ratio is selected to split the data.

A detailed discussion of how C4.5 uses the gain ratio measure to determine a best attribute choice is beyond the scope of our discussion. However, if you are interested in seeing how the gain ratio formulas are applied, Appendix C contains a detailed example for you to study. For our purposes we offer an intuitive approach to the process of attribute selection. Let's apply the simplified decision tree algorithm to the credit card promotion database defined in Chapter 2!

We follow our previous work with this dataset and designate *life insurance promotion* as the output attribute. Once again we wish to develop a predictive model. Therefore the input attributes are limited to *income range, credit card insurance, sex,* and *age.* Table 3.1 shows the training data. With the training data selected we can proceed to step 2 of the algorithm, which tells us to choose an input attribute to best differentiate the instances of the training data. Our choices are *income range, credit card insurance, sex,* and *age.* Let's look at each possibility.

For our first choice we consider *income range.* Figure 3.1 shows the partial tree created in step 3 of the algorithm provided income range is selected as the top-level

Table 3.1 • **The Credit Card Promotion Database**

Male N
Female Y

Income Range	Life Insurance Promotion	Credit Card Insurance	Sex	Age
40–50K	No	No	Male *N*	45
30–40K	Yes	No	Female *Y*	40
40–50K	No	No	Male *N*	42
30–40K	Yes	Yes	Male *N*	43
50–60K	Yes	No	Female *Y*	38
20–30K	No	No	Female *Y*	55
30–40K	Yes	Yes	Male *N*	35
20–30K	No	No	Male *N*	27
30–40K	No	No	Male *N*	43
30–40K	Yes	No	Female *Y*	41
40–50K	Yes	No	Female *Y*	43
20–30K	Yes	No	Male *N*	29
50–60K	Yes	No	Female *Y*	39
40–50K	No	No	Male *N*	55
20–30K	Yes	Yes	Female *Y*	19

Y: 9   Y: 3   Y: 7
N: 6   N: 12   N: 8

7F (6/1)
8M (5/3)
If F LIP = Y
if M LIP = N

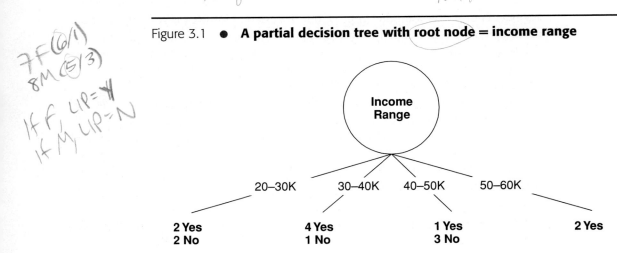

Figure 3.1 • **A partial decision tree with root node = income range**

Income Range

20–30K → **2 Yes / 2 No**
30–40K → **4 Yes / 1 No**
40–50K → **1 Yes / 3 No**
50–60K → **2 Yes**

node. The total *yes* and *no* counts for the output attribute (*life insurance promotion*) are shown at the bottom of each branch of the partial tree. To evaluate this choice we first make the value of each path of the partial tree the most frequently encountered class. We have two instances from each class following the branch given by *income range = 20–30K*. Therefore we can select either *life insurance promotion = no* or *life insurance promotion = yes* as the value of the path. To break the tie we opt for the most frequently occurring class, which is *life insurance promotion = yes*. For the branch showing *income range = 30–40K* we choose *life insurance promotion = yes* as the value of the path. For *income range = 40–50K* we choose *life insurance promotion = no*, and for *income range = 50–60K* we select *life insurance promotion = yes*.

Upon making these selections the partial tree correctly classifies 11 of the 15 training set instances. The result is a training set classification correctness of over 73%. This simple measure tells us something about the ability of the attribute to group the instances into the defined classes. However, the measure does not take into account the generalization capabilities of the attribute. For example, what happens when the training data contains an attribute, such as an identification number, that is unique to each instance? Obviously, each training instance is correctly classified by its unique identification number. Therefore the training set classification correctness score for the attribute will be 100%. However, picking such an attribute is a mistake, as the final decision tree will be a one-level structure having a unique path for each training instance!

A simple way to add a generalization factor to the accuracy measure is to divide training set accuracy by the total number of branches added to the tree as a result of the attribute choice. In this way attribute selections resulting in fewer additional tree branches will be favored. To apply this method to the income range attribute we divide the accuracy score of 11/15 by 4. This results in a goodness score for attribute income range of approximately 0.183.

Let's consider *credit card insurance* as a candidate for the top-level node of the decision tree. Figure 3.2 displays the partial tree created in step 3 of the algorithm provided *credit card insurance* is the selected attribute. Using the same reasoning as just discussed, we terminate the tree building process here and calculate the training set classification accuracy of the partial tree. For the branch *credit card insurance = no* we have six *yes* and six *no* responses to the life insurance promotion. Once again we break the tie by selecting the most frequently occurring class, which is *life insurance promotion = yes*. For the branch showing *credit card insurance = yes* we choose *life insurance promotion = yes*. To summarize, following either path of the tree we always make the choice *life insurance promotion = yes*. The resulting training set accuracy is 60% (9 of 15 correct choices). Dividing 0.60 by the number of branches added to the tree as a result of the attribute choice provides a goodness score of 0.30.

We now consider the numeric attribute *age* as a possible choice for the top-level node of the decision tree. A common method for processing numeric data is to sort

Figure 3.2   •   **A partial decision tree with root node = credit card insurance**

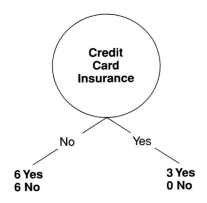

the values and consider binary splits between each pair of values. For our example, with Y denoting yes and N indicating no, the ages are first sorted as:

19	27	29	35	38	39	40	41	42	43	43	43	45	55	55
Y	N	Y	Y	Y	Y	Y	Y	N	Y	Y	N	N	N	N

A goodness score is then computed for each possible split point. That is, the score for a binary split between 19 and 27 is computed as is the score for a split between 27 and 29. This process continues until a score for the split between 45 and 55 is obtained. In this way each split point is treated as a separate attribute with two values. In making this computation for each choice point, our simple heuristic tells us that 43 results in the best split of the data. We associate *life insurance promotion = yes* with *age <= 43* and *life insurance promotion = no* with *age > 43*. The training set accuracy is 80% (12 of 15 correct), and the goodness score for this attribute is 0.40.

Finally, we consider attribute *sex* as a candidate top-level node. Choosing *sex* results in a goodness score of approximately 0.367. We leave the computational details for this selection as an exercise. Comparing the four results we see that attribute *age* offers the best score among the possible attribute selections. Therefore we make *age* the attribute of choice and execute step 3 of the decision tree algorithm. The partial tree with *age* as the top-level node is shown in Figure 3.3.

Step 4a of the algorithm requires us to examine each branch of the partial tree to determine if we are to continue the tree building process. The algorithm states two possibilities for terminating a path of the tree. First, if the instances following a

Figure 3.3 • **A partial decision tree with root node = age**

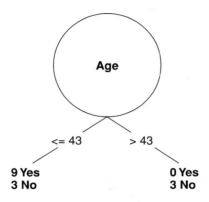

given branch satisfy a predetermined criterion, such as a minimum training set classification accuracy, the branch becomes a terminal path. The path is then assigned the value of the most frequently occurring class. An obvious termination criterion is that all instances following a specific path must be from the same class. A second possibility for terminating a path of the tree is the lack of an attribute for continuing the tree splitting process. To be sure, if a categorical attribute is selected, its values are able to divide the tree but once. However, a numerical attribute can be used to split the data several times. For our example the training instances following the branch having *age > 43* all have a value of *no* for life insurance promotion. Therefore we terminate this path and label the leaf node as *life insurance promotion = no.*

Next we consider the path with *age <= 43.* This path shows 9 instances having yes for the output attribute and 3 instances having no for the output attribute. As there is at least one more attribute to apply, we are able to continue building the tree. Notice that step 4b of the algorithm tells us the instances following this path are assigned as the new value of *T.* After the assignment for *T,* steps 2, 3, and 4 of the algorithm are repeated. This process continues until all paths meet the termination criteria or until all possibilities for attribute selections have been exhausted.

Decision Trees for the Credit Card Promotion Database

We applied two implementations of C4.5 to the data in Table 3.1. The versions vary slightly in their process for selecting attributes. The decision trees formed by each implementation are shown in Figures 3.4 and 3.5. The tree in Figure 3.4 contains

---

Figure 3.4 • **A three-node decision tree for the credit card database**

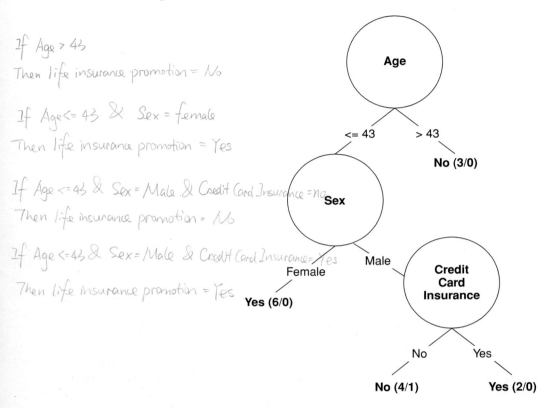

If Age > 43
Then life insurance promotion = No

If Age <= 43 & Sex = female
Then life insurance promotion = Yes

If Age <= 43 & Sex = Male & Credit Card Insurance = no
Then life insurance promotion = No

If Age <= 43 & Sex = Male & Credit Card Insurance = Yes
Then life insurance promotion = Yes

three nodes and was created by the most recent version of C4.5. It is worth noting that the gain ratio computation chose attribute *age* with a split at *age = 43* as the top-level node. Following the right branch of the tree we see individuals with age greater than 43 did not take advantage of the life insurance promotion. The *3* shown in parentheses indicates that three of the training instances follow this path. The *0* tells us that all three classifications are correct. Notice that the branch for *credit card insurance = no* shows one incorrect classification. The incorrect classification tells us that one male individual with age less than or equal to 43 did not purchase credit card insurance but said yes to the life insurance promotion. As all the other classifications are correct, the tree is able to accurately classify 14 of the 15 training instances.

The tree in Figure 3.5 has two rather than three nodes. As with the tree in Figure 3.4, the tree shows attributes *credit card insurance* and *sex*. However, the tree does not have a test for the *age* attribute. As you can see, the decision tree in Figure 3.5 incorrectly classifies two training instances.

Figure 3.5 • A two-node decision tree for the credit card database

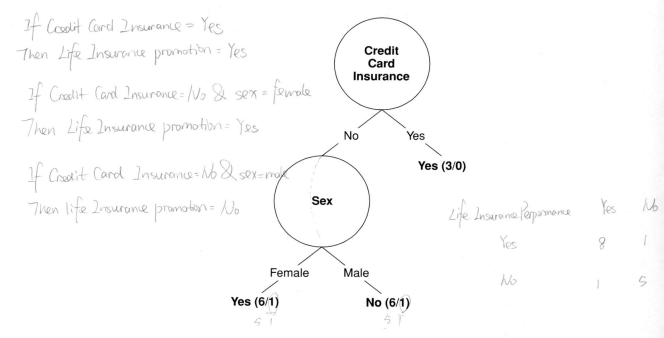

If Credit Card Insurance = Yes
Then Life Insurance promotion = Yes

If Credit Card Insurance = No & sex = female
Then Life Insurance promotion = Yes

If Credit Card Insurance = No & sex = male
Then life Insurance promotion = No

Life Insurance Performance	Yes	No
Yes	8	1
No	1	5

At first thought it seems highly unlikely to have a situation where a decision tree is unable to correctly classify all training instances. Let's use the decision tree in Figure 3.4 to see how this can happen. Table 3.2 displays the four training instances that follow the decision tree path in Figure 3.4 to *credit card insurance = no*. At this point the algorithm either decides the predefined criteria stated in step 4a of the algorithm have been satisfied or selects a new attribute to further subdivide the instances. Table 3.2 tells us that the first three instances have *life insurance promotion = no*. The fourth instance has *life insurance promotion = yes*. However, the fourth instance is identical to the second instance with the exception of the value for *life insurance promotion* and the value for *age*. As *life insurance promotion* is the output attribute, the only possible attribute choice is *age*. As noted earlier, once a categorical attribute has been selected as a tree node, it cannot be picked again. However, numerical attributes can be used several times provided a new split point is chosen each time the attribute is selected. Therefore the alternatives are to terminate further development of the path or to employ the attribute *age* and create a new node. As you can see, the algorithm chose to terminate the tree building process. Let's examine the alterative.

Table 3.2 shows an age of 29 for the single instance with *life insurance promotion = yes*. The only possibility for a split on age is to make one path with *age <= 29* and the second path having *age > 29*. The first and third instances of Table 3.2 follow *age > 29*.

Table 3.2 ● **Training Data Instances Following the Path in Figure 3.4 to Credit Card Insurance = No**

Income Range	Life Insurance Promotion	Credit Card Insurance	Sex	Age
40–50K	No	No	Male	42
20–30K	No	No	Male	27
30–40K	No	No	Male	43
20–30K	Yes	No	Male	29

As both instances show *yes* for life insurance promotion, the path is terminal. The path for *age <= 29* requires another split on the age attribute (*age <= 27* and *age > 27* are possibilities) for the tree to successfully classify all training instances. The end result is a decision tree with five nodes. However, instead of creating two new tree nodes to eliminate the incorrect classification, the logic of the algorithm gives preference to a more general tree structure and discounts the error.

Decision Tree Rules

In Chapter 1 you saw how a decision tree can be mapped to a set of production rules by writing one rule for each path of the tree. As rules tend to be more appealing than trees, several variations of the basic tree to rule mapping have been studied. Most variations focus on simplifying and/or eliminating existing rules. To illustrate the rule simplification process, consider the decision tree in Figure 3.4. A rule created by following one path of the tree is shown here:

> **IF** *Age <= 43 & Sex = Male & Credit Card Insurance = No*
> **THEN** *Life Insurance Promotion = No*

The antecedent conditions for this rule cover 4 of the 15 training set instances with a 75% accuracy. Let's simplify the rule by eliminating the antecedent condition for *age*. The simplified rule takes the form:

> **IF** *Sex = Male & Credit Card Insurance = No*
> **THEN** *Life Insurance Promotion = No*

By examining Table 3.1 we see the antecedent of the simplified rule covers six instances. As the rule consequent covers five of the six instances, the accuracy of the simplified rule is approximately 83.3%. Therefore the simplified rule is more general and more accurate than the original rule! At first thought it seems hard to believe that removing a conditional test can actually improve the accuracy of a rule. However, closer examination shows why eliminating the test gives a better result. To see this, notice that removing the *age* attribute from the rule is equivalent to deleting the attribute from the tree in Figure 3.4. In doing so, the three instances following the path *age > 43* must now follow the same path as those instances traversing *age <= 43*. All three instances with *age > 43* are members of the *life insurance promotion = no* class. Two of these three instances are of male gender with *credit card insurance = no*. Both instances satisfy the preconditions and consequent condition of the simplified rule. Because of this, the preconditions for the new rule are satisfied by six instances, five of which have *no* as the value of *life insurance promotion*.

Most decision tree implementations automate the process of rule creation and simplification. Once rules have been simplified and/or eliminated the rules are ordered so as to minimize error. Finally, a default rule is chosen. The default rule states the classification of an instance not meeting the preconditions of any listed rule.

Other Methods for Building Decision Trees

We just described the basics of C4.5—Quinlan's most recent noncommercial decision tree building algorithm. However, several other algorithms for building decision trees exist. ID3 (Quinlan, 1986) has been studied extensively and is the precursor to C4.5. CART (Breiman et al., 1984) is of particular interest as several commercial products implement variations of the algorithm. In addition, CART was the first system to introduce **regression trees.** Essentially, regression trees take the form of decision trees where the leaf nodes are numerical rather than categorical values.

CART is very similar to C4.5, but there are several differences. One notable difference is that CART always performs binary splits on the data regardless of whether attributes are categorical or numeric. A second difference is that CART invokes test data to help prune and therefore generalize a created binary tree, whereas C4.5 uses only training data to create a final tree structure. CHAID (Kass, 1980) is a second decision tree building algorithm of interest found in commercial statistical packages such as SAS and SPSS. CHAID differs from C4.5 and CART in that it is limited to working with categorical attributes. CHAID has a statistical flavor as it uses the X^2 statistical test of significance to determine candidate attributes for building the decision tree.

General Considerations

Decision trees have several advantages. Here is a list of a few of the many advantages decision trees have to offer.

- Decision trees are easy to understand and map nicely to a set of production rules.

- Decision trees have been successfully applied to real problems.

- Decision trees make no prior assumptions about the nature of the data.

- Decision trees are able to build models with datasets containing numerical as well as categorical data.

As with all data mining algorithms, there are several issues surrounding decision tree usage. Specifically,

- Output attributes must be categorical, and multiple output attributes are not allowed.

- Decision tree algorithms are **unstable** in that slight variations in the training data can result in different attribute selections at each choice point within the tree. The effect can be significant as attribute choices affect all descendent subtrees.

- Trees created from numeric datasets can be quite complex as attribute splits for numeric data are typically binary.

3.2 Generating Association Rules

Affinity analysis is the general process of determining which things go together. A typical application is market basket analysis, where the desire is to determine those items likely to be purchased by a customer during a shopping experience. The output of the market basket analysis is a set of associations about customer-purchase behavior. The associations are given in the form of a special set of rules known as association rules. The association rules are used to help determine appropriate product marketing strategies. In this section we describe an efficient procedure for generating association rules.

Confidence and Support

Association rules are unlike traditional classification rules in that an attribute appearing as a precondition in one rule may appear in the consequent of a second rule. In addition, traditional classification rules usually limit the consequent of a rule to a single attribute. Association rule generators allow the consequent of a rule to contain one or several attribute values. To show this, suppose we wish to determine if there are any interesting relationships to be found in customer purchasing trends among the following four grocery store products:

- Milk
- Cheese
- Bread
- Eggs

Possible associations include the following:

1. If customers purchase milk they also purchase bread.
2. If customers purchase bread they also purchase milk.
3. If customers purchase milk and eggs they also purchase cheese and bread.
4. If customers purchase milk, cheese, and eggs they also purchase bread.

The first association tells us that a customer who purchases milk is also likely to purchase bread. The obvious question is "How likely will the event of a milk purchase lead to a bread purchase?" To answer this each association rule has an associated **confidence**. For this rule confidence is the conditional probability of a bread purchase given a milk purchase. Therefore if a total of 10,000 customer transactions involve the purchase of milk, and 5000 of those same transactions also contain a bread purchase, the confidence of a bread purchase given a milk purchase is 5000/10,000 = 50%.

Now consider the second rule. Does this rule give us the same information as the first rule? The answer is an obvious no! With the first rule the transaction domain consisted of all customers who had made a milk purchase. For this rule the domain is the set of all customer transactions that show the purchase of a bread item. As an example, suppose we have a total of 20,000 customer transactions involving a bread purchase and of these, 5000 also involve a milk purchase. This gives us a confidence value for a milk purchase given a bread purchase of 25%.

Although the third and fourth rules are more complex, the idea is the same. The confidence for the third rule tells us the likelihood of a purchase of both cheese and bread given a purchase of milk and eggs. The confidence for the fourth rule tells us the likelihood of a bread purchase given the purchase of milk, cheese, and eggs.

One important piece of information a rule confidence value does not offer is the percent of all transactions containing the attribute values found in an association rule. This statistic is known as the **support** for a rule. Support is simply the minimum percentage of instances (transactions) in the database that contain all items listed in a specific association rule. In the next section you will see how item sets use confidence and support to set limits on the total number of association rules for a given dataset.

Mining Association Rules: An Example

Association rules can be generated using a traditional approach, however, when several attributes are present, this process becomes unreasonable because of the large number of possible conditions for the consequent of each rule. Special algorithms have been developed to generate association rules efficiently. One such algorithm is the *apriori* algorithm (Agrawal et al., 1993). This algorithm generates what are known as **item sets.** Item sets are attribute-value combinations that meet a specified coverage requirement. Those attribute-value combinations that do not meet the coverage requirement are discarded. Because of this, the rule generation process can be completed in a reasonable amount of time.

Apriori association rule generation is a two-step process. The first step is item set generation. The second step uses the generated item sets to create a set of association rules. We illustrate the idea with the subset of the credit card promotion database shown in Table 3.3. The *income range* and *age* attributes have been eliminated.

To begin, we set the minimum attribute-value coverage requirement at four items. The first item set table created contains single-item sets. Single-item sets represent individual attribute-value combinations extracted from the original dataset. We first consider the attribute *magazine promotion*. Upon examining the table values for *magazine promotion,* we see seven instances have a value of *yes* and three instances contain the value *no*. Therefore *magazine promotion = yes* represents a valid item set to be added to the single-item set table. As *magazine promotion = no* does not meet the coverage requirement, *magazine promotion = no* is not added to the single-item set table.

Table 3.3 • **A Subset of the Credit Card Promotion Database**

Magazine Promotion	Watch Promotion	Life Insurance Promotion	Credit Card Insurance	Sex
Yes	No	No	No	Male
Yes	Yes	Yes	No	Female
No	No	No	No	Male
Yes	Yes	Yes	Yes	Male
Yes	No	Yes	No	Female
No	No	No	No	Female
Yes	No	Yes	Yes	Male
No	Yes	No	No	Male
Yes	No	No	No	Male
Yes	Yes	Yes	No	Female

Table 3.4 • **Single-Item Sets**

Single-Item Sets	Number of Items
Magazine Promotion = Yes	7
Watch Promotion = Yes	4
Watch Promotion = No	6
Life Insurance Promotion = Yes	5
Life Insurance Promotion = No	5
Credit Card Insurance = No	8
Sex = Male	6
Sex = Female	4

Table 3.4 shows all single-item set values from Table 3.3 that meet the minimum coverage requirement.

We now combine single-item sets to create two-item sets with the same coverage restriction. We need only consider attribute value combinations derived from the single-item set table. Let's start with *magazine promotion = yes* and *watch promotion = yes*. As there are only three matches, this combination is not added to the two-item set table. Next we examine *magazine promotion = yes* and *watch promotion = no*. Four instances satisfy this combination, therefore this will be our first entry in the two-item set table. We then consider *magazine promotion = yes* and *life insurance promotion = yes*. As there are five instance matches, we add this combination to the two-item set table. We now try *magazine promotion = yes* and *life insurance promotion = no*. As there are only two matches, this combination is not a valid two-item set entry. Continuing this process results in a total of 11 two-item set table entries. Table 3.5 shows the complete two-item set table.

The next step is to use the attribute-value combinations from the two-item set table to generate three-item sets. Reading from the top of the two-item set table, our first possibility is

Magazine Promotion = Yes & Watch Promotion = No & Life Insurance Promotion = Yes.

As only one instance satisfies the three values, we do not add this combination to the three-item set table. In fact, the only three-item set that satisfies the coverage criterion is:

Watch Promotion = No & Life Insurance Promotion = No & Credit Card Insurance = No

---

Table 3.5 ● **Two-Item Sets**

Two-Item Sets	Number of Items
Magazine Promotion = Yes & Watch Promotion = No $C = \frac{4}{7}; S = \frac{4}{10}$	4
Magazine Promotion = Yes & Life Insurance Promotion = Yes $C = \frac{5}{7}, S = \frac{5}{10}$	5
Magazine Promotion = Yes & Credit Card Insurance = No $C = \frac{4}{7}; S = \frac{5}{10}$	5
Magazine Promotion = Yes & Sex = Male $C = \frac{4}{7}; S = \frac{4}{10}$	4
Watch Promotion = No & Life Insurance Promotion = No $C = \frac{4}{6}; S = \frac{4}{10}$	4
Watch Promotion = No & Credit Card Insurance = No $C = \frac{5}{6}, S = \frac{5}{10}$	5
Watch Promotion = No & Sex = Male $C = \frac{4}{6}; S = \frac{4}{10}$	4
Life Insurance Promotion = No & Credit Card Insurance = No $C = \frac{5}{5}, S = \frac{5}{10}$	5
Life Insurance Promotion = No & Sex = Male $C = \frac{4}{5}; S = \frac{4}{10}$	4
Credit Card Insurance = No & Sex = Male $C = \frac{4}{8}; S = \frac{4}{10}$	4
Credit Card Insurance = No & Sex = Female $C = \frac{4}{8}; S = \frac{4}{10}$	4

As there are no additional member set possibilities, the process proceeds from generating item sets to creating association rules. The first step in rule creation is to specify a minimum rule confidence. Next, association rules are generated from the two- and three–item set tables. Finally, any rule not meeting the minimum confidence value is discarded.

Two possible two–item set rules are:

IF *Magazine Promotion = Yes*
THEN *Life Insurance Promotion = Yes* (5/7)

IF *Life Insurance Promotion = Yes*
THEN *Magazine Promotion = Yes* (5/5)

The fractions at the right are used to compute rule confidence. For the first rule there are five instances where *magazine promotion* and *life insurance promotion* are both *yes*. There are seven total instances where *magazine promotion* = *yes*. Therefore in two situations the rule will be in error when predicting a life insurance promotion value of *yes* when *magazine promotion* = *yes*. If our minimum confidence setting is 80% this first rule will be eliminated from the final rule set. The second rule states that *magazine promotion* = *yes* any time *life insurance promotion* = *yes*. The rule confidence is 100%. Therefore the rule becomes part of the final output of the association rule generator.

Here are three of several possible three-item set rules:

IF *Watch Promotion = No & Life Insurance Promotion = No*
THEN *Credit Card Insurance = No* (4/4)

IF *Watch Promotion = No*
THEN *Life Insurance Promotion = No & Credit Card Insurance = No* (4/6)

IF *Credit Card Insurance = No*
THEN *Watch Promotion = No & Life Insurance Promotion = No* (4/8)

Exercises at the end of the chapter ask you to write additional association rules for this dataset. We conclude our discussion on association rules with some general considerations.

General Considerations

Association rules are particularly popular because of their ability to find relationships in large databases without having the restriction of choosing a single dependent variable. However, caution must be exercised in the interpretation of association rules since many discovered relationships turn out to be trivial.

As an example, let's suppose we present a total of 10,000 transactions for a market basket analysis. Also, suppose 70% of all transactions involve the purchase of milk and 50% of all transactions have a bread purchase. From this information we are likely to see an association rule of the form:

> *If customers purchase milk they also purchase bread.*

The confidence for this rule may be well above 40%. However, because most customers purchase both products, our association rule is of little value. That is, the rule does not give us additional marketing information telling us that it would be to our advantage to promote the purchase of bread with milk. However, there are two types of relationships found within association rules that are of interest:

- We are interested in association rules that show a lift in product sales for a particular product where the lift in sales is the result of its association with one or more other products. In this case we can use this information to help promote the product with increased sales as a result of the association.

- We are also interested in association rules that show a lower than expected confidence for a particular association. In this case a possible conclusion is the products listed in the association rule compete for the same market.

As a final point, volumes of data are often stored for market basket analysis. Therefore it is important to minimize the work required by an association rule generator. A good scenario is to specify an initially high value for the item set coverage criterion. If more rules are desired the coverage criterion can be lowered and the entire process repeated.

3.3   The K-Means Algorithm

The K-Means algorithm (Lloyd, 1982) is a simple yet effective statistical clustering technique. To help you better understand unsupervised clustering, let's see how the K-Means algorithm partitions a set of data into disjoint clusters.

Here is the algorithm:

1.   Choose a value for K, the total number of clusters to be determined.

2.   Choose K instances (data points) within the dataset at random. These are the initial cluster centers.

3.   Use simple Euclidean distance to assign the remaining instances to their closest cluster center.

4.   Use the instances in each cluster to calculate a new mean for each cluster.

5.   If the new mean values are identical to the mean values of the previous iteration the process terminates. Otherwise, use the new means as cluster centers and repeat steps 3–5.

The first step of the algorithm requires an initial decision about how many clusters we believe to be present in the data. Next, the algorithm randomly selects K data points as initial cluster centers. Each instance is then placed in the cluster to which it is most similar. Similarity can be defined in many ways, however, the similarity measure most often used is simple Euclidean distance.

Once all instances have been placed in their appropriate cluster, the cluster centers are updated by computing the mean of each new cluster. The process of instance classification and cluster center computation continues until an iteration of the algorithm shows no change in the cluster centers. That is, the algorithm terminates after j iterations if for each cluster C_i all instances found in C_i after iteration $j-1$ remain in cluster C_i upon the completion of iteration j.

An Example Using K-Means

To clarify the process, let's work through a partial example containing two attributes. Although most real datasets contain several attributes, the methodology remains the

Table 3.6 ● **K-Means Input Values**

Instance	X	Y
1	1.0	1.5
2	1.0	4.5
3	2.0	1.5
4	2.0	3.5
5	3.0	2.5
6	5.0	6.0

same regardless of the number of attributes. For our example we will use the six in-stances shown in Table 3.6. For simplicity we name the two attributes *x* and *y*, respectively, and map the instances onto an *x-y* coordinate system. The mapping is shown in Figure 3.6.

As the first step, we must choose a value for *K*. Let's assume we suspect two distinct clusters. Therefore we set the value for *K* at 2. The algorithm chooses two points at random to represent initial cluster centers. Suppose the algorithm selects instance 1 as one cluster center and instance 3 as the second cluster center. The next step is to classify the remaining instances.

Figure 3.6 ● **A coordinate mapping of the data in Table 3.6**

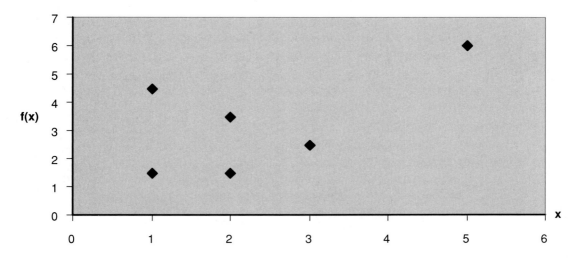

Recall the formula for computing the Euclidean distance between point A with coordinates (x_1, y_1) and point B with coordinates (x_2, y_2):

$$\text{Distance}(A - B) = \sqrt{(x_1 - x_2)^2 + (y_1 - y_2)^2}$$

Computations for the first iteration of the algorithm with $C_1 = (1.0, 1.5)$ and $C_2 = (2.0, 1.5)$ are as follows where $C_i - j$ is the Euclidean distance from point C_i to the point represented by instance j in Table 3.6.

Distance $(C_1 - 1) = 0.00$ Distance $(C_2 - 1) = 1.00$

Distance $(C_1 - 2) = 3.00$ Distance $(C_2 - 2) \approx 3.16$

Distance $(C_1 - 3) = 1.00$ Distance $(C_2 - 3) = 0.00$

Distance $(C_1 - 4) \approx 2.24$ Distance $(C_2 - 4) = 2.00$

Distance $(C_1 - 5) \approx 2.24$ Distance $(C_2 - 5) \approx 1.41$

Distance $(C_1 - 6) \approx 6.02$ Distance $(C_2 - 6) \approx 5.41$

After the first iteration of the algorithm we have the following clustering:

C_1 contains instances 1 and 2.

C_2 contains instances 3, 4, 5, and 6.

The next step is to recompute each cluster center.
For cluster C_1:

$x = (1.0 + 1.0) / 2 = 1.0$

$y = (1.5 + 4.5) / 2 = 3.0$

For cluster C_2:

$x = (2.0 + 2.0 + 3.0 + 5.0) / 4.0 = 3.0$

$y = (1.5 + 3.5 + 2.5 + 6.0) / 4.0 = 3.375$

Thus the new cluster centers are $C_1 = (1.0, 3.0)$ and $C_2 = (3.0, 3.375)$. As the cluster centers have changed, the algorithm must perform a second iteration.

Computations for the second iteration are:

Distance $(C_1 - 1) = 1.50$ Distance $(C_2 - 1) \approx 2.74$

Distance $(C_1 - 2) = 1.50$ Distance $(C_2 - 2) \approx 2.29$

Distance $(C_1 - 3) \approx 1.80$ Distance $(C_2 - 3) = 2.125$

Distance $(C_1 - 4) \approx 1.12$ Distance $(C_2 - 4) \approx 1.01$

Distance $(C_1 - 5) \approx 2.06$ Distance $(C_2 - 5) = 0.875$

Distance $(C_1 - 6) = 5.00$ Distance $(C_2 - 6) \approx 3.30$

The second iteration results in a modified clustering:

C_1 contains instances 1, 2, and 3.

C_2 contains instances 4, 5, and 6.

Next, we compute the new centers for each cluster.

For cluster C_1 :

$x = (1.0 + 1.0 + 2.0) / 3.0 \approx 1.33$

$y = (1.5 + 4.5 + 1.5) / 3.0 = 2.50$

For cluster C_2 :

$x = (2.0 + 3.0 + 5.0) / 3.0 \approx 3.33$

$y = (3.5 + 2.5 + 6.0) / 3.0 = 4.00$

Once again, this iteration shows a change in the cluster centers. Therefore the process continues to a third iteration with $C_1 = (1.33, 2.50)$ and $C_2 = (3.33, 4.00)$. We leave the computations for the third iteration as an exercise.

These computations have little meaning other than to demonstrate the workings of the algorithm. In fact, we may see a different final cluster configuration for each alternative choice of the initial cluster centers. Unfortunately, this is a general problem seen with the K–Means algorithm. That is, although the algorithm is guaranteed to cluster the instances into a stable state, the stabilization is not guaranteed to be optimal.

An optimal clustering for the K–Means algorithm is frequently defined as a clustering that shows a minimum summation of squared error differences between the instances and their corresponding cluster center. Finding a globally optimal clustering for a given value of K is nearly impossible as we must repeat the algorithm with alternative choices for the initial cluster centers. For even a few hundred data instances, it is not practical to run the K-Means algorithm more than a few times. Instead, the usual practice is to choose a terminating criterion, such as a maximum acceptable squared error value, and execute the K-Means algorithm until we achieve a result that satisfies the termination condition.

Table 3.7 shows three clusterings resulting from repeated application of the K-Means algorithm to the data in Table 3.6. Figure 3.7 displays the most frequently occurring clustering. This clustering is shown as outcome 2 in Table 3.7. Notice that the best clustering, as determined by a minimum squared error value, is outcome 3, where the single instance with coordinates (5,6) forms its own cluster and the remaining instances shape the second cluster.

General Considerations

The K-Means method is easy to understand and implement. However, there are several issues to consider. Specifically,

- The algorithm only works with real-valued data. If we have a categorical attribute in our dataset we must either discard the attribute or convert the attribute values to numerical equivalents. For example, suppose we have the attribute color with values red, blue, green, and brown. One possibility is to assign arbitrary numeric values to each color. However, there are several disadvantages to this solution. We address issues surrounding data conversion in Chapter 5.

- We are required to select a value for the number of clusters to be formed. This is an obvious problem if we make a poor choice. One way to cope with this issue is to run the algorithm several times with alternative values for K. In this way, we are more likely to get a "feel" for how many clusters may be present in the data.

Table 3.7 • Several Applications of the K-Means Algorithm ($K = 2$)

Outcome	Cluster Centers	Cluster Points	Squared Error
1	(2.67,4.67)	2, 4, 6	14.50
	(2.00,1.83)	1, 3, 5	
2	(1.5,1.5)	1, 3	15.94
	(2.75,4.125)	2, 4, 5, 6	
3	(1.8,2.7)	1, 2, 3, 4, 5	9.60
	(5,6)	6	

Figure 3.7   •   **A K-Means clustering of the data in Table 3.6 (K = 2)**

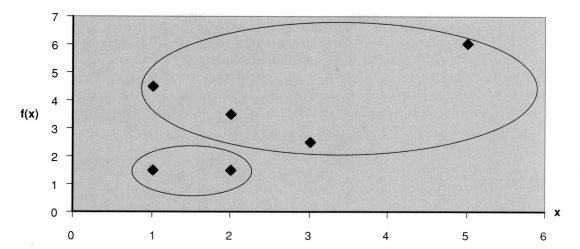

- The K-Means algorithm works best when the clusters that exist in the data are of approximately equal size. This being the case, if an optimal solution is represented by clusters of unequal size, the K-Means algorithm is not likely to find a best solution.

- There is no way to tell which attributes are significant in determining the formed clusters. For this reason several irrelevant attributes can cause less than optimal results.

- A lack of explanation about the nature of the formed clusters leaves us responsible for much of the interpretation about what has been found. However, we can use supervised data mining tools to help us gain insight into the nature of the clusters formed by unsupervised clustering algorithms.

Despite these limitations the K-Means algorithm continues to be a favorite statistical technique. In the section titled Genetic Algorithms and Unsupervised Clustering you will see a slightly different approach to numerical clustering that borrows several ideas from evolutionary science. Look closely and you will see similarities between the K-Means algorithm and the genetic learning approach to unsupervised clustering.

3.4   Genetic Learning

Genetic algorithms apply an evolutionary approach to inductive learning. The genetic algorithm learning model was initially developed by John Holland (1986) and is based on the Darwinian principle of natural selection. Genetic programming has been successfully applied to problems that are difficult to solve using conventional techniques. Common areas of application include scheduling problems, such as the traveling salesperson problem, network routing problems for circuit-switched networks, and problems in the area of financial marketing.

Genetic algorithms can be developed for supervised and unsupervised data mining. Here we present a basic genetic learning algorithm.

1.   Initialize a population *P* of *n* elements, often referred to as chromosomes, as a potential solution.

2.   Until a specified termination condition is satisfied:

   a.   Use a fitness function to evaluate each element of the current solution. If an element passes the fitness criteria, it remains in *P*.

   b.   The population now contains *m* elements (*m* <= *n*). Use genetic operators to create (*n* − *m*) new elements. Add the new elements to the population.

For data mining we think of elements as instances defined by attributes and values. A common technique for representing genetic knowledge is to transform elements into binary strings. To illustrate, consider the attribute *income range* given in Table 3.1. We can represent *income range* as a string of two bits by assigning "00" to 20–30K, "01" to 30–40K, "10" to 40–50K, and "11" to 50–60K. For a numeric attribute such as *age*, we have several options. A frequent approach is to map numeric values to discrete interval ranges and apply the same strategy as that used for categorical data.

The most widespread genetic operators are crossover and mutation. **Crossover** forms new elements for the population by combining parts of two elements currently in the population. The elements most often used for crossover are those destined to be eliminated from the population. **Mutation,** a second genetic operator, is sparingly applied to elements chosen for elimination. Mutation can be applied by randomly flipping bits (or attribute values) within a single element. Alternatively, the choice of whether to flip individual bits can be probability-based. **Selection** is a third genetic operator that is sometimes used. With selection, the elements deleted from the population are replaced by copies of elements that pass the fitness test with high scores. In this way the overall fitness of the population is guaranteed to increase. As selection supports specialization rather than generalization, it should be used with caution.

Genetic Algorithms and Supervised Learning

Figure 3.8 shows a plausible model for supervised genetic learning. Countless variations of the generalized model exist. However, the model suffices to help us explain the genetic learning process. Let's associate this model with the genetic algorithm defined earlier to obtain a better understanding of supervised genetic learning.

Figure 3.8 • **Supervised genetic learning**

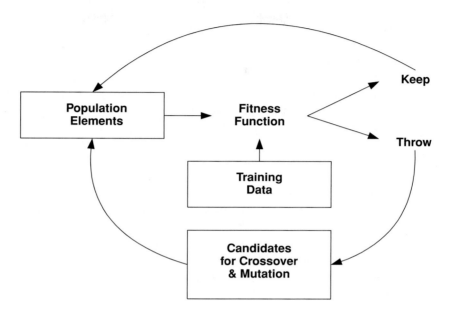

Step 1 of the algorithm initializes a population *P* of elements. The *P* referred to in the algorithm is shown in Figure 3.8 as the box labeled *population elements*. Figure 3.8 shows that the process of supervised genetic learning iteratively modifies the elements of the population. The algorithm tells us that this process continues until a termination condition is satisfied. The termination condition might be that all elements of the population meet some minimum criteria. As an alternative, the condition can be a fixed number of iterations of the learning process.

Step 2a of the algorithm applies a fitness function to evaluate each element currently in the population. Figure 3.8 shows us that the fitness function uses a set of training data to help with the evaluation. With each iteration of the algorithm, elements not satisfying the fitness criteria are eliminated from the population. The final result of a supervised genetic learning session is a set of population elements that best represents the training data.

Step 2b of the algorithm adds new elements to the population to replace any elements eliminated in step 2a. Figure 3.8 indicates that the new elements are formed from previously deleted elements by applying crossover and mutation. Although the selection operator is not specifically shown in Figure 3.8, it can be an option. If selection is used some elements with high fitness scores will be reproduced. In any case, a usual scenario holds the number of elements at a constant value. For example, if the population consists of 10 elements and 4 of these elements fail the fitness test, 4 new elements will be added to the population using some combination of crossover, mutation, and selection.

Now that we have a better understanding of what genetic learning is all about, let's look at a specific example that uses a subset of the credit card promotion database. Once again our goal is to create a model able to differentiate individuals who have accepted the life insurance promotion from those who have not. We must first generate an initial population for our model. As part of this selection process, it is our job to decide how many elements will be part of the population. For simplicity, let's suppose an initial population is represented by the four elements shown in Table 3.8. We require that after each iteration of the algorithm exactly two elements from each class (*life insurance promotion = yes* & *life insurance promotion = no*) remain in the population.

Notice that we have changed attribute values for *age* to discrete categories. This is to remove additional complexity from our explanation. Also, note the question mark as the value for *income range* in the third row of Table 3.8. A question mark is a "don't care" condition, meaning the attribute is not important to the learning process. This is one way to promote attribute significance within the population.

As stated in the algorithm, genetic training involves repeated modification of the population by applying a fitness function to each element. To implement the fitness function we compare each population element to the six training instances shown in Table 3.9. For a single population element E, we define our fitness function as follows:

1. Let N be the number of matches of the input attribute values of E with training instances from its own class.

2. Let M be the number of input attribute value matches to all training instances from the competing classes.

3. Add 1 to M.

4. Divide N by M.

Table 3.8 ● **An Initial Population for Supervised Genetic Learning**

Population Element	Income Range	Life Insurance Promotion	Credit Card Insurance	Sex	Age
1	20–30K	No	Yes	Male	30–39
2	30–40K	Yes	No	Female	50–59
3	?	No	No	Male	40–49
4	30–40K	Yes	Yes	Male	40–49

That is, the fitness score for any population element E is simply the ratio of the number of matches of the attribute values of E to its own class to the number of matches to all training instances from the competing classes. One is added to the denominator of each ratio to avoid a possible division by zero. If the fitness value of a particular element does not show a ratio score above a predefined value, it is eliminated from the population and becomes a candidate for crossover or mutation. If all currently selected elements meet or exceed the fitness score, elements are randomly chosen for removal. Alternatively, elements with the lowest fitness scores can be eliminated.

Now that our fitness function is defined, let's compute the fitness score for element 1. Element 1 is a member of the class *life insurance promotion = no*. Therefore N is computed as the number of matches element 1 has with the members in Table 3.9 having *life insurance promotion = no*. That is, for element 1 we compute N using the following information.

- *Income Range = 20–30K* matches with training instances 4 and 5.

- There are no matches for *Credit Card Insurance = Yes*.

- *Sex = Male* matches with training instances 5 and 6.

- There are no matches for *Age = 30–39*.

Therefore the value of N computes to 4. Next, we compute M by comparing element 1 with training instances 1, 2, and 3. The computation is as follows:

- There are no matches for *Income Range = 20–30K*.

- *Credit Card Insurance = Yes* matches with training instance 1.

Table 3.9 ● **Training Data for Genetic Learning**

Training Instance	Income Range	Life Insurance Promotion	Credit Card Insurance	Sex	Age
1	30–40K	Yes	Yes	Male	30–39
2	30–40K	Yes	No	Female	40–49
3	50–60K	Yes	No	Female	30–39
4	20–30K	No	No	Female	50–59
5	20–30K	No	No	Male	20–29
6	30–40K	No	No	Male	40–49

- *Sex = Male* matches with training instance 1.

- *Age = 30–39* matches with training instances 1 and 3.

As there are four matches with the training instances where *life insurance promotion = yes*, the value of *M* for instance 1 is 4. Next, we add 1 to *M*, giving us a final fitness score for element 1 of 4/5, or 0.80. The following is the list of fitness function values for the entire initial population. Any comparison with ? is considered a nonmatch. *F(i)* denotes the fitness value for population element *i*.

- $F(1) = 4 / 5 = 0.80$

- $F(2) = 6 / 7 = 0.86$

- $F(3) = 6 / 5 = 1.20$

- $F(4) = 5 / 5 = 1.00$

We now eliminate a subset of the population and use genetic operators to create new elements. To show the process, we remove elements 1 and 2 because each shows the lowest fitness score for its respective class. First, we use the crossover operator. Many crossover possibilities exist. Let's make the point of crossover after the *life insurance promotion* attribute. Therefore the attribute values for *income range* and *life insurance promotion* from element 1 are combined with the values for *credit card insurance, sex,* and *age* for element 2. A new second element is created in a similar fashion by combining the first part of element 2 with the last part of element 1. The complete crossover operation is shown in Figure 3.9. The resultant second-generation population is displayed in Table 3.10. Upon computing the fitness scores for these new elements, we find both fitness scores improve with $F(1) = 7/5$ and $F(2) = 6/4$.

As a second option, suppose the algorithm chooses to mutate the second element rather than perform the second crossover. A mutation will result in a modification of one or more attribute values of the original second element. For example, the 30–40K value for *income range* can be modified by randomly selecting any one of the alternative values for income range or the value can be replaced with a question mark. Clearly, a

---

Figure 3.9   •   **A crossover operation**

Population Element	Income Range	Life Insurance Promotion	Credit Card Insurance	Sex	Age
#1	20-30K	No	Yes	Male	30-39

Population Element	Income Range	Life Insurance Promotion	Credit Card Insurance	Sex	Age
#2	30-40K	Yes	Yes	Male	30-39

Population Element	Income Range	Life Insurance Promotion	Credit Card Insurance	Sex	Age
#2	30-40K	Yes	No	Fem	50-59

Population Element	Income Range	Life Insurance Promotion	Credit Card Insurance	Sex	Age
#1	20-30K	No	No	Fem	50-59

Table 3.10 ● A Second-Generation Population

Population Element	Income Range	Life Insurance Promotion	Credit Card Insurance	Sex	Age
1	20–30K	No	No	Female	50–59
2	30–40K	Yes	Yes	Male	30–39
3	?	No	No	Male	40–49
4	30–40K	Yes	Yes	Male	40–49

mutation is necessary if an income range value of 50–60K is to be seen in the element population. Countless variations of the stated processes for crossover and mutation are limited only by our imagination. The selection operator is not appropriate for this simple example because the number of elements for each class is limited to two.

Crossover and mutation continues until a termination condition is satisfied. Once the algorithm terminates we have a model for classifying new instances or predicting future outcome as appropriate. To use the model, we can compare a new unknown instance with the elements of the final population. A simple technique is to give the unknown instance the same classification as the population element to which it is most similar. A second possibility is for the model to keep track of the m elements from P most similar to the instance presented for classification. The algorithm then randomly chooses one of the m elements and gives the unknown instance the classification of the randomly selected element.

Genetic Algorithms and Unsupervised Clustering

Genetic learning is also a powerful unsupervised clustering technique. As a simple example, we can use unsupervised genetic learning to develop a set of clusters for numerical data in an n-dimensional space. Suppose there are P data instances within the space where each data instance consists of n attribute values. To formulate the problem, the algorithm is supplied with the number of clusters to be created. Suppose m clusters are desired. The model then generates k possible solutions. A specific solution contains m n-dimensional points, where each point is a best current representative element for one of the m clusters. Figure 3.10 illustrates the idea with $m = 2$. For example, S_2 represents one of the k possible solutions and contains two elements, E_{21} and E_{22}.

A crossover operation is accomplished by moving elements (n-dimensional points) from solution S_i to solution S_j. There are several possibilities for implementing mutation operations. One way to mutate solution S_i is to swap one or more point coordinates of the elements within S_i.

Figure 3.10   ●   **Unsupervised genetic clustering**

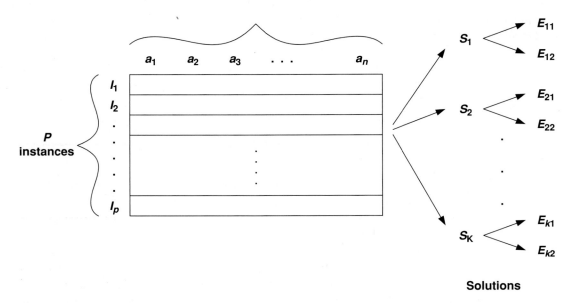

Solutions

An applicable fitness function for solution S_j is the average Euclidean distance of the P instances in the n-dimensional space from their closest element within S_j. That is, to compute the fitness value for solution S_j we take each instance I in P and compute the Euclidean distance from I to each of the m elements in S_j. The closest distance is saved and added to the sum total of closest values. The average of the summed distances is the fitness score for S_j. Clearly, lower values represent better fitness scores. Once genetic learning terminates, the best of the k possible solutions is selected as the final solution. Each instance in the n-dimensional space is then assigned to the cluster associated with its closest element in the final solution.

Let's see how the technique is applied to the six instances of Table 3.6. Assume we suspect the data contains two clusters and we instruct the algorithm to start with a solution set consisting of three plausible solutions ($k = 3$). With $m = 2$, $P = 6$, and $k = 3$, the algorithm generates the initial set of solutions, shown in Table 3.11. An element in the solution space contains a single representative data point for each cluster. For example, the data points for solution S_1 are (1.0,1.0) and (5.0,5.0).

To compute the fitness score of 11.31 for solution S_1 the Euclidean distance between each instance in Table 3.6 and its closest data point in S_1 is summed. To illustrate this, consider instance 1 in Table 3.6. The Euclidean distance between (1.0,1.0)

Table 3.11 • **A First-Generation Population for Unsupervised Clustering**

	S_1	S_2	S_3
Solution elements (initial population)	(1.0,1.0) (5.0,5.0)	(3.0,2.0) (3.0,5.0)	(4.0,3.0) (5.0,1.0)
Fitness score	11.31	9.78	15.55
Solution elements (second generation)	(5.0,1.0) (5.0,5.0)	(3.0,2.0) (3.0,5.0)	(4.0,3.0) (1.0,1.0)
Fitness score	17.96	9.78	11.34
Solution elements (third generation)	(5.0,5.0) (1.0,5.0)	(3.0,2.0) (3.0,5.0)	(4.0,3.0) (1.0,1.0)
Fitness score	13.64	9.78	11.34

and (1.0,1.5) is computed as 0.50. The distance between (5.0,5.0) and (1.0,1.5) is 5.32. The smaller value of 0.50 is therefore represented in the overall fitness score for solution S_1. Table 3.11 shows S_2 as the best first-generation solution.

The second generation is obtained by performing a crossover between solutions S_1 and S_3 with solution element (1.0,1.0) in S_1 exchanging places with solution element (5.0,1.0) in S_3. As the table shows, the result of the crossover operation improves (decreases) the fitness score for S_3 while the score for S_1 increases. The third generation is acquired by mutating S_1. The mutation interchanges the y-coordinate of the first element in S_1 with the x-coordinate of the second element. The mutation results in an improved fitness score for S_1. Mutation and crossover continue until a termination condition is satisfied. The terminating condition can be a maximum number of iterations of the algorithm or a minimum fitness score for one or several solutions. If the third generation is seen as terminal the final solution will be S_2. Computing the distances between the points in Table 3.6 and their closest element in S_2 results in instances 1, 3, and 5 forming one cluster and instances 2 and 6 forming the second cluster. As instance 4 is equidistant from both elements in S_2, it can be placed in either cluster.

General Considerations

Although few commercial data mining products contain a genetic learning component, genetic algorithms continue to gain popularity. Here is a list of considerations when using a problem-solving approach based on genetic learning:

- Genetic algorithms are designed to find globally optimized solutions. However, there is no guarantee that any given solution is not the result of a local rather than a global optimization.

- The fitness function determines the computational complexity of a genetic algorithm. A fitness function involving several calculations can be computationally expensive.

- Genetic algorithms explain their results to the extent that the fitness function is understandable.

- Transforming the data to a form suitable for a genetic algorithm can be a challenge.

In addition to being used for supervised learning and unsupervised clustering, genetic techniques can be used in conjunction with other learning techniques. For example, genetic algorithms can be applied to train feed-forward neural networks. Each chromosome or element in a population represents one possibility for the connection weights contained in the network. As genetic operators are then applied to the various elements, the connection weights of the network change. As a second example, in Chapter 5 you will see how genetic learning can be applied to help select a best set of input attributes for supervised learning.

3.5   Choosing a Data Mining Technique

It is apparent that when it comes to solving a particular problem we have several techniques to choose from. The question now becomes, how do we know which data mining technique to use? Let's examine this issue in more detail. A formal statement of the problem reads:

> *Given a set of data containing attributes and values to be mined together with information about the nature of the data and the problem to be solved, determine an appropriate data mining technique.*

The following questions may be useful in determining which techniques to apply:

- Is learning supervised or unsupervised?

- Do we require a clear explanation about the relationships present in the data?

- Is there one set of input attributes and one set of output attributes or can attributes interact with one another in several ways?

- Is the input data categorical, numeric, or a combination of both?

- If learning is supervised, is there one output attribute or are there several output attributes? Are the output attribute(s) categorical or numeric?

For a particular problem, these questions have obvious answers. For example, we know neural networks and regression models are black–box structures. Therefore these techniques are poor choices if an explanation about what has been learned is required. Also, association rules are usually a best choice when attributes are allowed to play multiple roles in the data mining process.

If the answers to these questions still leave us with several choices, we can try turning to the research community for direction. Several studies offer generalizations about the behavior of different data mining techniques (Quinlan, 1994; Shavlik et al., 1990). Unfortunately, many of these studies give conflicting results. Still, answers to several additional questions may provide some guidance. Specifically,

1. *Do we know the distribution of the data?*
   Datasets containing more than a few hundred instances can be a problem for data mining techniques that require the data to conform to certain standards. For example, many statistical techniques assume the data to be normally distributed.

2. *Do we know which attributes best define the data to be modeled?*
   Decision trees and certain statistical approaches can determine those attributes most predictive of class membership. Neural network, nearest neighbor, and various clustering approaches assume attributes to be of equal importance. This is a problem when several attributes not predictive of class membership are present in the data.

3. *Does the data contain several missing values?*
   Most data mining researchers agree that, if applicable, neural networks tend to outperform other models when a wealth of noisy data are present.

4. *Is time an issue?*
   Algorithms for building decision trees and production rules typically execute much faster than neural network or genetic learning approaches.

5. *Which technique is most likely to give a best classification accuracy?*

The last question is of particular interest, as a best accuracy is always a desirable feature of any model. As previous research has shown different levels of performance among data mining techniques, it seems reasonable to assume that a maximum classification accuracy is obtainable using an approach where several models built with the same training data vote on the classification of new unknown instances. An instance is then given the classification chosen by the majority of the competing models.

Unfortunately, our experience with a variety of data mining tools and several datasets, both large and small, has consistently shown a high degree of overlap among individual instance misclassifications for competing classifier models. Because of this, multiple model approaches making use of several data mining techniques are not likely to improve the results seen with an individual model. However, multiple model approaches that apply the same data mining technique for building each model have met with some success (Maclin and Opitz, 1997). We discuss multiple model approaches of this type in Chapter 11. Also, in Chapter 12 we show you how a rule-based expert system approach using some of the ideas presented here can be developed to help determine a best data mining technique.

3.6   Chapter Summary

Decision trees are probably the most popular structure for supervised data mining. A common algorithm for building a decision tree selects a subset of instances from the training data to construct an initial tree. The remaining training instances are then used to test the accuracy of the tree. If any instance is incorrectly classified the instance is added to the current set of training data and the process is repeated. A main goal is to minimize the number of tree levels and tree nodes, thereby maximizing data generalization. Decision trees have been successfully applied to real problems, are easy to understand, and map nicely to a set of production rules.

Association rules are able to find relationships in large databases. Association rules are unlike traditional production rules in that an attribute that is a precondition in one rule may appear as a consequent in another rule. Also, association rule generators allow the consequent of a rule to contain one or several attribute values. As association rules are more complex, special techniques have been developed to generate association rules efficiently. Rule confidence and support help determine which discovered associations are likely to be interesting from a marketing perspective. However, caution must be exercised in the interpretation of association rules because many discovered relationships turn out to be trivial.

The K-Means algorithm is a statistical unsupervised clustering technique. All input attributes to the algorithm must be numeric and the user is required to make a decision about how many clusters are to be discovered. The algorithm begins by randomly choosing one data point to represent each cluster. Each data instance is then placed in the cluster to which it is most similar. New cluster centers are computed and the process continues until the cluster centers do not change. The K-Means algorithm is easy to implement and understand. However, the algorithm is not guaranteed to converge to a globally optimal solution, lacks the ability to explain what has been found, and is unable to tell which attributes are significant in determining the formed clusters. Despite these limitations, the K-Means algorithm is among the most widely used clustering techniques.

Genetic algorithms apply the theory of evolution to inductive learning. Genetic learning can be supervised or unsupervised and is typically used for problems that cannot be solved with traditional techniques. A standard genetic approach to learning applies a fitness function to a set of data elements to determine which elements survive from one generation to the next. Those elements not surviving are used to create new instances to replace deleted elements. In addition to being used for supervised learning and unsupervised clustering, genetic techniques can be employed in conjunction with other learning techniques.

Here and in Chapter 2 we have previewed several data mining techniques. Later chapters introduce several additional techniques for you to study. Several factors, including the nature of the data, the role of individual attributes, and whether learning is supervised or unsupervised, help us determine the data mining technique most appropriate for a particular problem.

3.7   Key Terms

Affinity analysis. The process of determining which things are typically grouped together.

Confidence. Given a rule of the form "If A then B," confidence is defined as the conditional probability that B is true when A is known to be true.

Crossover. A genetic learning operation that creates new population elements by combining parts of two or more elements from the current population.

Genetic algorithm. A data mining technique based on the theory of evolution.

Item set. A set of several combinations of attribute-value pairs that cover a prespecified minimum number of data instances.

Mutation. A genetic learning operation that creates a new population element by randomly modifying a portion of an existing element.

Regression tree. A decision tree where the leaf nodes of the tree are numerical rather than categorical values.

Selection. A genetic learning operation that adds copies of current population elements with high fitness scores to the next generation of the population.

Support. The minimum percentage of instances in the database that contain all items listed in a given association rule.

Unstable algorithm. A data mining algorithm that is highly sensitive to small changes in the training data. As a result, the models built using the algorithm show significant changes in structure when slight changes are made to the training data.

3.8 Exercises

Review Questions

1. A decision tree built using the algorithm described in Section 3.1 allows us to choose a categorical attribute for data division only once. However, the same numeric attribute may appear several times in a decision tree. Explain how this is true.

2. How do association rules differ from traditional production rules? How are they the same?

3. What is the *usual* definition of an optimal clustering for the K-Means algorithm?

4. What do you suppose happens when selection is the only operator allowed for supervised genetic learning?

5. One of the problems with the K-Means algorithm is its inability to explain what has been found. Describe how you could apply a decision tree algorithm to a set of clusters formed by the K-Means algorithm to better determine the meaning of the formed clusters.

6. Describe how you would apply unsupervised genetic learning to cluster the instances of the credit card promotion database.

Computational Questions

1. Use the training data in Table 3.1 to construct a confusion matrix for the decision tree shown in Figure 3.5.

2. Answer the following;
    a. Write the production rules for the decision tree shown in Figure 3.4.
    b. Can you simplify any of your rules without compromising rule accuracy?

3. Repeat the previous question for the decision tree shown in Figure 3.5.

4. Using the attribute *age*, draw an expanded version of the decision tree in Figure 3.4 that correctly classifies all training data instances.

5. In the section titled An Algorithm for Building Decision Trees we defined a simple measure for decision tree attribute selection. Use our defined measure to compute a goodness score for using the attribute *sex* as the top-level node of a decision tree to be built from the data in Table 3.1.

6. Use the measure described in the section titled An Algorithm for Building Decision Trees to compute a goodness score for choosing *credit card insurance* as the node to follow the branch *income range = 20–30K* in Figure 3.1.

7. Use the data in Table 3.3 to give confidence and support values for the following association rule.

   IF *Sex = Male & Magazine Promotion = Yes* THEN *Life Insurance Promotion = Yes*

8. Use the information in Table 3.5 to list three two–item set rules. Use the data in Table 3.3 to compute confidence and support values for each of your rules.

9. List three rules for the following three–item set. Use the data in Table 3.3 to specify the confidence and support for each rule.

   Watch Promotion = No & Life Insurance Promotion = No & Credit Card Insurance = No

10. Perform the third iteration of the K–Means algorithm for the example given in the section titled An Example Using K–Means. What are the new cluster centers?

11. Use crossover and mutation as appropriate to compute third-generation elements for the population shown in Table 3.10. Compute fitness scores for the new population.

Chapter 4

An Excel-Based Data Mining Tool

Chapter Objectives

▶ Understand the structure of the iData Analyzer.

▶ Recognize how predictability and predictiveness scores help determine categorical attribute significance.

▶ Understand how attribute mean and standard deviation scores are used to compute numerical attribute significance.

▶ Know how to use ESX for building supervised learner models.

▶ Know how to perform unsupervised clustering with ESX.

▶ Know how to create production rules with RuleMaker.

▶ Understand how instance typicality is computed.

In this chapter we introduce the iData Analyzer (iDA) and show you how to use two of the learner models contained in your iDA software suite of data mining tools. Section 4.1 overviews the iDA Model for Knowledge Discovery. In Section 4.2 we introduce ESX, an exemplar-based data mining tool capable of both supervised learning and unsupervised clustering. In Section 4.3 we present the standard way of representing datasets for all iDA data mining tools. Section 4.4 shows you how to use ESX to perform unsupervised clustering. You will also learn how to generate production rules with RuleMaker. In Section 4.5 we show you how to build supervised learner models with ESX. Section 4.6 details RuleMaker's rule generation options. Section 4.7 introduces the concept of instance typicality. Section 4.8 offers additional information about features of the ESX learner model. The end-of-chapter exercises help you better understand how ESX and RuleMaker can create generalized models from data.

4.1   The iData Analyzer

The iData Analyzer (iDA) provides support for the business or technical analyst by offering a visual learning environment, an integrated tool set, and data mining process support. iDA consists of a preprocessor, three data mining tools, and a report generator. As iDA is an Excel add-on, the user interface is Microsoft Excel. Figure 4.1 shows the component parts of iDA. The following is a brief description of each component:

- **Preprocessor.** Before the data in a file is presented to one of the iDA mining engines, the file is scanned for several types of errors, including illegal numeric values, blank lines, and missing items. The preprocessor corrects several types of errors but does not attempt to fix numerical data errors. The preprocessor outputs a data file ready for data mining as well as a document informing us about the nature and location of unresolved errors.

- **Heuristic agent.** The heuristic agent responds to the presentation of data files containing several thousand instances. The heuristic agent allows us to decide if we wish to extract a representative subset of the data for analysis or if we desire to process the entire dataset.

- **ESX.** This component is an exemplar-based data mining tool that builds a concept hierarchy to generalize data.

- **Neural networks.** iDA contains two neural network architectures: a backpropagation neural network for supervised learning and a self-organizing feature map for unsupervised clustering. These neural network architectures are the topic of Chapter 9.

- **RuleMaker.** iDA's production rule generator provides several rule generating options.

- **Report generator.** The report generator offers several sheets of summary information for each data mining session. The contents of the individual sheets created by the report generator are detailed in this chapter.

As a final point, a major concern with neural network architectures is their lack of explanation about what has been discovered. Fortunately, a primary strength seen with the ESX learner model is its ability to output useful explanations about patterns within the data. Figure 4.1 illustrates that we can use ESX to help explain the output of an iDA neural network data mining session.

Installing iDA

In this section we show you how to install iDA. The software should install correctly with all current versions of MS Excel. However, if you are using MS Office 2000 or Office XP, the macro security level of your implementation may be set at *high*. If this is the case, the software will not install. Perform the following steps to check and possibly reset the security level:

- Open Excel and select *Tools.*

- Mouse to *Macro* and then select *Security.*

- If the security setting is *high,* change the setting to *medium* and click *OK.*

- Exit Excel and close all other applications.

The steps for installing iDA are as follows:

- Insert the CD that comes with the text into your CD drive.

- Mouse to *Start* and left-click on *Run.*

- Specify your CD drive and type *installiDA.exe.* For example, if your CD drive is D, type: *d:\installiDA.exe.*

- Press *Enter.*

- Select *Next,* read the license agreement, and select *Agree.*

- Select *Finish,* then *OK.*

- Answer *Yes* if asked "Would you like to enable macros?"

Figure 4.1 ● **The iDA system architecture**

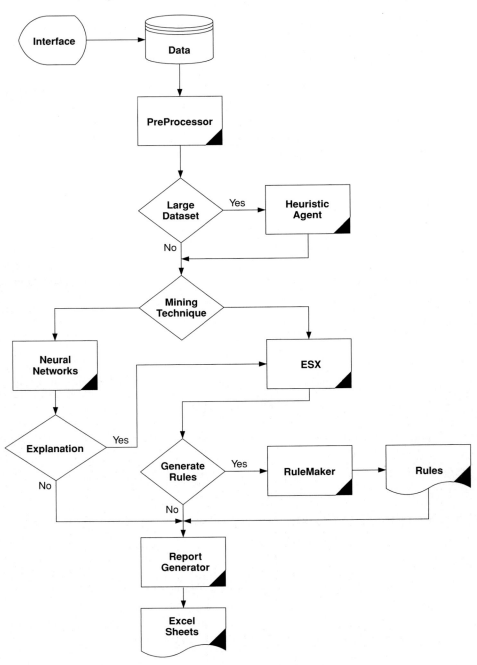

- Upon completion, a ReadMe file will appear on your screen. Once you close the file the installation is complete.

A successful installation adds the iDA drop-down menu item to the MS Excel spreadsheet environment, as shown in Figure 4.2.

The iDA neural networks are written in the Java programming language. Therefore to run the neural network software you must have Java installed on your machine. Java is free software, and the installation file for Java is contained on your CD. The instructions for installing Java are given in Appendix A. If you need to install Java, you can do so now or you can wait until you are ready to study Chapter 9. If you have any other problems with the installation, refer to Appendix A for additional assistance.

Figure 4.2 • **A successful installation**

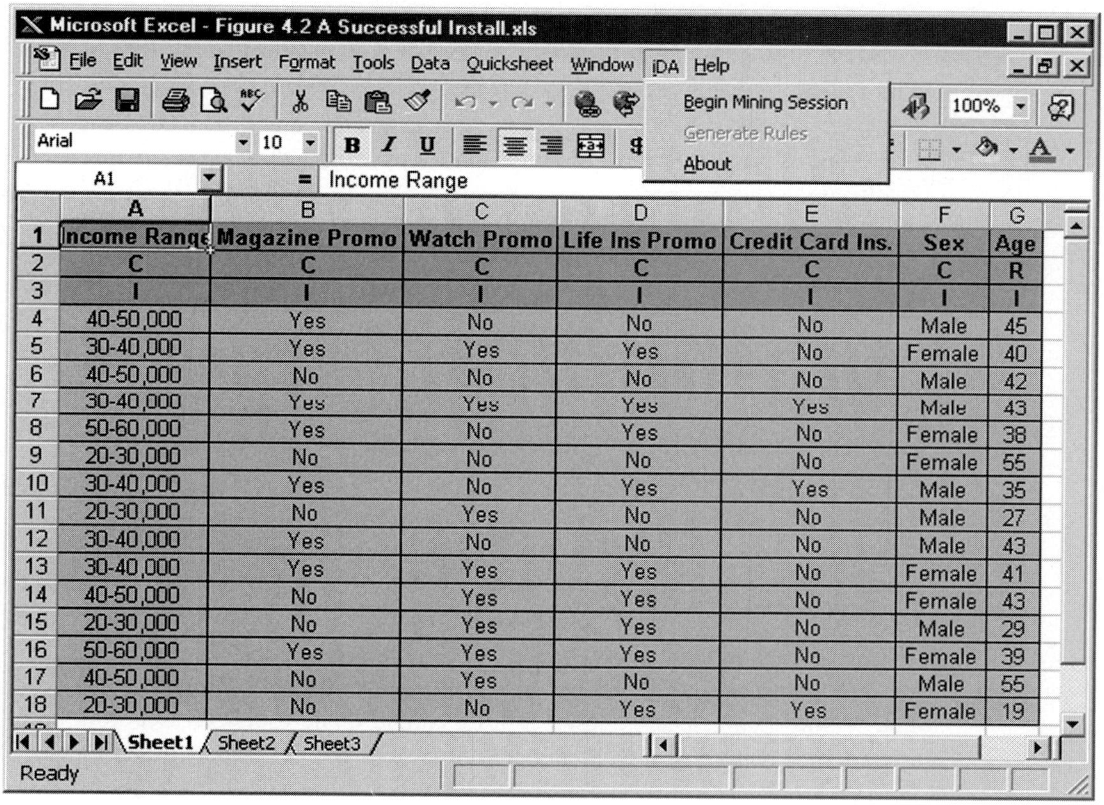

	A	B	C	D	E	F	G
1	Income Range	Magazine Promo	Watch Promo	Life Ins Promo	Credit Card Ins.	Sex	Age
2	C	C	C	C	C	C	R
3	I	I	I	I	I	I	I
4	40-50,000	Yes	No	No	No	Male	45
5	30-40,000	Yes	Yes	Yes	No	Female	40
6	40-50,000	No	No	No	No	Male	42
7	30-40,000	Yes	Yes	Yes	Yes	Male	43
8	50-60,000	Yes	No	Yes	No	Female	38
9	20-30,000	No	No	No	No	Female	55
10	30-40,000	Yes	No	Yes	Yes	Male	35
11	20-30,000	No	Yes	No	No	Male	27
12	30-40,000	Yes	No	No	No	Male	43
13	30-40,000	Yes	Yes	Yes	No	Female	41
14	40-50,000	No	Yes	Yes	No	Female	43
15	20-30,000	No	Yes	Yes	No	Male	29
16	50-60,000	Yes	Yes	Yes	No	Female	39
17	40-50,000	No	Yes	No	No	Male	55
18	20-30,000	No	No	Yes	Yes	Female	19

Limitations

The commercial version of iDA is bound by the size of a single MS Excel spreadsheet, which allows a maximum of 65,536 rows and 256 columns. The iDA input format uses the first three rows of a spreadsheet to house information about individual attributes. Therefore a maximum of 65,533 data instances in attribute-value format can be mined. The student version that comes with your text allows a maximum of 7000 data instances (7003 rows).

As each MS Excel column holds a single attribute, the maximum number of attributes allowed is 256. The maximum size of an attribute name or attribute value is 250 characters. Also, RuleMaker will not generate rules for more than 20 classes. Although not required, it is best to close all other applications while you use the iDA software suite of tools. This is especially true for applications containing more than a few hundred data instances.

4.2   ESX: A Multipurpose Tool for Data Mining

ESX can help create target data, find irregularities in data, perform data mining, and offer insight about the practical value of discovered knowledge. The following is a partial list of features seen with the ESX learner model:

- It supports both supervised learning and unsupervised clustering.

- It does not make statistical assumptions about the nature of data to be processed.

- It supports an automated method for dealing with missing attribute values.

- It can be applied in domains containing both categorical and numerical data.

- It can point out inconsistencies and unusual values in data.

- For supervised classification, ESX can determine those instances and attributes best able to classify new instances of unknown origin.

- For unsupervised clustering, ESX incorporates a globally optimizing evaluation function that encourages a best instance clustering.

The primary data structure used by ESX is a three-level concept hierarchy. Figure 4.3 shows the general form of this tree structure. The nodes at the instance level of the tree represent the individual instances that define the concept classes given at the concept level. The concept-level nodes store summary statistics about the attribute values found within their respective instance-level children. The root-level tree node stores summary information about all instances within the domain. Concept- and root-level

Figure 4.3 • **An ESX concept hierarchy**

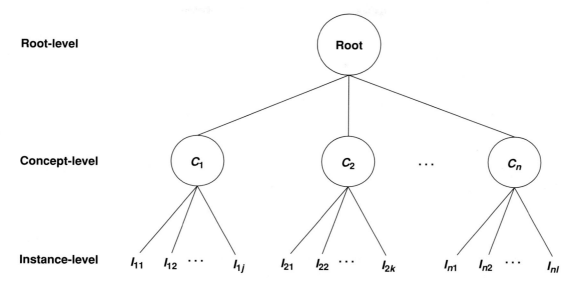

summary information is given to the report generator, which in turn outputs a summary report in spreadsheet format.

Class resemblance scores are stored within the root node and each concept-level node. Class resemblance scores form the basis of ESX's evaluation function. Class resemblance scores provide a measure of overall similarity for the exemplars making up individual concept classes. As ESX is commercial software, details about the class resemblance computation are not available. However, we can state the evaluation rule ESX uses for both supervised learning and unsupervised clustering.

1. Given:
   a. A set of existing concept-level nodes $C_1, C_2, \ldots C_n$.
   b. An average class resemblance score S, computed by summing the resemblance scores for each class $C_1, C_2, \ldots C_n$ and dividing by n.
   c. A new instance I to be classified.

2. Make I an instance of the concept node that results in the largest average increase or smallest average decrease for S.

3. When learning is unsupervised:
   If a better score is achieved by creating a new concept node, then create new node C_{n+1} with I as its only member.

That is, for each existing concept-level node C_k, a new instance to be classified is temporarily placed in the concept class represented by the node. A new class resemblance score is computed for C_k, as well as a new average class resemblance score. The winning concept class is the one that creates the largest increase (or smallest decrease) in average class resemblance. When learning is unsupervised, a score for creating a new concept-level node is also computed. As you can see, unlike the K-Means algorithm, we are not required to make a determination about the total number of clusters to be formed.

So much for theory! Let's work through a few simple examples so you can learn how the features of ESX help you create your own data models.

4.3   iDAV Format for Data Mining

ESX can build both unsupervised and supervised learner models. For the first example we use ESX and unsupervised clustering. Our example is based on the fictitious data defined in Chapter 2 about individuals who own credit cards issued by the Acme Credit Card Company. The data is displayed in Table 4.1 in *iDAV format* (iDA attribute-value format). This is the format required by all iDA data mining tools. Let's begin by taking a closer look at the structure of iDAV formatted files.

Setting up a data file in iDAV format is easy! The columns in the first row contain attribute names. Although Excel allows us to place multiple lines of data in a single cell, iDA does not. Be sure to reformat any data file cells with multiple lines before attempting a data mining session.

Table 4.1 shows a C or an R in each column of the second row. We place a C in a second-row column if the corresponding attribute data type is categorical (nominal). We place an R in a second-row column if the entered data is real-valued (numerical). Integers, decimal values, numbers formatted with scientific notation, as well as values containing dollar signs (\$57.30) or percent symbols (57.3%) are all valid numeric data items.

Categorical data includes all data not represented by numbers. We can sometimes treat numbers as categorical data. As a general rule, if there are but a few differing attribute values, we can and should treat numerical data as categorical. For example, an attribute representing the total number of household vehicles for individual families should be considered categorical.

The third row of Table 4.1 informs ESX about attribute usage. Table 4.2 displays the possibilities. To perform an unsupervised clustering we place an I in the third-row columns of attributes we wish to have ESX use as input attributes. If learning is supervised, exactly one attribute must contain an O in its third-row column. With ESX, an output attribute must be categorical. Categorical attributes having several unique values are of little predictive value and should be marked

Table 4.1 • **Credit Card Promotion Database: iDAV Format**

Income Range	Magazine Promotion	Watch Promotion	Life Insurance Promotion	Credit Card Insurance	Sex	Age
C	C	C	C	C	C	R
I	I	I	I	I	I	I
40–50K	Yes	No	No	No	Male	45
30–40K	Yes	Yes	Yes	No	Female	40
40–50K	No	No	No	No	Male	42
30–40K	Yes	Yes	Yes	Yes	Male	43
50–60K	Yes	No	Yes	No	Female	38
20–30K	No	No	No	No	Female	55
30–40K	Yes	No	Yes	Yes	Male	35
20–30K	No	Yes	No	No	Male	27
30–40K	Yes	No	No	No	Male	43
30–40K	Yes	Yes	Yes	No	Female	41
40–50K	No	Yes	Yes	No	Female	43
20–30K	No	Yes	Yes	No	Male	29
50–60K	Yes	Yes	Yes	No	Female	39
40–50K	No	Yes	No	No	Male	55
20–30K	No	No	Yes	Yes	Female	19

with a *U.* Attributes falling into this category include *last name*, *sequence number*, and *birthdate*.

Starting with the fourth row, we enter actual data. Each new row contains one data instance. There are two cautions when entering data to be mined:

- Each data item, whether it is an attribute name, value, or data type, must be entered in a single cell on one line. The preprocessor will flag any row containing multiple lines as an error.

- The preprocessor flags any data instance containing an illegal numeric value as an error. This is true even if the attribute is declared as unused. To be safe, place a *C* in the second-row column corresponding to an unused numeric attribute that is suspect of containing illegal values. In this way, the preprocessor will think the attribute is categorical and ignore any illegal numeric characters.

Table 4.2   ●   **Values for Attribute Usage**

Character	Usage
I	The attribute is used as an input attribute.
U	The attribute is not used.
D	The attribute is not used for classification or clustering, but attribute value summary information is displayed in all output reports.
O	The attribute is used as an output attribute. For supervised learning with ESX, exactly one categorical attribute is selected as the output attribute.

The next section offers an example using a five-step approach for unsupervised clustering with ESX. The example is written as a tutorial. We encourage you to use your iDA software to work through the example with us.

4.4   A Five-Step Approach for Unsupervised Clustering

Here is a five-step procedure for performing unsupervised clustering with ESX:

1. Enter data to be mined into a new Excel spreadsheet.

2. Perform a data mining session.

3. Read and interpret summary results.

4. Read and interpret results for individual clusters.

5. Visualize and interpret rules defining the individual clusters.

Let's apply the five-step approach to the credit card promotion database shown in Table 4.1!

Applying the Five-Step Approach for Unsupervised Clustering

STEP 1: ENTER THE DATA TO BE MINED

Two forms of the credit card promotion database are located in the iDA samples directory—CreditCardPromotion.xls and CreditCardPromotionNet.xls. We are interested in the first version of the dataset. The second version has been transformed by mapping categorical attribute values to numeric equivalents. We will use the second version of the dataset when we study neural networks in Chapters 8 and 9. Here's how to open Excel and load the CreditCardPromotion dataset:

1. Open Microsoft Windows Explorer.

2. Double-click on the *iDA* directory.

3. Double-click on the *Samples* directory.

4. Double-click on the file *CreditCardPromotion.xls*.

As an alternative, you may choose to mouse to *Start,* then to *Run* and type c:\iDA\Samples\CreditCardPromotion.xls. In either case, your spreadsheet should look like the one shown in Figure 4.4.

STEP 2: PERFORM A DATA MINING SESSION

Before mining the data make sure all attribute usage values show an *I*. The procedure to perform the data mining session is as follows:

1. Select the *iDA* menu item from the menu bar at the top of your MS Excel workbook.

2. Select *Begin Mining Session* from the drop-down list. If this does not start a data mining session, click on any cell and try a second time.

Figure 4.4 • **The credit card promotion database in MS Excel**

	A	B	C	D	E	F	G
1	Income Range	Magazine Promo	Watch Promo	Life Ins Promo	Credit Card Ins.	Sex	Age
2	C	C	C	C	C	C	R
3	I	I	I	I	I	I	I
4	40-50,000	Yes	No	No	No	Male	45
5	30-40,000	Yes	Yes	Yes	No	Female	40
6	40-50,000	No	No	No	No	Male	42
7	30-40,000	Yes	Yes	Yes	Yes	Male	43
8	50-60,000	Yes	No	Yes	No	Female	38
9	20-30,000	No	No	No	No	Female	55
10	30-40,000	Yes	No	Yes	Yes	Male	35
11	20-30,000	No	Yes	No	No	Male	27
12	30-40,000	Yes	No	No	No	Male	43
13	30-40,000	Yes	Yes	Yes	No	Female	41
14	40-50,000	No	Yes	Yes	No	Female	43
15	20-30,000	No	Yes	Yes	No	Male	29
16	50-60,000	Yes	Yes	Yes	No	Female	39
17	40-50,000	No	Yes	No	No	Male	55
18	20-30,000	No	No	Yes	Yes	Female	19

3. A message box indicating that you are registered to use the non-commercial version of iDA for 180 days will appear. This software allows you to mine the data in a spreadsheet having a maximum of 7000 instances. This message box is shown each time you initiate a new data mining session. Click *OK* to continue.

4. A message box appears asking you to select an unsupervised learner model. Select *ESX* and click *OK*.

5. You will then see the message box shown in Figure 4.5. You are asked to enter two values:

   ● The value for instance similarity encourages or discourages the creation of new clusters. A value closer to *100* encourages the formation of new clusters. A value closer to *0* favors new instances to enter existing classes. The default value is *65*. Notice that with ESX the terms *class* and *cluster* are used interchangeably.

   ● The real-valued tolerance setting helps determine the similarity criteria for real-valued attributes. A setting of *1.0* is usually appropriate. However, there are exceptions to this rule.

   For our example, use the defaults for both parameters and click *OK*.

6. Next you will see a message box indicating that eight clusters were formed. This tells you the data has been successfully mined. The box asks if we wish to generate the output report. As a general rule, an unsupervised clustering of more than five or six clusters is likely to be less than optimal. There are always exceptions. However, let's apply this rule and click *No*.

7. A message box reading "Dataset not mined" will appear. Click *OK*.

8. Let's try again. Repeat steps 1–4. For step 5, set the similarity value to *55*, leave the real-tolerance value at *1.0,* and click *OK*.

Figure 4.5 ● **Unsupervised settings for ESX**

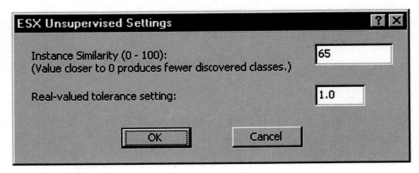

9. A message appears indicating three classes have been formed. Click *Yes* to generate the output report.

10. After a minute or two you will be presented with the message box shown in Figure 4.6. The message box asks you to choose settings for the rule generator. You can also bypass rule generation. For our example, we will generate rules. Set the minimum rule coverage at *30,* use the default settings for all other parameters, and click *OK*.

Once rule and report generation is complete you will see the output of the rule generator as displayed in Figure 4.7. By clicking inside the production rules window you can scroll the window and examine the rules for each cluster. Notice that the clusters have been respectively named: *Class 1, Class 2,* and *Class 3.* We examine each sheet of the output report in detail in the sections that follow.

STEP 3: READ AND INTERPRET SUMMARY RESULTS

The output of an unsupervised mining session appears in four new sheets. Sheet names are based on the name of the original sheet (in our case, Sheet1) as well as on their purpose. You can move from one sheet to the next by clicking on the sheet name given in the bottom tray of the current spreadsheet. Any sheet not appearing in the tray can be summoned by clicking on the left or right arrows found in the left-bottom portion of the spreadsheet. The description box titled

Figure 4.6 • **RuleMaker options**

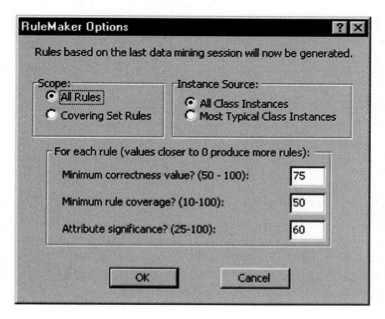

Figure 4.7   ●   **Rules for the credit card promotion database**

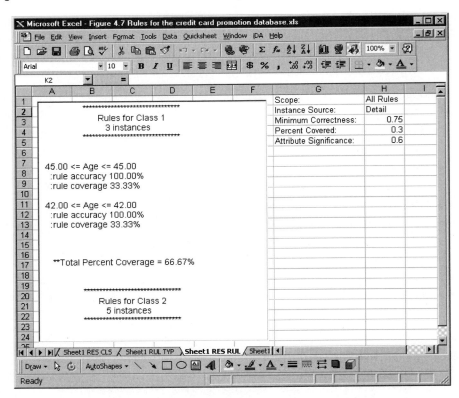

Output Reports: Unsupervised Clustering offers a brief explanation of the contents found within each sheet. We begin by examining the overall summary results of the data mining session.

To display the summary results on your screen left-click on the tray sheet labeled *Sheet1 RES SUM*. The first part of the output for the result summary sheet is displayed in Figure 4.8. We first examine the class resemblance statistics.

Class Resemblance Statistics

The *Class Resemblance Statistics* show us that ESX has partitioned the 15 instances into 3 clusters denoted as *Class 1, Class 2,* and *Class 3*. Row three lists the resemblance score (*Res. Score*) for each class as well as the resemblance score for the entire domain of instances. The class resemblance score offers a first indication about how well the instances within each cluster fit together. This score is a similarity value and should not be interpreted as a probability. Notice that the instances of Class 1 have a best within-class fit.

Figure 4.8 • **Summary statistics for the Acme credit card promotion database**

	X Microsoft Excel - Figure 4.8 Summary statistics for the Acme credit card promotion database.xls					
	A	B	C	D	E	F
1	**CLASS RESEMBLANCE STATISTICS**					
2		Class 1	Class 2	Class 3	Domain	
3	Res. Score:	0.81	0.529	0.66	0.46	
4	No. of Inst.	3	5	7	15	
5	Cluster Quality:	0.75	0.14	0.43		
6						
7	**DOMAIN STATISTICS FOR CATEGORICAL ATTRIBUTES**					
8	Number of Classes:	3				
9	Domain Res. Score:	0.46				
10						
11	Categorical Attribute Summary:	**Name**	**Value**	**Frequency**	**Predictability**	
12		Income Range	"40-50,000"	4	0.27	
13			"20-30,000"	4	0.27	
14			"30-40,000"	5	0.33	
15			"50-60,000"	2	0.13	
16						
17		Magazine Promo	Yes	8	0.53	
18			No	7	0.47	
19						
20		Watch Promo	No	7	0.47	
21			Yes	8	0.53	
22						
23		Life Ins Promo	No	6	0.40	
24			Yes	9	0.60	
25						
26		Credit Card Ins.	No	12	0.80	
27			Yes	3	0.20	

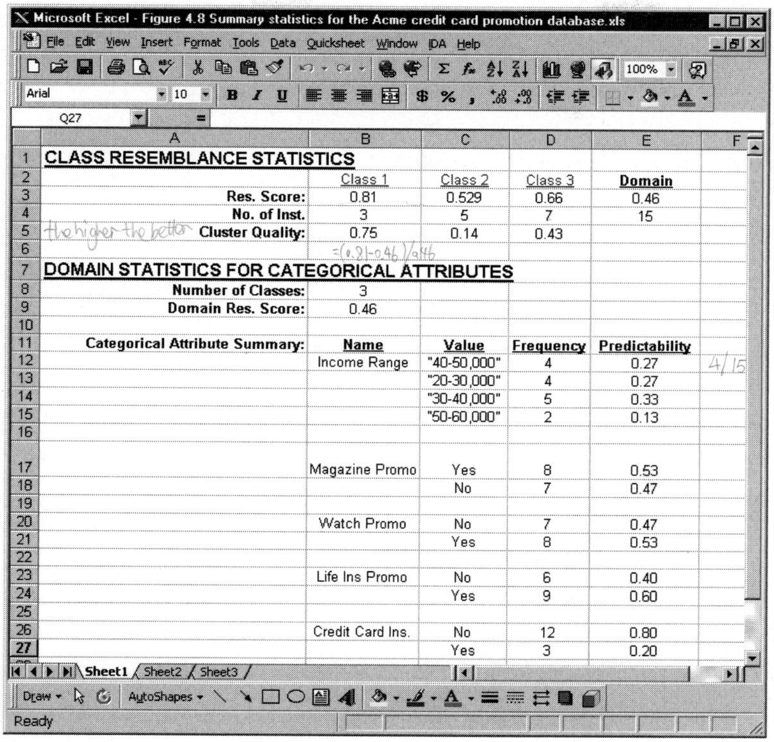

(handwritten annotations: "the higher the better", "=(0.81-0.46)/.46", "4/15")

The **domain resemblance** represents the overall similarity of all instances within the dataset. As a rule, it is important to see within-class resemblance scores that are higher than the domain resemblance value. This rule need not be true in all cases, but should apply to the larger classes. When learning is unsupervised, if within-class similarity scores are not generally higher than the domain similarity score, there are at least three possibilities:

1. The chosen attributes do a poor job of representing the instances. One way to test this is to choose other attributes and see if the results improve.

2. The instances chosen for the unsupervised clustering are not representative of typical instances found within the domain.

3. The domain does not contain definable classes and is not appropriate for unsupervised clustering.

Whether learning is supervised or unsupervised, poor class resemblance scores will likely result in poor model performance.

Finally, we see **cluster quality** scores listed directly below the instance count for each class. These values are percentages. The cluster quality for an individual class is simply the percent increase (or decrease) of the class resemblance score relative to the domain resemblance. Higher class resemblance scores relative to the domain resemblance result in higher values for cluster quality.

Domain Statistics for Categorical Attributes

Returning to Figure 4.8, the next section of the RES SUM sheet is titled *Domain Statistics for Categorical Attributes.* You will need to use the scroll bar to see all categorical attribute values. By examining the domain statistics for categorical data, we can locate duplicate categorical attribute names and values. For example, the attribute *income range* might be referenced in some instances as "Income Range" and in other instances as "income range." In addition, low frequency counts can help identify incorrect categorical attribute values.

We can make several initial deductions about categorical attributes by examining attribute-value *predictability scores*. Predictability scores are simple probabilities, but they can be confusing. Attribute-value predictability scores can be computed relative to the entire domain of instances. They can also be computed for each class or cluster found within a dataset. First we investigate **domain predictability.**

Given categorical attribute A with values v_1, v_2, v_3...v_n, the domain predictability of v_i tells us the percent of domain instances showing v_i as the value for A.

To illustrate, here are two potentially interesting domain predictability scores from Figure 4.8.

- Eighty percent of all credit card holders do not have credit card insurance.

- Sixty percent of all card holders took advantage of the life insurance promotion.

Output Reports: Unsupervised Clustering

Sheet1 RES SUM: This sheet contains summary statistics about attribute values and offers several heuristics to help us determine the quality of a data mining session.
Sheet1 RES CLS: This sheet has information about the clusters formed as a result of an unsupervised mining session.
Sheet1 RUL TYP: Instances are listed by their cluster number. The last column of this sheet shows a typicality value for each instance. The typicality of instance *I* is the average similarity of *I* to the other members of its cluster.
Sheet1 RES RUL: The production rules generated for each cluster are contained in this sheet.

A predictability score near 100% for a domain-level categorical attribute value indicates that the attribute is not likely to be useful for supervised learning or unsupervised clustering. This is true because a majority of instances will have an identical value for the attribute. However, if we are specifically looking for outliers within the dataset, we must exercise caution when eliminating attributes displaying large attribute-value predictability scores.

Domain Statistics for Numerical Attributes

Moving down the RES SUM sheet, we see the section labeled *Domain Statistics for Numerical Attributes*. Scroll the RES SUM sheet until your screen is similar to the output displayed in Figure 4.9. The summary provides useful information about class mean and standard deviation scores. The *attribute significance* value measures the predictive value of each numerical attribute. The computation of attribute significance is best illustrated by example. Here's how we compute the attribute significance score for attribute *age*.

- Subtract the smallest class mean (*Class 2 age* = 37.00) from the largest mean value (*Class 1 age* = 43.33).

- Divide this result by the domain standard deviation (sd = 9.51).

The result gives a final attribute significance of 0.67. Dividing by the standard deviation normalizes mean difference values, thus allowing us to compare the attribute significance scores for all numeric attributes. Numeric attributes with lower significance values (usually less than 0.25) will likely be of little value in differentiating one class from another.

Commonly Occurring Categorical Attributes

The final output for the RES SUM sheet displays the most commonly occurring categorical attribute values found within each cluster. Figure 4.9 shows the most commonly occurring categorical attribute summary for our application. This information offers initial insight about which categorical attributes are best able to differentiate the individual clusters.

STEP 4: READ AND INTERPRET INDIVIDUAL CLASS RESULTS

Sheet1 RES CLS displays statistics about the individual classes. We often find valuable knowledge within the class summary sheet that cannot be seen in the rules generated for each class. We limit our discussion to the output for Class 3.

Figure 4.10 shows a portion of the summary results for Class 3. To open this sheet click on Sheet1 RES CLS and scroll down until your spreadsheet matches the output shown in Figure 4.10. The initial information found within the RES CLS sheet repeats facts about the number of class instances and the class resemblance score. You will also see attribute values for the two most and two least typical class instances. **Typicality** is defined as the average similarity of an instance to all other members of its cluster or class. Scroll to the right if the typicality scores are not

Figure 4.9 ● **Statistics for numerical attributes and common categorical attribute values**

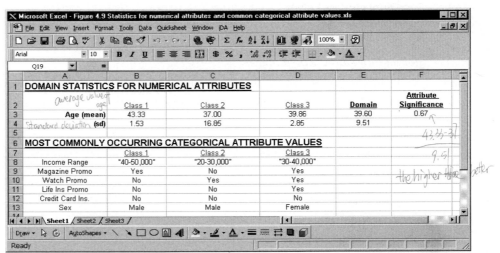

displayed on your spreadsheet. As you can see, the typicality score for each of the most typical instances is 0.76. Examining the most and least typical class instances gives us a first impression about the structure of the class.

Class Predictability and Predictiveness

Class predictiveness and predictability scores shown in Figure 4.10 for Class 3 merit detailed examination. Let's first consider the attribute *income range*. **Class predictability** can be defined as follows:

> Given categorical attribute *A* with values $v_1, v_2, v_3...v_n$, the class *C* predictability score for v_i tells us the percent of instances within class *C* showing v_i as the value for *A*. Class predictability is a within-class measure. The sum of the predictability scores for attribute *A* with values $v_1, v_2, v_3...v_n$ within class *C* is always equal to 1.

Class predictability tells us the percent of class instances having a particular value for a categorical attribute. To illustrate, Figure 4.10 shows the class predictability score for *income range = 30–40K* as 0.57. This predictability score informs us that 57% of all Class 3 instances make between $30,000 and $40,000 per year. Class predictability scores measure the degree of *necessity* for class membership.

Figure 4.10 • **Class 3 summary results**

	A	B	C	D	E	F	G	H	I
1	Class:	3							
2	Total Number of Instances:	7							
3	Class Resemblance Score:	0.66							
4									
5	Most Typical Instances:	Income Range	Magazine Promo	Watch Promo	Life Ins Promo	Credit Card Ins.	Sex	Age	Typicality
6		"30-40,000"	Yes	Yes	Yes	No	Female	40	0.76
7		"30-40,000"	Yes	Yes	Yes	No	Female	41	0.76
8									
9	Least Typical Instances:	Income Range	Magazine Promo	Watch Promo	Life Ins Promo	Credit Card Ins.	Sex	Age	Typicality
10		"40-50,000"	No	Yes	Yes	No	Female	43	0.57
11		"30-40,000"	Yes	No	Yes	Yes	Male	35	0.55
12									
13	Categorical Attribute Summary:	Name	Value	Frequency	Predictability	Predictiveness			
14		Income Range	"30-40,000"	4	0.57	0.80			
15			"50-60,000"	2	0.29	1.00			
16			"40-50,000"	1	0.14	0.25			
17									
18		Magazine Promo	Yes	6	0.86	0.75			
19			No	1	0.14	0.14			
20									
21		Watch Promo	Yes	5	0.71	0.63			
22			No	2	0.29	0.29			

Class predictiveness scores are more difficult to understand. An attribute-value predictiveness score is defined as the probability an instance resides in a specified class given the instance has the value for the chosen attribute. A formal definition for **class predictiveness** follows:

> Given class C and attribute A with values $v_1, v_2, v_3 \ldots v_n$, an attribute-value predictiveness score for v_i is defined as the probability an instance resides in C given the instance has value v_i for A. Predictiveness scores are between-class measures. The sum of the predictiveness scores for categorical attribute A with value v_i is always equal to 1.

To better understand class predictiveness, consider the attribute *income range* with value *50–60K*. Figure 4.10 shows that only 29% of all Class 3 instances have this value for income range. However, the predictiveness score of 1.00 tells us that all instances with *income range = 50–60K* reside in Class 3. We say that *income range = 50–60K* is a *sufficient* condition for Class 3 membership. Therefore if someone tells us that the value of *income range* for a particular instance is *50–60K*, we can predict with 100% certainty that the instance is from Class 3. Notice that *life insurance promotion = yes* has a predictability score of 1.00 and a predictiveness score of 0.78, making *life insurance promotion = yes* a best defining attribute value for

Class 3. Here are four useful observations relating to class predictability and predictiveness scores. For a given concept class *C:*

1. If an attribute value has a predictability and predictiveness score of 1.0, the attribute value is said to be *necessary and sufficient* for membership in C. That is, all instances within class C have the specified value for the attribute and all instances with this value for the attribute reside in class C.

2. If an attribute value has a predictiveness score of 1.0 and a predictability score less than 1.0, we conclude that all instances with the value for the attribute reside in class C. However, there are some instances in C that do not have the value for the attribute in question. We call the attribute value *sufficient but not necessary* for class membership.

3. If an attribute value has a predictability score of 1.0 and a predictiveness score less than 1.0, we conclude that all instances in class C have the same value for the chosen attribute. However, some instances outside of class C also have this same value for the given attribute. The attribute is said to be *necessary but not sufficient* for class membership.

In general, any categorical attribute with at least one highly predictive value should be designated as an input attribute. Also, a categorical attribute with little predictive value ought to be flagged as unused or display-only.

Necessary and Sufficient Attribute Values

The report generator lists attribute values with predictiveness scores greater than or equal to 0.80 as highly sufficient. Likewise, attribute values showing a predictability greater than or equal to 0.80 are listed as necessary attributes. Figure 4.11 presents a summary of necessary and sufficient attribute-value information for Class 3. Scroll the current RES CLS spreadsheet until you see the information displayed in the figure. As you can see, there are no categorical attribute values necessary and sufficient for Class 3 membership. Also, income range values *30–40K* and *50–60K* are highly sufficient for membership in Class 3. Finally, *magazine promotion = yes* and *life insurance promotion = yes* are highly necessary Class 3 attribute values.

STEP 5: VISUALIZE INDIVIDUAL CLASS RULES

In Chapter 2 you were introduced to RuleMaker, the production rule generator that comes with your iDA software package. In this section we review RuleMaker's output format by examining the production rules generated for Class 3. In Section 4.6 we will take a closer look at how to make optimal use of RuleMaker's features.

To examine the rules generated for Class 3, click on *Sheet1 RES RUL*. Figure 4.7 displays the initial output for this sheet. Click inside the rules window and scroll until you encounter the list of rules for Class 3. Here is an interesting Class 3 rule with one precondition:

Figure 4.11 • **Necessary and sufficient attribute values for Class 3**

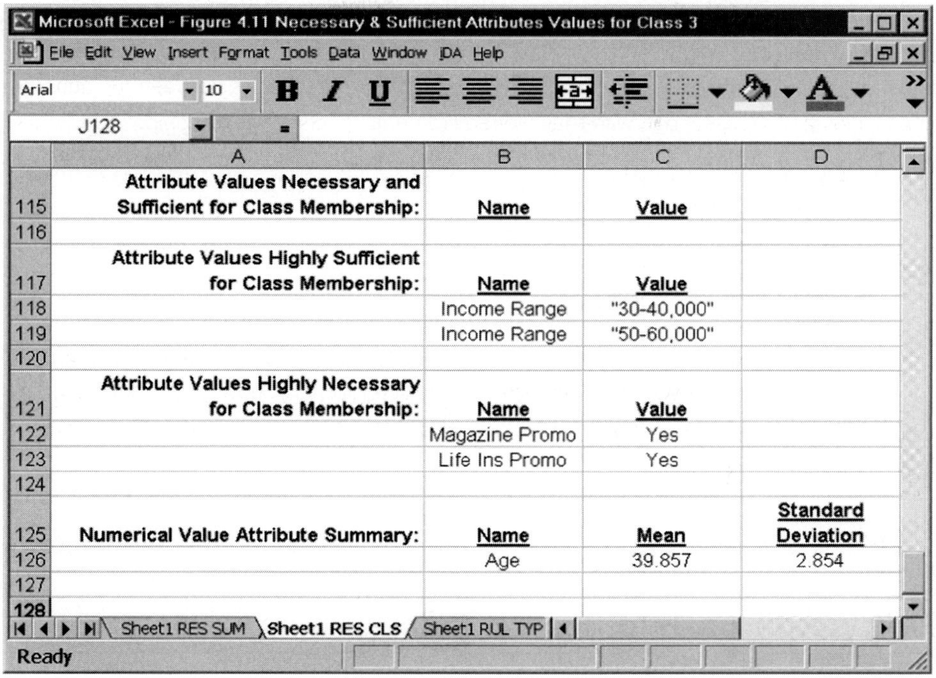

	A	B	C	D
115	**Attribute Values Necessary and Sufficient for Class Membership:**	**Name**	**Value**	
116				
117	**Attribute Values Highly Sufficient for Class Membership:**	**Name**	**Value**	
118		Income Range	"30-40,000"	
119		Income Range	"50-60,000"	
120				
121	**Attribute Values Highly Necessary for Class Membership:**	**Name**	**Value**	
122		Magazine Promo	Yes	
123		Life Ins Promo	Yes	
124				
125	**Numerical Value Attribute Summary:**	**Name**	**Mean**	**Standard Deviation**
126		Age	39.857	2.854
127				
128				

Sheet1 RES SUM \ Sheet1 RES CLS / Sheet1 RUL TYP

Life Ins Promo = Yes
:rule accuracy 77.78%
:rule coverage 100.00%

Notice the rule format is a variation of what we saw in Chapter 2. Each rule simply declares the precondition(s) necessary for an instance to be covered by the rule. The abbreviated rule format is preferred, as RuleMaker is designed to generate a wealth of rules for each concept class. An explicit form of the same rule is:

IF *Life Ins Promo = Yes*
THEN *Class = 3*
:rule accuracy 77.78%
:rule coverage 100.00%

Rule accuracy tells us the rule is accurate in 77.78% of all cases where it applies. That is, the rule will cause a misclassification with 22.22% of the training set instances. Rule coverage informs us that the rule applies to 100% of the Class 3 instances. In other words, everyone in Class 3 accepted the life insurance promotion.

Rarely are single conditionals able to cover a significant number of class instances. For this reason, RuleMaker is able to generate rules with multiple conditions. Rules with multiple conditions are interesting because they help uncover possible dependencies between the attributes. The following is a Class 3 rule with multiple requirements for class membership:

> 35.00 <= *Age* <=43.00
> and *Life Insurance Promo* = *Yes*
> :rule accuracy 100.00%
> :rule coverage 100.00%

This rule shows a relationship between the values of the attributes *age* and *life insurance promotion*. The rule covers all Class 3 instances and is 100% correct. For a real application, this result is strong supportive evidence for targeting the 35-to-43 age group for any new life insurance promotional offerings.

4.5   A Six-Step Approach for Supervised Learning

We now turn our attention toward supervised learning with ESX. For our example we once again employ the hypothetical database about credit card promotions. To follow our discussion, open the CreditCardPromotion.xls file and copy the dataset to a new spreadsheet file. Here is a six-step procedure for supervised learning with ESX.

1.   Enter data to be mined into an Excel spreadsheet and choose an output attribute.

2.   Perform a data mining session.

3.   Read and interpret summary results.

4.   Read and interpret test set results.

5.   Read and interpret results for individual classes.

6.   Visualize and interpret class rules.

Let's work through the credit card promotion example using the six-step approach just described.

Applying the Six-Step Approach for Supervised Learning

STEP 1: CHOOSE AN OUTPUT ATTRIBUTE

The output attribute forms the basis for supervised classification. Our understanding of the data and what we are trying to achieve determines the choice of an output attribute. Let's follow the theme of Chapters 2 and 3 and assume we are about to launch a fresh life insurance promotion. Therefore our goal is to build a model able to predict customers likely to take advantage of the new promotional offering. Since we want our model to be applicable to new card holders, we limit the input attribute selection to *income range, credit card insurance, sex,* and *age*.

STEP 2: PERFORM THE MINING SESSION

To begin, change the *I* in the third-row column for *life insurance promotion* to an *O*. Also, change the *I* in the third-row column for *magazine promotion* as well as *watch promotion* to *D,* indicating these will be display-only attributes. Here is the procedure for mining the data.

1. From the dropdown iDA menu, click on *Begin Mining Session.*

2. Click *OK* when your registration information appears.

3. A message box will appear asking you to choose a supervised learner model. Select *ESX* and click *OK.*

4. You will see a message box asking you to select the number of instances for training as well as a real-valued tolerance setting. Select *10* instances for training and *1.0* for the real-valued tolerance. Click *OK.*

5. Finally, use the default settings for the rule generator and click *OK.*

The output of a supervised mining session appears in either four or six sheets. The description box titled *Output Reports: Supervised Learning* gives a brief description of the output for each sheet. The contents of four of these sheets are similar to those described for unsupervised clustering The two additional sheets are created only when test data are present. We will examine the contents of the new sheets in step 4. We begin our analysis of the data with summary results. To open the summary results sheet, click on *Sheet1 RES SUM* located in the bottom tray of your spreadsheet.

STEP 3: READ AND INTERPRET SUMMARY RESULTS

The output summary sheet gives us results based on the training data. As a first test, we examine the class resemblance scores for each class. The highest class resemblance score is seen with the class represented by *life insurance promotion = yes* (0.575). The class for *life insurance promotion = no* displays a resemblance score of 0.525, and the domain resemblance shows 0.48. As the class resemblance scores are higher than the domain resemblance, we have some indication that differences exist between the two classes. *Domain Statistics for Categorical Attributes* tell us that 80% of the training instances represent individuals without credit card insurance.

Domain Statistics for Numerical Attributes* show attribute *age* with a significance score of 0.42. Finally, upon examining the *Most Commonly Occurring Categorical Attribute Values* for both classes, we see differences between the values for all categorical attributes except *credit card insurance.*

STEP 4: READ AND INTERPRET TEST SET RESULTS

To determine test set model performance, locate and open the sheet labeled *Sheet1 RES TST.* Finding the RES TST sheet may involve manipulating the arrows in the lower left of the Excel spreadsheet. This sheet lists each test set instance together with its computed class.

The RES TST output sheet for our experiment is shown in Figure 4.12. The last two columns are of interest. The last column offers the choices made by the model. The second-to-last column displays the correct classification for each instance. A star is placed to the right of those test instances correctly classified by the model. Notice three of the five test set instances have been correctly classified.

Next, find and open the sheet labeled *Sheet1 RES MTX.* This sheet displays the confusion matrix for the test data. RES MTX shows that three test set instances were correctly classified. Also, two instances from the class represented by *life insurance promotion = yes* were incorrectly classified as unlikely candidates for the promotional offer. Finally, the RES MTX sheet

---

Output Reports: Supervised Learning

Sheet1 RES MTX: This sheet shows the confusion matrix for test set data.

Sheet1 RES TST: This sheet contains individual test set instance classifications and is only seen when a test set is applied.

Sheet1 RES SUM: This sheet contains summary statistics about attribute values and offers several heuristics to help us determine the quality of a data mining session.

Sheet1 RES CLS: This sheet has information about the classes formed as a result of a supervised mining session.

Sheet1 RUL TYP: Instances are listed by their class name. The last column of this sheet shows a typicality value for each instance.

Sheet1 RES RUL: The production rules generated for each class are contained in this sheet.

Figure 4.12 • **Test set instance classification**

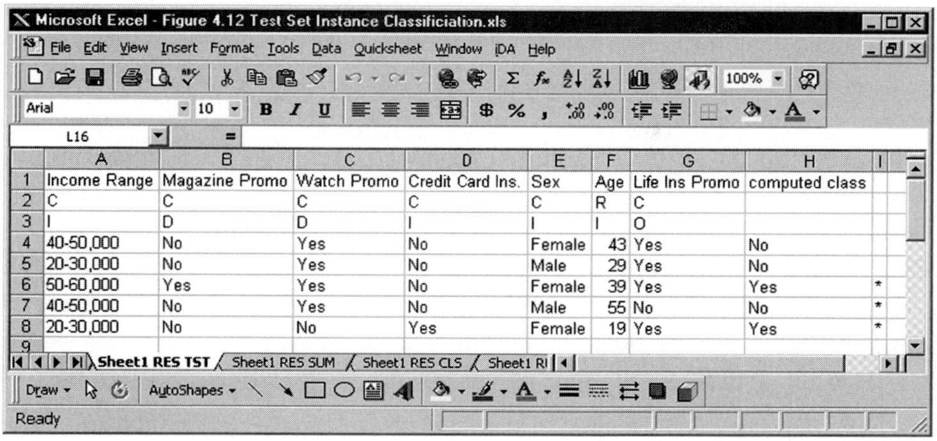

	A	B	C	D	E	F	G	H	I
1	Income Range	Magazine Promo	Watch Promo	Credit Card Ins.	Sex	Age	Life Ins Promo	computed class	
2	C	C	C	C	C	R	C		
3	I	D	D	I	I	I	O		
4	40-50,000	No	Yes	No	Female	43	Yes	No	
5	20-30,000	No	Yes	No	Male	29	Yes	No	
6	50-60,000	Yes	Yes	No	Female	39	Yes	Yes	*
7	40-50,000	No	Yes	No	Male	55	No	No	*
8	20-30,000	No	No	Yes	Female	19	Yes	Yes	*

gives the percent of test set instances classified correctly, as well as an upper and lower error bound for the test set classification. Notice that 60% of the test instances were correctly classified. The size of the test set must be relatively large ($n > 100$) for the upper and lower bound error rates to have meaning. For purposes of general explanation, the error bound gives us a confidence interval for the test set error rate. We offer a clear example of how the confidence interval is used in Section 4.8.

Lastly, a supervised model must be able to classify new instances of unknown origin. If we wish to classify instances whose classification is not known, we simply place the instances in the dataset as test set entries. As the instances are not really part of the test set per se, we leave the output attribute field blank. Once the data is mined the RES TST sheet will show the classification determined by the model for the unknown instances. Given that iDA denotes a missing field with an open square, the column specifying the correct class output will contain the open square symbol. In addition, since the unknown instance is without a predetermined class, the instance does not count as an incorrect classification.

STEP 5: READ AND INTERPRET RESULTS FOR INDIVIDUAL CLASSES

Section 4.4 showed you how to interpret individual class results with unsupervised clustering. The same information is relevant when learning is supervised. However, with supervised learning it is particularly important for us to examine both categorical attribute predictiveness scores and numeric attribute significance. In this way, when a wealth of available attributes exist, we can create new supervised models by employing only those attributes most predictive of class membership.

For our example the summary results for the two formed classes are given in the sheet labeled *Sheet1 RES CLS*. Notice that the attribute-value combination *credit card insurance = yes* as well as the attribute-value pair *income range = 50–60K* each show a predictiveness score of 1.00 for the class *life insurance promotion = yes*. Can you find any highly predictive categorical attribute-value combinations in the class *life insurance promotion = no*?

STEP 6: VISUALIZE AND INTERPRET CLASS RULES

Open the *Sheet1 RES RUL* sheet to visualize the rules for the two classes. By scrolling the rule window, we see that 100% of all instances from each class are covered by at least one rule. Although this may be an acceptable result, it often takes several iterations of rule generation parameter manipulation to create a satisfactory set of rules. For this reason, iDA has a rerule feature that allows us to generate a new rule set without repeating an entire mining session. Here is the procedure for generating a new set of rules.

1. Click on the *RUL TYP* sheet located in the lower tray of your Excel spreadsheet. Two MS Word document images appear on your screen. These documents contain information relevant to the rule generation process. There is no need to open either document.

2. Mouse to the *iDA Drop-Down Menu* and click on *Generate Rules*. Several windows appear and disappear as the rule generator prepares itself for another session.

3. When the rule dialog box appears, modify the rule generating parameters as desired and click *OK*.

To try this, follow the procedure and change the *Scope* setting from *All Rules* to *Covering Set Rules*. Also change the *Minimum Rule Coverage* parameter to *30*. When rule generation is complete, you will see two rules for the first listed class and one rule for the second class. Here is the first rule for class *life insurance promotion = no*:

> *Income Range = 40–50K*
> :rule accuracy 100.00%
> # covered = 2
> # remaining = 3

Notice the rule format has changed in that we are told the number of class instances covered by the rule and the number of instances remaining to be covered. In this way, instead of obtaining a list of all possible rules satisfying the parameter settings, we get a best set of covering rules.

The *Covering Set Rules* algorithm uses the following procedure to generate a set of rules.

1. Construct a best-covering rule for the current set of class instances.

2. Eliminate all class instances covered by the rule generated in step 1.

3. If additional class instances remain to be covered, and the minimum rule coverage criterion can be satisfied, repeat step 1.

Notice that each additional rule generation gives a new rule sheet. The first rerule will show new rules in *Sheet1 RUL TYP 2 RUL*. The second rerule will create *Sheet1 RUL TYP 3 RUL*. The pattern continues with each new set of rules. After several rule generations, it is best to delete previous rule sets. Simply right-click the bottom tray sheet you wish to delete and left-click *Delete*.

Before we look more closely at the options offered by the rule generator, a word of caution about the interpretation of rule accuracy values is merited. Although useful, the accuracy score is optimistic, as the score is computed based on training rather than test data. As of this writing, iDA does not support test set rule accuracy computations. The next section details the rule generation parameter settings and offers helpful hints when generating rules.

4.6 Techniques for Generating Rules

Many traditional rule generation programs follow a simple procedure for creating rules.

1. Choose an attribute that best differentiates all domain or subclass instances.

2. Use the attribute to further subdivide instances into classes.

3. For each subclass created in step 2:
   - If the instances in the subclass satisfy a predefined criteria, generate a defining rule for the subclass.
   - If the subclass does not satisfy the predefined criterion, repeat 1.

This algorithm works well for generating a best set of covering rules for a set of class instances. However, in a data mining environment we frequently wish to determine as many interesting class rules as possible. With RuleMaker we have this option. Alternatively, we can request RuleMaker to generate a best set of class covering rules. Let's look at all of the options available with RuleMaker.

Once a data mining session is complete, the dialog box shown in Figure 4.6 appears. We are asked to:

1. *Define the scope of the rules to be generated.*
   If we select the *All Rules* radio button, RuleMaker will generate all rules for all classes that meet the criteria of the other parameters. If we select the *Covering Set Rules* radio button, RuleMaker will generate a set of best–defining rules for each class. With the covering set option, the rule coverage percent is replaced by two values: #covered and #remaining. In this way, we clearly see the covering effect each rule has on a set of class instances.

2. *Choose whether we wish to use all class instances or only the most typical instances for rule generation.*

   If we choose the most typical instance option, we obtain a set of rules that best describe the most characteristic features of each class. However, some of the more atypical class instances may not be covered by the generated rules.

3. *Set a minimum correctness value.*

   We must input a value between 50 and 100. If we enter 100, the only rules generated by RuleMaker will be rules that are 100% correct. If we enter the value 80, the rules generated must have an error rate less than or equal to 20%.

4. *Define a minimum percent of instances to be covered.*

   We enter a value between 10 and 100. If we enter the value 10, RuleMaker will generate rules that cover 10% or more of the instances in each class. If we enter 80, only those rules covering 80% of the class instances will be covered.

5. *Choose an attribute significance value.*

   Values close to 100 will allow RuleMaker to consider only those attribute values most highly predictive of class membership for rule generation. A good choice for this value is extremely important in domains containing more than a few attributes. As a general rule, in domains containing several attributes, we should start with a value between 80 and 90. If an interesting set of rules is not generated, we can always use the rerule feature and try lower attribute significance values.

Some helpful hints for generating rules:

1. If you spend time manipulating rule generating parameters you can often find a best set of class defining rules. As a first attempt, generate rules for a dataset by using the default parameters. If you are satisfied with these results you need not proceed further. However, if the rules appear to be less than optimal or if one or more classes are without rules you should alter the parameters and try again.

2. For categorical data, you can take advantage of attribute value predictability and predictiveness scores to help find rule sets. Suppose class resemblance scores indicate an interesting classification, but one or more of the formed classes is without a set of rules. For any class without rules and containing at least one categorical attribute, attribute-value predictiveness scores can be examined to determine a lower-bound setting for the minimum rule correctness value.

3. Generating a covering set of rules can be difficult at times. Frequently, we achieve a desired result by manipulating the minimum correctness, coverage, and attribute significance attributes. First, try setting the coverage and signifi-

cance parameters at their minimal values. If you are still unsuccessful, try decreasing the parameter value for classification correctness.

4.7 Instance Typicality

Whether learning is supervised or unsupervised, each instance has an associated typicality score. The typicality score for instance *I* represents the average similarity of *I* to all other instances within its class. We can observe the typicality scores for all instances by opening Sheet1 RUL TYP. This sheet gives us a listing of the data instances ordered by their typicality scores. With supervised learning the instances are limited to those found in the training data. Figure 4.13 shows the contents of the RUL TYP sheet for the supervised learning example just presented. Notice the sheet also contains two MS Word document icons. These documents hold instance and attribute information for the rule generator and are not of interest to us.

Let's examine the RUL TYP sheet more closely. The left-most column contains sequential instance numbers. The second column gives the class for each instance. The next few columns show the attribute values for the individual instances. The final column displays typicality scores. Typicality scores range between 0 and 1, with higher scores being more typical class instances. The instances are ordered within each class from most to least typical. The first listed instance for each class is considered the **class prototype** as it is a

Figure 4.13 • **Instance typicality**

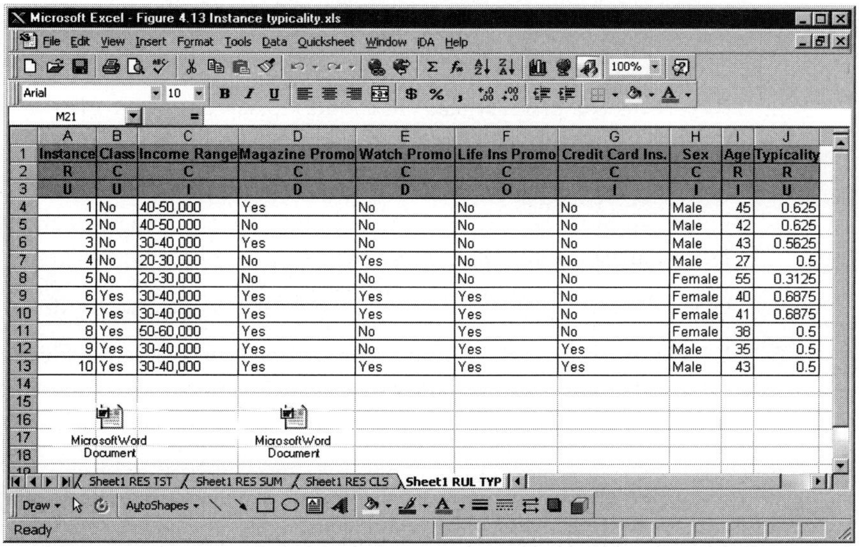

Instance	Class	Income Range	Magazine Promo	Watch Promo	Life Ins Promo	Credit Card Ins.	Sex	Age	Typicality
R	C	C		C	C	C	C	R	R
U	U	I	D	D	O	I	I	I	U
1	No	40-50,000	Yes	No	No	No	Male	45	0.625
2	No	40-50,000	No	No	No	No	Male	42	0.625
3	No	30-40,000	Yes	No	No	No	Male	43	0.5625
4	No	20-30,000	No	Yes	No	No	Male	27	0.5
5	No	20-30,000	No	No	No	No	Female	55	0.3125
6	Yes	30-40,000	Yes	Yes	Yes	No	Female	40	0.6875
7	Yes	30-40,000	Yes	Yes	Yes	No	Female	41	0.6875
8	Yes	50-60,000	Yes	No	Yes	No	Female	38	0.5
9	Yes	30-40,000	Yes	No	Yes	Yes	Male	35	0.5
10	Yes	30-40,000	Yes	Yes	Yes	Yes	Male	43	0.5

best single representative of the class in general. The last few class instances are candidate *outliers* as they are atypical class members. The exposure of class outliers can frequently lead to a better understanding about the nature of the domain under study.

Here are some ways in which typicality scores can be used.

- Typicality scores can identify prototypical class instances as well as outliers.
- Instance typicality can help select a best set of instances for supervised classification.
- Typicality scores can be used to compute individual instance classification confidence values.

The end-of-chapter exercises help you learn more about how typicality is used to build supervised learner models. Here we take a closer look at how typicality can be employed to compute instance classification confidence scores.

As an example, assume we have built a supervised model to distinguish individuals likely to respond to a promotion from those who would not respond. We present our model with a set of 1,000,000 new instances to be classified. We have a budget allowing us to send the promotional package to 10,000 individuals.

Suppose our model classifies 20,000 of the instances as good candidates for the promotional offer. Given our restriction, we need a mechanism for choosing a best set of 10,000 individuals from the group of candidate instances. Several models associate confidence factors with individual rules, but few models allow us to easily compute test set confidence scores for individual instances. Fortunately, typicality scores allow us to associate confidence factors with new classifications. The general procedure for computing a classification confidence score for instance *I* is as follows:

1. Open the RES TST sheet to determine the classification given for unknown instance *I*.

2. Return to the original data sheet and replace the blank output attribute cell for instance *I* with the computed class.

3. Initiate a new supervised mining session, but this time include the previously unknown instance as part of the training data. By doing this, the instance will receive an associated typicality score.

4. Open the RES TYP sheet to see the typicality score associated with instance *I*.

5. Divide the instance *I* typicality score by the typicality score for the most typical class instance. This value represents the classification confidence score for instance *I*.

When you have time, test this procedure by adding one or more new unknown instances to the credit card promotion database.

4.8 Special Considerations and Features

This section offers information about making your data mining sessions more productive. We also provide a short discussion on erroneous and missing data.

Avoid Mining Delays

The data within an Excel spreadsheet can be mined several times. However, each mining session creates several other Excel spreadsheets. To avoid confusion each of these sheets are numbered. To illustrate, the first mining session will result in a sheet titled Sheet1 RES 1 SUM. If we mine the same data a second time, Sheet1 RES 2 SUM will be created. After a few mining sessions it is easy to get confused with the numbers as they increase. In addition, prior to each new mining session, Excel must save the contents of the current spreadsheets. Therefore at some point it is best to simply copy the original data into another Excel spreadsheet before starting a new mining session.

The Deer Hunter Dataset

The Deer Hunter dataset contains information about 6059 individual deer hunters who were asked whether they would have taken any hunting trips during 1991 if the total cost of their trips was a specified amount more than what they had paid for the current year. Although each instance contains only one increase amount, there are a total of 10 possible dollar-increase values ranging from as little as $9.00 to as much as $953.00. The original data was obtained from a survey conducted by the U.S. Fish and Wildlife Service. We obtained a cleaned form of the datafile from Dr. John Whitehead. The cleaned dataset contains 20 input attributes and 1 output attribute indicating whether the hunter responded positively to the aforementioned question.

The dataset is interesting because it represents real data that can be used to monitor and develop profiles of deer hunters. For example, states might use the results of discovered relationships in the data to help determine future changes in permit and licensing fees. The dataset is a difficult data mining application because of the variable amounts for total trip-increase values. See Appendix B for a complete description of the attributes in the dataset as well as more information about the original data. The dataset is found in the iDA samples directory under the title DeerHunter.xls. ■

The Quick Mine Feature

Datasets having thousands of instances may take several minutes to mine. If a dataset contains more than 2000 instances, the iDA quick mine feature allows us to significantly reduce the time it takes to mine the data. The quick mine feature is useful because the performance of a model built from a random subset of the data is likely to give us results similar to those seen with a model constructed from the entire dataset.

When learning is supervised and we have more than 2000 training set instances, iDA asks us if we wish to conduct a *quick mine* of the data. If we choose the quick mine feature, the ESX concept hierarchy is built using a random subset of 500 training set instances. The test set data remains unchanged. When learning is unsupervised and more than 2000 data instances are presented for clustering, ESX is given a random selection of 500 instances from which to cluster the data. We use the quick mine feature to:

1. Obtain initial information about the predictive nature of the attributes within the domain.

2. Determine a setting for the similarity parameter (unsupervised learning).

3. Determine a value for the real-valued tolerance.

4. Determine settings for the rule generation parameters.

Two of the datasets that come with your software are quick mine candidates. The Deer Hunter dataset is an interesting dataset containing 6059 instances. Each instance of the dataset represents individual statistics gathered from a national survey conducted by the U.S. Fish and Wildlife Service (USFWS). The description box titled *The Deer Hunter Dataset* as well as a summary in Appendix B offers more details about this dataset.

The Titanic dataset is also a quick mine candidate. The dataset contains survival information for 2201 passengers and crew aboard the Titanic when it sank into the Atlantic ocean on April 15, 1912, while on its maiden voyage. The description box titled *The Titanic Dataset* as well Appendix B gives additional information about this dataset. Let's use the Titanic dataset to demonstrate iDA's quick mine feature.

Applying the Quick Mine Feature to the Titanic Dataset

1. Open Excel and load the Titanic.xls file.

2. Perform a supervised mining session with *class* as the output attribute. Use 2001 instances for training and the default real-tolerance setting.

3. When asked if you wish to perform a quick mine session, answer *Yes*.

4. Select *Cancel* when the rule generation menu is presented.

As the training data is randomly selected, your results will be similar to but not identical to our findings. Please examine the contents of your RES SUM and RES MTX output sheets to compare your results with ours.

When the mining session is complete, check the RES SUM sheet for the total number of instances used for training. Our results show that 180 of the training data instances represent survivors of the tragedy and 320 of the training data instances did not survive. This gives us a 36% survivor rate. This is relatively close to the survivor rate of 32% seen within the entire population.

Finally, the test set confusion matrix is of interest because we can achieve a better understanding of the meaning associated with upper and lower bound error rates. By clicking on the RES MTX sheet, our results show that 99% of the test set instances were correctly classified. Stated another way, the model test set error rate is 1%. The test data is biased toward non-survivor instances, as only 5% of the test instances represent survivors. The upper and lower bound error values give us a 95% confidence limit for the test set error rate. Our results show an upper-bound error of 1.5% and a lower-bound error of 0.5%. Therefore, we can be 95% confident that the test set error rate of 1% is actually somewhere between 0.5% and 1.5%. Stated another way, given a pool of data instances for testing, if we perform this experiment with the same model by applying randomly selected test data from this pool 100 times, we will see a test set classification error rate somewhere between 0.5% and 1.5% in at least 95 of the 100 experiments. Although we cannot be sure of the exact test set accuracy of our model, we can be 95% confident that the model test set performance is within the computed lower and upper error bound. We will address the issue of how confidence intervals and error rates are computed in Chapter 7.

The Titanic Dataset

The Titanic dataset contains 2201 data instances. Each data instance represents information about one passenger or crew member aboard the Titanic when it sank into the Atlantic Ocean on April 15, 1912. An individual instance has three input attribute values: the class of the individual (first, second, third, or crew), the individual's age (adult or child), and the sex of the individual. The fourth attribute is an output attribute that tells whether the individual survived to tell the story of the tragic event. The dataset is of historic interest and allows us to develop a profile of a "typical" survivor of this unusual event. The dataset is found in the iDA samples directory as Titanic.xls.

Erroneous and Missing Data

The preprocessor lets you know if an input data file contains errors. Incorrectly formatted data can take many forms. Common mistakes include:

- Blank lines without any valid data.

- Instances containing values in cells beyond the last attribute column.

- Numeric attributes containing invalid characters.

A blank cell indicates a missing data item. Rows containing valid data and one or more blank cells are not flagged as errors. The iDA mining tools have a built-in facility to process missing data items.

When we begin a mining session with a file containing one or more errors that cannot be resolved by the preprocessor, a message box informing us about the total number of errors appears on our screen. We are offered the option to continue the mining session with the valid data. In any case, the rows containing one or more unresolved errors are highlighted in red. Also, an MS Word document offering a general explanation about the location of the errors appears in the upper left of the Excel spreadsheet. Clicking on the document opens the file. You can delete the file by placing the mouse pointer over the document and striking the delete key.

Many real-world datasets contain a wealth of missing and/or erroneous information. The Spine Clinic Dataset that comes with your iDA software package fits this

The Spine Clinic Dataset

The dataset contains three-month follow-up information collected by a metropolitan spine clinic on 171 of their patients who have had back surgery. The dataset consists of 31 attributes. Several attributes relate to the condition of the patient before and during surgery. Other attributes store information about current patient health as well as general patient characteristics. The attribute *return to work* is of particular interest as it indicates whether the patient has returned to work. Ninety-seven of the patients had returned to work at the time of the survey.

The dataset is interesting because it contains information about real patients who have had major surgery. Also, although the dataset has several missing and erroneous entries, useful patterns differentiating patients who have and have not returned to work can be found. The dataset is located in the iDA samples directory as SpineData.xls. ■

category. The Spine Clinic Dataset consists of three-month follow-up information for patients who have had back surgery. Many of the data entries for individual patients are missing, and some attribute values are erroneous. The description box titled *The Spine Clinic Dataset* as well as Appendix B provide additional information about this dataset. Data Mining Exercise 5 asks you to profile patients who have returned to work after back surgery.

4.9   Chapter Summary

Data mining is an iterative process that involves a degree of art as well as science. Because of this, everyone develops their own special techniques for creating better models through data mining. In this chapter we offered a methodology for data mining using two of the data mining tools that are part of your iDA software package—ESX and RuleMaker. ESX forms a concept hierarchy from a set of instances to perform both supervised learning and unsupervised clustering. Whether learning is supervised or unsupervised, the following is a plausible strategy for analyzing a data mining session with ESX:

1. Examine class resemblance scores and individual class rules to see how well the input attributes define the formed classes.

2. Examine domain summary statistics to help locate attribute errors and to determine predictive numeric attributes.

3. Examine class summary statistics to locate predictive categorical attribute values.

4. Modify attribute or instance selections and parameter settings as appropriate and repeat the data mining process to create a best data model.

RuleMaker creates sets of production rules from instances of known classification. RuleMaker offers several rule generation parameters that include the option to obtain a listing of all possibly interesting rules. In the next chapter you will learn more about how ESX and RuleMaker create generalized models from data.

4.10   Key Terms

Class predictability. Given class C and categorical attribute A with values v_1, v_2, $v_3 \dots v_n$, the class C predictability score for v_i tells us the percent of instances showing v_i as the value for A in C.

Class predictiveness. Given class C and attribute A with values $v_1, v_2, v_3 \ldots v_n$. An attribute-value predictiveness score for v_i is defined as the probability an instance resides in C given the instance has value v_i for A.

Class prototype. The instance that best represents a class of instances.

Class resemblance. The average similarity of all instances within a class or cluster.

Cluster quality. For an individual class, cluster quality is the percent increase (or decrease) of the class resemblance score relative to the domain resemblance.

Domain predictability. Given attribute A with values $v_1, v_2, v_3 \ldots v_n$, the domain predictability score for v_i tells us the percent of all dataset instances showing v_i as the value for A.

Domain resemblance. The overall similarity of all instances within a dataset.

Necessary attribute value. Value v_i for categorical attribute A is necessary for membership in class C if and only if all instances of C have v_i as their value for A.

Sufficient attribute value. Value v_i for categorical attribute A is sufficient for membership in class C if and only if any instance having v_i as its value for A resides in C.

Typicality. The typicality of instance I is the average similarity of I to the other members of its cluster or class.

4.11   Exercises

Review Questions

1. Differentiate between the following terms.

   a. Domain resemblance and class resemblance

   b. Class predictiveness and class predictability

   c. Domain predictability and class predictability

   d. Typicality and class resemblance

   e. Within-class and between-class measure

2. Suppose you have used data mining to build a model able to differentiate between individuals likely and unlikely to default on a car loan. For each of the following, describe a categorical attribute value likely to display the stated characteristic.

   a. A categorical attribute value that is necessary but not sufficient for class membership.

b. A categorical attribute value that is sufficient but not necessary for class membership.

c. A categorical attribute that is both necessary and sufficient for class membership.

Data Mining Questions

LAB 1. This exercise demonstrates how erroneous data is displayed in a spreadsheet file.

a. Copy the CreditCardPromotion.xls dataset into a new spreadsheet.

b. Modify the instance on line 17 to contain one or more illegal characters for age.

c. Add one or more blank lines to the spreadsheet.

d. Remove values from one or more spreadsheet cells.

e. Using *life insurance promotion* as the output attribute, initiate a data mining session with ESX. When asked if you wish to continue mining the good instances, answer *No.* Open the Word document located in the upper-left corner of your spreadsheet to examine the error messages.

2. Suppose you suspect marked differences in promotional purchasing trends between female and male Acme credit card customers. You wish to confirm or refute your suspicion. Perform a supervised data mining session using the CreditCardPromotion.xls database with *sex* as the output attribute. Designate all other attributes as input attributes, and use all 15 instances for training. Because there is no test data, the RES TST and RES MTX sheets will not be created. Write a summary confirming or refuting your hypothesis. Base your analysis on:

a. Class resemblance scores

b. Class predictability and predictiveness scores

c. Rules created for each class. You may wish to use the rerule feature.

3. Repeat the previous exercise with *income range* as the output attribute.

LAB 4. For this exercise you will use ESX to perform a data mining session with the cardiology patient data described in Chapter 2. Load the CardiologyCategorical.xls file into a new MS Excel spreadsheet. This is the mixed form of the dataset containing both categorical and numeric data. Recall that the data contains 303 instances representing patients who have a heart condition (sick) as well as those who do not.

LAB Denotes exercise appropriate for a laboratory setting.

Save the spreadsheet to a new file and perform a supervised mining session using *class* as the output attribute. Use 1.0 for the real–tolerance setting and select 203 instances as training data. The final 100 instances represent the test dataset. Generate rules using the default settings for the rule generator. Answer the following based on your results:

a. Provide the domain resemblance score as well as the resemblance score for each class (sick and healthy).

b. What percent of the training data is female?

c. What is the most commonly occurring domain value for the attribute *slope*?

d. What is the average age of those individuals in the *healthy* class?

e. What is the most common *healthy* class value for the attribute *thal*?

f. Specify blood pressure values for the two most typical *sick* class instances.

g. What percent of the *sick* class is female?

h. What is the predictiveness score for the *sick* class attribute value *angina = true*? In your own words, explain what this value means.

i. List one *sick* class attribute value that is highly sufficient for class membership.

j. What percent of the test set instances were correctly classified?

k. Give the 95% confidence limits for the test set. State what the confidence limit values mean.

l. How many test set instances were classified as being sick when in reality they were from the *healthy* class?

m. List a rule with multiple conditions for the *sick* class that covers at least 50% of the instances and is accurate in at least 85% of all cases.

n. What is the most highly predictive numeric attribute?

5. The SpineClinic.xls data file has an attribute named *return to work*. A value of 1 for the attribute indicates the patient has returned to work. Load this dataset into an Excel spreadsheet and designate the *return to work* attribute as an output attribute. Perform a data mining session with ESX using all 171 patient records as training data. Generate rules in an attempt to find one or two interesting rules that differentiate individuals who have and have not returned to work. Use the rerule feature if necessary.

LAB 6. In this exercise you will use instance typicality to determine class prototypes. You will then employ the prototype instances to build and test a supervised learner model.

a. Open the CardiologyCategorical.xls spreadsheet file.

b. Save the file to a new spreadsheet.

c. Perform a supervised mining session on the *class* attribute. Use all instances for training.

d. When learning is complete, open the RES TYP sheet and copy the most typical sick class instance to a new spreadsheet. Save the spreadsheet and return to the RES TYP sheet.

e. Now, copy the most typical healthy class instance to the spreadsheet created in the previous step and currently holding the single most typical sick class instance. Save the updated spreadsheet file.

f. Delete columns A, B, and Q of the new spreadsheet file that now contains the most typical healthy class instance and the most typical sick class instance. Copy the two instances contained in the spreadsheet.

g. Return to the original sheet1 data sheet and insert two blank rows after row three. Paste the two instances copied in step f into sheet1.

h. Your sheet1 spreadsheet now contains 305 instances. The first instance in sheet1 (row 4) is the most typical sick class instance. The second instance is the most typical healthy class instance.

i. Perform a data mining session using the first *two* instances as training data. The remaining 303 instances will make up the test set.

j. Analyze the test set results by examining the confusion matrix. What can you conclude?

k. Repeat the above steps but this time extract the least typical instance from each class. How do your results compare with those of the first experiment?

7. Add one or more unknown data instances to the CreditCardPromotion.xls database. Use supervised learning on the *life insurance promotion* attribute together with the procedure described in Section 4.7 to compute classification confidence scores for the new instances.

LAB 8. Perform a supervised data mining session with the Titanic.xls dataset. Use 1500 instances for training and the remaining instances as test data.

a. Are any of the input attributes highly predictive of class membership for either class?

b. What is the test set accuracy of the model?

c. Use the confidence limits to state the 95% test set accuracy range.

d. Why is the classification accuracy so much lower for this experiment than for the quick mine experiment given in Section 4.8?

Computational Questions

1. Concept class C_1 shows the following information for the categorical attribute *color*. Use this information and the information in the table to answer the following questions:

Name	Value	Frequency	Predictability *[Coveracy]*	Predictiveness *[accuracy]*
Color	Red	30	*0.6*	0.4
	Black	20	*0.4*	1.0

   a. What percent of the instances in class C_1 have a value of *black* for the *color* attribute?   *20/(30+20) = 40%*

   b. Suppose that exactly one other concept class, C_2, exists. In addition, assume all domain instances have a color value of either *red* or *black*. Given the information in the table, can you determine the predictability score of *color = red* for class C_2? If your answer is yes, what is the predictability value? *=1.0*   *Yes. The predictiveness score for color = black in C_1 is 1.0, therefore all C_1 instances must have*

   c. Using the same assumption as in part b, can you determine the predictiveness score for *color = red* for class C_2? If your answer is yes, what is the predictiveness score? *color = red*   *the predictiveness score is 0.6. The predictiveness scores for color = red within*   *C_1 & C_2 = 1.0.*

   d. Once again, use the assumption stated in part b. How many instances reside in class C_2?

PART **II**

Tools for
Knowledge Discovery

RDB (relational data base)

Primary key - Unique ... ...

$1:1$

$1:M$

$M:M$

Chapter **5**

Knowledge Discovery in Databases

Chapter Objectives

▶ Know the seven-step KDD process.

▶ Know that data mining is one step of the KDD process.

▶ Understand techniques for normalizing, converting, and smoothing data.

▶ Understand methods for attribute elimination and creation.

▶ Recognize the advantages and disadvantages of methods for dealing with missing data.

▶ Become familiar with the Cross Industry Standard Process Model for Data Mining (CRISP-DM).

In Chapter 1 we described a simple data mining process model. In Section 5.1 of this chapter we introduce a formal seven-step KDD process. In Sections 5.2 through 5.8 we examine each step of this model in detail. In Section 5.9 we introduce a second knowledge discovery model known as the Cross Industry Standard Process for Data Mining (CRISP-DM). Section 5.10 offers two experiments with ESX that demonstrate the iterative nature of the data mining process.

5.1   A KDD Process Model

Knowledge Discovery in Databases (KDD) is an interactive, iterative procedure that attempts to extract implicit, previously unknown, and potentially useful knowledge from data. Several variations of what has come to be known as the KDD process model exist. These variations describe the KDD process in 4 to as many as 12 steps. Although the number of steps may differ, most descriptions show consistency in content. We prefer to characterize the KDD process as a seven-step approach to knowledge discovery. The seven-step KDD process model is shown in Figure 5.1. A brief description of each step follows:

1. **Goal identification.** The focus of this step is on understanding the domain being considered for knowledge discovery. We write a clear statement about what is to be accomplished. Hypotheses offering likely or desired outcomes can be stated.

2. **Creating a target data set.** With the help of one or more human experts and knowledge discovery tools, we choose an initial set of data to be analyzed.

3. **Data preprocessing.** We use available resources to deal with noisy data. We decide what to do about missing data values and how to account for time-sequence information.

4. **Data transformation.** Attributes and instances are added and/or eliminated from the target data. We decide on methods to normalize, convert, and smooth data.

5. **Data mining.** A best model for representing the data is created by applying one or more data mining algorithms.

6. **Interpretation and evaluation.** We examine the output from step 5 to determine if what has been discovered is both useful and interesting. Decisions are made about whether to repeat previous steps using new attributes and/or instances.

7. **Taking action.** If the discovered knowledge is deemed useful, the knowledge is incorporated and applied directly to appropriate problems.

Figure 5.1 • **A seven-step KDD process model**

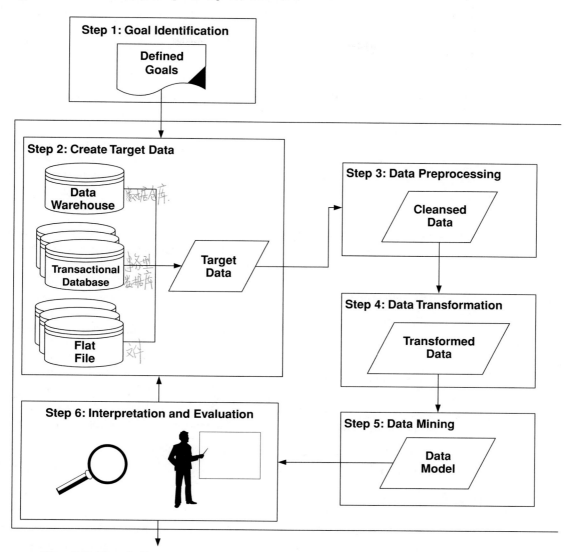

KDD has been described as the application of the **scientific method** to data mining. In 1620, Sir Francis Bacon first explained the scientific method in his book *Novum Organum* (*New Instrument*). He portrayed the scientific method as a four-step process:

1. Define the problem to be solved.

2. Formulate a hypothesis.

3. Perform one or more experiments to verify or refute the hypothesis.

4. Draw and verify conclusions.

Figure 5.2 shows the correspondence between the scientific method and the KDD process model. Let's take a closer look at each of the steps defining the knowledge discovery process.

Figure 5.2   ●   **Applying the scientific method to data mining**

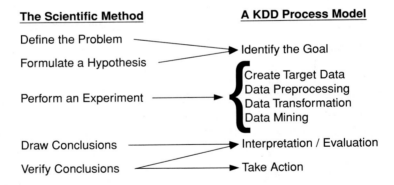

5.2   Step 1: Goal Identification

A main objective of goal identification is to clearly define what is to be accomplished. This first step is in many ways the most difficult, as decisions about resource allocations as well as measures of success need to be determined. Whenever possible, broad goals should be stated in the form of specific objectives. Here is a partial list of things to consider at this stage:

● A clear problem statement is provided as well as a list of criteria to measure success and failure. One or more hypotheses offering likely or desired outcomes may be established.

- The choice of a data mining tool or set of tools is made. The choice of a tool depends on several factors, including the level of explanation required and whether learning is supervised, unsupervised, or a combination of both techniques.

- An estimated project cost is determined. A plan for human resource management is offered.

- A project completion/product delivery date is given.

- Legal issues that may arise from applying the results of the discovery process are taken into account.

- A plan for maintenance of a working system is provided as appropriate. As new data becomes available, a main consideration is a methodology for updating a working model.

Our list is by no means exhaustive. As with any software project, more complex problems require additional planning. Of major importance is the location, availability, and condition of resource data.

5.3   Step 2: Creating a Target Dataset

A viable set of resource data is of primary importance for any data mining project to succeed. Figure 5.1 shows target data being extracted from three primary sources—a data warehouse, one or more transactional databases, or one or more flat files. Many data mining tools require input data to be in a flat file or spreadsheet format. If the original data is housed in a flat file, creating the initial target data is straightforward. Let's examine the other possibilities.

Database management systems (DBMS) store and manipulate transactional data. The computer programs in a DBMS are able to quickly update and retrieve information from a stored database. The data in a DBMS is often structured using the relational model. A **relational database** represents data as a collection of tables containing rows and columns. Each column of a table is known as an attribute, and each row of the table stores information about one data record. The individual rows are called **tuples.** All tuples in a relational table are uniquely identified by a combination of one or more table attributes.

A main goal of the relational model is to reduce data redundancy so as to allow for quick access to information in the database. A set of normal forms that discourage data redundancy define formatting rules for relational tables. If a relational table contains redundant data, the redundancy is removed by decomposing the table into two or more relational structures. In contrast, the goal of data mining is to uncover the inherent redundancy in data. Therefore one or more relational join operations are usually required to restructure data into a form amenable for data mining.

To see this, consider the hypothetical credit card promotion database we defined in Table 2.3 of Chapter 2. Recall the table attributes: *income range, magazine promotion, watch promotion, life insurance promotion, credit card insurance, sex,* and *age.* The data in Table 2.3 is not a database at all, but represents a flat file structure extracted from a database such as the one shown in Figure 5.3. The Acme credit card database contains tables about credit card billing information and orders, in addition to information about credit card promotions. As you can see, the promotional information shown in Table 2.3 is housed in two relational tables within the database. In Chapter 6 we detail the database pictured in Figure 5.3 and show you how the database can be restructured for a decision support environment.

Note that Figure 5.1 also offers the possibility of extracting data from multiple databases or files. If target data is to be extracted from more than one source, the transfer process can be tedious. Consider a simple example where one operational database

---

Figure 5.3 ● **The Acme credit card database**

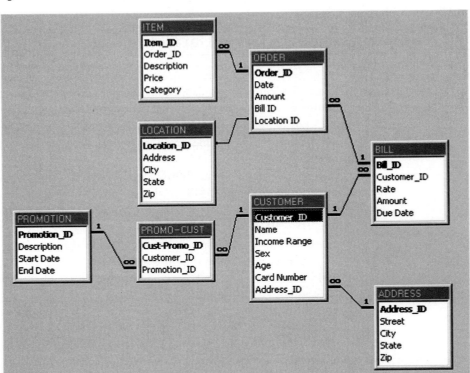

stores customer gender with the coding *male = 1, female = 2.* A second database stores the gender coding as *male = M* and *female = F.* The coding for *male* and *female* must be consistent throughout all records in the target data or the data will be of little use. The process of promoting this consistency when transporting the data is a form of **data transformation.** Other types of data transformations are discussed in Section 5.5.

Finally, a third possibility for harvesting target data is the data warehouse. Chapter 1 described the data warehouse as a historical database designed specifically for decision support. In Chapter 6 you will see how a well-structured data warehouse best supports the redundancy required to build learner models through the process of data mining.

5.4   Step 3: Data Preprocessing

Most data preprocessing is in the form of **data cleaning,** which involves accounting for noise and dealing with missing information. Ideally, the majority of data preprocessing takes place before data is permanently stored in a structure such as a data warehouse.

Noisy Data

Noise represents random error in attribute values. In very large datasets, noise can come in many shapes and forms. Common concerns with noisy data include the following:

- How do we find duplicate records?

- How can we locate incorrect attribute values?

- What data smoothing operations should be applied to our data?

- How can we find and process outliers?

Locating Duplicate Records

Suppose a certain weekly publication has 100,000 subscribers and 0.1% of all mailing list entries have erroneous dual listings under a variation of the same name (e.g., Jon Doe and John Doe). Therefore 100 extra publications are processed and mailed each week. At a processing and mailing cost of $2.00 for each publication, the company spends over $10,000 each year in unwarranted costs. Ideally, errors such as these are uncovered as data are moved from an operational environment to a data warehouse facility. Automated graphical tools to assist with data cleaning and data movement do exist. However, the responsibility for data transition still lies in the hands of the data warehouse specialist.

Locating Incorrect Attribute Values 查找错误的属性值

Finding errors in categorical data presents a problem in large datasets. Some data mining tools offer a summary of frequency values and/or predictability scores for categorical attributes. We should consider attribute values having predictability scores near 0 as error candidates.

A numeric value of 0 for an attribute such as blood pressure or weight is an obvious error. Such errors often occur when data is missing and default values are assigned to fill in for missing items. In some cases such errors can be seen by examining class mean and standard deviation scores. However, if the dataset is large and only a few incorrect values exist, finding such errors can be difficult. Some data analysis tools allow the user to input a valid range of values for numerical data. Instances with attribute values falling outside the valid range limits are flagged as possible error candidates.

Data Smoothing

Data smoothing is both a data cleaning and data transformation process. Several data smoothing techniques attempt to reduce the number of values for a numeric attribute. Some classifiers, such as neural networks, use functions that perform data smoothing during the classification process. When data smoothing is performed during classification, the data smoothing is said to be internal. External data smoothing takes place prior to classification. Rounding and computing mean values are two simple external data smoothing techniques. Mean value smoothing is appropriate when we wish to use a classifier that does not support numerical data and would like to retain coarse information about numerical attribute values. In this case all numerical attribute values are replaced by a corresponding class mean.

Another common data smoothing technique attempts to find and possibly remove atypical instances from the dataset. As we mentioned in Chapter 2, it is always useful to identify outliers in data, but it may be counterproductive to remove outliers from the database. Recall that with iDA we can identify outliers by examining instance typicality. Outliers represent those instances with the lowest typicality scores.

Missing Data

Missing data items present a problem that can be dealt with in several ways. In most cases missing attribute values indicate lost information. For example, a missing value for the attribute *age* certainly indicates a data item that exists but is unaccounted for. However, a missing value for *salary* may be taken as an unentered data item, but it could also indicate an individual who is unemployed. Some data mining techniques are able to deal directly with missing values. However, many classifiers require all attributes to contain a value. The following are possible options for dealing with missing data *before* the data is presented to a data mining algorithm.

- **Discard records with missing values.** This method is most appropriate when a small percent of the total number of instances contain missing data and we can be certain that missing values do indeed represent lost information.

- **For real–valued data, replace missing values with the class mean.** In most cases this is a reasonable approach for numerical attributes. Options such as replacing missing numeric data with a zero or some arbitrarily large or small value is generally a poor choice.

- **Replace missing attribute values with the values found within other highly similar instances.** This technique is appropriate for either categorical or numeric attributes.

Some data mining techniques allow instances to contain missing values. Here are three ways that data mining techniques deal with missing data while learning:

1. **Ignore missing values.** Several data mining algorithms, including neural networks and Bayes classifier (Chapter 10), use this approach.

2. **Treat missing values as equal comparisons.** This approach is dangerous with very noisy data in that dissimilar instances may appear to be very much alike.

3. **Treat missing values as unequal comparisons.** This is a pessimistic approach but may be appropriate. Two similar instances containing several missing values will appear dissimilar. This is the approach used by ESX.

Finally, a slightly different approach is to use supervised learning to determine likely values for missing data. When the missing attribute is categorical, we designate the attribute with missing values as an output attribute. The instances with known values for the attribute are used to build a classification model. The created model is then summoned to classify the instances with missing values. For numerical data we can use an estimation mining tool, such as a neural network, and apply the same strategy.

5.5 Step 4: Data Transformation

Data transformation can take many forms and is necessary for a variety of reasons. We offer a description of some familiar data transformations in the following sections.

Data Normalization

A common data transformation involves changing numeric values so they fall within a specified range. Classifiers such as neural networks do better with numerical data scaled to a range between 0 and 1. Normalization is particularly appealing with distance-based classifiers, because by normalizing attribute values, attributes with a wide range of values are less likely to outweigh attributes with smaller initial ranges. Four common normalization methods include:

- **Decimal scaling.** Decimal scaling divides each numerical value by the same power of 10. For example, if we know the values for an attribute range between –1000 and 1000, we can change the range to −1 and 1 by dividing each value by 1000.

- **Min–Max normalization.** Min-Max is an appropriate technique when minimum and maximum values for an attribute are known. The formula is,

$$newValue = \frac{originalValue - oldMin(newMax - newMin) + newMin}{oldMax - oldMin}$$

where *oldMax* and *oldMin* represent the original maximum and minimum values for the attribute in question. *NewMax* and *newMin* specify the new maximum and minimum values. *NewValue* represents the transformation of *originalValue*. This transformation is particularly useful with neural networks where the desired range is [0,1]. In this case the formula simplifies to,

$$newValue = \frac{originalValue - oldMin}{oldMax - oldMin}$$

- **Normalization using Z-scores.** Z-score normalization converts a value to a standard score by subtracting the attribute mean (μ) from the value and dividing by the attribute standard deviation (σ). Specifically,

$$newValue = \frac{originalValue - \mu}{\sigma}$$

This technique is particularly useful when maximum and minimum values are not known.

- **Logarithmic normalization.** The base *b* logarithm of a number *n* is the exponent to which *b* must be raised to equal *n*. For example, the base 2 logarithm of 64 is 6 because $2^6 = 64$. Replacing a set of values with their logarithms has the effect of scaling the range of values without loss of information.

Data Type Conversion

Many data mining tools, including neural networks and some statistical methods, cannot process categorical data. Therefore converting categorical data to a numeric equivalent is a common data transformation. On the other hand, some data mining techniques are not able to process numeric data in its original form. For example, most decision tree algorithms discretize numeric values by sorting the data and considering alternative binary splits of the data items.

Attribute and Instance Selection

Classifiers vary in their ability to deal with large volumes of data. Some data mining algorithms have trouble with a large number of instances, whereas other algorithms cannot analyze data containing more than a few attributes. Also many data mining algorithms are unable to differentiate between relevant and irrelevant attributes. This is a problem, as it has been shown that the number of training instances needed to build accurate supervised learner models is directly affected by the number of irrelevant attributes in the data. To overcome these problems, we must make decisions about which attributes and instances to use when building our data mining models. The following is a possible algorithm to help us with attribute selection:

1. Given N attributes, generate the set S of all possible attribute combinations.
2. Remove the first attribute combination from set S and generate a data mining model M using these attributes.
3. Measure the goodness of model M.
4. Until S is empty
    a. Remove the next attribute combination from S and build a data mining model using the next attribute combination in S.
    b. Compare the goodness of the new model with the saved model M. Call the better model M and save this model as the best model.
5. Model M is the model of choice.

This algorithm will surely give us a best result. The problem with the algorithm lies in its complexity. If we have a total of n attributes, the total number of attribute combinations is $2^n - 1$. The task of generating and testing all possible models for any dataset containing more than a few attributes is not possible. Let's investigate a few techniques we can apply.

Eliminating Attributes

Data mining algorithms do not generally perform well with data containing a wealth of attributes that are not predictive of class membership. Some statistical as well as nonstatistical classifiers have attribute selection techniques included as part of the model building process. Classifiers with built-in attribute selection are less likely to suffer from the effects of datasets containing attributes of little predictive value. Unfortunately, many data mining algorithms, including neural networks and nearest neighbor classifiers, give equal weight to all attributes during the model building phase. With these classifiers, attribute selection needs to take place before the data mining process begins. Several steps can be taken to help determine which attributes to eliminate from consideration:

1. Input attributes highly correlated with other input attributes are redundant. Most data mining tools build better models when only one attribute from a set of highly correlated attributes is designated as an input value.

2. For categorical data, any attribute containing value v_i with a domain predictability score greater than a chosen threshold can be considered for elimination. This is the case because most domain instances will have v_i as their value for the attribute. As the domain predictability score of v_i increases, the ability of v_i to differentiate the individual classes decreases.

3. When learning is supervised, numerical attribute significance can be determined by comparing class mean and standard deviation scores. Recall that the numerical attribute significance measure employed by ESX computes attribute significance scores by comparing standardized differences between class means.

The first two techniques can be applied to supervised learning or unsupervised clustering. Unfortunately, with unsupervised clustering numerical attribute significance cannot be computed because predefined classes do not exist. However, we can experiment with subsets of likely attribute choices and use a suitable measure of cluster quality to help us determine a best set of numerical attributes.

An interesting approach to attribute selection makes use of genetic learning. The method is appealing, because by incorporating an evaluation function, we eliminate the combinatorial problems seen with the try-everything approach but are still able to achieve satisfactory results. The approach is especially useful when a wealth of irrelevant attributes exist in the data. The method is best illustrated by example.

Let's consider the credit card promotion database described in Chapter 2. Once again, we assume the output attribute is *life insurance promotion*. Table 5.1 shows an initial population of three elements. Each element tells us which attributes to use when building the associated learner model. A "1" indicates the attribute is an input attribute and a "0" specifies the attribute as unused. The technique is as follows:

1. Choose appropriate training and test data.

2. Use a random selection process to initialize a population of elements.

Table 5.1 • **An Initial Population for Genetic Attribute Selection**

Population Element	Income Range	Magazine Promotion	Watch Promotion	Credit Card Insurance	Sex	Age
1	1	0	0	1	1	1
2	0	0	0	1	0	1
3	0	0	0	0	1	1

3. Build a supervised learner model for each population element. Each model is constructed with the attributes specified by the corresponding element from the population. For example, the learner model for population element 1 uses input attributes: *income range, credit card insurance, sex,* and *age.*

4. Evaluate each element by applying the corresponding model to test data. A possible evaluation function is test set model accuracy.

5. If the termination condition has been met, choose one element from the population to build a final supervised model from the training data.

6. If the termination condition is not satisfied, apply genetic operators to modify one or more population elements and repeat steps 3–5.

Although this technique is guaranteed to converge, the convergence is not necessarily optimal. Because of this, several executions of the algorithm may be necessary to achieve a desired result.

Creating Attributes

Attributes of little predictive power can sometimes be combined with other attributes to form new attributes with a high degree of predictive capability. As an example, consider a database consisting of data about stocks. Conceivable attributes include current stock price, 12-month price range, company growth rate, quarterly earnings, market capitalization, company sector, and the like. The attributes price and earnings are of some predictive value in determining a future target price. However, the ratio of price to earnings (P/E ratio) is known to be more useful. A second created attribute likely to effectively predict a future stock price is the stock P/E ratio divided by the company growth rate. Here are a few transformations commonly applied to create new attributes:

• Create a new attribute where each value represents a ratio of the value of one attribute divided by the value of a second attribute.

- Create a new attribute whose values are differences between the values of two existing attributes.

- Create a new attribute with values computed as the percent increase or percent decrease of two current attributes. Given two values v_1 and v_2 with $v_1 < v_2$, the percent increase of v_2 with respect to v_1 is computed as

$$Percent\ Increase(v_2, v_1) = \frac{v_2 - v_1}{v_1}$$

If $v_1 > v_2$, we subtract v_2 from v_1 and divide by v_1, giving a percent decrease of v_2 with respect to v_1.

New attributes representing differences and percent increases or decreases are particularly useful with time-series analysis. **Time-series analysis** models changes in behavior over a time interval. For this reason, attributes created by computing differences between one time interval and the next time interval are important. In Chapter 11 you will see how to build models for solving time-series problems.

Instance Selection

Data used for the training phase of supervised learning are often randomly chosen from a pool of instances. The only criterion affecting the random process is that instances are selected so as to guarantee representation from each concept class to be learned. As you saw in Chapter 2, decision tree algorithms go a step further by initially choosing a random subset of the selected training instances to build a first classifier. The classifier is then tested on the remaining training instances. Those instances incorrectly classified by the decision tree are added to the subset of training data. The process is repeated until the training set is exhausted or a classifier that correctly classifies all training data is constructed.

An exception to this rule applies to **instance-based classifiers.** Instance-based classifiers do not create generalized classification models. Instead, they save a subset of representative instances from each class. A new instance is classified by comparing its attribute values with the values of saved instances. Unknown instance i is placed in the class whose representative instances are most similar to i. It is obvious that the instances chosen to represent each class determine the predictive accuracy of the model.

Instance typicality scores can be used to choose a best set of representative instances from each class. We have performed several experiments using instance typicality to help select training data for supervised learning. Our experiments show that a best test set classification accuracy can be achieved with all types of classifiers by forming training sets containing an overweighted selection of highly and moderately typical training instances (Roiger and Cornell, 1996).

Unsupervised clustering can also benefit from instance selection. A simple technique is to determine a typicality score for each domain instance. As predefined classes do not exist, each typicality score is computed relative to all domain instances. By eliminating the most atypical domain instances, an unsupervised learner is better able to form well-defined clusters. Once quality clusters have been formed, atypical instances can then be presented to the clustering system. The clustering model will either form new clusters with the instances or place the instances in existing clusters.

5.6   Step 5: Data Mining

The experimental and iterative nature of knowledge discovery is most apparent during steps 5 and 6 of the knowledge discovery process. Here is a typical scenario for building a supervised or unsupervised learner model:

1.   Choose training and test data from the pool of available instances.

2.   Designate a set of input attributes.

3.   If learning is supervised, choose one or more attributes for output.

4.   Select values for the learning parameters.

5.   Invoke the data mining tool to build a generalized model of the data.

Once data mining is complete, the model is evaluated (step 6). If an acceptable result is not seen, the just-described steps may be repeated several times. Because of this, the total number of possible learner models created from one set of data is infinite. Fortunately, the nature of the experimental process combined with the fact that data mining techniques are able to create acceptable models with less than perfect data increases our likelihood for success.

5.7   Step 6: Interpretation and Evaluation

The purpose of interpretation and evaluation is to determine whether a learner model is acceptable and can be applied to problems outside the realm of a test environment. If acceptable results are achieved, it is at this stage where acquired knowledge is translated into terms understandable by users.

Interpretation and evaluation can take many forms, some of which include:

- **Statistical analysis.** Such analysis is useful for determining if significant differences exist between the performance of various data mining models created using distinct sets of attributes and instances.

- **Heuristic analysis.** *Heuristics* are rules of thumb that generally give good enough solutions to problems. Most data mining tools offer numerically computed heuristics to help us decide the degree to which discovered knowledge is of value. Two examples include the class resemblance heuristic computed by ESX and the sum of squared error computation associated with the K–Means algorithm.

- **Experimental analysis.** Neural network techniques as well as the K–Means algorithm build slightly different models each time they are invoked with the same set of parameters and the same data. Other methods build distinct models with slight variations in data selection or parameter settings. Because of this, experimenting with various attribute or instance choices as well as alternative parameter settings can give markedly different results.

- **Human analysis.** The human component of result analysis reminds us that we are in control of the experimental process. In the final analysis, we must decide whether the knowledge gained from a data mining process can be successfully applied to new problems.

Chapter 2 showed you how to evaluate supervised learner models by incorporating a training/test set scenario. We also showed how lift can help determine the value of supervised models designed for marketing applications. In Chapter 7 we offer several formal evaluation methods, some of which are based on statistical analysis and others that provide a more intuitive approach.

5.8   Step 7: Taking Action

An ultimate goal of data mining is to apply what has been learned. It is at this point where we see our return on investment. A number of possible actions may result from successful application of the knowledge discovery process:

- Creation of a report or technical article about what has been discovered.

- Relocation of retail items for purchase or placement of selected items on sale together.

- The mailing of promotional information to a bias sampling of a customer population.

- Incorporation of a developed learner model as a front-end system designed to detect fraudulent credit card usage.

- Funding of a new scientific study motivated by what has been learned from a knowledge discovery process.

The possibilities are limited only by our ability to gather, preprocess, and effectively analyze data. In the next section we outline a data mining process model especially designed for the business community.

5.9   The CRISP-DM Process Model

A second process model that has proven application is the Cross Industry Standard Process for Data Mining (CRISP-DM). CRISP-DM is a product-neutral data mining model developed by a consortium of several companies. The CRISP-DM process model consists of six phases:

1. **Business understanding.** The center of attention is the project objectives and requirements from a business perspective. A data mining problem definition is given and an initial plan is developed.

The Credit Card Screening Dataset

The Credit Card Screening dataset contains information about 690 individuals who applied for a credit card. The dataset includes 15 input attributes and 1 output attribute indicating whether an individual credit card application was accepted (+) or rejected (–). All input attribute names and values have been changed to meaningless symbols to protect the confidentiality of the data. The original dataset was submitted by Ross Quinlan to the machine learning dataset repository referenced in Appendix B.

The dataset is interesting for several reasons. First, the instances represent real data about credit card applications. Second, the dataset offers a nice mix of categorical and numeric attributes. Third, 5% of the dataset records contain one or more pieces of missing information. Finally, as the attributes and values are without semantic meaning, we cannot introduce biases about which attributes we believe to be important. The dataset is found in the iDA samples directory under the name CreditScreening.xls. ■

2. **Data understanding.** The focus is on data collection and hypothesis formation.

3. **Data preparation.** Tables, records, and attributes are selected. The data is cleansed for the chosen modeling tools.

4. **Modeling.** This phase focuses on selecting and applying one or more data mining techniques.

5. **Evaluation.** An analysis of results determines if the developed model achieves the business objectives. A determination about the future use of the model is reached.

6. **Deployment.** If the model achieves the business objectives, a plan of action is developed to apply the model.

Taken together, steps 1 and 2 represent the KDD process of goal identification. Step 3 combines steps 2, 3, and 4 of the KDD process model. Finally, steps 4, 5, and 6 map respectively to steps 5, 6, and 7 of the KDD process model. If you want to learn more about the CRISP-DM process model, visit the Web site http://www.crisp-dm.org.

5.10   Experimenting with ESX

In this section we provide two experiments with ESX. The first experiment shows you how to use unsupervised clustering to determine if the input attributes defined for the Credit Card Screening Dataset are able to differentiate between the values of the output attribute. The second experiment highlights the role that parameters can play in the knowledge discovery process. As our datasets have been preprocessed and we do not have an opportunity to apply a developed model, we use a simplified four-step version of the KDD process model for our experiments. Our revised model has the following steps:

A Four-Step Process Model for Knowledge Discovery

1. Identify the goal.

2. Prepare the data.

3. Apply data mining.

4. Interpret and evaluate the results.

We encourage you to use your iDA software to work through the experiments with us.

Experiment 1: Attribute Evaluation

Our first experiment uses a dataset holding information about individuals who were either accepted or rejected when they applied for a credit card (see *The Credit Card Screening Dataset* description box). The dataset contains 690 instances, 307 of which represent individuals who were approved to receive a credit card. The remaining 383 individuals had their credit card application rejected. We want to know how well the input attributes define the classes contained in the data. Stated another way, we wish to test the possibility of building an accurate supervised learner model with the data. The attributes and values have been mapped to a set of meaningless symbols to protect the confidentiality of the data. However, because the mapping is consistent, we should be able to apply data mining to analyze the dataset.

The Satellite Image Dataset

The Satellite Image Dataset contains instances representing a digitized satellite image of a portion of the earth's surface. The dataset consists of 300 pixels for which ground truth has been established. Each data instance has been classified into exactly 1 of 15 categories: Urban, Agriculture 1, Agriculture 2, Turf/Grass, Southern Deciduous, Northern Deciduous, Coniferous, Shallow Water, Deep Water, Marsh, Shrub Swamp, Wooded Swamp, Dark Barren, Barren 1, and Barren 2. Each category contains approximately 20 instances.

Our ability to analyze satellite image data is of primary importance because it allows us to monitor changes in regions of the earth's surface as they occur. The capacity to see changes in specific regions has implications for both the scientific and business communities. By monitoring changes to the earth's surface, the scientist is able to better understand environmental control issues. The business analyst can use obtained knowledge about regional changes to help make decisions about whether to support additional commercial development in the specified area.

Many datasets available for data mining experiments contain instances having two or three classes. Unlike these datasets, the satellite image data is of special interest because it allows us to build and test data mining models for a large number of well-defined classes. Also, as each class contains a limited number of instances, we are able to easily see the differences that slight adjustments in learner model parameter settings can make in model performance. Finally, the dataset is entirely numeric and can therefore be used to build and test neural network models. Two versions of the dataset are contained in the iDA samples directory. The file titled sonar.xls is for supervised learning, and the file sonaru.xls can be employed to build unsupervised learner models. ∎

One way to accomplish our goal is to use a training/test set scenario and measure classifier test set accuracy. A second and sometimes more useful technique is to employ unsupervised clustering to see how well the set of input attributes are able to define the classes known to be in the data. If the input attributes define the output classes, we will see the instances naturally cluster so as to separate the known classes. This technique is particularly useful if we initially build a supervised model with the data and encounter a less than optimal test set accuracy. If the unsupervised clustering also fails to naturally cluster the known classes, we conclude that the attribute choices are poor. For our experiment, we choose the unsupervised approach.

Applying the Four-Step Process Model to the Credit Card Screening Dataset

STEP 1: IDENTIFY THE GOAL

The Credit Card Screening Dataset contains 690 data instances, each of which has 15 input attributes and 1 output attribute. The output attribute indicates whether an individual credit card application was accepted (+) or rejected (−). All input attribute names and values have been changed to meaningless symbols to protect confidentiality of the data. Our goal is to determine if the defined input attributes are appropriate choices for building a supervised learner model. We pursue our goal by applying unsupervised clustering to see if the two classes (*accept/reject*) naturally form two clusters.

STEP 2: PREPARE THE DATA

The dataset is housed within the samples directory as CreditScreening.xls. The input attribute types and designations should be correct. However, as our experiment calls for unsupervised clustering, we must change the usage of the *class* attribute to display-only. In this way, we will be able to tell how many instances from each class are contained in the formed clusters. Here's what to do:

- Open Excel and load the CreditScreening.xls file.
- Save the file under a new name. In this way, the original file remains intact.
- Change the usage on the *class* attribute from *O* to *D*.

STEP 3: APPLY DATA MINING

- Initiate an unsupervised clustering with ESX.
- Set the similarity parameter at 45 to form 2 classes.

- Use the default value for the real-valued tolerance setting.

- Begin the mining session.

- Generate rules using the default settings.

STEP 4: INTERPRET AND EVALUATE THE RESULTS

Let's explore the results by following the strategy for analyzing a data mining session outlined in the Chapter 4 summary. Here we list the steps of the strategy described in Chapter 4 and provide our analysis.

1. Examine class resemblance scores and individual class rules to see how well the input attributes define the formed classes.

   - Two clusters of approximately equal size were formed. One cluster contains 321 instances. The second cluster has 369 instances.

   - The resemblance scores for each of the two clusters exceeds the domain resemblance value. This gives initial positive evidence of a well-defined clustering.

   - A wealth of rules can be seen for both clusters. This provides further evidence supporting well-defined clusters.

2. Examine domain summary statistics to help locate attribute errors and to determine predictive numeric attributes.

   - Missing categorical attribute values are shown as a small square (■).

   - Numeric attributes *eight* and *eleven* show the highest significance scores. Attributes *fourteen* and *fifteen* offer the least predictive power.

   - The table of most commonly occurring categorical attributes shows that attributes *nine, ten,* and *twelve* have different values.

3. Examine class summary statistics to locate predictive categorical attribute values.

   - Categorical attributes *nine* and *ten* have relatively high attribute-value predictability and predictiveness scores.

   - Of primary interest is the fact that 84% of the instances in cluster 1 are from the credit card application *accept* class. Also, 90% of the credit card *reject* class instances are housed in cluster 2. These facts, taken together, offer strong supportive evidence that the input attributes define the two classes found within the data.

4. Modify attribute or instance selections and parameter settings as appropriate and repeat the data mining process to create a best data model.

● As our results give positive support that a subset of the input attributes determine the value of the output attribute, a logical next step is to use a training/test set scenario to build and test a supervised learner model.

● Consideration should be given to limiting the attributes used to build the supervised model to those deemed most predictive of class membership.

To provide additional support for the ability of the input attributes to build an accurate supervised model, we applied a training/test set scenario to the data. We used 350 instances for training and 340 test set instances to build the supervised learner model. Approximately 45% of the total dataset instances represent approved applications. This same percent holds for the first 350 instances. Therefore we simply designated the first 350 data instances as the training data. The resultant model showed a 78% test set classification accuracy. The confusion matrix for this experiment is shown in Table 5.2.

Next we applied three additional experiments to the data. For the first experiment, we used the same training and test data but flagged all but the most predictive categorical and numeric data as unused. Specifically, we limited the attribute selection to attributes *eight, nine, ten,* and *eleven.* The experiment showed a 77% test set accuracy. Although model performance did not improve, it is clear that we achieved the same test set accuracy by using a subset of four input attributes. For the second experiment, we flagged the four most predictive attributes as unused and used the remaining input attributes to build the supervised model. The resultant test set accuracy was 58%. This result is expected because the best predictors of class membership have been removed.

For the final experiment we used all input attributes but limited the training data to the 20 most typical training set instances from each class. The results of the experiment showed a 76.5% classification correctness. The confusion matrix for the experiment is displayed in Table 5.3. It is interesting to note that the model accepts only 25 individuals that should have been rejected. It is also interesting that a supervised model built with 40 of the most typical data instances is able to perform as well as the model created using 350 training instances. This is, at least in part, a direct result of the fact that the instances from the two classes naturally form separate clusters. The Deer Hunter Dataset introduced in the previous chapter does not have this characteristic. Building an acceptable supervised learner model for the Deer Hunter Dataset is much more of a challenge (see Data Mining Exercise 1).

Table 5.2   ●   **A Confusion Matrix for Credit Card Screening**

	Computed Accept	Computed Reject
Accept	115	38
Reject	35	152

Table 5.3 • **Test Set Results for a Most Typical Training Model**

	Computed Accept	Computed Reject
Accept	98	55
Reject	25	162

Experiment 2: Parameter Evaluation

Our second example uses a dataset containing pixels representing a digitized satellite image of a portion of the earth's surface. The training and test data consist of 300 pixels for which ground truth has been established. These data have been classified into 15 categories: Urban, Agriculture 1, Agriculture 2, Turf/Grass, Southern Deciduous, Northern Deciduous, Coniferous, Shallow Water, Deep Water, Marsh, Shrub Swamp, Wooded Swamp, Dark Barren, Barren 1, and Barren 2. Each category contains approximately 20 instances. Each pixel is represented by six numeric values consisting of the multispectral reflectance values in six bands of the electromagnetic spectrum: blue (0.45–0.52 m), green (0.52–0.60 m), red (0.63–.069 m), near infrared (0.76–0.90 m), and two middle infrared (1.55–1.75 m and 2.08–2.35 m). For additional information on the dataset, see *The Satellite Image Dataset* description box.

Many learning schemes are controlled by one or more user-set parameters. Recall that ESX uses the real-valued tolerance parameter to help compute similarity scores for numeric data. Experimental results have shown that the default setting of 1.0 is usually a best value for this parameter. However, in cases where numeric attributes have little within-class variation relative to overall domain variation, lower (more stringent) settings are necessary for a best result. One of the purposes of our second experiment is to see the marked effect this parameter can have on test set classification correctness with ESX.

Applying the Four-Step Process Model to the Satellite Image Dataset

STEP 1: IDENTIFY THE GOAL

Our goal is to develop an accurate supervised learner model for classifying pixel images taken from a satellite image of a region of the earth's surface. Once accepted, the model will be used to locate regional ground changes for the specified area. A marked urban advance within the area will initiate investigation into the possibility of additional business development projects for the region.

STEP 2: PREPARE THE DATA

Before performing the experiment, we need to load and prepare the data:

- To begin, open Excel and load the sonar.xls spreadsheet file.

- The output data is currently formatted for the iDA backpropagation neural network. As our experiment uses ESX, we must modify the third row of the spreadsheet file.

- Copy the workbook to a new Excel spreadsheet.

- We will perform a supervised classification on the *class* attribute. Change the *class* attribute usage from *U* to *O* and change the usage for attributes *output1*, *output2*, *output3*, and *output4* to *U*. Figure 5.4 shows the correct format for the spreadsheet data. We are now ready to begin mining the data.

STEP 3: APPLY DATA MINING

- Perform a supervised classification with ESX. Use 150 data instances for training.

- Let the real-valued tolerance setting default to 1.0.

Figure 5.4 • **Satellite image data**

	A	B	C	D	E	F	G	H	I	J	K
1	blue	green	red	nred	ir1	ir2	class	output1	output2	output3	output4
2	R	R	R	R	R	R	C	R	R	R	R
3	I	I	I	I	I	I	O	U	U	U	U
4	104	43	49	65	80	43	urban	1	1	1	1
5	115	50	62	68	83	43	urban	1	1	1	1
6	106	46	56	47	76	42	urban	1	1	1	1
7	106	44	55	63	79	41	urban	1	1	1	1
8	104	45	55	66	76	41	urban	1	1	1	1
9	105	46	59	65	79	44	urban	1	1	1	1
10	103	44	54	68	81	45	urban	1	1	1	1
11	118	48	59	62	80	46	urban	1	1	1	1
12	112	49	62	54	79	47	urban	1	1	1	1
13	115	46	58	72	87	47	urban	1	1	1	1
14	82	34	30	35	78	23	agriculture	1	1	1	0
15	81	34	29	37	76	22	agriculture	1	1	1	0
16	82	34	28	34	75	22	agriculture	1	1	1	0
17	82	34	29	35	77	21	agriculture	1	1	1	0
18	81	33	29	37	73	21	agriculture	1	1	1	0
19	78	34	28	31	74	22	agriculture	1	1	1	0
20	81	25	28	35	76	22	agriculture	1	1	1	0
21	79	34	29	33	75	20	agriculture	1	1	1	0
22	81	34	29	29	77	21	agriculture	1	1	1	0
23	82	35	29	36	75	24	agriculture	1	1	1	0
24	84	34	32	19	76	24	agriculture	1	1	0	0

STEP 4: INTERPRET AND EVALUATE THE RESULTS

Because a test set has been applied, a logical first step is to examine the confusion matrix. Open the RES MTX sheet to check the confusion matrix for this experiment. Notice that the test set classification correctness is 65%.

A first reaction could easily be that the dataset is not amenable for data mining. After all, 150 training instances for a 15-class dataset allows an average of only 10 training instances per class! However, many factors may be responsible for the poor result. Therefore we conduct a thorough investigation before drawing any final conclusions. We follow the strategy for analyzing a data mining session outlined in the Chapter 4 summary. As with the first experiment, we list the steps of the strategy and provide our analysis.

1. Examine class resemblance scores and individual class rules to see how well the input attributes define the formed classes.

   - The fact that a majority of the class resemblance scores are at or near 1.0 is suspect.

   - A wealth of rules exists for most classes, indicating a training set of well-defined classes.

2. Examine domain summary statistics to help locate attribute errors and to determine predictive numeric attributes.

   - All numeric attributes show attribute significance scores over 1.90 with some significance values above 3.5.

   - This indicates a very well-defined set of class attributes.

3. Examine class summary statistics to locate predictive categorical attribute values.

   - The data does not contain categorical attributes.

4. Modify attribute or instance selections and parameter settings as appropriate and repeat the data mining process to create a best data model.

   - Our conclusion tells us the training data contains well-defined classes as measured by large attribute significance scores and a wealth of class rules. We also see unusually high class resemblance scores.

   - A viable course of action is to make an attempt at lowering class resemblance scores by modifying the real-valued tolerance parameter.

Initially, the action suggested in step 4 seems counterintuitive. However, the fact that the resemblance scores are so high, together with the poor test set result, indicates that the model is unable to differentiate between instances from alternative classes. Therefore we must make the similarity criteria more stringent by lowering the value of the tolerance parameter. Let's follow the suggested action and repeat the experiment, but this time set the real-valued tolerance at 0.30.

When data mining is complete, check the confusion matrix resulting from the classification. Your confusion matrix should show a classification correctness of 98%. Next we check the class resemblance scores. Surprisingly, the scores are still above 0.90. However, the fact that we have improved performance indicates the tolerance setting isn't causing overly optimistic similarity computations. As a final note, if the input data is strictly categorical and a similar initial result is seen, a separate course of action is required. This is true because categorical data do not have tolerance settings. Additional options for improving results for both categorical and numeric data include adding or deleting attributes, choosing a new set of training instances, increasing or decreasing the number of training instances, and transforming current attributes to create new features.

Both experiments in this section applied the four-step process model to datasets having a well-defined output attribute. This same process model can be applied to datasets where an output attribute is not defined. A particularly interesting dataset that does not have an output attribute specified is the Gamma-Ray Burst Dataset. You can read about this dataset in the description box titled *Gamma-Ray Burst Dataset*. Data mining exercise 4 asks you to perform several experiments with this dataset.

5.11   Chapter Summary

Knowledge discovery can be modeled as a seven-step process that includes goal identification, target data creation, data preprocessing, data transformation, data mining, result interpretation and evaluation, and knowledge application. A clear statement about what is to be accomplished is a good starting point for successful knowledge discovery. Creating a target dataset often involves extracting data from a warehouse or a transactional database. Transactional databases do not store redundant data, as they are modeled to quickly update and retrieve information. Because of this, the structure of the data in a transactional database must be modified before data mining can be applied.

Prior to exercising a data mining tool, the gathered data is preprocessed to remove noise. Missing data is of particular concern because many data mining algorithms are unable to process missing items. In addition to data preprocessing, data transformation techniques can be applied before data mining takes place. Data transformation methods such as data normalization and attribute creation or elimination are often necessary for a best result. An attribute selection technique of particular interest makes use of genetic learning to help us decide on a best choice of attributes.

Once a data mining process has been completed, the results are evaluated. If the results are acceptable, the created model can be applied. If the results are less than optimal, one or more steps of the knowledge discovery process are repeated. Fortunately,

The Gamma-Ray Burst Dataset

Gamma-ray bursts are brief gamma-ray flashes with origins outside of our solar system. More than 1000 such events have been recorded. The gamma-ray burst data in this dataset are from the BATSE 4B catalog. The bursts in the BATSE 4B catalog were observed by the Burst And Transient Source Experiment (BATSE) aboard NASA's Compton Gamma-Ray Observatory between April 1991 and March 1993. Although many attributes have been measured for these bursts, the dataset is limited to seven attributes. Attribute *burst* gives the assigned burst number. All other attributes have been preprocessed by applying a logarithmic normalization. Normalized attributes *T90* and *T50* measure burst duration (burst length), *P256* and *fluence* measure burst brightness, and *HR321* and *HR32* measure burst hardness.

This dataset is interesting for several reasons. First, the dataset allows astronomers to develop and test various hypotheses about the nature of gamma-ray bursts. In doing so, astronomers have an opportunity to learn more about the structure of the universe. Second, the raw gamma-ray burst data had to be preprocessed and transformed several times before a set of significant attributes were developed. The dataset clearly demonstrates the importance of data preprocessing and data transformation. Finally, because the data is strictly real-valued, we can study this data using a neural network approach. The dataset is found in the iDA samples directory under the name Grb4u.xls. If you would like more information about the BATSE project, visit the Web site at http://www.batse.msfc.nasa.gov/batse/grb/catalog/.■

an iterative approach involving model creation and model testing will often lead to an acceptable result.

A second knowledge discovery process model that has a proven track record is the CRISP-DM process model. CRISP-DM is a product–neutral model developed specifically for the business community.

5.12 Key Terms

Data cleaning. A data preprocessing technique that accounts for noisy and missing data.

Data normalization. A data transformation where numeric values are modified to fall within a specified range.

Data preprocessing. The step of the KDD process that deals with noisy and missing data.

Data transformation. The step of the KDD process that deals with data normalization and conversion as well as the addition and/or elimination of attributes.

Decimal scaling. A data transformation technique for a numeric attribute where each value is divided by the same power of 10.

Instance-based classifier. Any classifier that models data by saving a subset of instances from each class.

Logarithmic normalization. A data transformation method for a numeric attribute where each numeric value is replaced by its base b logarithm.

Min-Max normalization. A data transformation method that is used to transform a set of numeric attribute values so they fall within a specified numeric range.

Noise. Random error in data.

Relational database. A database where data is represented as a collection of tables containing rows and columns. Each column of the table is known as an attribute, and each row of the table stores information about one data record.

Scientific method. A four-step approach to problem solving that includes defining a problem, forming a hypothesis, performing an experiment, and drawing conclusions.

Time-series analysis. Any technique that models changes in behavior over a period of time.

Tuple. An individual row of a table in a relational database.

Z-score normalization. A data normalization technique for a numeric attribute where each numeric value is replaced by its standardized difference from the mean.

5.13   Exercises

Review Questions

1.   Differentiate between the following terms:

   a.   Data cleaning and data transformation

   b.   Internal and external data smoothing

   c.   Decimal scaling and Z-score normalization

2.   In Section 5.4 you learned about three basic ways that data mining techniques deal with missing data while learning. Decide which technique is best for the following problems. Explain each choice.

   a.   A model designed to accept or reject credit card applications.

   b. A model for determining who should receive a promotional flyer in the mail.

   c. A model designed to determine those individuals likely to develop colon cancer.

   d. A model to decide whether to drill for oil in a certain region.

   e. A model for approving or rejecting candidates applying to refinance their home.

Data Mining Questions

1. Use the Deer Hunter Dataset to perform the following tasks.

   a. Repeat the experiment described in Section 5.10, which uses unsupervised clustering, to determine if the defined set of input attributes are appropriate for building a supervised learner model. Follow the four-step model and write a short description of what was found at each step of the process. Be sure to designate the *yes* attribute as display-only. Because the dataset is relatively large, you should initially use the quick mine feature to achieve a setting for the similarity score that will result in two formed classes.

   b. Attempt to build a supervised learner model using the first 4000 data instances for training. What is your test set result?

   c. Choose the most predictive categorical and numeric attributes together with the first 4000 instances to build a second supervised model. What is your test set result? Is the result an improvement over the result in part b?

   d. Build a final model using the 50 most typical instances from each class as training data. Compare your test set results with the results obtained in parts b and c.

LAB 2. Perform an unsupervised clustering using the sonaru.xls data file. Experiment with the instance similarity and real-tolerance parameters in an attempt to form 15 well-defined clusters similar to the actual classes contained in the data. Be sure to designate the class attribute as display-only.

   a. Does the clustering show a class structure similar to the actual classes found within the data?

   b. Which classes show instances that naturally cluster together?

   c. Which classes tend to intermix their instances with the instances of other classes?

LAB Denotes exercise appropriate for a laboratory setting.

LAB 3.   The CardiologyNumerical.xls data file contains the same instances as the CardiologyCategorical.xls file but the categorical attributes have been changed to numeric equivalents.

   a.   Load the CardiologyNumerical.xls file into Excel. Please refer to Table 2.1 to see how the categorical attributes are mapped to corresponding numerical equivalents. For example, the table shows that values male and female for attribute sex are replaced with a 1 and a 0. Likewise the values angina, abnormal angina, noTang, and asymptomatic for attribute chest pain type are respectively replaced with 1,2,3, and 4. Note that the class attribute represents an instance of the healthy class with a 1 and an instance of the sick class with a 0.

   b.   Perform the first experiment in Section 5.10 using this dataset. Follow the four-step model and write a short description of what was found at each step of the process. Be sure to designate the *class* attribute as display-only. You may have to manipulate the real-tolerance setting to get a best result. Do the *healthy* and *sick* instances cluster together?

LAB 4.   The iDA samples directory includes a file named grb4u.xls. Read about this dataset in the description box titled *The Gamma-Ray Burst Dataset* located at the end of this chapter.

   a.   Use ESX to perform four unsupervised clusterings of this data. Vary the similarity parameter setting so as to create two, three, four, and five clusters. Be sure to save each clustering in a new spreadsheet.

   b.   For each of the four clusterings, examine the domain and class statistics as well as the rules generated for individual clusters. Choose one or two of the clusterings and provide a brief written description of the nature of the bursts falling into each cluster. Indicate any marked differences you find in average burst length, burst brightness, and burst hardness.

   c.   Use some combination of class resemblance scores, generated rules, and attribute significance values to make a decision about which clustering is a best representation of the data. Justify your answer.

   d.   List one rule from each of the clusters for the clustering you believe to be a best choice.

   5.   Visit the FTP site: ftp://ftp.ics.uci.edu/pub/machine-learning-databases/ (or any of the Web sites listed in Appendix B) and select a dataset that interests you. Download and format the data in an Excel spreadsheet. Use ESX and the four-step process model defined in Section 5.10 to perform one or more data mining experiments with the data.

Computational Questions

1. Set up a general formula for a Min-Max normalization as it would be applied to the attribute *age* for the data in Table 2.3. Transform the data so the new minimum value is 0 and the new maximum value is 1. Apply the formula to determine a transformed value for *age* = 35.

2. The price of a certain stock increases from $25.00 to $40.00. Compute the percent increase in the stock price.

3. You are to apply a base 2 logarithmic normalization to a certain numeric attribute whose current range of values falls between 2,300 and 10,000. What will be the new range of values for the attribute once the normalization has been completed? $\log_2^{2300} - \log_2^{10000} = 11.674 - 13.288$

4. Apply a base 10 logarithmic normalization to the values for attribute *age* in Table 2.3. Use a table to list the original values as well as the transformed values.

5. Use the CreditCardPromotion.xls data file together with the initial element population shown in Table 5.1 to perform the first iteration of the genetic algorithm for attribute selection. Specify life insurance promotion as the output attribute. Use 10 instances for training and the remaining instances as a test set. Use classification correctness on the test data as your fitness function. List the fitness scores for each of the three elements of the initial population.

6. Based on the experiments with ESX in this chapter, can you hypothesize an inverse relationship between a setting for the real-tolerance parameter and numerical attribute significance?

Chapter **6**

The Data Warehouse

Chapter Objectives

▶ Understand why transactional databases do not support the redundancy required for decision support.

▶ Know that a data warehouse is implemented using a multidimensional or relational architecture.

▶ Understand how a star schema is used for data warehouse modeling.

▶ Know how on-line analytical processing can be applied to analyze the multidimensional data stored in a warehouse.

▶ Understand how Microsoft Excel pivot tables can be used to model multidimensional data.

Data mining can, has, and will continue to take place in environments not supporting a data warehouse. However, as volumes of data continue to be collected for purposes of decision support, the need for organized, efficient data storage and retrieval architectures has become quite apparent. The result of this need has sparked the birth of the data warehouse.

In this chapter we provide an overview of the major concepts and issues that surround data warehouse design. Although several warehousing architectures exist, we focus on the most common design forms. We also introduce on-line analytical processing—a powerful decision support tool offering a multidimensional approach for data analysis. In Section 6.1 you will learn about the inherent problems in analyzing data stored in a transactional database. In Section 6.2 we define data warehousing and detail a popular model for data warehouse design. Section 6.3 shows how on-line analytical processing can be used to test human-generated hypotheses about data stored in a warehouse. We conclude this chapter with an introduction to MS Excel pivot tables.

Several books have been written about designing and implementing a data warehouse. Two excellent sources for additional information about data warehousing are *Object-Oriented Data Warehouse Design* (Giovinazzo, 2000) and *The Data Warehouse Lifecycle Toolkit: Expert Methods for Designing, Developing, and Deploying Data Warehouses* (Kimball et al., 1998).

6.1   Operational Databases

We have seen that one possibility for gathering data for analysis is to extract data directly from one or more operational databases. Operational, or transactional, databases are designed to process individual transactions quickly and efficiently. This type of transaction-based interaction is known as **on-line transactional processing,** or simply **OLTP**.

In contrast, decision support systems are subject oriented. They incorporate facilities for reporting, analyzing, and mining data about a particular topic such as credit card promotions, automotive engine repairs, or heart disease. Because of the difference in intent between an operational and a decision support setting, models built for one methodology are not appropriate for the other. To demonstrate, let's take a quick look at the structures used for modeling an operational database environment.

Data Modeling and Normalization

The first step toward building a transactional database is data modeling. A **data model** documents the structure of the data to be placed into a system independent of how the data will be used. A common notation for data modeling is the **entity relationship diagram (ERD).** An ERD shows the structure of the data in terms of entities and relationships between entities. An **entity** is like a concept in that it represents a class of persons, places, or things. An entity may contain one or several attributes. A key represented by a combination of one or more attributes uniquely identifies each instance of an entity.

Relationships between entities are either **one-to-one**, **one-to-many,** or **many-to-many.** In a monogamous society, the *husband–wife* relationship is one-to-one. The *father–child* relationship is one-to-many because a father may have one or several children, but a child has one and only one biological father. Finally, *student–teacher* is a many-to-many relationship because a teacher can have several students and a student is likely to have more than one teacher.

Figure 6.1 depicts a hypothetical ERD for two entities *vehicle-type* and *customer*. The key for each entity is marked with a dot. That is, *type ID* uniquely identifies a vehicle of a specific make and year and *customer ID* is a unique identifier for the customer entity. The crows feet on *customer* indicate that the relationship between the two entities is one-to-many. That is, each customer owns exactly one vehicle, but several customers can own a vehicle having the same make and year.

If crows feet also appear on the link to *vehicle-type,* the relationship is many-to-many, thus allowing one customer to own more than one vehicle. Many-to-many relationships are typically mapped as two one-to-many relationships by creating an **intersection entity** whose existence depends solely on the many-to-many relationship. Figure 5.3 in Chapter 5 depicts an ERD using the notation adopted by Microsoft Access. Attributes representing keys are highlighted and crows feet are replaced by the symbol for infinity (∞). Figure 5.3 shows that *promotion-customer* is an

---

Figure 6.1 • **A simple entity-relationship diagram**

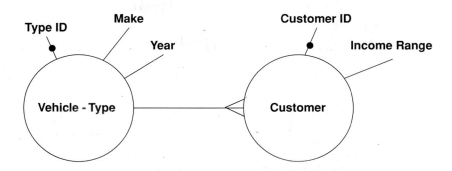

intersection entity formed by a many-to-many relationship between *promotion* and *customer.* The relationship is many-to-many because several customers can take advantage of a single promotion and an individual customer may choose to purchase several promotional offerings.

Once an ERD has been completed, the model is analyzed for possible improvements. A main part of the analysis involves **normalization.** Normalization is a multistep process designed to remove any redundancies that may be present in the current model. Several normal forms have been defined. **First normal form (1NF)** requires all attributes to have a single value. An entity is in **second normal form (2NF)** if it is in first normal form and all nonkey attributes are dependent on the full primary key. The check for 2NF is relevant only when the key field is made up of more than one attribute. An entity is in **third normal form (3NF)** if it is in 2NF and the following condition is met:

> *Every nonprimary key attribute is dependent on the primary key, the whole primary key, and nothing but the primary key.*

That is, 3NF requires that the values for all nonkey attributes are dependent solely on the complete primary key. Although higher normal forms have been defined, most data models are considered acceptable if all entities are in 3NF.

The Relational Model

ERDs map naturally to the relational model. Table 6.1a shows the relational table for *vehicle-type,* and Table 6.1b displays the relational table for *customer.* Notice the one-to-many relationship between *vehicle-type* and *customer* is supported by placing the key field for *vehicle-type* as an attribute in *customer.* When an intersection entity is mapped to a relational table, it contains the key field from the two entities making up the original many-to-many relationship. This is seen in Figure 5.3 where the intersection entity *promotion-customer* holds both *customer-ID* and *promotion-ID.*

Relational databases are well suited for transactional processing because they can efficiently collect and manage data without loss of information. However, data mining and other forms of decision support are interested in analyzing rather than processing data. As the purpose of data analysis is to examine and uncover redundancies in data, the uniqueness constraints placed on the relational model by the normalization process are not desirable for a decision support environment. An example will make this point clear.

Let's consider the relations shown in Tables 6.1a and 6.1b. The relational *join* operator is used to combine two relational tables by matching the values of an attribute common to both tables. We can join Tables 6.1a and 6.1b on the common attribute

Table 6.1a • **Relational Table for *Vehicle-Type***

Type ID	Make	Year
4371	Chevrolet	1995
6940	Cadillac	2000
4595	Chevrolet	2001
2390	Cadillac	1997

Table 6.1b • **Relational Table for *Customer***

Customer ID	Income Range ($)	Type ID
0001	70–90K	2390
0002	30–50K	4371
0003	70–90K	6940
0004	30–50K	4595
0005	70–90K	2390

type ID. Table 6.2 displays the table resulting from the join operation. We can make at least two observations. First, Table 6.2 is denormalized, because any combination of one or more attributes chosen as the key field will violate the functional dependency requirement. For example, creating a combined key field with attributes *customer ID* and *type ID* violates 2NF because *make, income range,* and *year* are each dependent on part of, but not the entire, key field.

A second observation is the relationship between an individual's salary and the type of car he or she owns. Although this relationship is not of interest in a transactional environment, it is of primary importance to decision support. Relationships showing this type of redundancy can only be observed by denormalizing the data. The long and short of this is that in a transactional environment a significant amount of denormalization in the form of combining entities is necessary to prepare data for decision support. This in turn leads to new questions about which entities to combine, as well as how and where to store and maintain the combined entities. A better choice is to have one mechanism for storing, maintaining, and processing transactional data and a second to house data for decision support.

Table 6.2   •   **Join of Tables 6.1a and 6.1b**

Customer ID	Income Range ($)	Type ID	Make	Year
0001	70–90K	2390	Cadillac	1997
0002	30–50K	4371	Chevrolet	1995
0003	70–90K	6940	Cadillac	2000
0004	30–50K	4595	Chevrolet	2001
0005	70–90K	2390	Cadillac	1997

6.2   Data Warehouse Design

When transactional data is no longer of value to the operational environment, it is removed from the database. If a business is without a decision support facility, the data is archived and eventually destroyed. However, if there is a decision support environment, the data is transported to some type of interactive medium commonly referred to as a data warehouse.

In Chapter 1 we defined the data warehouse as a historical database designed for decision support. A more precise definition is given by W. H. Inmon (1996). Specifically,

> *"A data warehouse is a subject-oriented, integrated, time-variant, and nonvolatile collection of data in support of management's decision making process."*

As the definition implies, significant variations in structure and intent exist between an OLTP database and a data warehouse. A few of the major differences are:

- The data in a warehouse is subject oriented and based on one or more central themes. OLTP databases are process oriented and organized so as to maximize data update and retrieval.

- Warehouse data is denormalized and integrated, the data in an OLTP database is normalized and separated.

- An OLTP system supports data processing, collection, and management. A data warehouse stores data to be reported on, analyzed, and tested.

- OLTP deals with data necessary for the efficient day-to-day operation of a business or organization. Data records in a transactional database are subject to multiple access and constant update. In contrast, the data in a warehouse exists in part because the data is no longer of use to the OLTP environment. The majority of data in a warehouse is historical, time-stamped, and not subject to change (read-only).

- **Granularity** is a term used to describe the level of detail of stored information. Operational data represents the lowest level of granularity as each data item contains information about an individual transaction. The level of granularity for data stored in a warehouse is a design issue dependent on the desires of the user as well as on the amount of data being collected.

A data warehouse can also be viewed as a process for gathering, storing, managing, and analyzing data (Gardner, 1998). Figure 6.2 displays the key components of the warehousing process. Let's take a closer look at how data moves from the external environment into the data warehouse.

Entering Data into the Warehouse

Figure 6.2 shows data entering the data warehouse from three main sources. External data represents items such as economic indicators, weather information, and the like that are not specific to the internal organization. An **independent data mart** is a data store that is similar to a warehouse but limits its focus to a single subject. An independent data

---

Figure 6.2 • **A data warehouse process model**

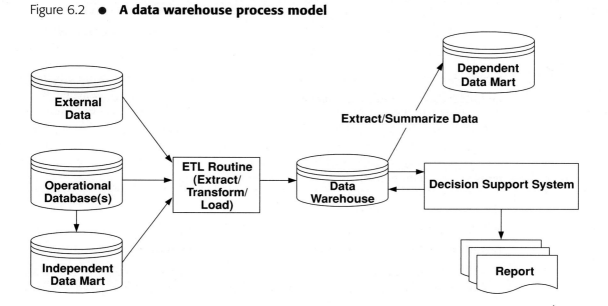

mart is structured using operational data as well as external data sources. The data stored in a data mart can be loaded into the central data warehouse for use by other facets of the organization. Regardless of the external data source, the process of moving data into the warehouse will likely involve some low-level procedural programming.

Figure 6.2 illustrates that prior to entering the warehouse, data is processed by an **ETL** (extract, transform, and load) routine. The primary responsibilities of the ELT process include: extracting data from one or more of the input sources shown in Figure 6.2, cleaning and transforming the extracted data as necessary, and loading the data into the warehouse. Data transformations are often used to resolve granularity issues, correct data inconsistencies between multiple operational databases, and to time-stamp individual data records. Once transformed and cleaned, the data enters the warehouse where it is stored in a relational or multidimensional format.

As a rule, once data enters the warehouse it is not subject to change. An obvious exception to this rule is when errors are detected in the data. But what about special situations such as when an individual changes their address or their marital status? Let's consider a data warehouse storing customer transactions for credit card purchases. Suppose a customer changes their marital status from single to married. A first thought is to simply change the marital status of all warehouse records referencing the customer. The problem with this solution is that any analysis that makes use of marital status information is processing corrupted data, as purchases made by the individual when they were single are considered as purchases made by a married customer. So how is such a change of information recorded? Several solutions have been proposed. One solution recommends creating record fields to hold previous as well as current values for each attribute. A second method suggests creating a new record each time an attribute value changes in an existing record. The existing record and the new record are then linked with a key field. A general solution for reflecting changing record status within the warehouse remains an unsolved problem.

The warehouse also stores another type of data known as **metadata.** Metadata is technically defined as data about data. The purpose of metadata is to allow for a better understanding of the nature of the data contained in the warehouse. Two general types of metadata have been defined: structural and operational. Structural metadata emphasizes data descriptions, data types, representation rules, and relationships between data items. Operational metadata is primarily responsible for describing the quality and usage of data. A major difference between structural and operational data is that the latter is in a constant state of change whereas the former is static.

Structuring the Data Warehouse: The Star Schema

Broadly speaking, two general techniques have been adopted for implementing a data warehouse. One method is to structure the warehouse model as a multidimensional array. In this case the data is stored in a form similar to the format used for presentation to the user. In Section 6.3 you will learn more about the advantages and disadvantages of the multidimensional database model. A more common approach stores the warehouse data using the relational model and invokes a relational database engine to present the data to the user in a multidimensional format. Here we discuss a popular relational modeling technique known as the **star schema.**

Figure 6.3 outlines a star schema created from the Acme credit card database of Figure 5.3. The theme of the star schema is credit card purchases. At the center of the star schema is the **fact table.** The fact table defines the dimensions of the multidimensional space. The fact table seen in Figure 6.3 has four dimensions—*cardholder, purchase, location,* and *time.* Each record of the fact table contains two types of information—dimension keys and facts. The dimension keys are system-generated values that taken together uniquely define each record of the fact table. The dimension keys

Figure 6.3 • **A star schema for credit card purchases**

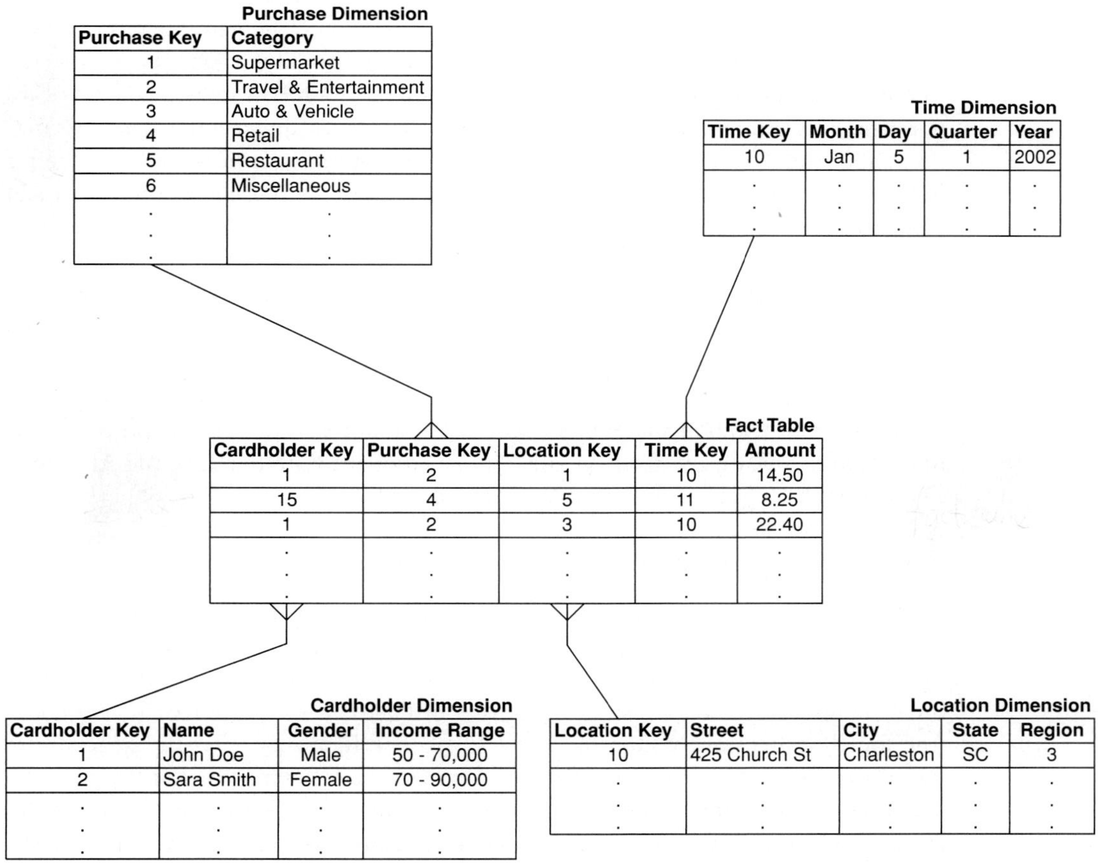

Purchase Dimension

Purchase Key	Category
1	Supermarket
2	Travel & Entertainment
3	Auto & Vehicle
4	Retail
5	Restaurant
6	Miscellaneous
.	.

Time Dimension

Time Key	Month	Day	Quarter	Year
10	Jan	5	1	2002
.	.	.	.	.

Fact Table

Cardholder Key	Purchase Key	Location Key	Time Key	Amount
1	2	1	10	14.50
15	4	5	11	8.25
1	2	3	10	22.40
.	.	.	.	.

Cardholder Dimension

Cardholder Key	Name	Gender	Income Range
1	John Doe	Male	50 - 70,000
2	Sara Smith	Female	70 - 90,000
.	.	.	.

Location Dimension

Location Key	Street	City	State	Region
10	425 Church St	Charleston	SC	3
.	.	.	.	.

determine the coordinates of the multidimensional structure represented by the star schema.

Each dimension of the fact table may have one or more associated **dimension tables.** The dimension tables make up the points of a star whose center is the fact table—hence the name star schema. The dimension tables contain data specific to each dimension. The relationship between a dimension table and the fact table is one-to-many. Therefore the dimension tables will be significantly smaller than the central fact table. Although the fact table is in 3NF, the dimension tables are not normalized. Instead, the choice of attributes comprising a dimension table is largely determined by the nature of the analytical questions to be answered by the star schema. Finally, the dimensions of the star schema are often referred to as **slowly changing dimensions.** This is because it is the dimension tables whose information is subject to the types of infrequent changes discussed in the previous section. Let's examine the dimension tables associated with the star schema for the Acme credit card database.

The star schema of Figure 6.3 shows four dimension tables. The *cardholder* dimension table is linked to the *cardholder* dimension and contains the name, gender, and income range of each customer stored in the database. The dimension table connected to the *purchase* dimension includes the possible categories for an individual credit card purchase. The dimension table associated with the *location* dimension stores information about the location of a purchased item. The *location* dimension holds a value for state as well as region. The model assumes four regions, with each state being part of one and only one region. Finally, the dimension table for *time* allows us to view time in terms of days, months, quarters, or years.

In addition to dimension key fields, the fact table may associate one or more facts with each record. The fact table displayed in Figure 6.3 has one fact representing the purchase amount for each credit card transaction. We can now read the first entry in the fact table. The credit card purchase was made by John Doe, a male cardholder who makes between $50,000 and $70,000 a year. The purchase was a travel and entertainment item and was made January 5, 2002. The amount of the purchase was $14.50.

The Multidimensionality of the Star Schema

Let's take a closer look at the multidimensional nature of the star schema. The fact table in Figure 6.3 defines a four-dimensional space. Figure 6.4 maps three of the four dimensions—*purchase, location,* and *time*—to a three-dimensional coordinate system. A three-dimensional structure such as the one in Figure 6.4 exists for each cardholder (the fourth dimension) within the star schema. The figure indicates the general case where the ith cardholder is given as C_i.

Every record contained in the fact table is represented by exactly one point in this four-dimensional space. The point for the first fact table record ($C_i = 1$) with coordi-

Figure 6.4 • **Dimensions of the fact table shown in Figure 6.3**

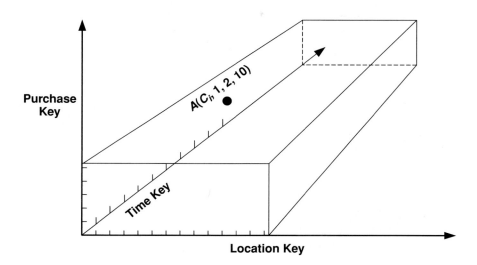

nates $(C_i, 1, 2, 10)$ is marked in Figure 6.4 by the letter A. The cell labeled A contains the value \$14.50. You will notice that the dimension tables of the star schema are not shown in Figure 6.4. Although the dimension tables are not explicitly displayed in the figure, the contents of any dimension table are easily obtained by performing a join operation with the central fact table.

The granularity of the fact table is at the transaction level. That is, all credit card purchases made by each cardholder are individually recorded in the fact table. To increase the granularity, we could record a summary of all purchases of a single type by each customer for a single day. By doing this, the fact table in Figure 6.3 will contain one entry for the two purchases made by the customer with *cardholder key* = 1, *purchase key* = 2, and *time key* = 10. The purchase amount for the combined entry will be recorded as \$36.90. An even higher level of granularity is achieved if we record total purchases by category for each customer on a monthly basis. If we choose this level of granularity, the attribute *day* would be removed from the *time* dimension table. To determine the level of granularity, we need a clear understanding about the level of detail required by the individuals who will be using the system. For any problem, a higher granularity will benefit system performance, as an increase in granularity allows for a decrease in the total number of fact table records.

Additional Relational Schemas

The **snowflake schema** is a variation of the star schema where some of the dimension tables linked directly to the fact table are further subdivided. This permits the dimension tables to be normalized, which in turn means less total storage. The advantage of this is increased storage efficiency because there is less redundancy. In addition, because the relational tables are smaller, join operations will show an improvement in performance. However, an increase in the total number of tables extends the complexity of the data queries required to extract the same information as is stored in tables that have not been normalized.

A second variation of the star schema that accounts for models requiring more than one central fact table is the **constellation schema.** A data warehouse supporting several subjects benefits most from the constellation schema. To illustrate, let's suppose we wish to include promotional information with the credit card purchase database defined in Figure 6.3. One possibility is to design a constellation schema having the current fact table for credit card purchases and a second fact table for information about promotional purchases. Figure 6.5 displays one configuration for a constellation schema that supports both credit card purchases and credit card promotions.

Figure 6.5 shows each record of the promotion fact table storing a cardholder key together with a *promotion key,* a *time key,* and a *response.* Notice that data redundancy is minimized by having the cardholder key dimension for both fact tables share the cardholder dimension table. The promotion dimension table describes each promotion in detail and links with the promotion dimension key. The time dimension key found within the promotion fact table links with the shared time dimension table. The time link signifies the start date for each promotional offering. As we have assumed a promotion duration of one month, a second time dimension indicating a promotion termination date is not necessary. However, if individual promotional offerings were to vary in duration, a second time dimension indicating promotion termination dates would be required. Finally, every record of the promotion fact table stores a single fact—denoted in Figure 6.5 as *response*—that indicates whether a cardholder did or did not take advantage of a specific promotion. As you can see, the credit card promotion database first described in Chapter 2 can be made readily available by querying the tables defined by the constellation schema of Figure 6.5.

Decision Support: Analyzing the Warehouse Data

The primary function of the data warehouse is to house data for decision support. Figure 6.2 shows that data is copied from the data warehouse for analysis by the decision support system. We also see data entering the data warehouse from the decision environment. Any data entering the warehouse from the decision support system will be in the form of metadata created from information gained through one or more decision support processes.

Figure 6.5 • **A constellation schema for credit card purchases and promotions**

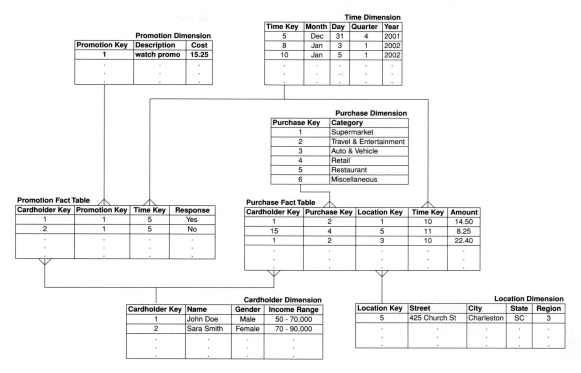

Three categories of decision support can be defined. Specifically,

1. **Reporting data.** Reporting is considered the lowest level of decision support. However, a reporting facility capable of generating informative reports for a variety of clientele is of utmost importance for the successful operation of any business.

2. **Analyzing data.** Data analysis is usually accomplished with some form of multidimensional data analysis tool. Multidimensional data analysis is the topic of the next section.

3. **Knowledge discovery.** Knowledge discovery typically takes place through data mining. However, manual data mining techniques involving repeated query and data analysis can sometimes uncover interesting patterns in data.

Besides storing data for decision support, the warehouse is a data store for creating smaller departmental warehouses known as **dependent data marts**. A dependent data mart is typically about a single subject and designed for a specific purpose. In addition, the data mart is likely to contain summary information showing a higher level of granularity than that of the data warehouse.

6.3   On-line Analytical Processing

On-line analytical processing (OLAP) is a query-based methodology that supports data analysis in a multidimensional environment. OLAP is a valuable tool for verifying or refuting human-generated hypotheses and for performing manual data mining. A complete treatment of OLAP would take several chapters at best. Our discussion here offers a basic understanding of the types of problems that can be solved with a strategy based on OLAP technology.

An OLAP engine logically structures multidimensional data in the form of a cube like the one shown in Figure 6.6. The cube displays three dimensions—*purchase category, time in months,* and *region.* You will notice that the dimensions are a subset of attributes taken from the star schema shown in Figure 6.3. A three-dimensional cube such as the one in Figure 6.6 is easy to visualize. However, it is often difficult to picture a data cube having more than three dimensions. To help paint a clear image of a four-dimensional cube, we can visualize four dimensions by thinking of n three-dimensional cubes where n is the total number of possible attribute values for the fourth dimension. To conceptualize higher-level dimensions, the process is repeated as necessary.

As an OLAP cube is designed for a specific purpose, it is not unusual to have several cubes structured from the data in a single warehouse. The design of a data cube includes decisions about which attributes to include in the cube as well as the granularity of each attribute. A well-designed cube is configured so as to avoid situations where data cells do not contain useful information. For example, a cube with two time dimensions, one for month and a second for fiscal quarter (Q_1, Q_2, Q_3, Q_4), is a poor choice because cell combinations such as (January, Q_4) or (December, Q_1) will always be empty.

One important feature of an OLAP technology is its underlying data store, which can be relational or multidimensional. If the data warehouse is relational, the internal representation of the OLAP cube is likely to be a star schema. With a multidimensional data store, the data is logically stored in arrays. Each storage method has its advantages. A relational data store allows the user to view the data at the detail level defined within the star schema. A second advantage of a relational data store is that the contents of the cells within a cube can be easily modified, even while the cube is in use. The primary advantage of a multidimensional data store is performance as measured by query speed. Whether the data store is relational or multidimensional, the user views the data as a multidimensional structure.

Another important feature of an OLAP system is the design of the user interface. Although several variations exist for the user interface, the usual structure is a modified spreadsheet format. A useful interface allows the user to display the data

Figure 6.6 ● **A multidimensional cube for credit card purchases**

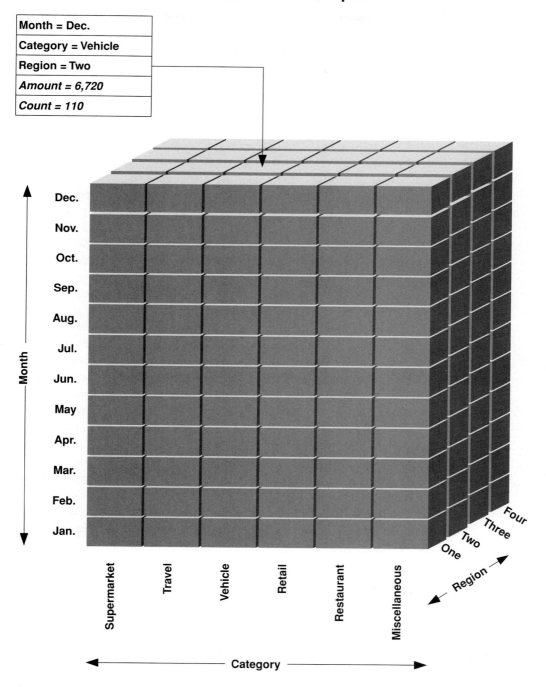

| Month = Dec. |
| Category = Vehicle |
| Region = Two |
| *Amount = 6,720* |
| *Count = 110* |

from different perspectives, perform statistical computations and tests, query the data into successively higher and/or lower levels of detail, cross-tabulate the data, and view the data with graphs and charts. The capabilities of OLAP are best described with an example.

OLAP: An Example

Once again, we'll consider the credit card application described throughout the text. Let's use OLAP to help us make decisions about times and locations for promotional offerings.

For our example we return to Figure 6.6, which shows a three-dimensional data cube created from the star schema displayed in Figure 6.3. The cube contains $12 \times 6 \times 4 = 288$ cells. Stored within each cell is the total amount spent within a given category by all credit card customers for a specific month and region. If an average purchase amount is to be computed, the cube will also contain a count representing the total number of purchases for each month, category, and region. The arrow in Figure 6.6 points to a cube holding the total amount and the total number of vehicle purchases in region two for the month of December.

Each attribute of an OLAP cube may have one or more associated **concept hierarchies.** A concept hierarchy defines a mapping that allows the attribute to be viewed from varying levels of detail. Figure 6.7 displays a concept hierarchy for the attribute *location*. As you can see, *region* holds the highest level of generality within the hierarchy. The second level of the hierarchy tells us that one or more states make up a region. The third and fourth levels show us that one or more cities are contained in a state and one or more addresses are found within a city. By definition, the hierarchy shows that each state is contained entirely within one and only one region and each city is part of exactly one state. Let's create a scenario where our OLAP cube, together with the concept hierarchy of Figure 6.7, will be of assistance in a decision-making process.

Suppose we wish to determine a best situation for offering a luggage and hand-bag promotion for travel. Our goal is to determine when and where the promotional offering will have its greatest impact on customer response. We can do this by finding those times and locations where relatively large amounts have been previously spent on travel. Once determined, we then designate the best regions and times for the promotional offering so as to take advantage of the likelihood of ensuing travel purchases. Here is a list of common OLAP operations together with a few examples for our travel promotion problem:

1.   The **slice** operation selects data on a single dimension of an OLAP cube. For the cube in Figure 6.6, a slice operation leaves two of the three dimensions in-

Figure 6.7 • **A concept hierarchy for location**

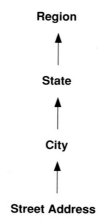

tact, while a selection on the remaining dimension creates a subcube from the original cube. Two queries for the slice operator are:

a. Provide a spreadsheet of *month* and *region* information for all cells pertaining to *travel*.

b. Select all cells where *purchase category* = *restaurant* or *supermarket*.

2. The **dice** operation extracts a subcube from the original cube by performing a select operation on two or more dimensions. Here are three queries requiring one or more dice operations:

a. Identify the month of peak travel expenditure for each region.

b. Is there a significant variation in total dollars spent for travel and entertainment by customers in each region?

c. Which month shows the greatest amount of total dollars spent on travel and entertainment for all regions?

3. **Roll-up**, or aggregation, is a combining of cells for one of the dimensions defined within a cube. One form of roll-up uses the concept hierarchy associated with a dimension to achieve a higher level of generalization. For our example, this is illustrated in Figure 6.8 where the roll-up is on the *time* dimension. The cell pointed to in the figure contains region one supermarket data for the months of October, November, and December. A second type of roll-up operator actually eliminates an entire dimension. For our example, suppose we choose to eliminate the *location* dimension. The end result is a spreadsheet of total purchases delineated by month and category type.

Figure 6.8 • **Rolling up from months to quarters**

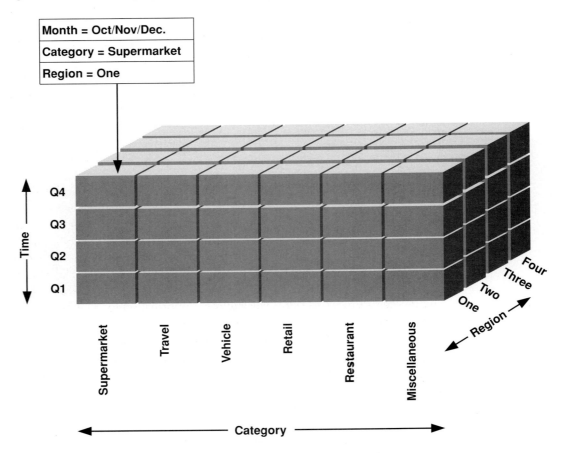

4. **Drill-down** is the reverse of a roll-up and involves examining data at some level of greater detail. Drilling down on *region* in Figure 6.6 results in a new cube where each cell highlights a specific category, month, and state.

5. **Rotation,** or pivoting, allows us to view the data from a new perspective. For our example, we may find it easier to view the OLAP cube in Figure 6.6 by having months displayed on the horizontal axis and purchase category on the vertical axis.

General Considerations

Most useful strategies for analyzing a cube require a sequence of two or more operations. For example, consider the cube in Figure 6.8. To view Q_4 totals for travel and entertainment purchases in regions one and two, we can roll-up the original cube on the *time* dimension, then dice the resultant cube on *category* and *region*. Alternatively, the dice operator may be replaced by two slice operations, one on *region* and a second on *purchase category*. As a second example, as travel and entertainment are grouped into a single category, we can't be sure about the amount of money spent on items such as airline tickets as compared to tickets to the local ballpark. We can attempt to isolate overnight travel expenses by finding those times where large travel and entertainment purchases correlate with increased restaurant purchases and decreased supermarket purchases. To do this, we first slice the cube in Figure 6.6 to create a subcube where *purchase category* is limited to *supermarket, restaurant,* and *travel & entertainment*. After this, we rank *travel & entertainment* purchases and perform a statistical analysis to better determine those times within the various regions that see significant increases in travel and restaurant purchases together with decreases in supermarket sales. The level of sophistication for the user interface together with the flexibility of the OLAP engine will, to a large extent, determine the time needed to design solutions requiring multiple queries.

MS Excel provides an interface that allows us to view OLAP cubes created from data stored in a relational database. The information contained in the cube can be displayed and manipulated in Excel as a **pivot table.** Pivot tables are easy to use and offer many of the same features seen with more complex OLAP interface tools. Pivot tables also provide us with a powerful tool for analyzing spreadsheet data. Pivot table features include the ability to summarize data, group data in various ways, and display data using several alternative formats. Pivot tables are the topic of the next section.

6.4   Excel Pivot Tables for Data Analysis

The best way for you to understand how pivot tables are used is to work through a few examples. The following examples offer a good starting point for learning about pivot tables. We leave it up to you to further investigate the capabilities of this useful analysis tool.

Excel 97, Excel 2000, and Excel XP use different procedures for creating pivot tables. Our examples explain how pivot tables work in Excel 2000. Although there are differences, methods for creating pivot tables with Excel 2000 and Excel XP are quite similar. However, several marked differences exist between pivot table creation with Excel 2000 and Excel 97. Therefore we have provided the steps for working through these same examples with Excel 97 in Appendix E.

Creating a Simple Pivot Table

We start with a simple example using the credit card promotion database to show how pivot tables summarize data for the attribute *income range*.

1. To begin, load the CreditCardPromotion.xls file into an Excel spreadsheet. Copy the data into a new spreadsheet so as to leave the original data file intact.

2. Delete the second and third rows of the spreadsheet data as they are not relevant to our analysis.

3. Make sure the cursor is positioned in one of the cells containing data. Proceed to the *Data* dropdown menu and select *PivotTable and PivotChart Report*. A three-step *PivotTable and PivotChart Wizard* will appear.

4. Select the *Microsoft Excel list or database* radio button. This indicates that the data to be analyzed is housed within an Excel spreadsheet. We have the option of creating a PivotTable or a PivotChart. Select the *PivotTable* option and click *Next* to continue.

5. In step 2 we are asked for the data range parameters to be used for creating the pivot table. As we initially placed the cursor in a cell containing data, the data range should be correct. Click *Next* to continue to step 3.

6. In step 3 we specify the location of the pivot table. Select the *New worksheet* radio button and click *Finish* to continue.

Figure 6.9 shows the display screen resulting from the application of the PivotTable wizard. The display contains two areas. The rectangular area located in the top portion of the screen is for placing data items and data fields. The bottom area of the screen holds a toolbar labeled *PivotTable*. The toolbar lists the attribute names contained in the first row of the original spreadsheet. The toolbar menu also offers several report generating options. Let's use the toolbar together with the data drop area to generate a summary report for attribute *income range*.

7. Use your mouse to drag *income range* from the toolbar into the area specified by *Drop Row Fields Here*. Next, return to the toolbar and drag *income range* into the area specified by *Drop Data Items Here*.

The result of this action produces the pivot table shown in Figure 6.10. The report tells us, among other things, that the majority of credit card customers have an income ranging between $30,000 and $40,000 dollars. Next, we'll use the toolbar to modify the format of the pivot table. First, we change the pivot table display format:

1. Single-click on the *Format Report* square located in the first row of the toolbar.

2. A box labeled *AutoFormat* will appear. The box offers 10 report formats and 10 table formats from which to choose.

Figure 6.9 • **A pivot table template**

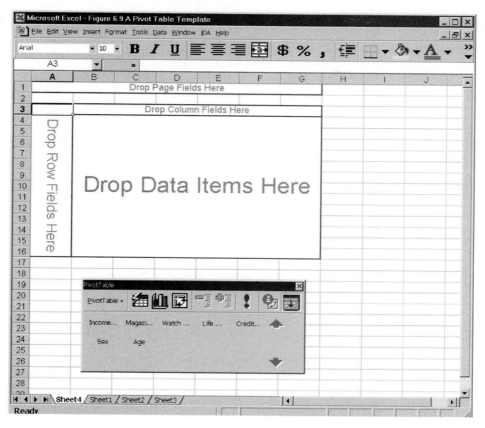

3. Experiment with several of the report and table formats. Choose a final format for use in completing this example.

Now let's change the output format for the total column (currently a count) to a percent:

1. Single-click on *Count of Income Range*.

2. Single-click on the *Field Settings* square located in the top-right portion of the pivot table toolbar. A *PivotTable Field* box will appear.

3. Single-click on *options* >> and examine the options in the *Show data as:* dropdown menu.

4. Select *% of column* and click *OK*.

The data in the total column will now appear as a percent.

Figure 6.10   ●   **A summary report for *income range***

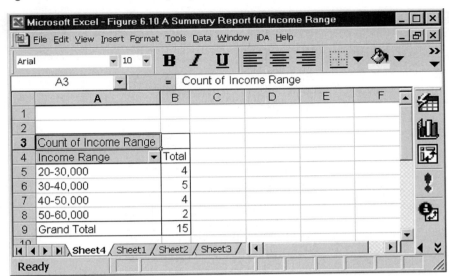

Finally, let's make a pie chart to complement the table output:

1. Begin by highlighting the percent scores for the four income range values.

2. Next, single-click on the *Chart Wizard* located in the top-left portion of the pivot table toolbar. A bar chart representing the four income range values will appear. However, we wish to have a pie chart showing the values. To accomplish this, single-click on the *Chart Wizard* a second time.

3. Choose one of the pie chart types and click on *Finish*.

Note that the pie chart is housed in a new sheet titled *chart1*. The pivot table output remains in *Sheet4*. The format for your output will depend on your pie chart selection. In any case, your output should be similar to the chart displayed in Figure 6.11. Note that the pivot table toolbar has been vertically repositioned to the right of the pie chart. This is accomplished by dragging the toolbar to the right until it fits next to the vertical scroll bar.

Next we use the pivot table *drill-down* feature to display the records of those individuals in a particular salary range:

1. Click on *Sheet4* in the bottom tray to display the pivot table.

2. Double-click on the cell containing the percent for the desired salary range (e.g., 20–30K). All instances within the chosen salary range will appear in a new spreadsheet.

3. To return to the pivot table, click on *Sheet4*.

Figure 6.11 • **A pie chart for *income range***

Total

Count of Income Range

Series "Total" Point "20-30,000"
Value: 26.67% (27%)

Income Range
■ 20-30,000
■ 30-40,000
□ 40-50,000
□ 50-60,000

This completes our first example. Once you have deleted *Sheet4, Sheet5,* and *Chart1,* you are ready to begin the second example!

Pivot Tables for Hypothesis Testing

The Acme Credit Card Company has decided to solicit by telephone select cardholders who received their credit card within the last year and who did not purchase credit card insurance with their initial mail-in application. Their data analyst believes that there is a relationship between a cardholder's age and whether the cardholder has credit card insurance. Specifically, the analyst wishes to test the hypothesis that younger cardholders purchase credit card insurance whereas more senior cardholders do not. If the hypothesis is true, only those cardholders under a certain age will be selected for the telephone solicitation.

To test the hypothesis we will use a pivot table and our imagination and assume that the credit card promotion database contains a much larger sampling of cardholders. The following steps test the hypothesis claiming a relationship between age and credit card insurance status:

1. To begin, make sure the cursor is positioned in one of the cells of *Sheet1* that contains data. Proceed to the *Data* dropdown menu and select *PivotTable and PivotChart Report* and select *Finish.*
2. Move *age* to the area labeled *Drop Row Fields Here.* Move *credit card insurance* to the area labeled *Drop Column Fields Here.*
3. Move *credit card insurance* to the area labeled *Drop Data Items Here.* The resultant pivot table is given in Figure 6.12.

The pivot table is informative in that it tells us that very few individuals currently have credit card insurance. However, the distribution of ages is such that it is difficult to make any conclusions about a relationship between age and credit card insurance. We can use the *group* function to develop a clearer picture about any possible relationship between the two attributes. The method is as follows:

Figure 6.12 • **A pivot table showing age and credit card insurance choice**

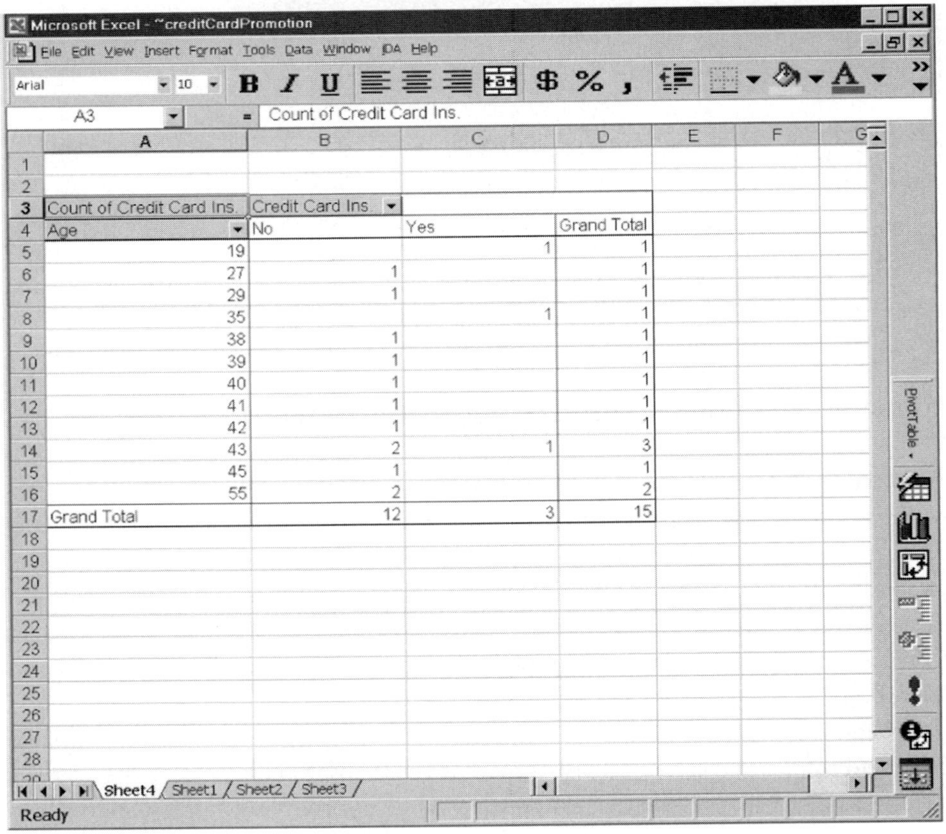

Count of Credit Card Ins.	Credit Card Ins		
Age	No	Yes	Grand Total
19		1	1
27	1		1
29	1		1
35		1	1
38	1		1
39	1		1
40	1		1
41	1		1
42	1		1
43	2	1	3
45	1		1
55	2		2
Grand Total	12	3	15

1. Single-click on the *age* attribute within the pivot table.

2. Single-click on the *Data* dropdown menu.

3. Mouse to *Group and Outline* and then to *Group*. Single-click on *Group*. A grouping box that allows you to select a *Starting at*, *Ending at,* and *By* value will appear.

4. Click on *OK* to select the default values.

The new pivot table is displayed in Figure 6.13. Although our data set is too small to draw valid conclusions, grouping the data by age allows us to obtain a clearer picture of the relationship between the two attributes. To undo the grouping, single-click on the *Data* dropdown menu, mouse to *Group and Outline,* and click on *ungroup*.

A second method for determining if a relationship between age and credit card insurance exists. This method computes the average ages for those individuals with and without credit

---

Figure 6.13 • **Grouping the credit card promotion data by age**

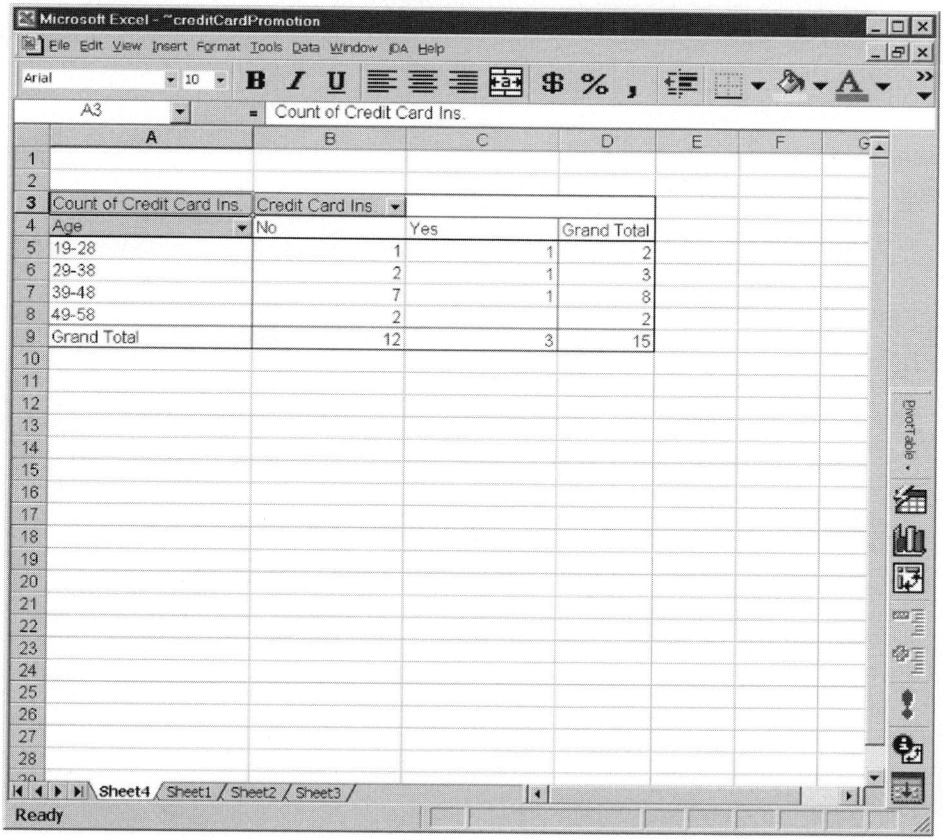

Count of Credit Card Ins.	Credit Card Ins		
Age	No	Yes	Grand Total
19-28	1	1	2
29-38	2	1	3
39-48	7	1	8
49-58	2		2
Grand Total	12	3	15

card insurance. Instead of starting with the original credit card promotion database, we'll modify the current pivot table by invoking the *PivotTable Wizard* from the toolbar as follows:

1. Locate the *PivotTable Wizard* in the top row of the toolbar.

2. Single-click on the wizard. This action invokes the step 3 display of the *PivotTable Wizard*.

3. Locate and left-click on *layout*. The current pivot table layout is displayed within the *PivotTable Layout Wizard*. Figure 6.14 shows the current layout. Figure 6.14 should be familiar to those of you who have previously used pivot tables with Excel 97.

4. Use your mouse to remove attribute *age* from the *Row* area and drag it to the *age* button located on the far right of the layout display window. Next, drag *credit card insurance* from the *Column* area to the *Row* area.

5. Remove *Count of Credit Card Insurance* from the data area and place *age* in the data area.

6. Double-click on *Sum of age* within the data area. A *PivotTable Field* box will appear.

7. Single-click on *Average* within the *Summarize by:* box. Click on *OK*. This returns you to the *PivotTable Layout Wizard.*

Figure 6.14   •   **PivotTable Layout Wizard**

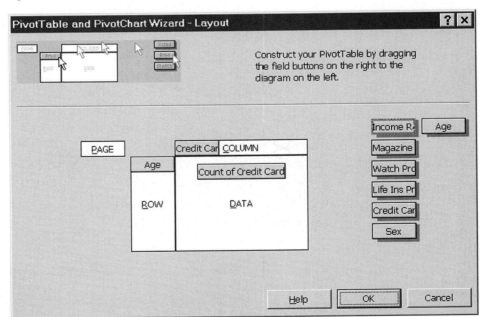

8. Click on *OK* from within the *PivotTable Layout Wizard*. Finally, click on *Finish* within the step 3 display of the *PivotTable Wizard*.

The resultant pivot table shows the average age for *credit card insurance = no* is approximately 41.42, whereas the average age for *credit card insurance = yes* is approximately 32.33.

This completes our second example. Once you have deleted *Sheet4*, you may begin the final example!

Creating a Multidimensional Pivot Table

For this example, we will use a pivot table to investigate relationships between the *magazine, watch,* and *life insurance* promotions relative to customer gender and *income range.* We will do this by creating a three-dimensional cube like the one shown in Figure 6.15. Each cell of the cube contains a count of the number of customers who either did or did not take part in

Figure 6.15 • **A credit card promotion cube**

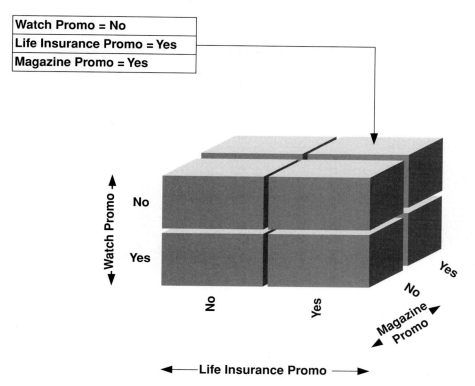

the promotional offerings. The arrow in Figure 6.15 points to the cell holding the total number of customers who took advantage of the life insurance promotion and the magazine promotion, but who did not take advantage of the watch promotion. We include *sex* and *income range* in our analysis by designating these attributes as *page* variables. Here's the procedure:

1. To begin, make sure the cursor is positioned in one of the cells of *Sheet1* that contains data. Proceed to the *Data* dropdown menu and select *PivotTable and PivotChart Report* and then *Finish.*

2. Use your mouse to drag *watch promotion* and *life insurance promotion* to the area labeled *Drop Row Fields Here.* Drag *magazine promotion* to the area labeled *Drop Column Fields Here*.

3. Drag *life insurance promotion, watch promotion,* and *magazine promotion* to the area labeled *DropData Items Here.*

4. Finally, drag *sex* and *income range* to the area labeled *Drop Page Fields Here.*

The resultant pivot table appears in Figure 6.16. The 24 highlighted cells correspond to the cells of the cube shown in Figure 6.15. In addition to the 24 cells representing the cube,

Figure 6.16 • **A pivot table with page variables for credit card promotions**

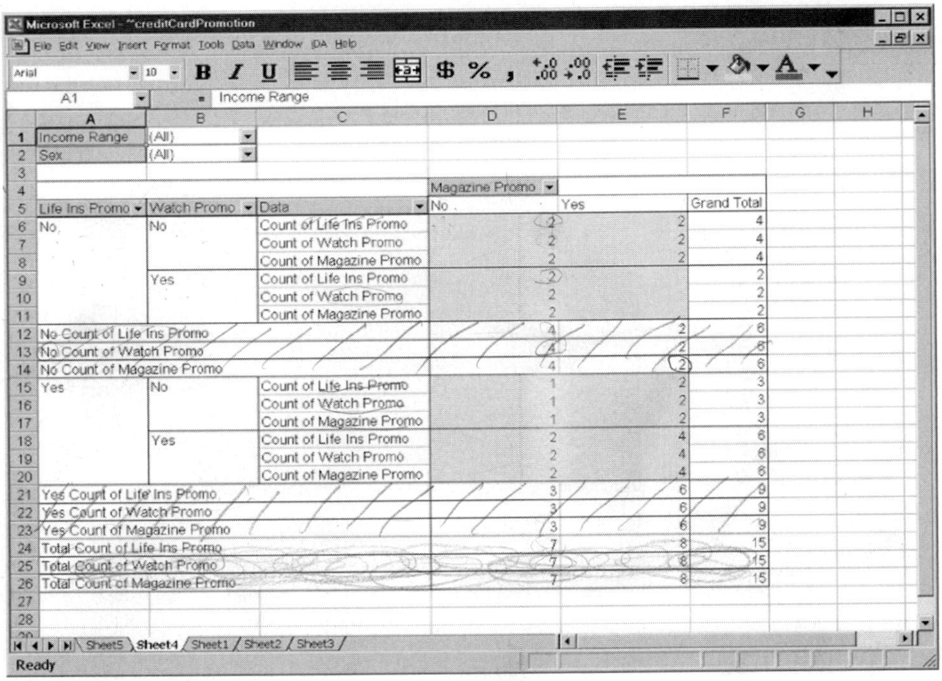

Row	A	B	C	D	E	F
1	Income Range	(All)				
2	Sex	(All)				
3						
4				Magazine Promo		
5	Life Ins Promo	Watch Promo	Data	No	Yes	Grand Total
6	No	No	Count of Life Ins Promo	2	2	4
7			Count of Watch Promo	2	2	4
8			Count of Magazine Promo	2	2	4
9		Yes	Count of Life Ins Promo	2		2
10			Count of Watch Promo	2		2
11			Count of Magazine Promo	2		2
12	No Count of Life Ins Promo			4	2	6
13	No Count of Watch Promo			4	2	6
14	No Count of Magazine Promo			4	2	6
15	Yes	No	Count of Life Ins Promo	1	2	3
16			Count of Watch Promo	1	2	3
17			Count of Magazine Promo	1	2	3
18		Yes	Count of Life Ins Promo	2	4	6
19			Count of Watch Promo	2	4	6
20			Count of Magazine Promo	2	4	6
21	Yes Count of Life Ins Promo			3	6	9
22	Yes Count of Watch Promo			3	6	9
23	Yes Count of Magazine Promo			3	6	9
24	Total Count of Life Ins Promo			7	8	15
25	Total Count of Watch Promo			7	8	15
26	Total Count of Magazine Promo			7	8	15

the pivot table also shows total *yes* and *no* counts for each promotion together with summary totals. Let's use the pivot table to help us determine relationships among the three promotions.

First, we'll use the table to find the customer count for the cell designated in Figure 6.15:

1. Find the area to the far left within the pivot table that shows *life insurance promotion = yes.* This is given in Figure 6.16 by rows 15 through 20.

2. Within this same area, locate the subregion that has *watch promotion = no.*

3. Finally, follow this subregion to the right until you reach the column for *magazine promotion = yes.*

The contents of the cell show a 2 for all three promotions. This tells us that a total of two customers took advantage of the life insurance and magazine promotions but did not purchase the watch promotion.

We can drill-down to examine the individual records represented by the cell. Simply double-click on any one of the cells containing the value 2. By default, the records will be displayed in *Sheet5.* To return to the pivot table, click on *Sheet4* in the bottom tray.

Because a pivot table maintains a connection to the original data, a change made to the original spreadsheet data will also be seen in the pivot table. To have a change that has been made reflected within the pivot table, simply click on the exclamation mark shown on the PivotTable toolbar. You may wish to test this feature before continuing.

Next let's look at the *paging* feature. In the upper-left corner of the pivot table, you will see the paging variables (*sex* and *income-range*) specified with the table definition. We can use the page feature to answer questions about the relationship between the attributes given as page variables and the promotional offerings. For example, let's say we wish to examine the relationship between income range and promotional offerings for female customers. The procedure is as follows:

1. Single-click on the dropdown menu for *sex,* highlight *female,* and click *OK.*

2. Single-click on the dropdown menu for *income range,* highlight *20-30,000,* and click *OK.*

The pivot table displays the promotional summary data for females making between $20,000 and $30,000 dollars. The table shows two female customers within the specified income range. Neither female took advantage of the watch or magazine promotions, but one female did purchase the life insurance promotional offering. By examining the remaining income range data, you will see that females with an annual salary between $30,000 and $40,000 dollars have traditionally been the best candidates for promotional offerings. It is obvious that the paging feature adds one more dimension to the analysis capabilities of Excel pivot tables.

Here we have introduced pivot tables as a tool for data analysis. Several of the end-of-chapter exercises will help you become more familiar with how pivot tables are able to summarize data. For more information about pivot tables, we encourage you to read the documents available with the MS Excel Help facility.

6.5   Chapter Summary

Operational databases are designed to process individual transactions quickly and efficiently. To accomplish this, operational data is often stored as a set of normalized relational tables. The normalization minimizes data redundancy, thus allowing for effective data processing. Once transactional data is no longer useful, it is transferred from the operational environment to a secondary storage medium. If a decision support facility exists, the storage facility will likely be a data warehouse. W. H. Inmon (1992) describes the data warehouse as a "subject oriented, integrated, nonvolatile, time variant collection of data in support of management's decisions."

Two methods have been developed for organizing a data warehouse. One method structures the data as a multidimensional array. A second method uses the relational model for data storage and retrieval. In either case, the user views the data as a multidimensional data store. Although each method has advantages, the relational approach—implemented with a star schema—is the more popular technique. The star schema supports a central fact table and several dimension tables. The fact table defines the dimensions of the multidimensional space. Individual dimension tables store detailed information about their associated fact table dimensions. One variation of the star schema is the snowflake schema, which encourages the structuring of normalized dimension tables. A second variation is the constellation schema, which can be used to accommodate a data warehouse containing several fact tables.

The primary function of warehoused data is for decision support. Three categories of decision support are *reporting data, analyzing data,* and *knowledge discovery.* A data reporting facility must be capable of generating detailed reports about the data stored in the warehouse. Knowledge discovery is accomplished through data mining. Data analysis is performed with the help of OLAP, a query-based methodology that supports data analysis in a multidimensional environment. OLAP tools contain a friendly user interface and are capable of displaying data from different perspectives, performing statistical analysis, and querying data at successively lower and/or higher levels of detail. MS Excel pivot tables offer many of the same features seen with more complex OLAP tools. Pivot table features include the ability to summarize and group data and display data in several formats.

6.6   Key Terms

Concept hierarchy. A mapping that allows attributes to be viewed from varying levels of detail.

Constellation schema. A variation of the star schema that allows more than one central fact table.

Data model. A notational language that documents the structure of data independent of how the data will be used.

Dependent data mart. A departmental warehouse designed for a specific purpose and created from the data in a larger warehouse structure.

Dice. An OLAP operation on two or more dimensions that extracts a subcube from the original cube.

Dimension table. A relational table containing information about one of the dimensions of a star schema.

Drill-down. An OLAP operation performed on a data cube that allows for examining data at some level of greater detail.

Entity relationship diagram (ERD). A data modeling tool that shows the structure of the data in terms of entities and relationships between entities. Relationships between entities can be one-to-one, one-to-many, or many-to-many.

Entity. A generic representation for a class of persons, places, or things.

ETL routine. Any process that cleans, transforms, and loads data into a warehouse.

Fact table. A relational table that defines the dimensions of the multidimensional space within a star schema.

First normal form (1NF). A rule that requires all attributes within an entity to have a single value.

Granularity. A term used to describe the level of detail of stored information.

Independent data mart. A data store that is similar to a warehouse but limits its focus to a single subject. An independent data mart can be structured using operational data as well as external data sources.

Intersection entity. An entity created by mapping a many-to-many relationship to two one-to-many relationships.

Many-to-many relationship. A relationship between two entities, *A* and *B*, where each instance of *A* is associated with one or several instances of *B*, and each instance of *B* is associated with one or several instances of *A*.

Metadata. Data about data.

Normalization. A multistep process designed to remove redundancies from a data model.

One-to-one relationship. A relationship between two entities, *A* and *B*, where each instance of *A* is associated with exactly one instance of *B*.

One-to-many relationship. A relationship between two entities, *A* and *B*, where each instance of *A* is associated with one or several instances of *B*.

On-line transactional processing (OLTP). Database procedures designed to process individual transactions quickly and efficiently.

Pivot table. An MS Excel-based data analysis tool that can be used to summarize data, group data in various ways, and display data using several alternative formats.

Roll-up. An OLAP operation that combines the cells of a data cube to form a higher-level view of the data.

Rotation. An OLAP operation that allows the user to examine data from several perspectives.

Second normal form (2NF). An entity is in 2NF if it is in 1NF and all nonkey attributes are dependent on the full primary key.

Slice. An OLAP operation that creates a subcube by performing a selection on a single dimension of a data cube.

Slowly changing dimension. A dimension whose attributes change over time.

Snowflake schema. A variation of the star schema where some of the dimension tables linked directly to the fact table are further subdivided. This permits the dimension tables to be normalized, which in turn means less total storage.

Star schema. A multidimensional data warehouse model implemented within a relational database. The model consists of a fact table and one or more dimension tables.

Third normal form (3NF). An entity is in 3NF if it is in 2NF and every nonkey attribute is dependent entirely on the primary key.

6.7   Exercises

Review Questions

1. Differentiate between the following terms:

    a. Independent data mart and dependent data mart

    b. Fact table and dimension table

    c. Slice and dice

    d. Drill-down and roll-up

e. OLTP and OLAP

2. Specify each relationship as one-to-one, one-to-many, or many-to-many. Justify each answer.

a. Employer–Employee

b. Automobile–License Plate

c. Pastor–Parish

d. Course–Instructor

e. Home–Owner

3. Consider the star schema in Figure 6.3. Suppose an individual customer would like us to extract a list of the specific items he or she purchased during a given month and year. Will you be able to accommodate the customer? Explain your answer.

4. Think of ways to incorporate promotions into the star schema of Figure 6.3 without creating a second fact table. What are the positive and negative aspects of each approach?

5. Sketch the OLAP cubes created from the slice and dice operations described in Section 6.3.

Computational Questions

1. Sketch a three-dimensional OLAP cube from the star schema in Figure 6.3 where the dimensions are *purchase category, sex,* and *income range.* Describe several slice, dice, and rotation operations for extracting useful information from the data cube.

LAB 2. Construct a pivot table with the *CardiologyCategorical.xls* database file. Make *angina* and *thal* row attributes and *class* a column attribute. Place *class, angina,* and *thal* in the data area. Specify *slope, sex,* and *#colored vessels* as page variables. Use the pivot table to answer the following questions:

a. How many healthy males are in the database?

b. How many healthy females have three or more colored vessels?

c. Determine values for *#colored vessels* and *angina* that are sufficient for defining a sick individual.

d. Verify or refute the hypothesis: The majority of individuals with *#colored vessels = 0* are healthy.

e. Verify or refute the hypothesis: A typical healthy individual will show no symptoms of angina and will have a value of *normal* for attribute *thal.*

LAB Denotes exercise appropriate for a laboratory setting.

LAB 3.   Recreate the pivot table shown in Figure 6.16 to answer the following:

a.   How many cardholders did not purchase a single promotional offering?

b.   How many cardholders took advantage of the magazine and watch promotions but did not purchase the life insurance promotion?

c.   How many male cardholders make between $50,000 and $60,000?

d.   Verify or refute the hypothesis: Individuals who purchased all three promotional offerings also purchased credit card insurance.

Chapter 7

Formal Evaluation Techniques

Chapter Objectives

▶ Determine confidence intervals for model test set accuracy.

▶ Use statistical evaluation to compare the accuracy of two supervised learner models.

▶ Apply hypothesis testing to determine numerical attribute significance.

▶ Know how correlation coefficients and scatterplot diagrams identify redundant numerical attributes.

▶ Understand how cross validation and bootstrapping are applied to evaluate supervised learner models.

▶ Know how unsupervised clustering is used for supervised evaluation.

▶ Use supervised learning to evaluate the results of an unsupervised clustering.

▶ Understand how attribute analysis can be used to evaluate the results of an unsupervised clustering.

▶ Evaluate supervised models having numerical output.

In previous chapters we showed how test set error rates, confusion matrices, and lift charts can help us evaluate supervised learner models. You also saw how supervised learning can be used to evaluate the results of an unsupervised clustering. In this chapter we continue our discussion of performance evaluation by focusing on formal evaluation methods for supervised learning and unsupervised clustering. Most of the methods introduced in this chapter are of a statistical nature. The advantage of this approach is that it permits us to associate a level of confidence with the outcome of our data mining experiments.

We emphasize the practical application of standard statistical and nonstatistical methods rather than the theory behind each technique. Our goal is to provide the necessary tools to enable you to develop a clear understanding of which evaluation techniques are appropriate for your data mining applications. The methods presented here are enough to meet the needs of most interested readers. However, Appendix D provides additional material for the reader who desires a more complete treatment of statistical evaluation techniques.

In Section 7.1 we highlight the component parts of the data mining process that are responsive to an evaluation. In Section 7.2 we provide an overview of several foundational statistical concepts such as mean and variance scores, standard error computations, data distributions, populations and samples, and hypothesis testing. Section 7.3 offers a method for computing test set confidence intervals for classifier error rates. Section 7.4 shows you how to employ classical hypothesis testing together with test set error rates to compare the classification accuracy of competing models. In Section 7.5 you learn how to apply a classical hypothesis testing model to determine numerical attribute significance. Section 7.6 offers several methods for evaluating the results of an unsupervised clustering. In Section 7.7 we show you how to evaluate supervised learner models having numerical output. As you read and work through the examples of this chapter, keep in mind that a best evaluation is accomplished by applying a combination of statistical, heuristic, experimental, and human analyses.

7.1   What Should Be Evaluated?

Figure 7.1 shows the major components used to create and test a supervised learner model. All elements contribute in some way to the performance of a created model. When a model fails to perform as expected, an appropriate strategy is to evaluate the effect every component has on model performance. The individual elements of Figure 7.1 have each been a topic of discussion in one or more of the previous chapters. The following is a list of the components shown in the figure together with additional considerations for evaluation.

1.   **Supervised model.** Supervised learner models are usually evaluated on test data. Special attention may be paid to the cost of different types of misclassification. For example, we might be willing to use a loan application model that

Figure 7.1 ● **Components for supervised learning**

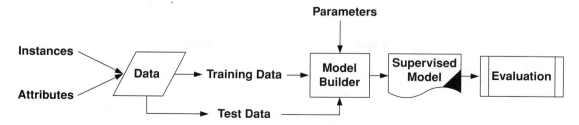

rejects borderline individuals who would likely pay off a loan provided the model does not accept strong candidates for loan default. In this chapter we add to your evaluation toolbox by showing you how to compute test set error rate confidence intervals for supervised models having categorical output.

2. **Training data.** If a supervised learner model shows a poor test set accuracy, part of the problem may lie with the training data. Models built with training data that does not represent the set of all possible domain instances or contains an abundance of atypical instances are not likely to perform well. A best preventative measure is to randomly select training data, making sure the classes contained in the training data are distributed as they are seen in the general population. The procedure for ensuring an appropriate distribution of data is known as **stratification.** A second technique for ensuring representative instance selections is to examine training instance typicality scores.

3. **Attributes.** Attribute evaluation focuses on how well the attributes define the domain instances. In Section 7.5 we review attribute evaluation procedures, provide an additional statistical tool for numerical attribute evaluation, and show you how to identify redundant numerical attributes.

4. **Model builder.** It has been shown that supervised learner models built with alternative learning techniques tend to show comparable test set error rates. However, there may be situations where one learning technique is preferred over another. For example, neural networks tend to outperform other supervised learning techniques when the training data contains a wealth of missing or noisy data items. In Section 7.4 we show you how to decide if two supervised learner models built with the same training data show a significant difference in test set performance.

5. **Parameters.** Most data mining models support one or more user-specified learning parameters. As you saw in Chapter 5, parameter settings can have a marked effect on model performance. The technique used to compare supervised learner models built with different data mining techniques can also be applied to

compare models constructed with the same data mining method but alternate settings for one or more learning parameters.

6. **Test set evaluation.** The purpose of test data is to offer a measure of future model performance. Test data should be selected randomly, with stratification applied as appropriate.

Figure 7.1 also applies to unsupervised clustering, with the exception that we are without test data containing instances of known classification. In Section 7.6 we review unsupervised evaluation techniques and explore additional methods for evaluating an unsupervised clustering.

7.2   Tools for Evaluation

Statistics are a part of our everyday lives. The results of statistical studies help us make decisions about how to invest our hard-earned money, when to retire, where to place our gambling bets, and even whether to have a certain surgical procedure. The following are several interesting statistical findings that have been reported during the past year:

- 60% of the 100,000,000 households in the United States have credit card debt of $6000 or more.

- 50% of all adults in the United States are not invested in the stock market.

- 70% of all felons come from homes without a father.

- One in 700,000 deaths is caused by dog bite.

- One in 15 men will get prostate cancer.

- The average age when a woman becomes a widow is 56.

- Of every 100 people who turn age 65, one has wealth in excess of $5 million dollars, four are financially independent ($1 to $4 million dollars), 41 are still working, and 54 are dead broke.

Sometimes, the results of statistical studies must be interpreted with a degree of caution. For example, the average age when a woman becomes a widow may be 56, however the *median* age when a woman is widowed is likely to be higher as well as more informative.

Findings such as those just listed are often gathered through a process of random sampling. The first statement fits this category. It is simply too difficult to poll each and every American family to determine the amount of household credit card debt. Therefore experts poll a sample of individual households and report findings in terms of the general population along with a margin of error. As you will see, we can apply the techniques developed to conduct statistical studies to our data mining problems. The advantage of a statistical approach is that it allows us to associate levels of confidence with the outcomes of our data mining experiments.

Before investigating several useful statistics for evaluating and comparing data mining models, we review the fundamental notions of mean, variance, and population distributions.

Single-Valued Summary Statistics

A population of numerical data is uniquely defined by a mean, a standard deviation, and a frequency or probability distribution of values occurring in the data. The **mean,** or average value, denoted by μ, is computed by summing the data and dividing the sum by the number of data items.

Whereas the mean designates an average value, the **variance** (σ^2) represents the amount of dispersion about the mean. To calculate the variance, we first compute the sum of squared differences from the mean. This is accomplished by subtracting each data value from the mean, squaring the difference, and adding the result to an accumulating sum. The variance is obtained by dividing the sum of squared differences by the number of data items. The **standard deviation,** denoted by σ, is simply the square root of the variance.

When computing a mean, variance, or standard deviation score for a sampling of data, symbol designations change. We adopt the following notation for sample mean and variance scores:

$$\text{Sample mean} = \overline{X}$$
$$\text{Sample variance} = V$$

The mean and variance are useful statistics for summarizing data. However, two populations can display very similar mean and variance scores yet show a marked variation between their individual data items. Therefore to allow for a complete understanding of the data, knowledge about the distribution of data items within the population is necessary. With a small amount of data, the data distribution is easily obtainable. However, with large populations the distribution is often difficult to determine.

The Normal Distribution

A fundamentally important data distribution that is well understood is the **normal distribution,** also known as the Gaussian curve or the normal probability curve. Several useful statistics have been developed for populations showing a normal distribution.

The normal, or bell-shaped, curve was discovered by accident in 1733 by the French mathematician Abraham de Moivre while solving problems for wealthy gamblers. The discovery came while recording the number of heads and tails during a coin-tossing exercise. For his experiment, he repeatedly tossed a coin 10 times and recorded the average number of heads. He found that the average as well as the most frequent number of heads tossed was five. Six and four heads appeared with the same frequency and were the next most frequently occurring numbers. Next, three and seven heads occurred equally often, followed by two and eight and so on. Since Moivre's initial discovery, many phenomenon such as measures of reading ability, height, weight, intelligence quotients, and job satisfaction ratings, to name a few, have been found to be distributed normally. The general formula defining the normal curve for continuous data is uniquely determined by a population mean and standard deviation and can be found in Appendix D.

A graph of the normal curve is displayed in Figure 7.2. The *x*-axis shows the arithmetic mean at the center in position 0. The integers on either side of the mean indicate the number of standard deviations from the mean. To illustrate, if data is normally distributed, approximately 34.13% of all values will lie between the mean and one standard deviation above the mean. Likewise, 34.13% of all values are seen between the mean and one standard deviation below the mean. That is, we can expect approximately 68.26% of all values to lie within one standard deviation on either side of the mean score.

As an example, suppose the scores on a test are known to be normally distributed with a mean of 70 and a standard deviation of 5. Knowing this, we can expect 68.26% of all students to have a test score somewhere between 65 and 75. Likewise, we should see over 95% of the student scores falling somewhere between 60 and 80. Stated another way, we can be 95% confident that all student test scores lie between two standard deviations above and below the mean score of 70.

As most data is not normally distributed, you may wonder as to the relevance of this discussion to data mining. After all, even if one attribute is known to be normally distributed, we must deal with instances containing several numeric values, most of which

Figure 7.2   ●   **A normal distribution**

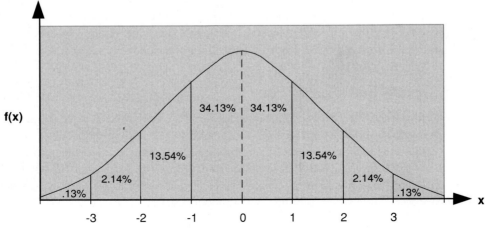

are not likely to be distributed normally. Our discussion of the normal distribution serves two purposes. First, some data mining models assume numeric attributes to be normally distributed. We discuss one such model in Chapter 10. More importantly, as you will see in the remaining sections of this chapter, we can use the properties of the normal distribution to help us evaluate the performance of our data mining models.

Normal Distributions and Sample Means

Most interesting populations are quite large, making experimental analysis extremely difficult. For this reason, experiments are often performed on subsets of data randomly selected from the total population. Figure 7.3 shows three sample datasets each containing three elements that have been taken from a population of 10 data items.

When sampling from a population, we cannot be sure that the distribution of values in the sample is normal. This is the case even if the population is normally distributed. However, there is a special situation where we are guaranteed a normal distribution. Specifically,

> *For a given population, a distribution of means taken from random sets of independent samples of equal size are distributed normally.*

To better understand the importance of this statement, let's consider the problem of determining the average American household credit card debt. There are approximately 100,000,000 American households. We have neither the time or resources to poll each and every household. Therefore we sample a random subset of 10,000,000 homes to obtain an average household credit card debt figure. We generalize our findings by reporting the obtained value as the average amount of American household credit card debt. An obvious question is: How confident can we be that the average computed from the sample data is an accurate estimate of the average household credit card debt for the general population?

To help answer this question, suppose we repeat this experiment several times, each time recording the average household credit card debt for a new random sample of 10,000,000 homes. Our statement tells us that the average values we obtain from the repeated process are normally distributed. Stated in a formal manner, we say that any one of the obtained sample means is an unbiased estimate of the mean for the general population. Also, the average of sample means taken over all possible samples of equal size is exactly equal to the population mean.

We now know that the average credit card debt computed from the initial sample mean of 10,000,000 households is an unbiased estimate of the average for the population. We still do not have a confidence in the computed average value. Although we cannot unequivocally state our computed value as an exact average debt figure for the general population, we can use the sample variance to easily obtain a confidence interval for the computed average value.

Figure 7.3   ● **Random samples from a population of 10 elements**

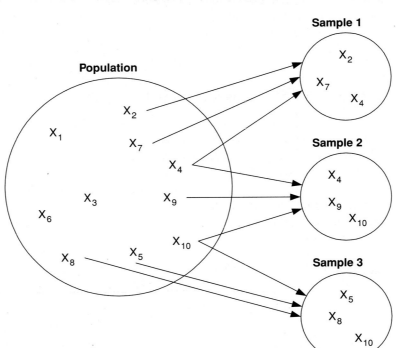

First, we estimate the variance of the population. The population variance is estimated by v/n, where v is the sample variance and n is the number of sample instances. Next we compute the **standard error.** The standard error *(SE)* is simply the square root of the estimated population variance. The formula for computing standard error is given as:

$$SE = \sqrt{v / n}$$ (7.1)

As the population of sample means is normally distributed and the standard error is an estimate of the population variance, we can make the following claim:

Any sample mean will vary less than plus or minus two standard errors from the population mean 95% of the time.

For the household credit card debt problem, this means that we can be 95% confident that the actual average household credit card debt lies somewhere between two standard errors above and two standard errors below the computed sample mean. For our example, suppose the average household debt for our sample of 10,000,000 households is $6000 with a standard error of 100. Our statement tells us that we can be 95% certain that the actual average American household credit card debt for the general population lies somewhere between $5800 and $6200.

We can use this technique as well as the hypothesis testing model introduced in the next section to help us compute confidence intervals for test set error rates, compare the classification error rates of two or more data mining models, and determine those numerical attributes best able to differentiate individual classes or clusters.

A Classical Model for Hypothesis Testing

You will recall that a hypothesis is an educated guess about the outcome of some event. Hypothesis testing is commonplace in the fields of science and medicine as well as in everyday situations dealing with politics and government. Let's take a look at a standard experimental design using a hypothetical example from the field of medicine.

Suppose we wish to determine the effects of a new drug, treatment X, that was developed to treat the symptoms associated with an allergy to house dust. For the experiment, we randomly choose two groups from a select population of individuals who suffer from the allergy. To perform the experiment, we pick one group as the **experimental group.** The second group is designated as the **control group.** Treatment X is applied to the experimental group and a placebo in the form of a sugar pill is distributed to the control group. We take care to make sure individual patients are not aware of their group membership. The average increase or decrease in the total number of allergic reactions per day is recorded for each patient in both groups. After a period of time, we apply a statistical test to determine if a significant difference in the measured parameter is seen between the two groups of patients.

A usual procedure is to state a hypothesis to be tested about the outcome of the experiment. Typically, the outcome is stated in the form of a **null hypothesis.** The null hypothesis takes a negative point of view in that it asserts any relationship found as a result of the experiment is due purely by chance. For our example, the null hypothesis declares the outcome will show no significant difference between the two groups of patients. A plausible null hypothesis for our experiment is:

> *There is no significant difference in the mean increase or decrease of total allergic reactions per day between patients in the group receiving treatment X and patients in the group receiving the placebo.*

Notice that the null hypothesis specifies no significant difference rather than no significant improvement. The reason for this is that we have no *a priori* guarantee that treatment X will not cause an adverse reaction and worsen the symptoms associated with the allergy.

Once the experiment is performed and the data showing the results of the experiment have been gathered, we test if the outcome shows a significant difference between the two groups of patients. A classical model to test for a significant difference between the mean scores of a measured parameter such the one for our experiment is given as:

$$P = \frac{\left|\overline{X}_1 - \overline{X}_2\right|}{\sqrt{(v_1 / n_1 + v_2 / n_2)}} \qquad (7.2)$$

where

P is the significance score

$\overline{X}_1$ and $\overline{X}_2$ are sample means for the independent samples

v_1 and v_2 are variance scores for the respective means

n_1 and n_2 are corresponding sample sizes

The term in the numerator is the absolute difference between the two sample means. To test for a significant difference between the mean scores, the difference is divided by the standard error for the distribution of mean differences. As the two samples are independent, the standard error is simply the square root of the sum of the two variance scores associated with the two sample means. To be 95% confident that the difference between two means is not due to chance, the value for P in the equation must be greater than or equal to 2. The model is valid because, like the distribution of means taken from sets of independent samples of equal size, the distribution of differences between sample means is also normal.

A 95% level of confidence still leaves room for error. With hypothesis testing two general types of error are defined. A **type 1 error** is seen when a true null hypothesis is rejected. A **type 2 error** is observed when a null hypothesis that should have been rejected is accepted. These two possibilities are shown in the confusion matrix of Table 7.1. For our experiment, a type 1 error would have us believing that treatment X has a significant impact on the average number of allergic reactions to dust when it does not. Likewise, a type 2 error would state that treatment X does not affect the mean number of allergic reactions when indeed it does.

A requirement of this methodology is that each mean is computed from an independent dataset. With data mining, the usual case is to compare models with the help of a single test set of data. Fortunately, we can employ a slight modification of the classical model to situations where we are limited to one test dataset.

7.3   Computing Test Set Confidence Intervals

Training and test data may be supplemented by **validation data.** One purpose of validation data is to help us choose one of several models built from the same training set. Once trained, each model is presented with the validation data, whereby the model showing a best classification correctness is chosen as the final model. Validation

Table 7.1 • **A Confusion Matrix for the Null Hypothesis**

	Computed Accept	Computed Reject
Accept Null Hypothesis	True Accept	Type 1 Error
Reject Null Hypothesis	Type 2 Error	True Reject

[我们认为药品X对于这些过敏反应在平均水量有显著影响,实际上并没有]

[错误,虚假设被接受的时候]

正确,虚假设被拒绝的时候

[我们认为药品X并不改变过敏反应在平均水量,但它实际上确实有影响]

data can also be used to optimize the parameter settings of a supervised model so as to maximize classification correctness.

Once a supervised learner model has been validated, the model is evaluated by applying it to the test data. The most general measure of model performance is **classifier error rate.** Specifically,

$$\text{Classifier Error Rate } (E) = \frac{\text{\# of test set errors}}{\text{\# of test set instances}} \quad (7.3)$$

The purpose of a classifier error rate computation is to give an indication as to the likely future performance of the model. How confident can we be that this error rate is a valid measure of actual model performance? To answer this question, we can use the standard error statistic to calculate an error rate confidence interval for model performance. To apply the standard error measure, we treat classifier error rate as a sample mean. Although the error rate is actually a proportion, if the number of test set instances is sufficiently large (say $n > 100$), the error rate can represent a mean value.

To determine a confidence interval for a computed error rate, we first calculate the standard error associated with the classifier error rate. The standard error together with the error rate is then used to compute the confidence interval. The procedure is as follows:

1. Given a test set sample S of size n and error rate E

2. Compute the sample variance as:
    $\text{Variance}(E) = E(1 - E)$

3. Compute the standard error (SE) as the square root of $\text{Variance}(E)$ divided by n.

4. Calculate an upper bound for the 95% confidence interval as $E + 2(SE)$.

5. Calculate a lower bound for the 95% confidence interval as $E - 2(SE)$.

Let's look at an example to better understand how the confidence interval is computed. Suppose a classifier shows a 10% error rate when applied to a random sample of 100 test set instances. We set $E = 0.10$ and compute the sample variance as:

$$Variance(0.10) = 0.10(1 - 0.10) = 0.09$$

With a test set of 100 instances, the standard error computation is:

$$SE = \sqrt{(0.09 / 100)} = 0.03$$

We can be 95% confident that the actual test set error rate lies somewhere between two standard errors below 0.10 and two standard errors above 0.10. This tells us that the actual test set error rate falls between 0.04 and 0.16, which gives a test set accuracy between 84 and 96 percent.

If we increase the number of test set instances, we are able to decrease the size of the confidence range. Suppose we increase the test set size to 1000 instances. The standard error becomes:

$$SE = \sqrt{(0.09 / 1000)} \approx .0095$$

Making the same computations as in the previous example, the test set accuracy range is now between 88 and 92 percent. As you can see, the size of the test dataset has a marked effect on the range of the confidence interval. This is to be expected, because as the size of the test dataset becomes infinitely large, the standard error measure approaches zero. Three general comments about this technique are:

1.   The confidence interval is valid only if the test data has been randomly chosen from the pool of all possible test set instances.

2.   Test, training, and validation data must represent disjoint sets. 不相连的基搭集

3.   If possible, the instances in each class should be distributed in the training, validation, and test data as they are seen in the entire dataset.

If ample test data are not available, we can apply a technique known as **cross validation.** With this method, all available data are partitioned into n fixed-size units. $n - 1$ of the units are used for training, whereas the nth unit is the test set. This process is repeated until each of the fixed-size units has been used as test data. Model test set correctness is computed as the average accuracy realized from the n training-testing trials. Experimental results have shown a value of 10 for n to be maximal in most situations. Several applications of cross validation to the data can help ensure an equal distribution of classes within the training and test datasets.

Bootstrapping is an alternative to cross validation. With bootstrapping, we allow the training set selection process to choose the same training instance several times. This happens by placing each training instance back into the data pool after it has been selected for training. It can be shown mathematically that if a dataset containing n instances is sampled n times using the bootstrap technique, the training set will contain approximately two-thirds of the n instances. This leaves one-third of the instances for testing.

As a final point, in Chapter 2 you learned that the test set error rate is but one of several considerations when determining the value of a supervised learner model. To emphasize this point, let's assume that an average of 0.5% of all credit card purchases are fraudulent. A model designed to detect credit card fraud that always states a credit card purchase is valid will show a 99.5% accuracy. However, such a model is worthless as it is unable to perform the task for which it was designed. In contrast, a model that correctly detects all cases of credit card fraud at the expense of showing a high rate of false positive classifications is of much more value.

One way to deal with this issue is to assign weights to incorrect classifications. With the credit card example, we could assign a large weight to incorrect classifications that allow a fraudulent card to go undetected and a smaller weight to the error of incorrectly identifying a credit card as fraudulent. In this way, a model will have its classification error rate increase if it shows a bias toward allowing fraudulent card usage to go undetected. In the next section we show you how test set classification error rate can be employed to compare the performance of two supervised learner models.

7.4 Comparing Supervised Learner Models

We can compare two supervised learner models constructed with the same training data by applying the classical hypothesis testing paradigm. Our measure of model performance is once again test set error rate. Let's state the problem in the form of a null hypothesis. Specifically,

> *There is no significant difference in the test set error rate of two supervised learner models, M_1 and M_2, built with the same training data.*

Three possible test set scenarios are:

1. The accuracy of the models is compared using two independent test sets randomly selected from a pool of sample data.

2. The same test set data is employed to compare the models. The comparison is based on a pairwise, instance-by-instance computation.

3. The same test data is used to compare the overall classification correctness of the models.

From a statistical perspective, the most straightforward approach is the first one, as we can directly apply the classical hypothesis testing model described in Section 7.2.

This approach is feasible only if an ample supply of test set data are available. With large datasets, the prospect of extracting independent test set data is real. However, with smaller-sized data, a single test set may be the only possibility.

When the same test set is applied to the data, one option is to perform an instance-by-instance pairwise matching of the test set results. This approach is described in Appendix D. Here we describe a simpler technique that compares the overall classification correctness of two models. The method can be applied to both the two independent (scenario 1) or single test set (scenario 3) cases. The most general form of the statistic for comparing the performance of two classifier models M_1 and M_2 is

$$P = \frac{\left|E_1 - E_2\right|}{\sqrt{q(1-q)(1/n_1 + 1/n_2)}} \tag{7.4}$$

where

E_1 = The error rate for model M_1

E_2 = The error rate for model M_2

$q = (E_1 + E_2)/2$

n_1 = the number of instances in test set A

n_2 = the number of instances in test set B

Notice that $q(1-q)$ is a variance score computed using the average of the two error rates. With a single test set of size n, the formula simplifies to:

$$P = \frac{\left|E_1 - E_2\right|}{\sqrt{q(1-q)(2/n)}} \tag{7.5}$$

With either Equation 7.4 or 7.5, if the value of $P \geq 2$, we can be 95% confident that the difference in the test set performance of M_1 and M_2 is significant.

Let's look at an example. Suppose we wish to compare the test set performance of learner models M_1 and M_2. We test M_1 on test set A and M_2 on test set B. Each test set contains 100 instances. M_1 achieves an 80% classification accuracy with set A, and M_2 obtains a 70% accuracy with test set B. We wish to know if model M_1 has performed significantly better than model M_2. The computations are:

- for model M_1: $E_1 = 0.20$

- for model M_2: $E_2 = 0.30$

- q is computed as:

    $(0.20 + 0.30)/2 = 0.25$

- the combined variance $q(1 - q)$ is:

$$0.25(1.0 - 0.25) = 0.1875$$

- the computation for P is:

$$P = \frac{\left| 0.20 - 0.30 \right|}{\sqrt{0.1875(1 / 100 + 1 / 100)}}$$

$$P \approx 1.633$$

As $P < 2$, the difference in model performance is not considered to be significant. We can increase our confidence in the result by switching the two test sets and repeating the experiment. This is especially important if a significant difference is seen with the initial test set selection. The average of the two values for P is then used for the significance test.

7.5   Attribute Evaluation

In Chapter 4 we showed you how attribute-value predictability and predictiveness scores help determine the significance of categorical attributes. We stated that a categorical attribute with at least one highly predictive value should be designated as an input attribute. An alternative measure of categorical attribute significance computes the product of attribute-value predictiveness and predictability. Attributes having at least one value showing a score larger than a user-specified threshold are chosen as input attributes. The advantage of this method is that an attribute is selected only when it supports a predictive value occurring with some frequency within a class. This measure eliminates the possibility that a nonpredictive attribute having a noisy value appearing in one or two instances will be selected.

In Chapter 4 you saw how ESX computes attribute significance scores for numerical data by employing class mean and domain standard deviation scores. In Chapter 5 we highlighted the importance of eliminating redundant attributes and outlined a genetic algorithm for selecting a best set of input attributes. In this section we broaden our discussion about numerical attribute elimination by demonstrating how to use attribute correlations and scatterplot diagrams created with MS Excel to uncover attribute redundancies. We also demonstrate how the classical hypothesis testing model can be applied to uncover numerical attributes of little predictive value.

In Chapter 5 you saw how supervised learning can be applied to estimate values for missing data items. In the end-of-chapter exercises we show you how the same technique can be applied to uncover redundancies between categorical as well as numeric data.

Locating Redundant Attributes with Excel

A **correlation coefficient** (designated by *r* for a sample or by ρ, the greek letter *rho*, for a population) measures the degree of linear association between two numeric attributes. Correlation coefficients take on values ranging between −1 and 1 inclusive. A **positive correlation** means two attributes increase or decrease in unison. Height and weight are two attributes that exhibit a high positive correlation. Two attributes have a **negative correlation** if as one attribute increases, the other decreases. Age and running speed display a high negative correlation. If *r* is near zero, the two attributes are not linearly correlated. Caution must be exercised in making deductions from correlational evidence. Although a marked correlation between two variables implies that they are related, the relationship may or may not be of a causal nature.

Computing Correlation Coefficients

If two candidate input attributes are highly correlated in a positive or a negative direction, only one of the attributes should be selected for data mining. The attribute with the larger significance score (see the second part of Section 7.5) is the attribute of choice. We can use MS Excel to compute correlation coefficients for numeric attributes. Let's work through an example using the mixed form of the cardiology patient database (CardiologyCategorical.xls).

Computing Attribute Correlations with MS Excel

We will use Excel's *CORREL* function to calculate the degree of correlation between *cholesterol level* and *blood pressure.* The procedure is as follows:

1. Open MS Excel and load the CardiologyCategorical.xls database file.

2. Mouse to any blank cell (cell O1 for example). Once step 3 has been completed, the correlation value will appear in the chosen cell.

3. Place your cursor in the Excel formula bar and type: =CORREL(D4:D306,E4:E306). As the first valid data point is in the fourth row, we start with D4 rather than D1.

4. Read the correlation coefficient in the cell selected in step 2.

The cell should display the value *0.123174.* This value is close to zero, which indicates little correlation between the values of the two attributes.

Making Scatterplot Diagrams

A correlation coefficient only measures the degree of linear relationship between two variables. Two attributes having a low *r* value may still have a **curvilinear** (curved line) relationship. If we suspect a relationship between two attributes lacking a linear correlation, we can view a **scatterplot diagram** to determine if two numeric attributes are related in a curvilinear fashion. A scatterplot diagram offers a two-dimensional plot of corresponding pairs of attribute values. The scatterplot will also show any linear relationship between two attributes.

Figure 7.4 displays a scatterplot diagram for two attributes having a perfect positive correlation. Figure 7.5 illustrates a perfect negative correlation. Figure 7.6 shows a scatterplot diagram of two attributes having no linear correlation. However, as the figure clearly illustrates, the attributes support a curvilinear relationship.

Figure 7.4 ● **A perfect positive correlation (r = 1)**

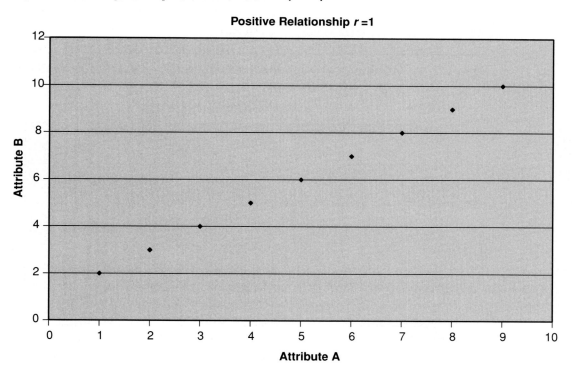

Figure 7.5   ●   **A perfect negative correlation (r = −1)**

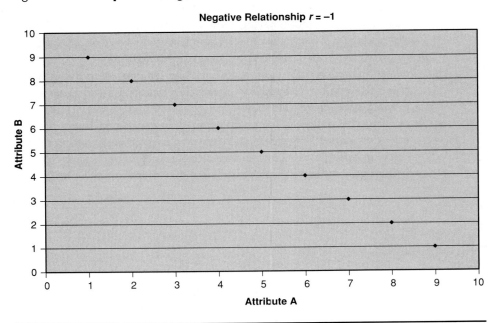

Figure 7.6   ●   **Attributes with no linear correlation (r = 0) but a substantial curvilinear relationship**

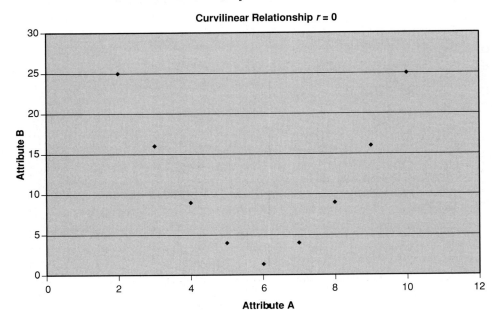

Creating a Scatterplot Diagram with MS Excel

Let's create a scatterplot diagram with MS Excel for the values *cholesterol level* and *blood pressure*. The procedure is as follows:

1. Open MS Excel and load the CardiologyCategorical.xls database file.

2. Mouse to the MS Excel menu bar. Locate and left-click on *Insert*.

3. Mouse down the menu bar and left-click on *Chart*.

4. Find chart type, left-click on *XY(Scatter)*, then left-click on *Next*.

5. In the box labeled *Data Range* type: *=D4:D103,E4:E103*.
   This will give you a scatterplot diagram of the two attributes for the first 100 data instances. Make sure the *Columns* radio button is highlighted, then click on *Next*.

6. Give the chart a title. Label the *x*-axis with *Blood Pressure* and the *y*-axis with *Cholesterol*. Left-click on *Next*.

7. Save the chart in a new sheet or as an object in the current sheet and click *Finish*.

Figure 7.7 shows the resultant scatterplot diagram. Based on the previously computed correlation value of 0.123174 and the scatterplot diagram, we conclude the two attributes are not related.

Figure 7.7 • **A scatterplot diagram relating blood pressure and cholesterol**

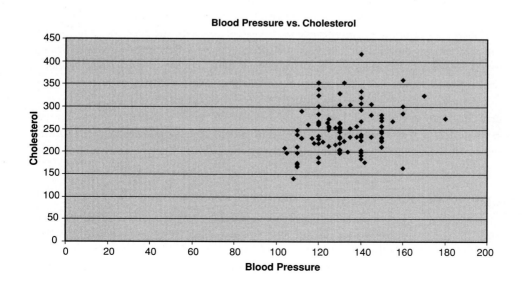

Hypothesis Testing for Numerical Attribute Significance

We can use the classical hypothesis testing model to determine numerical attribute significance through the following technique:

1. Given
   - Numerical attribute A whose significance is to be determined
   - n classes C_1, C_2, ..., C_n with corresponding means $\overline{X}_1, \overline{X}_2, ..., \overline{X}_n$ for Attribute A
2. For each pair of classes C_i and C_j, compute

$$P_{ij} = \frac{\left| \overline{X}_i - \overline{X}_j \right|}{\sqrt{(v_i / n_i + v_j / n_j)}} \qquad (7.6)$$

   where

   $\overline{X}_i$ is the class i mean and $\overline{X}_j$ is the class j mean for attribute A

   v_i is the class i variance and v_j is the class j variance for attribute A

   n_i is the number of instances in C_i and n_j is the number of instances in C_j

3. Compare. If any one of the values for P_{ij} is $>= 2$, the attribute is labeled as significant.

Notice that the test states that if *any* pair of class comparisons shows a significant difference, the attribute should be considered significant to the classification.

To illustrate the technique, we applied the hypothesis test for attribute significance to the numerical attributes within the mixed form of the cardiology patient dataset. Table 7.2 displays the computed values of P_{ij} for each numerical attribute. The table also shows corresponding significance scores calculated with the ESX attribute significance heuristic. Recall that the ESX heuristic considers attributes with significance scores less than 0.25 as being of little predictive value. The hypothesis testing model as well as the ESX heuristic show all attributes except *cholesterol* to be significant.

To summarize, when several numerical attributes appear in the data, it is best to first eliminate attributes that do not significantly affect the performance of a learner model. After this, the remaining attributes should be tested for correlational relationships and removed as appropriate.

7.6   Unsupervised Evaluation Techniques

Supervised learning and unsupervised clustering complement one another in that each approach can be applied to evaluate the opposite strategy. In this section we review both possibilities and offer additional evaluation methods for unsupervised clustering.

Table 7.2 • **Cardiology Patient Data: Numerical Attribute Significance**

	Class Sick	Class Healthy	ESX Attribute Significance	Hypothesis Test for Significance
Age (Mean)	56.50	52.50	0.45	4.08
(sd)	7.96	9.55		
BP (Mean)	134.40	129.30	0.29	2.51
(sd)	18.73	16.17		
Chol (Mean)	251.09	242.23	0.17	1.50
(sd)	49.46	53.55		
MHR (Mean)	139.10	158.47	0.85	7.96
(sd)	22.60	19.17		
Peak (Mean)	1.59	0.58	0.86	8.00
(sd)	1.30	0.78		

Unsupervised Clustering for Supervised Evaluation

When unsupervised clustering is adopted for supervised evaluation, the data instances selected for supervised training are presented to an unsupervised clustering technique with the output attribute flagged as display-only. If the instances cluster into the predefined classes contained in the training data, a supervised learner model built with the training data is likely to perform well. If the instances do not cluster into their known classes, a supervised model constructed with the training data is apt to perform poorly. In Section 5.10 you saw how ESX was used to apply this method to the credit card screening dataset.

Although this approach is straightforward, depending on the clustering technique it may be several iterations before an evaluation can be made. For example, suppose we decide to utilize the K-Means algorithm for the evaluation. The clusters formed by an application of the K-Means algorithm are highly affected by the initial selection of cluster means. For a single iteration, the algorithm is likely to experience a less-than-optimal convergence. With a nonoptimal convergence, a single cluster could contain a mixture of instances from several classes. This would in turn give us a false impression about the efficacy of the domain for supervised learning. Likewise, if ESX is the unsupervised technique, several iterations may be required just to obtain a best choice for parameter settings.

As the unsupervised evaluation is based solely on the training data, a quality clustering is no guarantee of acceptable performance on test set instances. For this reason, the technique complements other evaluation methods and is most valuable for identifying a rationale for supervised model failure. As a general rule, we see an inverse relationship between the value of this approach and the total number of predefined classes contained in the training data.

Supervised Evaluation for Unsupervised Clustering

In Chapter 2 we showed you how supervised learning can help explain and evaluate the results of an unsupervised clustering. This method is particularly appealing because it is independent of the technique used for the unsupervised clustering. Let's review the procedure:

1. Designate each formed cluster as a class.

2. Build a supervised learner model by choosing a random sampling of instances from each class.

3. Test the supervised learner model with the remaining instances.

As many unsupervised techniques lack an explanation facility, the supervised classification helps explain and analyze the formed clusters. A slight variation of this technique is to build the supervised model with the first n prototype instances from each cluster. Following this procedure allows us to observe model performance from the perspective of the instances that best define each cluster.

Additional Methods for Evaluating an Unsupervised Clustering

Unsupervised evaluation is often a two-step process. A first evaluation is internal and involves repeating the clustering process until we are satisfied that any user-defined parameters hold optimal values.

The second evaluation is external and independent of the model creating the clusters. The following is a short list of several additional external evaluation methods.

1. *Use a supervised learning approach as described in the previous section, but designate all instances as training data.*
   This variation is appropriate if a complete explanation about between-cluster differences is of primary importance. A supervised learner capable of generating production rules is particularly appealing for purposes of explanation.

2. *Apply an alternative technique's measure of cluster quality.*
   For example, suppose we use ESX to create a clustering of n classes for a set of numeric data. We then analyze the results by computing the mean and the sum of squared errors from the mean statistic for each cluster.

3. *Create your own measure of cluster quality.*
   Agglomerative clustering is an unsupervised technique that merges instances at each step of the clustering process until a terminating condition is satisfied. In Chapter 10 we describe agglomerative clustering along with two heuristic techniques to help determine when the merge process should terminate.

4. *Perform a between-cluster attribute-value comparison.*
   If between–cluster attribute values differ significantly, we conclude that between-cluster instance differences are also significant.

As you can well imagine, this list is by no means exhaustive. We encourage you to use this list as a starting point for developing your own tool kit for unsupervised evaluation.

7.7   Evaluating Supervised Models with Numeric Output

Thus far our discussion has been limited to models giving categorical output. However, we can use the techniques just described to help us evaluate models whose output is numerical. To apply the aforementioned techniques, we need a performance measure for models giving numerical output that is equivalent to classifier error rate. Several such measures have been defined, most of which are based on differences between actual and computed output. In each case, a smallest possible difference represents a best scenario. We will limit our discussion to three common methods for evaluating numeric output: the *mean squared error*, the *root mean squared error*, and the *mean absolute error*.

The **mean squared error** (*mse*) is the average squared difference between actual and computed output, as shown in Eq. 7.7.

$$mse = \frac{(a_1 - c_1)^2 + (a_2 - c_2)^2 + ... + (a_i - c_i) + ... + (a_n - c_n)^2}{n} \qquad (7.7)$$

where for the ith instance,

a_i = actual output value

c_i = computed output value

The **root mean squared error** (*rms*) is simply the square root of the mean squared error. By applying the square root, we reduce the dimensionality of the *mse* to that of the actual error computation. The backpropagation neural network model described in Chapter 9 uses *rms* as a measure of network convergence. Notice that for values less than 1.0, *rms* > *mse*.

The **mean absolute error** (*mae*) finds the average absolute difference between actual and computed output values. An advantage of *mae* is that it is less affected by large deviations between actual and computed output values. In addition, *mae* maintains the dimensionality of the error value. Equation 7.8 shows the formula.

$$mae = \frac{|a_1 - c_1| + |a_2 - c_2| + \dots + |a_n - c_n|}{n} \qquad (7.8)$$

In Chapter 2 we applied the iDA backpropagation neural network to the credit card promotion data where *life insurance promotion* was designated as the output attribute. Table 7.3 repeats the actual and computed output values for the experiment and displays the absolute and squared error output scores for each data instance. Although the values in the table are the result of applying training rather than test set data to the trained network, the example is useful for illustrative purposes. The computations for *mse, mae,* and *rms* using the table data are as follows:

$$mse = \frac{(0.0 - 0.024)^2 + (1.0 - 0.998)^2 + \dots + (1.0 - 0.999)^2}{15}$$

$$\approx \frac{0.1838}{15} \approx 0.0123$$

$$mae = \frac{|0.0 - 0.024| + |1.0 - 0.998| + \dots + |1.0 - 0.999|}{15}$$

$$\approx \frac{0.9060}{15} \approx 0.0604$$

To compute *rms* we simply take the square root of 0.0123. The computation gives an *rms* of 0.1107.

Finally, if your interests in numeric model testing lie beyond our discussion here, formulas and examples for computing test set confidence intervals as well as comparing supervised learner models having numeric output can be found in Appendix D.

7.8 Chapter Summary

A model's performance is influenced by several components, including training data, input attributes, learner technique, and learner parameter settings to name just a few. Each component that in some way dictates model performance is a candidate for evaluation.

Table 7.3 • **Absolute and Squared Error (Output Attribute = Life Insurance Promotion)**

Instance Number	Actual Output	Computed Output	Absolute Error	Squared Error
1	0.0	0.024	0.024	0.0005
2	1.0	0.998	0.002	0.0000
3	0.0	0.023	0.023	0.0005
4	1.0	0.986	0.014	0.0002
5	1.0	0.999	0.001	0.0000
6	0.0	0.050	0.050	0.0025
7	1.0	0.999	0.001	0.0000
8	0.0	0.262	0.262	0.0686
9	0.0	0.060	0.060	0.0036
10	1.0	0.997	0.003	0.0000
11	1.0	0.999	0.001	0.0000
12	1.0	0.776	0.224	0.0502
13	1.0	0.999	0.001	0.0000
14	0.0	0.023	0.023	0.0005
15	1.0	0.999	0.001	0.0000

Supervised model performance is most often evaluated with some measure of test set error. For models having categorical output, the measure is test set error rate computed as the ratio of test set errors to total test set instances. For models whose output is numeric, the error measure is usually the mean squared error, the root mean squared error, or the mean absolute error.

Although most data is not normally distributed, the distribution of sample means taken from a set of independent samples of the same size is distributed normally. We can take advantage of this fact by treating test set error rate as a sample mean and applying the properties of normal distributions to compute error rate confidence intervals. We can also apply classical hypothesis testing to compare test set error rate values for two or more supervised learner models. These statistical techniques offer us a means to associate measures of confidence with the output of our data mining sessions.

If two candidate numeric input attributes are related, only one of the attributes should be selected for data mining. Two numeric attributes may be related in a linear or curvilinear fashion or may not show a relationship. We can measure the degree of linear relationship between two attributes by computing a correlation coefficient. We can determine if two numeric attributes show a curvilinear or a linear relationship by examining their associated scatterplot diagram.

Unsupervised clustering techniques often support their own internal evaluation criteria. As many unsupervised techniques offer minimal explanation about the nature of the formed clusters, the evaluation of an unsupervised clustering should include an explanation about what has been discovered. Supervised learning can help explain and evaluate the results of an unsupervised clustering. Another effective evaluative procedure is to perform a between-cluster, attribute-value comparison to determine if the instances contained within the alternative clusters differ significantly.

7.9   Key Terms

Bootstrapping. Allowing instances to appear more than once in a training set.

Classifier error rate. The number of test set errors divided by the number of test set instances.

Control group. In an experiment, the group not receiving the treatment being measured. The control group is used as a benchmark for measuring change in the group receiving the experimental treatment.

Correlation coefficient. A correlation coefficient measures the degree of linear association between two numeric attributes. Correlation coefficients may take on values between −1 and 1 inclusive. A **positive correlation** means two attributes increase or decrease in unison. Two attributes show a **negative correlation** if as one attribute increases, the other decreases.

Cross validation. Partitioning a dataset into n fixed-size units. $n - 1$ units are used for training and the nth unit is used as a test set. This process is repeated until each of the fixed-size units has been used as test data. Model test set correctness is computed as the average accuracy realized from the n training-testing trials.

Curvilinear relationship. Two numeric variables that show a curved line (as compared to a linear) relationship to one another.

Experimental group. In a controlled experiment, the group receiving the treatment whose effect is being measured.

Mean. The average of a set of numerical values.

Mean absolute error. Given a set of instances each with a specified numeric output, the mean absolute error is the average of the sum of absolute differences between the classifier predicted output for each instance and the actual output.

Mean squared error. Given a set of instances each with a specified numeric output, the mean squared error is the average of the sum of squared differences between the classifier predicted output and actual output.

Normal distribution. A distribution of data is considered normal if a frequency graph of the data shows a bell-shaped or symmetrical characteristic.

Null hypothesis. The hypothesis of no significant difference.

Root mean squared error. The square root of the mean squared error.

Sample data. Individual data items drawn from a population of instances.

Scatterplot diagram. A two-dimensional graph plotting the relationship between two numeric attributes.

Standard deviation. The square root of the variance.

Standard error. A measure of dispersion computed by dividing a sample variance by the total number of sample instances and taking the square root of the result.

Stratification. Selecting data in a way so as to ensure that each class is properly represented in both the training and test set.

Type 1 error. Rejecting a null hypothesis when it is true.

Type 2 error. Accepting a null hypothesis when it is false.

Validation data. A set of data that is applied to optimize parameter settings for a supervised model or to help choose from one of several models built with the same training data.

Variance. The average squared deviation from the mean.

7.10   Exercises

Review Questions

1.   Differentiate between the following terms:

    a.   Validation data and test set data

    b.   Positive correlation and negative correlation

    c.   Control group and experimental group

    d.   Mean squared error and mean absolute error

    e.   Cross validation and bootstrapping

2.   For each of the following scenarios, state the type I and type II error. Also, decide whether a model that commits fewer type I or type II errors would be a best choice. Justify each answer.

    a.   A model for predicting if it will snow.

    b.   A model for selecting customers likely to purchase a television.

    c.   A model to decide likely telemarketing candidates.

    d.   A model to predict whether a person should have back surgery.

3. Section 7.5 describes a measure of categorical attribute significance computed by multiplying an attribute-value predictiveness and predictability score. What are the advantages and disadvantages of this measure of categorical attribute significance?

4. When a population is normally distributed, we can be more than 95% confident that any value chosen from the population will be within two standard deviations of the population mean. What is the confidence level that any value will fall within three standard deviations on either side of the population mean?

Data Mining Questions

1. Open Excel and load the Sonar.xls data file. Copy the data to a new Excel spreadsheet. Set the *class* attribute as an output attribute and flag attributes *output1* through *output4* as unused. Perform a supervised mining session with ESX. Set the *real-valued tolerance* at 0.75. Use the first 150 instances for training and the remaining 150 instances for testing. Record the test set error rate. Repeat the experiment but this time use 0.50 as the tolerance score. Use Equation 7.5 to determine if the test set error rate difference between the two models is significant.

2. Open Excel and load the CreditScreening.xls data file. Perform a supervised mining session with ESX using *class* as the output attribute. Use all data instances for training. Apply the hypothesis test for numerical attribute significance described in the second part of Section 7.5 to compute attribute significance scores for the two numeric attributes having the highest attribute significance score as determined by ESX. Does either value of P indicate that one or both attributes are significant predictors of class membership?

LAB 3. Load the CardiologyNumerical.xls data file into a new Excel spreadsheet. Use the *CORREL* function to determine the linear correlation between the attributes *#colored vessels* and *thal*. Create a scatterplot diagram to graphically depict the relationship between the two attributes. Assuming both attributes are significant in predicting class outcome, does the correlation value or the scatterplot diagram support eliminating one of the attributes?

4. Open Excel and load the DeerHunter.xls data file. Perform two supervised mining sessions with ESX as follows:

   a. Use the first 3000 instances for training and the remaining instances for testing. Say *yes* to the quick mine option. Record the confusion matrix and the test set error rate confidence interval.

LAB Denotes exercise appropriate for a laboratory setting.

b. Repeat part a, but this time say *no* to the quick mine option.

c. Compare the two test set accuracy values. What can you conclude?

LAB 5. We can apply supervised learning to locate redundancies between pairs of categorical or pairs of numeric attributes. We can also apply supervised learning to find redundancies between one categorical and one numeric attribute. Try the following experiment.

a. Load the CardiologyCategorical.xls file into a new Excel spreadsheet. Rename the spreadsheet so as to preserve the original file.

b. Specify *thal* as an output attribute and *#colored vessels* for input. Flag all other attributes, including the *class* attribute, as unused.

c. Use ESX together with the first 200 data instances to create a supervised learner model. When learning is complete and the test data has been classified, check the *RES MTX* sheet. What is the test set accuracy? What can you conclude?

d. Repeat the experiment with *maximum heart rate* as the sole input attribute and *chest pain type* as the output attribute. What can you conclude?

e. Outline a general procedure for applying supervised learning to locate redundant attributes. Explain the advantages and disadvantages of your approach.

PART **III**

Advanced Data Mining Techniques

Chapter 8

Neural Networks

Chapter Objectives

- ▶ Understand how feed-forward networks are used to solve estimation problems.

- ▶ Know how input and output data conversions are performed for neural networks.

- ▶ Understand how feed-forward neural networks learn through backpropagation.

- ▶ Know how genetic learning is applied to train feed-forward neural networks.

- ▶ Know how self-organizing neural networks perform unsupervised clustering.

- ▶ List the strengths and weaknesses of neural networks.

Neural networks continue to grow in popularity within the business, scientific, and academic worlds. This is because neural networks have a proven track record in predicting numeric or continuous outcomes. An excellent overview of neural network applications is given in Widrow, Rumelhart, and Lehr (1994).

Although several neural network architectures exist, we limit our discussion to two of the more popular structures. For supervised classification, we examine feed-forward neural networks trained with backpropagation or genetic learning. For unsupervised clustering, we discuss Kohonen self-organizing maps.

Section 8.1 introduces you to some of the basic concepts and terminology for neural networks. Neural networks require numeric input values ranging between 0 and 1 inclusive. As this can be a problem for some applications, we discuss neural network input and output issues in detail. In Section 8.2 we offer a conceptual overview of how supervised and unsupervised neural networks are trained. Neural networks have been criticized for their inability to explain their output. Section 8.3 looks at some of the techniques that have been developed for neural network explanation. Section 8.4 offers a list of general strengths and weaknesses found with all neural networks. Section 8.5 presents detailed examples of how backpropagation and self-organizing neural networks are trained. If your interests do not lie in a precise understanding of how neural networks learn, you may want to skip Section 8.5.

8.1   Feed-Forward Neural Networks

Neural networks offer a mathematical model that attempts to mimic the human brain. Knowledge is often represented as a layered set of interconnected processors. These processor nodes are frequently referred to as **neurodes** so as to indicate a relationship with the neurons of the brain. Each node has a weighted connection to several other nodes in adjacent layers. Individual nodes take the input received from connected nodes and use the weights together with a simple function to compute output values.

Neural network learning can be supervised or unsupervised. Learning is accomplished by modifying network connection weights while a set of input instances is repeatedly passed through the network. Once trained, an unknown instance passing through the network is classified according to the value(s) seen at the output layer.

Figure 8.1 shows a fully connected **feed-forward** neural network structure together with a single input instance [1.0,0.4,0.7]. Arrows indicate the direction of flow for each new instance as it passes through the network. The network is **fully connected** because nodes at one layer are connected to all nodes in the next layer.

The number of input attributes found within individual instances determines the number of input layer nodes. The user specifies the number of hidden layers as well as the number of nodes within a specific hidden layer. Determining a best choice for

Figure 8.1 • **A fully connected feed-forward neural network**

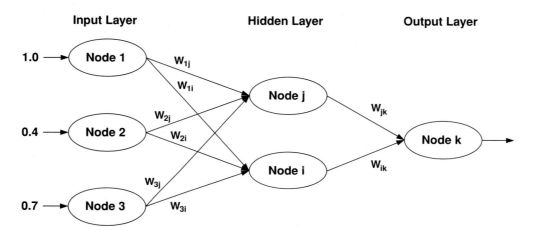

these values is a matter of experimentation. In practice, the total number of hidden layers is usually restricted to two. Depending on the application, the output layer of the neural network may contain one or several nodes.

Neural Network Input Format

The input to individual neural network nodes must be numeric and fall in the closed interval range [0,1]. Because of this, we need a way to numerically represent categorical data. We also require a conversion method for numerical data falling outside the [0,1] range.

There are several choices for categorical data conversion. A straightforward technique divides the interval range into equal-size units. To illustrate, consider the attribute *color* with possible values of red, green, blue, and yellow. Using this method, we might make the assignments: red = 0.00, green = 0.33, blue = 0.67, and yellow = 1.00. Although this technique can be used, it has an obvious pitfall. The modification incorporates a measure of distance not seen prior to the conversion. This is shown in our example in that the distance between red and green is less than the distance between red and yellow. Therefore it appears as though the color red is more similar to green than it is to yellow.

A second technique for categorical to numerical conversion requires the use of additional input nodes. Once again, consider the attribute *color* with the four values assigned as in the previous example. By adding an additional input node for *color*, we can represent the four colors as follows: red = [0,0], green = [0,1], blue = [1,0], and yellow

= [1,1]. Using the two-input-node scheme, we eliminate the bias seen with the previous technique.

Now let's consider the conversion of numerical data to the required interval range. Suppose we have the values 100, 200, 300, and 400. An obvious conversion method is to divide all attribute values by the largest attribute value. For our example, dividing each number by 400 gives the converted values: 0.25, 0.5, 0.75, and 1.0. The problem with this method is that we cannot take advantage of the entire interval range unless we have at least some values close to zero. A slight modification of this technique offers the desired result, as shown in Eq. 8.1.

$$newValue = \frac{originalValue - minimumValue}{maximumValue - minimumValue} \tag{8.1}$$

where

$newValue$ is the computed value falling in the [0,1] interval range

$originalValue$ is the value to be converted

$minimumValue$ is the smallest possible value for the attribute

$maximumValue$ is the largest possible attribute value

Applying the formula to the values above gives us 0.0, 0.33, 0.66, and 1.0.

A special case exists when maximum values cannot be determined. One possible solution is to use an arbitrarily large value as a divisor. Once again, dividing by an arbitrary number leaves us with the possibility of not covering the entire interval range. Finally, highly skewed data may cause less than optimal results unless variations of these techniques are applied. A common approach with skewed data is to take the base 2 or base 10 logarithm of each value before applying one of the previous transformations.

Neural Network Output Format

The output nodes of a neural network represent continuous values in the [0,1] range. However, the output can be transformed to accommodate categorical class values. To illustrate, suppose we wish to train a neural network to recognize new credit card customers likely to take advantage of a special promotion. We design our network architecture with two output layer nodes, node 1 and node 2. During training, we indicate a correct output for customers that have taken advantage of previous promotions as *1* for the first output node and *0* for the second output node. A correct output for customers that traditionally do not take advantage of promotions is designated by a node 1, node 2 combination of *0* and *1,* respectively. Once trained, the neural network will recognize a node 1, node 2 output combination of 0.9, 0.2 as a new customer likely to take advantage of a promotion.

This method has certain disadvantages in that node output combinations such as 0.2, 0.3 have no clear classification. Various approaches have been proposed for this situation. One method suggests the association of certainty factors with node output values. A popular method uses a special test dataset to help with difficult to interpret output values. This method also allows us to build a neural network with a single output layer node even when the output is categorical. An example illustrates the method.

Suppose we decide on a single output node for the credit card customer example just discussed. We designate *1* as an ideal output for customers likely to take advantage of a special promotion and a *0* for customers likely to pass on the offer. Once we have trained the network we can be confident about classifying an output value of 0.8 as a customer likely to take advantage of the promotion. However, what do we do when the output value is 0.45? The special test dataset helps with our dilemma. Prior to applying the network to unknown instances, we present the test set to the trained network and record the output values for each test instance. We then apply the network to the unknown instances. When unknown instance x shows an uncertain output value v, we classify x with the category shown by the majority of test set instances clustering at or near v.

Finally, when we wish to use the computed output of a neural network for prediction, we have another problem. Let's assume a network has been trained to help us predict the future price of our favorite stock. As the output of the network gives a result between 0 and 1, we need a method to convert the output into an actual future stock price.

Suppose the actual output value is 0.35. To determine the future stock price, we need to undo the original [0,1] interval conversion. The process is simple. We multiply the training data range of the stock price by 0.35 and add the lowest price of the stock to this result. If the training data price range is $10.00 to $100.00, the computation is:

$$(90.00)(0.35) + \$10.00$$

This gives a predicted future stock price of $41.50. All commercial and some public domain neural network packages perform these numeric conversions to and from the [0,1] interval range. This still leaves us with the responsibility of making sure all initial input is numeric.

The Sigmoid Function

The purpose of each node within a feed-forward neural network is to accept input values and pass an output value to the next higher network layer. The nodes of the input layer pass input attribute values to the hidden layer unchanged. Therefore for the input instance shown in Figure 8.1, the output of node 1 is 1.0, the output of node 2 is 0.4, and the output of node 3 is 0.7.

Table 8.1 • **Initial Weight Values for the Neural Network Shown in Figure 8.1**

W_{1j}	W_{1i}	W_{2j}	W_{2i}	W_{3j}	W_{3i}	W_{jk}	W_{ik}
0.20	0.10	0.30	−0.10	−0.10	0.20	0.10	0.50

A hidden or output layer node n takes input from the connected nodes of the previous layer, combines the previous layer node values into a single value, and uses the new value as input to an evaluation function. The output of the evaluation function is a number in the closed interval [0,1]. This value represents the output of node n.

Let's look at an example. Table 8.1 shows sample weight values for the neural network of Figure 8.1. Consider node j. To compute the input to node j, we determine the sum total of the multiplication of each input weight by its corresponding input layer node value. That is:

Input to node j = (0.2)(1.0) + (0.3)(0.4) + (−0.1)(0.7) = 0.25

Therefore 0.25 represents the input value for node j's evaluation function.

The first criterion of an evaluation function is that the function must output values in the [0,1] interval range. A second criterion is that the function should output a value close to 1 when sufficiently excited. In this way, the function propagates activity within the network. The **sigmoid function** meets both criteria and is often used for node evaluation. The sigmoid function is computed as:

$$f(x) = \frac{1}{1 + e^{-x}} \qquad (8.2)$$

where

e is the base of natural logarithms approximated by 2.718282.

Figure 8.2 shows the graph of the sigmoid function. Notice values of x less than zero provide little output activation. For our example, $f(0.25)$ evaluates to 0.562, which represents the output of node j.

8.2 Neural Network Training: A Conceptual View

In this section we discuss two methods for training feed-forward networks and one technique for unsupervised neural net clustering. Our discussion is limited in that we do not detail how the algorithms work. For most readers, the discussion here is

Figure 8.2 • **The sigmoid function**

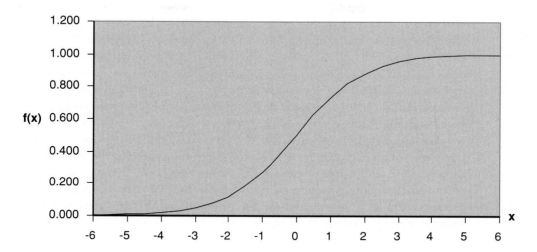

enough to satisfy basic curiosities about neural network learning. However, for the more technically inclined individual, Section 8.5 offers specific details about how neural networks learn.

Supervised Learning with Feed-Forward Networks

Supervised learning involves both training and testing. During the training phase, training instances are repeatedly passed through the network while individual weight values are modified. The purpose of changing the connection weights is to minimize training set error rate. Network training continues until a specific terminating condition is satisfied. The terminating condition can be convergence of the network to a minimum total error value, a specific time criterion, or a maximum number of iterations.

Training a Neural Network: Backpropagation Learning

Backpropagation learning is most often used to train feed-forward networks. For each training instance, backpropagation works by first feeding the instance through the network and computing the network output value. Recall that one output value is computed for each output layer node. To illustrate backpropagation learning, we use Figure 8.1 together with the input instance shown in the figure.

We previously determined that the computed output for the instance in Figure 8.1 is 0.582. Now suppose that the target output associated with the instance is 0.65. Obviously the absolute error between the computed and target value is 0.068. However, a problem is seen when we attempt to determine why the error occurred. That is, we do not know which of the network connection weights is to blame for the error. It is possible that changing just one of the weights will provide us with a better result the next time the instance passes through the network. It is more likely that the problem lies with some combination of two or more weight values. Still another possibility is that the error is to some degree the fault of every network connection associated with the output node.

The backpropagation learning algorithm assumes this last possibility. For our example, the output error at node k is propagated back through the network, and all eight of the associated network weights change value. The amount of change seen with each connection weight is computed with a formula that makes use of the output error at node k, individual node output values, and the derivative of the sigmoid function. The formula has a way of smoothing the actual error value so as not to cause an overcorrection for any one training instance.

Given enough iterations the backpropagation learning technique is guaranteed to converge. However, there is no guarantee that the convergence will be optimal. Therefore several applications of the algorithm may be necessary to achieve an acceptable result.

Training a Neural Network: Genetic Learning

Genetic learning is also a choice for training feed-forward neural nets. The general idea is straightforward. We first randomly initialize a population of elements where each element represents one possible set of network connection weights. Table 8.2 displays a set of plausible population elements for the network architecture seen in Figure 8.1. Once the element population is initialized, the neural network architecture is populated with the weights of the first element. The training data is passed through the created network once and the output error for each training instance is recorded. After all training instances have passed through the network, an average squared or absolute error is computed. The computed error is the fitness score for the population element. This process repeats for each element of the population.

As soon as the entire element population has been used to build and train a network structure, some combination of crossover, mutation, and selection is applied and the process repeats. Network convergence is seen when at least one element of the population builds a network that achieves an acceptable fitness score. When training is complete, the network is given the weights associated with the element having a best fitness score. As with backpropagation learning, this technique is guaranteed to converge. However, there is no guarantee that the convergence will be optimal. Once

Table 8.2 • **A Population of Weight Elements for the Network in Figure 8.1**

Population Element	W_{1j}	W_{1i}	W_{2j}	W_{2i}	W_{3j}	W_{3i}	W_{jk}	W_{ik}
1	0.20	0.10	0.30	−0.10	−0.10	0.20	0.10	0.50
2	0.14	0.38	0.19	0.25	−0.17	0.27	0.11	0.54
3	0.20	0.10	0.38	−0.16	−0.16	0.24	0.12	0.53
4	0.23	0.10	0.39	−0.18	−0.17	0.26	0.15	0.54

again, several applications of the genetic learning algorithm offers a best chance of achieving an acceptable result.

Unsupervised Clustering with Self-Organizing Maps

Teuvo Kohonen (1982) first formalized neural network unsupervised clustering in the early 1980s when he introduced Kohonen feature maps. His original work focused on mapping images and sounds. However, the technique has been effectively used for unsupervised clustering. Kohonen networks are also known as self-organizing maps (SOMs).

Kohonen networks support two layers. The input layer contains one node for each input attribute. Nodes of the input layer have a weighted connection to all nodes in the output layer. The output layer can take any form but is commonly organized as a two-dimensional grid. Figure 8.3 shows a simple Kohonen network with two input layer and nine output layer nodes.

During network learning, input instances are presented to each output layer node. When an instance is presented to the network, the output node whose weight connections most closely match the input instance *wins* the instance. The node is rewarded by having its weights changed to more closely match the instance. At first, neighbors to the winning node are also rewarded by having their weight connections modified to more closely match the attribute values of the current instance. However, after the instances have passed through the network several times, the size of the neighborhood decreases until finally only the winning node gets rewarded.

Each time the instances pass through the network, the output layer nodes keep track of the number of instances they win. The output nodes winning the most instances during the last pass of the data through the network are saved. The number of output layer nodes saved corresponds to the number of clusters believed to be in the data. Finally, those training instances classified with deleted nodes are once again presented to the network and classified with one of the saved nodes. The nodes, together

Figure 8.3   •   **A 3 × 3 Kohonen network with two input layer nodes**

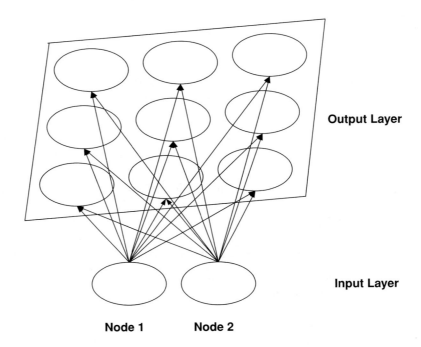

Output Layer

Input Layer

Node 1   Node 2

with their associated training set instances, characterize the clusters in the dataset. Alternatively, test data may be applied, and the clusters formed by these data are then analyzed to help determine the meaning of what has been found.

8.3   Neural Network Explanation

A major disadvantage seen with the neural network architecture is a lack of understanding about what has been learned. One possibility for neural network explanation is to transform a network architecture into a set of rules. Algorithms designed to extract rules from a neural network typically involve removing weighted links that minimally affect classification correctness. Unfortunately, rule extraction methods have met with limited success.

Sensitivity analysis is a technique that has been successfully applied to gain insight into the effect individual attributes have on neural network output. There are several variations to the approach. The general process consists of the following steps:

1. Divide the data into a training set and a test dataset.

2. Train the network with the training data.

3. Use the test set data to create a new instance I. Each attribute value for I is the average of all attribute values within the test data.

4. For each attribute:

   a. Vary the attribute value within instance I and present the modification of I to the network for classification.

   b. Determine the effect the variations have on the output of the neural network.

   c. The relative importance of each attribute is measured by the effect of attribute variations on network output.

A sensitivity analysis allows us to determine a rank ordering for the relative importance of individual attributes. However, the approach does not offer an explicit set of rules to help us understand more about what has been learned.

One method that has merit as a generalized explanation tool for unsupervised clustering is the **average member technique.** With this method, the average or most typical member of each class is computed by finding the average value for each class attribute. A more informative alternative is to apply the method described in Chapter 2 where supervised learning is employed to interpret the results of an unsupervised clustering. Here is the procedure as it applies to unsupervised neural network learning:

1. Perform any data transformations necessary to prepare the data for the unsupervised clustering.

2. Present the data to the unsupervised network model.

3. Call each cluster created by the neural network a class and assign each cluster an arbitrary class name.

4. Use the newly formed classes as training instances for a supervised classification model containing a rule generator.

5. Examine the generated rules to determine the nature of the concept classes formed by the clustering algorithm.

This method holds an advantage over the average member technique in that we are offered a generalization about differences as well as similarities of the formed clusters. In addition, rules can be generated to describe each cluster in detail. In Chapter 9 we use the iDA neural network software to apply this technique to the deer hunter dataset.

8.4   General Considerations

The process of building a neural network is both an art and a science. A reasonable approach is to conduct several experiments while varying attribute selections and learning parameters. The following is a partial list of choices that affect the performance of a neural network model:

- What input attributes will be used to build the network?

- How will the network output be represented?

- How many hidden layers should the network contain?

- How many nodes should there be in each hidden layer?

- What condition will terminate network training?

There are no right answers to these questions. However, we can use the experimental process to help us achieve desired results. In Chapter 9 you will learn how to better answer these questions by experimenting with your iDA neural network software. Here we provide a list of strengths and weaknesses for the neural network approach to knowledge discovery.

Strengths

- Neural networks work well with datasets containing large amounts of noisy input data. Neural network evaluation functions such as the sigmoid function naturally smooth input data variations caused by outliers and random error.

- Neural networks can process and predict numeric as well as categorical outcome. However, categorical data conversions can be tricky.

- Neural networks can be used for applications that require a time element to be included in the data (see Chapter 11).

- Neural networks have performed consistently well in several domains.

- Neural networks can be used for both supervised learning and unsupervised clustering.

Weaknesses

- Probably the biggest criticism of neural networks is that they lack the ability to explain their behavior.

- Neural network learning algorithms are not guaranteed to converge to an optimal solution. With most types of neural networks, this problem can be dealt with by manipulating various learning parameters.

- Neural networks can easily be overtrained to the point of working well on the training data but poorly on test data. This problem can be monitored by consistently measuring test set performance.

8.5   Neural Network Training: A Detailed View

Here we provide detailed examples of how two popular neural network architectures modify their weighted connections during training. In the first section we provide a partial example of backpropagation learning and state a general form of the backpropagation learning algorithm. In the second section we show you how Kohonen self-organizing maps are used for unsupervised clustering.

The Backpropagation Algorithm: An Example

Backpropagation is the training method most often used with feed-forward networks. Backpropagation works by making modifications in weight values starting at the output layer and then moving backward through the hidden layers. The process is best understood with an example. We will follow one pass of the backpropagation algorithm using the neural network of Figure 8.1, the input instance shown in the figure, and the initial weight values from Table 8.1.

Let's assume the target output for the specified input instance is 0.65. The first step is to feed the instance through the network and determine the computed output for node k. We apply the sigmoid function to compute all output values, as shown in the following calculations.

Input to node j = (0.2)(1.0) + (0.3)(0.4) + (−0.1)(0.7) = 0.250
   Output from node j = 0.562
Input to node i = (0.1)(1.0) + (−0.1)(0.4) + (0.2)(0.7) = 0.200
   Output from node i = 0.550
Input to node k = (0.1)(0.562) + (0.5)(0.550) = 0.331
   Output from node k = 0.582

Next we compute the observed error at the output layer of the network. The output layer error is computed as:

$$Error(k) = (T - O_k)[f'(x_k)] \tag{8.3}$$

where

T = The target output

O_k = The computed output at node k

$(T - O_k)$ = The actual output error

$f'(x_k)$ = The first-order derivative of the sigmoid function

x_k = the input to the sigmoid function at node k

Equation 8.3 shows that the actual output error is multiplied by the first-order derivative of the sigmoid function. The multiplication scales the output error, forcing stronger corrections at the point of rapid rise in the sigmoid curve. The derivative of the sigmoid function at x_k conveniently computes to $O_k(1 - O_k)$. Therefore:

$$Error(k) = (T - O_k)O_k(1 - O_k) \tag{8.4}$$

For our example, *Error(k)* is computed as:

$$Error(k) = (0.65 - 0.582)(0.582)(1 - 0.582) = 0.017$$

Computing the output errors for hidden layer nodes is a bit more intuitive. The general formula for the error at node j is:

$$Error(j) = \left(\sum_k Error(k)W_{jk}\right)f'(x_j) \tag{8.5}$$

where

$Error(k)$ = The computed output error at node k

W_{jk} = The weight associated with the link between node j and output node k

$f'(x_j)$ = The first-order derivative of the sigmoid function

x_j = The input to the sigmoid function at node j. As in Eq. 8.3, $f'(x_j)$ evaluates to $O_j(1 - O_j)$

Notice that the computed error is summed across all output nodes. For our example, we have a single output node. Therefore:

$$Error(j) = (0.017)(0.1)(0.562)(1 - 0.562) = 0.00042$$

We leave the computation of *Error(i)* as an exercise.

The final step in the backpropagation process is to update the weights associated with the individual node connections. Weight adjustments are made using the **delta rule** developed by Widrow and Hoff (Widrow and Lehr, 1995). The objective of the delta rule is to minimize the sum of the squared errors, where error is defined as the distance between computed and actual output. We will give the weight adjustment formulas and illustrate the process with our example. The formulas are as follows:

$$w_{jk}(new) = w_{jk}\,(current) + \Delta w_{jk} \tag{8.6}$$

where Δw_{jk} is the value added to the current weight value.

Finally, Δw_{jk} is computed as:

$$\Delta w_{jk} = (r)[Error(k)](O_j) \tag{8.7}$$

where

r = The learning rate parameter with $1 > r > 0$

$Error(k)$ = The computed error at node k

O_j = The output of node j

Here are the parameter adjustments for our example with $r = 0.5$.

- $\Delta w_{jk} = (0.5)(0.017)(0.562) = 0.0048$
  The updated value for $w_{jk} = 0.1 + 0.0048 = 0.1048$
- $\Delta w_{1j} = (0.5)(0.00042)(1.0) = 0.0002$
  The updated value for $w_{1j} = 0.2 + 0.0002 = 0.2002$
- $\Delta w_{2j} = (0.5)(0.00042)(0.4) = 0.000084$
  The updated value for $w_{2j} = 0.3 + 0.000084 = 0.300084$
- $\Delta w_{3j} = (0.5)(0.00042)(0.7) = 0.000147$
  The updated value for $w_{3j} = -0.1 + 0.000147 = -0.099853$

We leave adjustments for the links associated with node i as an exercise. Now that we have seen how backpropagation works, we state the general backpropagation learning algorithm.

1. Initialize the network.
    a. Create the network topology by choosing the number of nodes for the input, hidden, and output layers.
    b. Initialize weights for all node connections to arbitrary values between −1.0 and 1.0.

    c. Choose a value between 0 and 1.0 for the learning parameter.

    d. Choose a terminating condition.

2. For all training set instances:

    a. Feed the training instance through the network.

    b. Determine the output error.

    c. Update the network weights using the previously described method.

3. If the terminating condition has not been met, repeat step 2.

4. Test the accuracy of the network on a test dataset. If the accuracy is less than optimal, change one or more parameters of the network topology and start over.

The terminating condition can be given as a total number of passes (also called **epochs**) of the training data through the network. Alternatively, termination can depend on the degree to which learning has taken place within the network. A generalized form of the *root mean squared error* introduced in Chapter 2 is often used as a standard measure of network learning. The general formula to calculate *rms* is given as the square root of the following value.

$$\frac{\sum_{n}\sum_{i}(T_{in} - O_{in})}{ni} \qquad (8.8)$$

where

n = the total number of training set instances

i = the total number of output nodes

T_{in} = the target output for the nth instance and the ith output node

O_{in} = the computed output for the nth instance and i^{th} output node

As you can see, the *rms* is simply the square root of the average of all instance output error values. A common criterion is to terminate backpropagation learning when the *rms* is less than 0.10. Variations of the just–stated approach exist. One common variation is to keep track of training data errors but wait to update network weight connections only after all training instances have passed through the network. Regardless of the methodology, several iterations of the process are often necessary for an acceptable result.

Kohonen Self-Organizing Maps: An Example

To see how unsupervised clustering is accomplished, we consider the input layer nodes and two of the output layer nodes for the Kohonen feature map shown in Figure 8.3. The situation is displayed in Figure 8.4.

Figure 8.4 • **Connections for two output layer nodes**

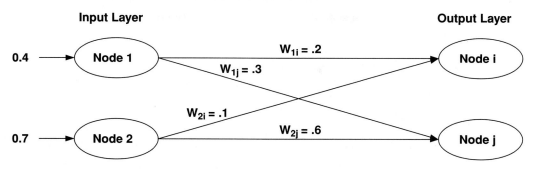

Recall that when an instance is presented to the network, a score for classifying the instance with each of the output layer nodes is computed. The score for classifying a new instance with output node j is given by:

$$\sqrt{\sum_i (n_i - w_{ij})^2} \qquad (8.9)$$

where n_i is the attribute value for the current instance at input node i, and w_{ij} is the weight associated with the ith input node and output node j. That is, the output node whose weight vectors most closely match the attribute values of the input instance is the winning node.

Let's use the formula to compute the score for the two output nodes shown in Figure 8.4 using the input instance [0.4, 0.7]. The score for inclusion with output node i is:

$$\sqrt{(0.4 - 0.2)^2 + (0.7 - 0.1)^2} = 0.632$$

Likewise, the score for inclusion with output node j is computed as:

$$\sqrt{(0.4 - 0.3)^2 + (0.7 - 0.6)^2} = 0.141$$

As you can see, node j is the winner as its weight vector values are more similar to the input values of the presented instance. As a result, the weight vectors associated with the output node are adjusted so as to reward the node for winning the instance. The following formula is used to adjust the values of the weight vectors:

$$w_{ij}(new) = w_{ij}(current) + \Delta w_{ij} \qquad (8.10)$$

where

$$\Delta w_{ij} = r(n_i - w_{ij})$$

$$0 < r <= 1$$

The winning output node has its weight vectors adjusted in the direction of the values contained within the new instance. For our example, with $r = 0.5$ the weight vectors of node j are adjusted as follows:

- $\Delta w_{1j} = (0.5)(0.4 - 0.3) = .05$

- $\Delta w_{2j} = (0.5)(0.7 - 0.6) = .05$

- $w_{1j}(new) = 0.3 + .05 = 0.35$

- $w_{2j}(new) = 0.6 + .05 = 0.65$

Output layer nodes within a specified neighborhood of the winning node also have their weights adjusted using the same formula. A square grid typically defines the neighborhood. The center of the grid contains the winning node. The size of the neighborhood as well as the learning rate r is specified when training begins. Both parameters are decreased linearly over the span of several iterations. Learning terminates after a preset number of iterations or after instance classifications do not vary from one iteration to the next.

To complete the clustering, the output nodes have their connection weights fixed and all but the n most populated output nodes are deleted. After this, the original training data or a previously unseen test dataset is fed through the output layer one last time. Finally, the clusters formed by the training or test data are analyzed in order to determine what has been discovered.

8.6   Chapter Summary

A neural network is a parallel computing system of several interconnected processor nodes. The input to individual network nodes is restricted to numeric values falling in the closed interval range [0,1]. Because of this, categorical data must be transformed prior to network training.

Developing a neural network involves first training the network to carry out the desired computations and then applying the trained network to solve new problems. During the learning phase, training data is used to modify the connection weights between pairs of nodes so as to obtain a best result for the output node(s).

The feed-forward neural network architecture is commonly used for supervised learning. Feed-forward neural networks contain a set of layered nodes and weighted connections between nodes in adjacent layers.

Feed-forward neural networks are often trained using a backpropagation learning scheme. Backpropagation learning works by making modifications in weight values starting at the output layer then moving backward through the hidden layers of the network. Genetic learning can also be applied to train feed-forward networks.

The self-organizing Kohonen neural network architecture is a popular model for unsupervised clustering. A self-organizing neural network learns by having several output nodes compete for the training instances. For each instance, the output node whose weight vectors most closely match the attribute values of the input instance is the winning node. As a result, the winning node has its associated input weights modified to more closely match the current training instance. When unsupervised learning is complete, output nodes winning the most instances are saved. After this, test data is applied and the clusters formed by the test set data are analyzed to help determine the meaning of what has been found.

A central issue surrounding neural networks is their inability to explain what has been learned. Despite this, neural networks have been successfully applied to solve problems in both the business and scientific world. Although we have discussed the most popular neural network models, several other architectures and learning rules have been developed. Jain, Mao, and Mohiuddin (1996) provide a good starting point for learning more about neural networks.

8.7   Key Terms

Average member technique. An unsupervised clustering neural network explanation technique where the most typical member of each cluster is computed by finding the average value for each class attribute.

Backpropagation learning. A training method used with many feed-forward networks that works by making modifications in weight values starting at the output layer then moving backward through the hidden layer.

Delta rule. A neural network learning rule designed to minimize the sum of squared errors between computed and target network output.

Epoch. One complete pass of the training data through a neural network.

Feed-forward neural network. A neural network architecture where all weights at one layer are directed toward nodes at the next network layer. Weights do not cycle back as inputs to previous layers.

Fully connected. A neural network structure where all nodes at one layer of the network are connected to all nodes in the next layer.

Kohonen network. A two-layer neural network used for unsupervised clustering.

Neural network. A parallel computing system consisting of several interconnected processors.

Neurode. A neural network processor node. Several neurodes are connected to form a complete neural network structure.

Sensitivity analysis. A neural network explanation technique that allows us to determine a rank ordering for the relative importance of individual attributes.

Sigmoid function. One of several commonly used neural network evaluation functions. The sigmoid function is continuous and outputs a value between 0 and 1.

8.8   Exercises

Review Questions

1. Draw the nodes and node connections for a fully connected feed-forward network that accepts three input values, has one hidden layer of five nodes, and an output layer containing four nodes.

2. Section 8.1 describes two methods for categorical data conversion. Explain how you would use each method to convert the categorical attribute *income range* with possible values 10–20K, 20–30K, 30–40K, 40–50K ... 90–100K to numeric equivalents. Which method is most appropriate?

3. The average member technique is sometimes used to explain the results of an unsupervised neural network clustering.

    a. List the advantages and disadvantages of this approach.

    b. Do you see similarities between this explanation technique and the K-Means algorithm?

Computational Questions

1. We have trained a neural network to predict the future price of our favorite stock. The one-year stock price range is a low of $20 and a high of $50.

    a. Use Eq. 8.1 to convert the current stock price of $40 to a value between 0 and 1.

    b. Suppose we apply the network model to predict a new price for some time period in the future. The neural network gives an output price value of 0.3. Convert this value to a predicted price we can understand.

2. Consider the feed-forward network in Figure 8.1 with the associated connection weights shown in Table 8.1. Apply the input instance [0.5,0.2,1.0] to the feed-forward neural network. Specifically,

    a. Compute the input to nodes i and j.

    b. Use the sigmoid function to compute the initial output of nodes i and j.

    c. Use the output values computed in part b to determine the input and output values for node k.

Chapter **9**

Building Neural Networks with iDA

Chapter Objectives

▶ Perform supervised neural network learning with iDA's backpropagation neural network.

▶ Perform unsupervised clustering with iDA's self-organizing neural network architecture.

▶ Employ the ESX supervised learner model to interpret the meaning of clusters formed by an unsupervised neural network data mining session.

In this chapter we show you how to use the neural network tools that are part of your iDA software package. The iDA neural network software allows you to create supervised classification models using backpropagation learning and unsupervised clustering models using a self-organizing map architecture. In Section 9.1 we examine iDA's feed-forward neural network with backpropagation learning. In Section 9.2 the emphasis is on unsupervised clustering with iDA's self-organizing map architecture. In Section 9.3 we illustrate how ESX can be employed to help explain the meaning of the clusters formed by an unsupervised neural network data mining session.

To run the iDA neural net software, you must have a Java interpreter installed on your computer. The CD that comes with your book contains a self-extracting executable for installing Java. As an alternative, you can obtain a free copy of Java by visiting the *www.javasoft.com* Web site. Instructions for installing Java are given in Appendix A.

9.1 A Four-Step Approach for Backpropagation Learning

In this section we work through two examples using a simple four-step procedure for performing supervised backpropagation learning with iDA. The steps of the procedure are as follows:

1. Prepare the data to be mined.

2. Define the network architecture.

3. Watch the network train.

4. Read and interpret summary results.

We begin with an interesting example that requires little data preparation on our part.

Example 1: Modeling the Exclusive-OR Function

Most of us are familiar with the basic logical operators. Common operators include *and, or, implication, negation,* and *exclusive or* (XOR). The definition of the XOR function is shown in Table 9.1. We can think of the XOR function as defining two classes. One class is denoted by the two instances with XOR function output equal to 1. The second class is given by the two instances with function output equal to 0.

Figure 9.1 offers a graphical interpretation of the output. The *x*-axis represents values for *input 1,* and the *y*-axis denotes values for *input 2.* The instances for the class with XOR equal to 1 are denoted in Figure 9.1 by an *A.* Likewise, instances for the class with XOR equal to 0 are denoted with a *B.* The XOR function is of particular interest because, unlike the other logical operators, the XOR function is not **linearly separable**.

Table 9.1 • **The Exclusive-OR Function**

Input 1	Input 2	XOR
1	1	0
0	1	1
1	0	1
0	0	0

This is seen in Figure 9.1, as we cannot draw a straight line to separate the instances in class A from those in class B.

The first neural networks, known as **perceptron networks,** consisted of an input layer and a single output layer. The XOR function causes trouble for these early networks because they are able to converge only when presented with problems having linearly separable solutions. The development of the backpropagation network architecture, which is able to model nonlinear problems, contributed to a renewed interest in neural network technology.

Figure 9.1 • **A graph of the XOR function**

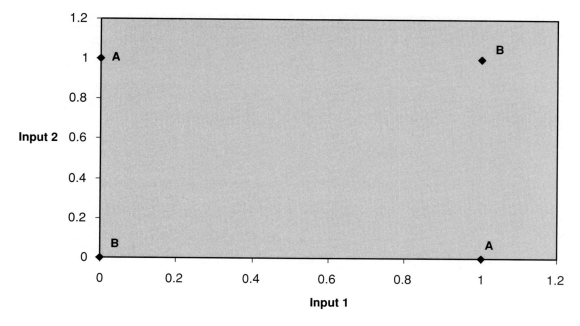

Applying the Four-Step Approach to the XOR Function

Let's build a backpropagation network to model the XOR function using the four-step procedure outlined at the beginning of the section. Fortunately, we can use our familiar Excel-based
interface to access the iDA backpropagation network building tool.

STEP 1: PREPARE THE DATA TO BE MINED

To produce the training data for the XOR function, create a new Excel spreadsheet identical to
the one shown in Figure 9.2. The first row shows the attribute names. The second row specifies
the attribute data types. Recall that all neural network input and output must be real-valued. The
third row indicates attribute usage. Attributes *input 1* and *input 2* are denoted as input attributes. The XOR function represents the output attribute.

STEP 2: DEFINE THE NETWORK ARCHITECTURE

Defining the network architecture requires us to make several choices. The description box titled *Parameter Settings for Backpropagation Learning* offers a brief description of each choice.
The following steps define the network architecture for the XOR function:

Figure 9.2 • **XOR training data**

	A	B	C	D	E	F	G
1	Input 1	Input 2	XOR				
2	R	R	R				
3	I	I	O				
4	1	1	0				
5	1	0	1				
6	0	1	1				
7	0	0	0				
8							
9							
10							

X Microsoft Excel - Figure 9.2 XOR Training Data.xls

File Edit View Insert Format Tools Data Quicksheet Window iDA Help

P28

Sheet1 / Sheet2 / Sheet3 /

Ready

1. Click on the iDA dropdown menu. The dialog box shown in Figure 9.3 will appear.

2. Choose the *Create a New Backpropagation Neural Network* option and click *OK*. A backpropagation options box similar to the one displayed in Figure 9.4 will appear.

3. Modify the parameters shown in the options box to match those shown in Figure 9.4. That is, change the value in the epochs options box to *10000* and set the convergence value to *0.001*.

4. Click *OK* to initiate network training.

Figure 9.3 • **Dialog box for supervised learning**

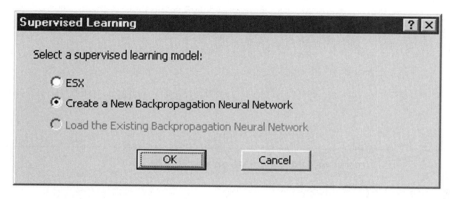

Figure 9.4 • **Training options for backpropagation learning**

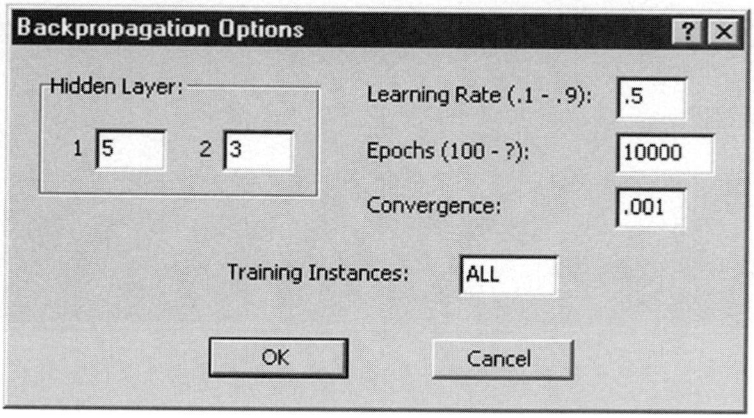

STEP 3: WATCH THE NETWORK TRAIN

Figure 9.5 shows the network execution window. As training proceeds, the window displays the total number of epochs and the current root mean squared error. The *rms* will usually decrease during network training. Several factors, including initial weight settings, the appropriateness of the chosen attributes, output attribute format, choice of training instances, number of epochs, and the learning rate, to name a few, determines a final value for *rms*.

When program execution is terminated, a message indicating that training and testing is complete will appear in the execution window. After this message appears, we can view the output of the neural network. Here's what to do:

1. If the execution window does not automatically close, left-click on the *X* in the upper-right corner of the execution window. This closes the window.

2. A box requesting you to click *OK* when training is complete appears. Click *OK* to display the output of the network.

The network output is shown in the Excel sheet titled *SHEET1 RES NN.* Figure 9.6 displays the output produced by our execution of the backpropagation network for the XOR problem.

Figure 9.5 ● **Neural network execution window**

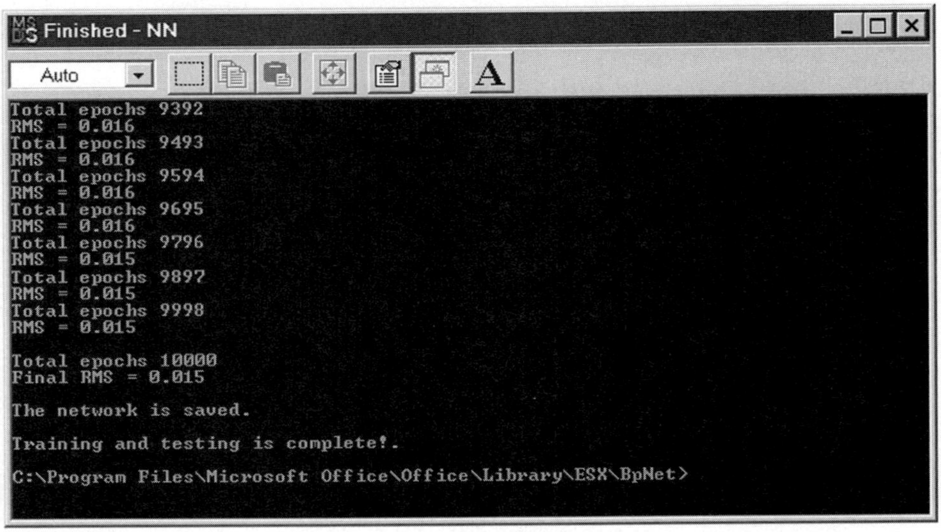

Figure 9.6 • **XOR output file for Experiment 1**

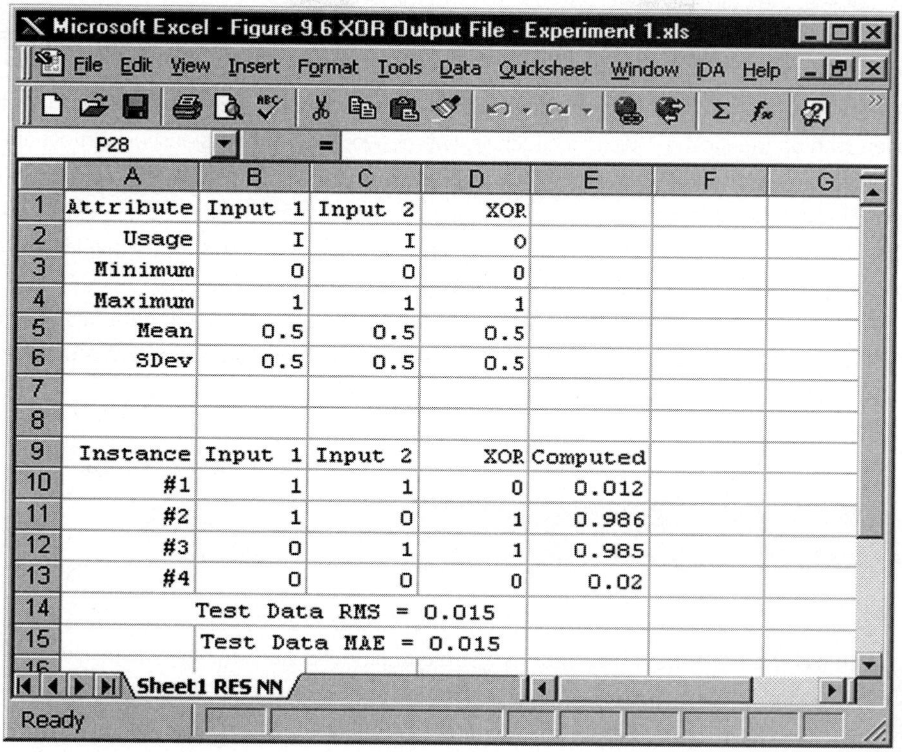

	A	B	C	D	E	F	G
1	Attribute	Input 1	Input 2	XOR			
2	Usage	I	I	O			
3	Minimum	0	0	0			
4	Maximum	1	1	1			
5	Mean	0.5	0.5	0.5			
6	SDev	0.5	0.5	0.5			
7							
8							
9	Instance	Input 1	Input 2	XOR	Computed		
10	#1	1	1	0	0.012		
11	#2	1	0	1	0.986		
12	#3	0	1	1	0.985		
13	#4	0	0	0	0.02		
14		Test Data RMS = 0.015					
15		Test Data MAE = 0.015					

STEP 4: READ AND INTERPRET SUMMARY RESULTS

The first six rows of your output sheet should be identical to the first six rows of the spreadsheet displayed in Figure 9.6. The first row gives the names of the attributes used to build the network. The second row specifies the usage for each attribute. The third and fourth rows offer minimum and maximum values for the individual attributes. The fifth and sixth rows show attribute mean and standard deviation scores for the training data.

The ninth row repeats the attribute names. The last column of the ninth row is titled *Computed*. Each row of this column contains the output value computed by the network for the corresponding instance. Beginning with the tenth row, the attribute values for each test set instance, together with the network-computed output, is specified. Row 10 tells us that the correct output for instance #1 is 0 and the computed output for instance #1 is 0.012. The final two output lines show the *rms* and *mae* for the test data. When all instances are specified for training, the training, data is also used to test the network.

The computed results shown in Figure 9.6 will be similar to the computed values seen with your execution of this experiment. The variation in output is due to the fact that the connection weights given to initialize the neural network are randomly generated values. Therefore even with an identical network architecture, two network training sessions will almost always show some variation in computed results. To see a more dramatic change in output values, let's modify the network architecture and repeat the experiment. Run the experiment a second time, but this time design the network architecture to have *two* nodes for hidden layer 1 and *zero* nodes for hidden layer 2. Leave the remaining parameters unchanged.

Our results for this experiment are displayed in Figure 9.7. Notice that the first instance shows a computed output of 0.142. This represents a relatively large error and is due in part

Parameter Settings for Backpropagation Learning

Hidden layers. An iDA network can have one or two hidden layers. We specify the number of hidden-layer nodes to be contained in each hidden layer.

Learning rate. The learning rate can range between .1 and .9. In general, lower learning rates will require more training iterations. A higher learning rate allows the network to converge more rapidly; however, the chances of a nonoptimal solution are greater.

Epochs. The number of epochs gives the total number of times the entire set of training data will pass through the network.

Convergence. The convergence setting allows us to choose a maximum root mean squared error for training termination. A reasonable setting for the convergence parameter is 0.10. The convergence parameter should be set at an arbitrarily low value if we wish to base training termination on the number of epochs.

Training instances. If the data file contains *n* instances and we specify *m* instances for training, the first *m* instances will be used to train the network and the remaining instances (*n* – *m*) will test the network. If *n* instances are specified for training, the training data will also be used to test the network.

Figure 9.7 • **XOR output file for Experiment 2**

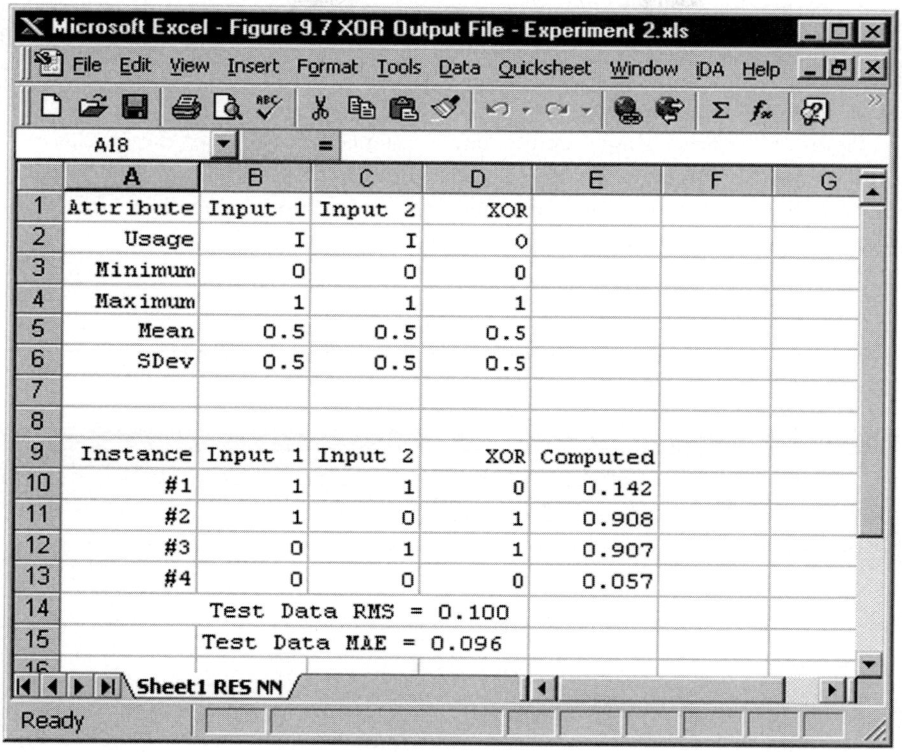

	A	B	C	D	E	F	G
1	Attribute	Input 1	Input 2	XOR			
2	Usage	I	I	O			
3	Minimum	0	0	0			
4	Maximum	1	1	1			
5	Mean	0.5	0.5	0.5			
6	SDev	0.5	0.5	0.5			
7							
8							
9	Instance	Input 1	Input 2	XOR	Computed		
10	#1	1	1	0	0.142		
11	#2	1	0	1	0.908		
12	#3	0	1	1	0.907		
13	#4	0	0	0	0.057		
14		Test Data RMS = 0.100					
15		Test Data MAE = 0.096					

to the fact that we used two rather than five hidden layer 1 nodes. Let's try one more experiment to see if increasing the number of epochs from 10,000 to 100,000 improves our results. Once again, model the network with *two* hidden layer 1 nodes and *zero* hidden layer 2 nodes. Use 100,000 rather than 10,000 epochs for training. Leave the remaining parameters unchanged.

The *rms* for our experiment was a much improved value of 0.027. Did your experiment show an improved *rms*? If not, run the experiment several times until you achieve a better result.

Example 2: The Satellite Image Dataset

Our next example uses the dataset first described in Chapter 5 that contains pixels from a digitized satellite image of a portion of the earth's surface. Recall that this dataset is listed in the iDA samples directory as Sonar.xls. An interesting aspect of this dataset is the fact that there are 15 output classes. We use an output layer consisting of 4 nodes to model the 15 classes.

Figure 9.8 shows a single representative instance from each of the 15 classes. The output sequence for each class has been arbitrarily chosen. Also, as each instance is from a different class, no two instances have the same output values. Let's use the four-step procedure defined earlier to experiment with the sonar dataset.

Figure 9.8   ●   **Satellite image data**

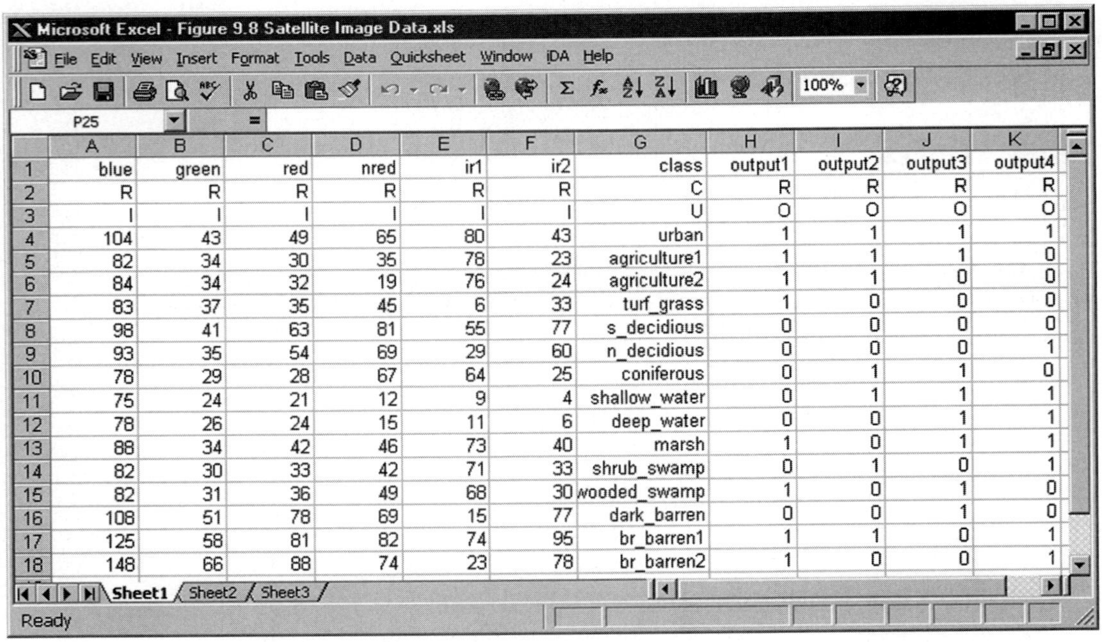

	A	B	C	D	E	F	G	H	I	J	K
	blue	green	red	nred	ir1	ir2	class	output1	output2	output3	output4
1	blue	green	red	nred	ir1	ir2	class	output1	output2	output3	output4
2	R	R	R	R	R	R	C	R	R	R	R
3	I	I	I	I	I	I	U	O	O	O	O
4	104	43	49	65	80	43	urban	1	1	1	1
5	82	34	30	35	78	23	agriculture1	1	1	1	0
6	84	34	32	19	76	24	agriculture2	1	1	0	0
7	83	37	35	45	6	33	turf_grass	1	0	0	0
8	98	41	63	81	55	77	s_decidious	0	0	0	0
9	93	35	54	69	29	60	n_decidious	0	0	0	1
10	78	29	28	67	64	25	coniferous	0	1	1	0
11	75	24	21	12	9	4	shallow_water	0	1	1	1
12	78	26	24	15	11	6	deep_water	0	0	1	1
13	88	34	42	46	73	40	marsh	1	0	1	1
14	82	30	33	42	71	33	shrub_swamp	0	1	0	1
15	82	31	36	49	68	30	wooded_swamp	1	0	1	0
16	108	51	78	69	15	77	dark_barren	0	0	1	0
17	125	58	81	82	74	95	br_barren1	1	1	0	1
18	148	66	88	74	23	78	br_barren2	1	0	0	1

Applying the Four-Step Approach to the Satellite Image Dataset

STEP 1: PREPARE THE DATA TO BE MINED

To begin the experiment, open Excel with the Sonar.xls spreadsheet file and copy the *Sheet1* data into a new spreadsheet. Check the attribute type and usage declarations to make sure they match the values shown in Figure 9.8. As the four output attributes are used to define the class structure, the *class* attribute should be declared as unused.

STEP 2: DEFINE THE NETWORK ARCHITECTURE

Figure 9.9 displays the settings for defining the network architecture for our experiment. The dataset contains 300 data instances with approximately 20 instances representing each class. The data is divided evenly with the first 150 instances having 10 instances from each class. For the experiment, we use 150 instances for training and 150 instances for testing. Notice we use a two-hidden-layer architecture with eight hidden layer 1 and three hidden layer 2 nodes. To run the experiment, fill in the parameter settings as shown in Figure 9.9 and click *OK* to begin network training.

Figure 9.9 • **Backpropagation learning parameters for the satellite image data**

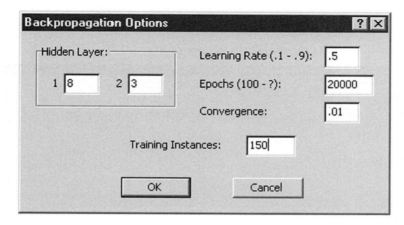

STEP 3: WATCH THE NETWORK TRAIN

As network training takes a few minutes, you have an opportunity to watch the *rms* value as it changes. Unless you get lucky, you will not see an *rms* of 0.1 or less. There are several reasons for this. A main reason is the fact that we have 15 classes with approximately 10 instances from each class for training. We are asking a lot to expect the network to converge to a reasonable value when we have so many classes and so few instances for training.

The final *rms* for our experiment was 0.270 for the training data and 0.294 for the test data. Do not be discouraged if you see a final *rms* of 0.30 or more. As an exercise, you may wish to run this experiment several times with varying parameter settings to obtain a best result.

STEP 4: READ AND INTERPRET SUMMARY RESULTS

Figure 9.10 offers the mean and standard deviation scores as well as minimum and maximum values for each attribute. The mean and standard deviation values for your experiment should be identical to the values seen in Figure 9.10. Figure 9.11 gives the test set classification of the first 24 instances. Figure 9.11 shows a column for the *class* attribute (column B). Because the *class* attribute was declared as unused, this column was not part of the network-generated output. However, we copied the *class* attribute column from the original spreadsheet to help us determine test set classification correctness.

To determine if a particular test set instance has been correctly classified, we examine the four output values and compare each output to the corresponding computed output. In Figure 9.11, *output1* corresponds with the computed output in column G, *output2* matches with the computed output in column H. Likewise, *output3* matches with column I and *output4* corresponds to column J.

Figure 9.10 • **Statistics for the satellite image data**

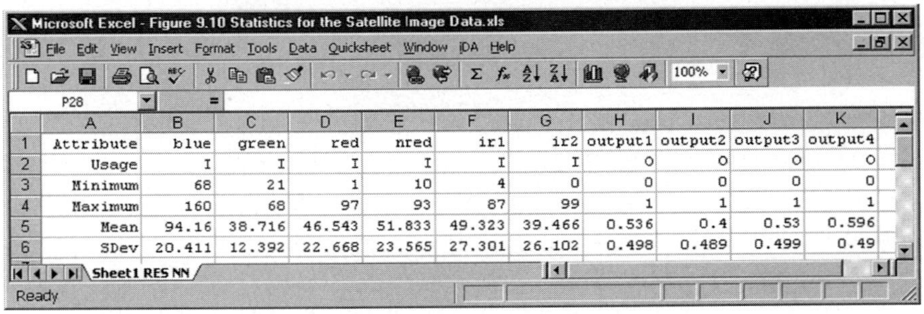

	A	B	C	D	E	F	G	H	I	J	K
1	Attribute	blue	green	red	nred	ir1	ir2	output1	output2	output3	output4
2	Usage	I	I	I	I	I	I	O	O	O	O
3	Minimum	68	21	1	10	4	0	0	0	0	0
4	Maximum	160	68	97	93	87	99	1	1	1	1
5	Mean	94.16	38.716	46.543	51.833	49.323	39.466	0.536	0.4	0.53	0.596
6	SDev	20.411	12.392	22.668	23.565	27.301	26.102	0.498	0.489	0.499	0.49

Figure 9.11 • **Satellite image data: Actual and computed output**

	A	B	C	D	E	F	G	H	I	J
1	Instance	Class	output1	output2	output3	output4	Computed	Computed	Computed	Computed
2	#1	br_barren2	1	0	0	1	0.981	0.016	0	0.992
3	#2	br_barren1	1	1	0	1	0.999	0.98	0	0.999
4	#3	br_barren1	1	1	0	1	0.999	0	0	0
5	#4	br_barren1	1	1	0	1	0.997	0.833	0	0.999
6	#5	br_barren1	1	1	0	1	0.998	0.985	0	0.999
7	#6	br_barren1	1	1	0	1	0.999	0.999	0	0.161
8	#7	br_barren1	1	1	0	1	0.999	0	0	0
9	#8	br_barren1	1	1	0	1	0.999	0.992	0	0.999
10	#9	br_barren1	1	1	0	1	0.999	0.999	0	0.993
11	#10	br_barren1	1	1	0	1	0.999	0.998	0	0.983
12	#11	br_barren1	1	1	0	1	0.999	0.999	0	0.994
13	#12	urban	1	1	1	1	0.999	0.988	0.999	0
14	#13	urban	1	1	1	1	0.999	0.996	0.995	0
15	#14	urban	1	1	1	1	0.999	0.998	0.985	0
16	#15	urban	1	1	1	1	0.999	0.997	0.993	0
17	#16	urban	1	1	1	1	0.999	0.997	0.995	0
18	#17	urban	1	1	1	1	0.999	0.997	0.995	0
19	#18	urban	1	1	1	1	0.999	0.997	0.995	0
20	#19	urban	1	1	1	1	0.999	0.997	0.994	0
21	#20	urban	1	1	1	1	0.999	0.997	0.992	0
22	#21	urban	1	1	1	1	0.999	0.997	0.995	0
23	#22	agriculture1	1	1	1	0	0.999	0.996	0.996	0
24	#23	agriculture1	1	1	1	0	0.999	0.996	0.995	0
25	#24	agriculture1	1	1	1	0	0.999	0.997	0.995	0

Test set instance #1 represents a correct classification because each corresponding computed output closely matches the actual output value. This is also the case for test set instance #2. However, test set instance #3 is an incorrect classification because *output2* has a value of 1 and a computed output of 0. Also, *output4* has a value of 1, whereas the computed output (column J) shows a value of 0.

As we continue to examine the output, we see that the instances through instance #11, excepting instance #7, are correctly classified. However, starting with instance #12 through instance #21 (the *urban* class), we see large discrepancies between actual and computed *output4* values. The instances of the *urban* class are partially responsible for the less than optimal *rms*. To improve these results, we may consider repeating the experiment with an increased value for the epochs parameter and/or a new network architecture.

Finally, we can use a trained neural network to classify instances whose output values are not known. To determine the classification of an unknown instance, simply include the instance as part of the test set data. Leave cells that would normally contain actual output values blank. In this way, we can use the neural network to compute output values for instances of unknown origin.

General Considerations

Building neural networks is both an art and a science. Because of this, determining a best set of parameter choices for network training usually involves a combination of creativity and rational reasoning. The novice often finds the process of constructing useful neural network models a bit tedious, as a great deal of experimental trial and error may be necessary. However, as with most things, time and patient effort are often rewarded with acceptable problem solutions.

Of special concern with backpropagation learning is the possibility of overtraining a network. When this happens, the network model does an excellent job of estimating output values for the training data but shows a poor performance when estimating output values for test set instances. This scenario is most readily observed when we obtain an acceptable *rms* for the training instances but an unacceptable *rms* for the test set data. One way to help overcome this problem is to retrain the network with fewer epochs. A second consideration is to make sure the training data are representative of the overall instance population. Finally, continued experimentation with the parameters defining a network architecture often leads to an acceptable result.

9.2   A Four-Step Approach for Neural Network Clustering

In this section we show you how to perform unsupervised clustering with your iDA neural net software. Fortunately, we can apply the same four-step procedure used for backpropagation learning to build unsupervised learner models.

An Example: The Deer Hunter Dataset

We employ the deer hunter dataset first described in Chapter 4 to illustrate the process of unsupervised network clustering with iDA. Recall that the deer hunter dataset contains a single output attribute named *yes* that indicates whether an individual hunter is willing to pay a higher total cost for their hunting trips. The added cost is variable and is given in the attribute column labeled *a*.

For our experiment, we will perform an unsupervised clustering by designating the attribute *yes* as display-only. We hypothesize that the instances having *yes* = *1* will form one well-defined cluster and the instances with *yes* = *2* will form a second cluster. If this is the case, we conclude that the input attributes are able to differentiate between the values of the output attribute. If the formed clusters do not group the instances in this way, we conclude that the input attributes are not useful for predicting output attribute values. Let's use the four-step process to see what happens.

Applying the Four-Step Approach to the Deer Hunter Dataset

STEP 1: PREPARE THE DATA TO BE MINED

Several attributes of the deer hunter dataset are listed as categorical. However, the actual values for all categorical attributes are numeric. Therefore we can simply change the designation of each categorical attribute we wish to use to real.

1. Open Excel and load the samples directory file titled DeerHunter.xls.

2. Copy and paste the deer hunter data into a new spreadsheet.

3. Change the type of any attributes designated as categorical to real.

4. Designate the usage of attribute *wtdeer* as unused (*U*) and attribute *yes* as display-only (*D*). Specify all other attributes for input.

5. Click on the iDA dropdown menu and select *Begin mining session*.

6. Highlight the *Kohonen neural network* option and click *OK* to display the options box for designing the structure of the network.

STEP 2: DEFINE THE NETWORK ARCHITECTURE

Figure 9.12 gives the options for creating the network architecture used with this experiment. The options box offers several choices, which are outlined in the description box titled *Parameter Settings for Unsupervised Network Clustering*. Figure 9.12 shows we have chosen a 3 × 3 output layer grid for the experiment. Therefore a total of nine initial clusters will be formed during network training. Because we specify two output clusters, once training is complete, all but the two most populated output layer nodes will be deleted.

Figure 9.12 also shows that we have chosen to use the entire dataset for network training. In this case, the final network clustering will include all data instances. However, if we select a subset of the total instance population for training, only the remaining instances (test set data) are used to form the final data clusters. In our case, the training data is employed to determine the network connection weights, and to establish the final output clustering.

Finally, notice the choice of 200 epochs for network training. Unlike the backpropagation model, which typically requires several thousand training iterations, the unsupervised model will

Figure 9.12   •   **Learning parameters for unsupervised clustering**

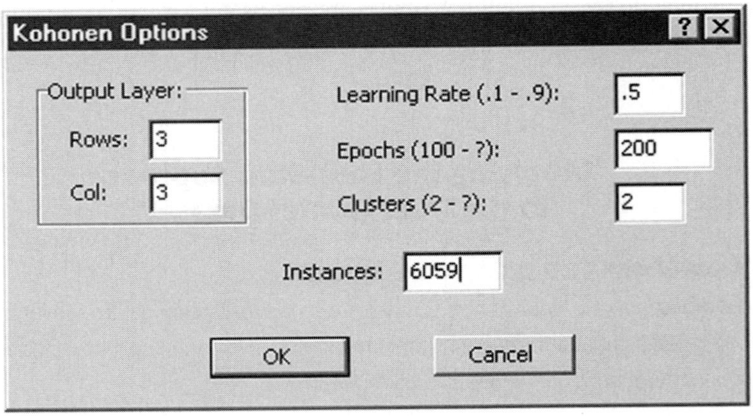

Parameter Settings for Unsupervised Network Clustering

Output rows and columns. The row and column parameters define the size of the output layer grid. Although not required, it is usually best to choose the same number of rows and columns.

Learning rate. The learning rate can range between .1 and .9. As with backpropagation, lower learning rates require more training iterations. A higher learning rate allows the network to converge more rapidly; however, higher learning rates increase the chances for a nonoptimal solution.

Epochs. Epochs represent the total number of times the entire set of training data will pass through the network structure.

Clusters. The value of the clusters parameter determines the total number of clusters created by the network. Suppose we specify *n* clusters. When training terminates, the algorithm sorts the output layer nodes from most to least populated. Only the *n* most populated output layer nodes are saved for network testing.

Instances. The instances parameter determines the total number of training instances. Once training is complete, network weight values become fixed and the test data is used to create a final clustering. If all data instances are specified for training, the training data are also used for testing the network. With unsupervised clustering, it is common practice to use the same data for network training and testing.

usually converge with a minimum number of training iterations. This is a positive aspect, because as the size of the output grid expands, the time for network training increases significantly.

To continue with the experiment, modify the parameter settings in your Kohonen options dialog box to match those seen in Figure 9.12 and click *OK* to initiate network training.

STEP 3: WATCH THE NETWORK TRAIN

Figure 9.13 shows the network execution window for the first few training iterations. As with backpropagation learning, the window displays the total number of epochs and the current root mean squared error. However, of more interest is the value given for **total delta.** This value represents the total absolute change in network connection weights for each pass of the training data through the network. That is, on the 49th training iteration, the total amount of absolute change in network connection weights was approximately 1935.163. During the 199th iteration, the change is shown as 0.0. In reality, at least some minimal accumulated change takes place during each pass of the training data through the network. However, the important point is that when the total change in network weights falls below a minimal value (such as 1.0), the network has converged. Although network convergence is assured, we cannot be certain that any given convergence is optimal. For this reason, it is best to experiment with several network architectures before choosing a final model to represent the data.

When training is complete, left-click on the *X* shown in the upper-right corner of the execution window. The window will close and a message box will appear. Click *OK* to display the sheet showing the output summary statistics.

Figure 9.13 ● **Network execution window**

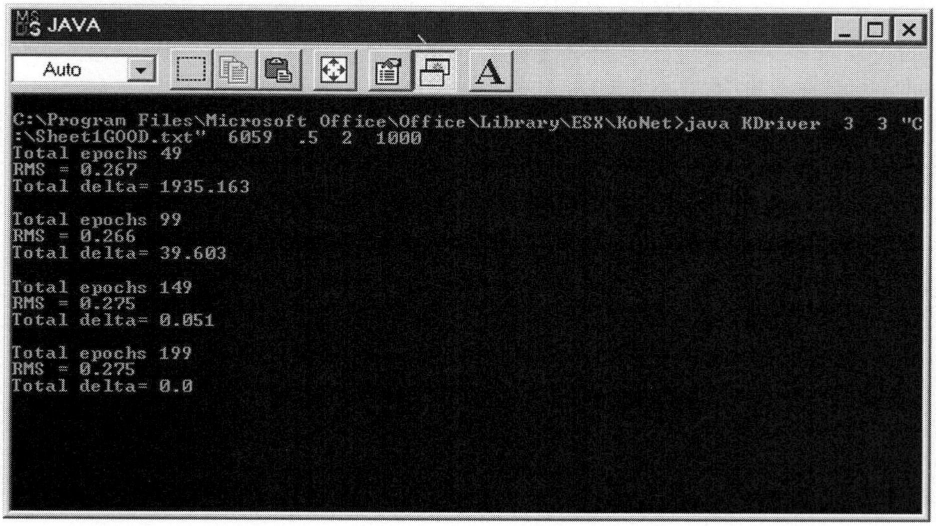

STEP 4: READ AND INTERPRET SUMMARY RESULTS

Figure 9.14 shows the sheet containing output summary statistics for our experiment. The name of the sheet with this information is titled *Sheet1 RES NN*. The first six rows of your output sheet should be identical to the sheet shown in Figure 9.14. The first two rows list the attribute names and their usage. The third and fourth rows show the minimum and maximum value for each attribute. The fifth and sixth rows give attribute mean and standard deviation scores.

The root mean squared error for the final clustering is given in the eighth row. The *rms* has a slightly different interpretation for unsupervised clustering as output attributes do not exist. *Rms* is determined by computing average squared differences between vector weights and instance attribute values. Although a lowest possible *rms* value is desired, a more important aspect is whether the *rms* converges toward a value or continues to vary during network training.

Notice the *rms* of 0.275 displayed in the eighth row of Figure 9.14 is identical to the *rms* shown in Figure 9.13. However, it is not unusual to see a larger error in the final output as the last clustering eliminates all but two of the most highly populated output layer nodes. Therefore each instance associated with an eliminated cluster must become part of a new cluster for which it may not be as well suited.

Figure 9.15 shows a partial listing of the original data together with an added column giving the cluster number for each instance. The output sheet containing this information is titled *Sheet1 RES NN DET.* The first row lists all attributes found within the dataset, the second row specifies attribute types, and the third row shows the usage of each attribute. Rows four and beyond list the data instances. The final column of each row gives a numerical value representing the cluster number for the associated instance. The cluster number tells us where each instance has been placed in the output grid during the final training iteration. Our experiment shows that all data instances have been classified with either output node 2 or output node 3. Although your output sheet will also show two output clusters, the actual cluster number designations will likely differ.

Figure 9.14 • **Deer hunter data: Unsupervised summary statistics**

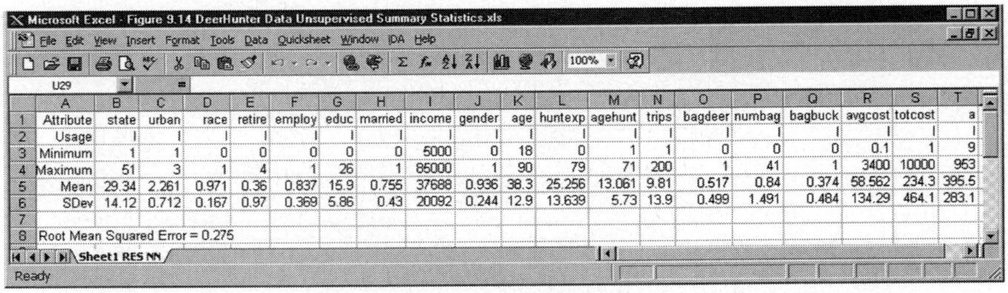

	A	B	C	D	E	F	G	H	I	J	K	L	M	N	O	P	Q	R	S	T
1	Attribute	state	urban	race	retire	employ	educ	married	income	gender	age	huntexp	agehunt	trips	bagdeer	numbag	bagbuck	avgcost	totcost	a
2	Usage	I	I	I	I	I	I	I	I	I	I	I	I	I	I	I	I	I	I	I
3	Minimum	1	1	0	0	0	0	0	5000	0	18	0	1	1	0	0	0	0.1	1	9
4	Maximum	51	3	1	4	1	26	1	85000	1	90	79	71	200	1	41	1	3400	10000	953
5	Mean	29.34	2.261	0.971	0.36	0.837	15.9	0.755	37688	0.936	38.3	25.256	13.061	9.81	0.517	0.84	0.374	58.562	234.3	395.5
6	SDev	14.12	0.712	0.167	0.97	0.369	5.86	0.43	20092	0.244	12.9	13.639	5.73	13.9	0.499	1.491	0.484	134.29	464.1	283.1
7																				
8	Root Mean Squared Error = 0.275																			

Figure 9.15 • **Output clusters for the deer hunter dataset**

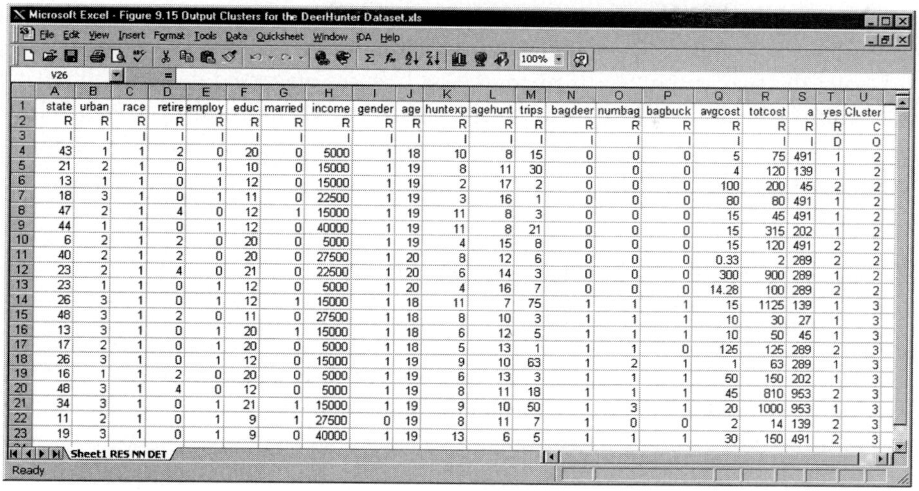

	A	B	C	D	E	F	G	H	I	J	K	L	M	N	O	P	Q	R	S	T	U
1	state	urban	race	retire	employ	educ	married	income	gender	age	huntexp	agehunt	trips	bagdeer	numbag	bagbuck	avgcost	totcost	a	yes	Cluster
2	R	R	R	R	R	R	R	R	R	R	R	R	R	R	R	R	R	R	R	R	C
3	I	I	I	I	I	I	I	I	I	I	I	I	I	I	I	I	I	I	I	D	O
4	43	1	1	2	0	20	0	5000	1	18	10	8	15	0	0	0	5	75	491	1	2
5	21	2	1	0	1	10	0	15000	1	19	8	11	30	0	0	0	4	120	139	1	2
6	13	1	1	0	1	12	0	15000	1	19	2	17	2	0	0	0	100	200	45	2	2
7	18	3	1	0	1	11	0	22500	1	19	3	16	1	0	0	0	80	80	491	1	2
8	47	2	1	4	0	12	1	15000	1	19	11	8	3	0	0	0	15	45	491	1	2
9	44	1	1	0	1	12	0	40000	1	19	11	8	21	0	0	0	15	315	202	1	2
10	6	2	1	2	0	20	0	5000	1	19	4	15	8	0	0	0	15	120	491	2	2
11	40	2	1	2	0	20	0	27500	1	20	8	12	6	0	0	0	0.33	2	289	2	2
12	23	2	1	4	0	21	0	22500	1	20	6	14	3	0	0	0	300	900	289	1	2
13	23	1	1	0	1	12	0	5000	1	20	4	16	7	0	0	0	14.28	100	289	2	2
14	26	3	1	0	1	12	1	15000	1	18	11	7	75	1	1	1	15	1125	139	1	3
15	48	3	1	2	0	11	0	27500	1	18	8	10	3	1	1	1	10	30	27	1	3
16	13	3	1	0	1	20	1	15000	1	18	6	12	5	1	1	1	10	50	45	1	3
17	17	2	1	0	1	20	0	5000	1	18	5	13	1	1	1	0	125	125	289	2	3
18	26	3	1	0	1	12	0	15000	1	19	9	10	63	1	2	1	1	63	289	1	3
19	16	1	1	2	0	20	0	5000	1	19	6	13	3	1	1	1	50	150	202	1	3
20	48	3	1	4	0	12	0	5000	1	19	8	11	18	1	1	1	45	810	953	2	3
21	34	3	1	0	1	21	1	15000	1	19	9	10	50	1	3	1	20	1000	953	1	3
22	11	2	1	0	1	9	1	27500	0	19	8	11	7	1	0	0	2	14	139	2	3
23	19	3	1	0	1	9	0	40000	1	19	13	6	5	1	1	1	30	150	491	2	3

To examine the individual instances for each cluster, simply scroll the output sheet. If your results are similar to ours, you will notice little consistency in the clustering of data instances with respect to the values for attribute *yes.* This is a first indication that our initial hypothesis indicating that hunters willing to accept added fees for hunting privileges will cluster together is not correct. Beyond this observation, we will need additional help to determine the patterns found within the clusters. Fortunately, Section 9.3 offers the required assistance.

Leave your current spreadsheet open, as it will be used in Section 9.3 to further analyze the unsupervised neural network clustering.

General Considerations

When selecting a network architecture, a first consideration is the size of the output grid. As a general rule, the size of the grid should vary directly with the number of clusters in the final output. It is best to specify an output grid significantly larger than the size of the final clustering. For example, suppose we suspect two clusters to be present in the data. Knowing this, we select a 2×2 output grid and specify two clusters for the final output. Even though the 2×2 grid gives us twice as many output nodes as final clusters, the choice inhibits neighborhood training and limits the total number of options for instance cluster formation. In this case, a 3×3 or 4×4 grid is likely to be a better choice.

A second consideration is the optimality of network convergence. Experimenting with several network architectures before choosing a final model gives some insight into the optimality of the clustering formed with each mining session. As a general rule, smaller *rms* values indicate higher-quality clusters.

Finally, the two output sheets presented with an unsupervised network clustering supply a limited amount of explanation about any interesting patterns that may have been discovered. Let's see how ESX can help us find the patterns formed by an unsupervised network clustering.

9.3   ESX for Neural Network Cluster Analysis

You may have noticed that the *Sheet1 RES NN DET* created in the experiment with the deer hunter dataset is specially formatted for supervised classification with ESX. Let's use supervised learning to help us better understand the structure of the clusters created for the deer hunter dataset.

Applying Supervised Learning to Evaluate Neural Network Clustering

1. Open the *Sheet1 RES NN DET* workbook containing the results of the unsupervised clustering.

2. Several of the categorical attributes in the original dataset were designated as *real* so that the dataset could be used for unsupervised network training. Change these attributes back to their original *categorical* designation. Make sure output attribute *yes* is shown as categorical, display-only.

3. The spreadsheet is now ready for a supervised data mining session on attribute *cluster*. Click on the iDA dropdown menu, select *ESX*, use all data instances for training, and employ the default value for the tolerance setting.

4. Click *No* when asked if you would like to perform a quick mine session. As the dataset is large, the data mining session will take a few minutes.

5. For rule generation, use a minimum correctness setting of 70 and a minimum rule coverage of 20.

We explore our results by following the first three steps of the strategy for analyzing a data mining session outlined in the Chapter 4 summary. As an exercise, follow the analysis below to see if your results are similar to ours.

1. Examine class resemblance scores and individual class rules to see how well the input attributes define the formed clusters.

- The two formed clusters show resemblance scores of .667 with 2952 (cluster 2) instances and .634 with 3134 (cluster 3) instances. The domain resemblance is given as 0.60. This provides initial evidence that the formed clusters are of interest.

- Both clusters are uniquely defined by a single rule. Specifically,
  If *bagdeer* = *0* Then *Class* = *2*.
  If *bagdeer* = *1* Then *Class* = *3*.

2. Examine domain summary statistics to help locate attribute errors and to determine predictive numeric attributes.

   - The most predictive numeric attribute is *numbag*. This attribute represents the total number of deer bagged by each hunter.

   - Other numeric attributes of some predictive value are *totalcost, agehunt,* and *trips*.

3. Examine class summary statistics to locate predictive categorical attribute values.

   - Categorical attribute value *bagdeer* = *0* is necessary and sufficient for membership in class 2. Likewise, *bagdeer* = *1* is necessary and sufficient for membership in class 3.

   - The values for categorical attribute *yes* are not predictive of class membership for either cluster. For example, in cluster 2, 1563 instances have *yes* = *1* and 1362 instances show *yes* = *2*.

To summarize, the instances of the deer hunter dataset do form meaningful clusters. However, the instance clustering is based on the *bagdeer* attribute rather than on the attribute indicating whether a deer hunter is willing to pay more for his next hunting trip. It is clear that building a model able to differentiate hunters willing to pay an added fee for their hunting trips will require additional work.

9.4   Chapter Summary

The iDA feed-forward backpropagation neural network tool allows us to build supervised models for estimation and prediction. IDA backpropagation learning can be described as a four-step procedure that consists of preparing the data, defining the network architecture, watching the network train, and interpreting summary results. To design the network architecture, we must decide on whether one or two hidden layers will be used for network training. We also specify the number of nodes in each hidden layer, a network convergence criterion, and a learning rate.

The output of a backpropagation mining session shows actual and network-computed output values. To help determine model accuracy, the output also provides root mean squared error and mean absolute error values. When test data are not available, the training data is employed to test model accuracy. A trained network can also be used to estimate output values for instances of unknown origin.

The iDA unsupervised clustering neural network tool is based on the two-layer Kohonen architecture. The same four-step process used with backpropagation learning can be applied to unsupervised clustering. During the network design phase, we are responsible for determining the initial size of the output layer, the number of clusters present in the data, the learning rate, and the amount of network training.

One of the output sheets generated by an unsupervised network clustering is specially formatted for supervised learning with ESX. Because of this, we can apply ESX to help us interpret the meaning of the formed clusters.

9.5   Key Terms

Linearly separable. Two classes, A and B, are said to be linearly separable if a straight line can be drawn to separate the instances of class A from the instances of class B.

Perceptron neural network. A simple feed-forward neural network architecture consisting of an input layer and a single output layer.

Total delta. The total absolute change in network connection weights for each pass of the training data through a neural network.

9.6   Exercises

Data Mining Questions

LAB 1. Create a backpropagation network to model one of the three logical operators shown in the table. Because these operators are linearly separable, we might hypothesize that it takes fewer epochs to train a network to recognize each operator. Run several experiments with one or more of these operators to affirm or reject this hypothesis.

Input 1	Input 2	And	Or	Implication
1	1	1	1	1
0	1	0	1	1
1	0	0	1	0
0	0	0	0	1

LAB Denotes exercise appropriate for a laboratory setting.

LAB 2. Use the numerical form of the credit card promotion database (CreditCard PromotionNet.xls) and backpropagation learning to build a model for estimating the likelihood of a new credit card customer accepting a new life insurance promotion. As the model is for predictive purposes, be sure to flag *magazine promotion* and *watch promotion* as unused. To perform the experiment, add the five instances, representing new customers, listed in the table below to the end of the dataset. Be sure to leave the cells for *magazine promotion, watch promotion,* and *life insurance promotion* blank. Use the original 15 instances to train the network. Which customers listed in the table are likely candidates for the new life insurance promotion?

Income Range	Magazine Promotion	Watch Promotion	Life Ins Promo	Credit Card Ins	Sex	Age
30000				0	0	33
40000				1	1	42
20000				0	0	19
30000				0	1	50
40000				1	0	48
30000				0	0	31

3. Use the numerical form of the cardiology patient data (CardiologyNumerical.xls) to perform backpropagation learning. Define a plausible network architecture. Use 200 instances for training and the remaining 103 instances to test the created network. Repeat the experiment several times using architectures containing one as well as two hidden layers. Do the one or two hidden-layer architectures give a better test set result?

LAB 4. Use the numerical form of the cardiology patient data (CardiologyNumerical.xls) to perform an unsupervised network clustering. Use a 5 × 5 output layer and indicate two final clusters. Limit the total number of epochs to 1000 or less. Make sure you specify the *class* attribute as display-only. Follow the procedure outlined in Section 9.3 to answer the following questions.

a. Do the instances from the *healthy* and *sick* classes form separate clusters?

b. Are the input attributes appropriate for differentiating healthy and sick patients?

5. Repeat the backpropagation experiment with the satellite image data described in the second part of Section 9.1. Use the parameter settings specified in Figure 9.9, but increase the number of epochs to 100,000.

    a. Examine the test set values and list the three classes that show a large number of classification errors.

    b. Employ ESX to perform a supervised classification using the same 150 instances for training. Make sure the *output1* through *output4* attributes are denoted as unused and that the *class* attribute is specified as an output attribute. Set the real-valued tolerance at 0.30. Examine the confusion matrix and list the three classes having a highest classification error rate.

    c. Do the classes you listed in part a correspond to the classes incorrectly classified by ESX?

6. This exercise uses the satellite image data found in Sonaru.xls to perform an unsupervised neural network clustering.

    a. Copy the Sheet1 data in the Sonaru.xls file into a new spreadsheet.

    b. Specify the *class* attribute as display-only.

    c. Begin an unsupervised neural network training session.

    d. Use a 12 × 12 output-layer architecture, use all instances for training, set the epochs value at 1000, and specify six final clusters.

    e. Once training is complete, follow the procedure in Section 9.3 to analyze the output.

    f. What is the class resemblance score for each cluster? How do the class resemblance scores compare with the domain resemblance?

    g. Are there any clusters that contain a single class? Which classes group together in the same cluster? What does this tell you?

LAB 7. Copy the grb4u.xls file found in the samples directory into a new spreadsheet. Use the Kohonen network to perform an unsupervised clustering. Specify the number of output rows and columns as five each. Specify the number of clusters as three. Use ESX to help you describe the three clusters formed by the network. Give your description in terms of burst length, brightness, and hardness. Repeat the experiment, but specify four rather than three final clusters.

8. Copy the grb4u.xls file found in the samples directory into a new spreadsheet. Specify *T50* and *T90* as output attributes. Use backpropagation learning and 640 training instances to see how well burst length can be predicted by the attributes for burst brightness and burst hardness.

9. In question 2 of the Data Mining Questions at the end of Chapter 2 we asked you to keep track of your credit card purchases for one or more months.

    a. Create appropriate attributes and place this information in attribute-value format in a new Excel spreadsheet. Perform data transformations as necessary so you can use your neural network software to analyze the data. Add an output attribute to each record whose value is 1 to indicate this is a purchase you have made.

b. Add several new hypothetical purchases to the end of your list that are both typical and atypical of your current purchases.

c. Use your iDA supervised backpropagation neural network tool to build a model representing your credit card purchases. For test data, include some of your actual purchases as well as all of the hypothetical purchases added to the list.

d. What values do the atypical purchases show for the output attribute?

e. As a second experiment, flag the output attribute as unused and perform an unsupervised neural network clustering. Use all data instances to train the network. Specify two final output clusters. Do the atypical purchases cluster with your actual purchases or do they form their own cluster?

Chapter **10**

Statistical Techniques

Chapter Objectives

- ▶ Understand when linear regression is an appropriate data mining technique.

- ▶ Know how to perform linear regression with Microsoft Excel's LINEST function.

- ▶ Know that logistic regression can be used to build supervised learner models for datasets having a binary outcome.

- ▶ Understand how Bayes classifier is able to build supervised models for datasets having categorical data, numeric data, or a combination of both data types.

- ▶ Know how agglomerative clustering is applied to partition data instances into disjoint clusters.

- ▶ Understand that conceptual clustering is an unsupervised data mining technique that builds a concept hierarchy to partition data instances.

- ▶ Know that the EM algorithm uses a statistical parameter adjustment technique to cluster data instances.

- ▶ Understand the basic features that differentiate statistical and machine learning data mining methods.

In this chapter we provide a detailed overview of several common statistical data mining techniques. It is not necessary for you to study each technique in detail to obtain an overall understanding of this field. For this reason, each section of this chapter is self-contained. Several of the experiments conducted here and in Chapter 11 use free downloadable software from the Weka (Waikato Environment for Knowledge Analysis) project developed at the University of Waikato in New Zealand.

Section 10.1 covers linear regression and regression trees. In addition, we show you how to perform multiple linear regression with Excel's LINEST function. In Section 10.2 we discuss logistic regression and how it is applied to build supervised learner models for datasets with a binary outcome. In Section 10.3 you learn how Bayes classifier builds supervised learner models for categorical and real-valued data. In Section 10.4 we present three popular unsupervised clustering techniques. In Section 10.5 we differentiate between statistical and machine learning data mining methods.

10.1 Linear Regression Analysis

Statistical **regression** is a supervised technique that generalizes a set of numeric data by creating a mathematical equation relating one or more input attributes to a single output attribute. With **linear regression,** we attempt to model the variation in a dependent variable as a linear combination of one or more independent variables. A linear regression equation is of the form:

$$f(x_1, x_2, x_3...x_n) = a_1 x_1 + a_2 x_2 + a_3 x_3 + ...a_n x_n + c \qquad (10.1)$$

where $x_1, x_2, x_3...x_n$ are independent variables and $a_1, a_2, a_3...a_n$ and c are constants. $f(x_1, x_2, x_3...x_n)$ represents the dependent variable and is often shown simply as y. In general, linear regression is appropriate when the relationship between the dependent and independent variables is nearly linear.

Simple Linear Regression

The simplest form of the linear regression equation allows but a single independent variable as the predictor of the dependent variable. This type of regression is appropriately named **simple linear regression.** The regression equation is written in **slope-intercept form.** Specifically,

$$y = ax + b \qquad (10.2)$$

where x is the independent variable and y depends on x. The constants a and b are computed via supervised learning by applying a statistical criterion to a dataset of known values for x and y. The graph of Equation 10.2 is a straight line with slope a and y-intercept b.

A common statistical measure used to compute a and b is the *least-squares criterion*. The least-squares criterion minimizes the sum of squared differences between actual and predicted output values. Deriving a and b via the least squares method requires a knowledge of differential calculus. Therefore we simply state the formulas for computing a and b. For a total of n instances we have:

$$b = \frac{\sum xy}{\sum x^2} \qquad\qquad a = \frac{\sum y}{\sum n} - \frac{b\sum y}{n} \qquad (10.3)$$

Simple linear regression is both easy to understand and to apply. However, the fact that it allows but a single independent variable makes the technique of limited use for most data mining applications.

Multiple Linear Regression with Excel

Microsoft Excel contains a regression analysis tool that enables us to perform simple and multiple linear regressions. Here we describe Excel's LINEST function with a tutorial example taken from the Excel Help document. The LINEST function uses the least-squares criterion to perform linear regression. A complete description of Excel's regression analysis tool can be found by typing the word "regression" in the text box associated with Excel's Help menu.

Applying the LINEST Function

To illustrate the LINEST function, we consider the sample data in Table 10.1 taken from an example in the Microsoft Excel Help document. Each row of data represents information about a particular office building in an established business district. A commercial developer wishes to use linear regression to estimate the value of a specific office building based on the table data. The independent variables are given as *floor space* in square feet, *number of offices*, *number of entrances,* and *building age*. The dependent variable is the *assessed value* of the office building. The following steps show how to perform a linear regression analysis with the table data.

1. Open a new Excel spreadsheet. Use columns A through E and rows 1 through 12 to enter the data in Table 10.1. Make sure the first row of your spreadsheet contains the attribute names as they appear in the table.

2. The output of the LINEST function is shown in an $n \times n$ array where n is the total number of variables used for the regression. For our problem, $n = 5$. Use your mouse

Table 10.1   ●   **District Office Building Data**

Space	Offices	Entrances	Age	Value
2310	2	2	20	$142,000
2333	2	2	12	$144,000
2356	3	1.5	33	$151,000
2379	3	2	43	$150,000
2402	2	3	53	$139,000
2425	4	2	23	$169,000
2448	2	1.5	99	$126,000
2471	2	2	34	$142,900
2494	3	3	23	$163,000
2517	4	4	55	$169,000
2540	2	3	22	$149,000

to highlight an area of at least five rows and five columns below or to the right of the input data. This area represents the array to contain the output of the regression analysis. The highlighted area must have the same number of rows as columns.

3. To perform the regression, type the following expression into the Excel formula bar:

=LINEST(E2:E12,A2:D12,TRUE,TRUE)

Be sure to include the equal sign as the first character in your expression.

4. Next, hold down the *Ctrl* and *Shift* keys while striking the *Enter* key. This allows the output of the regression analysis to appear in the highlighted area of your Excel spreadsheet.

Before we explore the output of the regression, an additional explanation of the LINEST function is warranted. The first function parameter is for the dependent variable. Specifically, E2:E12 states that the dependent variable resides in column E and that the data for this vari-able are found in rows 2 through 12. The second parameter gives LINEST the data range for the independent variables. For our example, values for the independent variables reside in col-umn A row 2 through column D row 12.

If the third parameter is TRUE or omitted, the constant term in the regression formula is computed normally. If the value FALSE is assigned to the third parameter, the constant term is set to 0. If the fourth parameter is assigned the value FALSE, LINEST returns only the coeffi-

Table 10.2 • **Regression Statistics for the Office Building Data**

−234.2371645	2553.211	12529.77	27.64139	52317.83
13.26801148	530.6692	400.0668	5.429374	12237.36
0.996747993	970.5785	#N/A	#N/A	#N/A
459.7536742	6	#N/A	#N/A	#N/A
1732393319	5652135	#N/A	#N/A	#N/A

cients for the regression equation. If the parameter is seen as TRUE, the output array also contains several statistics that help determine the efficacy of the regression equation. Now that we see how the LINEST function is applied, it is time to examine the output of the regression analysis!

The output of the regression analysis, as it appears in the highlighted area of your Excel spreadsheet, is shown in Table 10.2. We read the coefficients for the regression equation directly from the table. The coefficients appear in the first row of the table and are given in reverse order. That is, the left-most entry is the coefficient for the right-most independent variable. The

Figure 10.1 • **A simple linear regression equation**

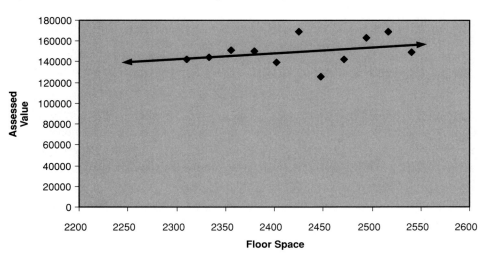

right-most entry represents the constant term. The regression equation for estimating the value of same district office buildings is:

$$Value = 27.64 Space + 12529.77 Offices + 2553.21 Entrances - 234.24 Age + 52317.83$$

An obvious question is how accurate the regression equation is at estimating assessed values. With simple linear regression, we can partially answer this question by viewing a scatterplot diagram together with a two-dimensional graph of the created regression equation. For example, Figure 10.1 shows the scatterplot diagram and graph of the regression equation for *assessed value* using the single independent variable *floor space*. The figure clearly indicates a linear relationship between the independent and dependent variables. However, with more than one independent variable, we turn to basic statistical analysis to help determine the extent to which the independent variables are linearly related to the dependent variable. The information we need is contained in the third and fourth rows of Table 10.2.

The first entry in the third row of the table is the **coefficient of determination.** This represents the correlation between actual and estimated values for the dependent variable. A score of 1.0 indicates no difference between actual and computed variable values. For our example, we see a value of 0.9967. Although the correlation is high, we must be cautious in assuming that the regression equation is a good predictor of actual assessed values, as the determination coefficient is computed using training rather than test set data. The second entry in the third row is the standard error for the estimate of the dependent variable.

The first entry in the fourth row is the F statistic for the regression analysis. The F statistic helps establish if the coefficient of determination given in the third row is significant. To interpret the F statistic, we must access a table of F critical values, found in most statistics books. The F statistic requires two measures for degrees of freedom. The measures are often denoted in an F table of critical values as $v1$ and $v2$. $v1$ is the total number of independent variables. For our example, $v1 = 4$. $v2$ is computed by subtracting the total number of variables in the analysis from the total number of training instances. For our example, $v2 = (11 - 5) = 6$. $v2$ is also shown as the second entry in the fourth row of Table 10.2.

Examining a one-tailed F table with $v1 = 4$ and $v2 = 6$ gives a 0.05 significance score of 4.53. The F value of 459.75 in the third row is obviously significant. This tells us that the regression equation is able to accurately determine assessed values of the office buildings that are part of the training data. Once again, we must exercise caution in making generalizations about the ability of the equation to accurately estimate assessed values for unseen data instances. The regression equation can be safely used on new data provided we are confident that the same linear relationship seen with the training data is also found with previously unobserved data.

Finally, the values in the second row of Table 10.2 determine the usefulness of individual independent variables in predicting assessed building values. For a complete discussion of how these values are used, please direct your attention to the LINEST Help document.

Regression Trees 回归树.

Regression trees represent an alternative to statistical regression. Regression trees get their name from the fact that most statisticians refer to any model that predicts numeric output as a regression model. Essentially, regression trees take the form of decision trees where the leaf nodes of the tree are numeric rather than categorical values. The value at an individual leaf node is computed by taking the numeric average of the output attribute for all instances passing through the tree to the leaf node position.

Regression trees are more accurate than linear regression equations when the data to be modeled is nonlinear. However, regression trees can become quite cumbersome and difficult to interpret. For this reason, regression trees are sometimes combined with linear regression to form what are known as **model trees.** With model trees, each leaf node of a partial regression tree represents a linear regression equation rather than an average of attribute values. By combining linear regression with regression trees, the regression tree structure can be simplified in that fewer tree levels are necessary to achieve accurate results.

Figure 10.2 presents a generic model tree structure containing four tests on real-valued attributes and five leaf nodes each representing a linear regression equation.

Figure 10.2 • **A generic model tree**

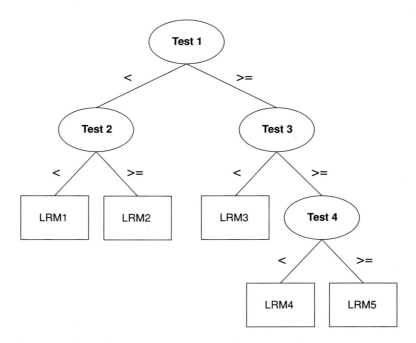

Figure 10.3 • **A model tree for the deer hunter dataset (output attribute yes)**

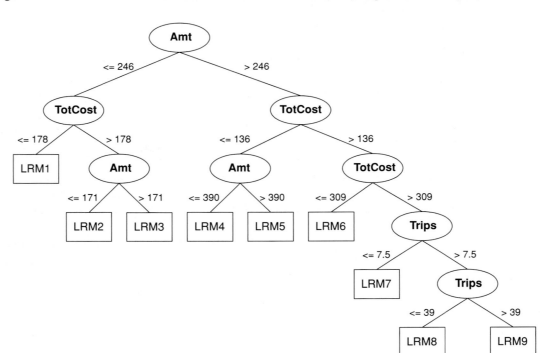

The complexity of a model tree depends on the degree of linearity seen between the dependent and independent variables. As an experiment, we created two model trees, one using the numeric form of the cardiology patient data and a second using the deer hunter dataset.

The model tree for the cardiology patient data contained one node representing a multiple linear regression equation. This result tells us that the relationship between the independent variables and the dependent variable for the cardiology patient dataset is linear. The model tree for the deer hunter dataset is displayed in Figure 10.3. The tree shows eight attribute tests and nine linear regression equations. The complexity of the tree indicates a lack of linearity between the dependent and independent variables.

10.2 Logistic Regression

In Chapter 2 we used multiple linear regression with the credit card promotion database to develop an equation for determining values for output attribute *life insurance promotion*. As linear regression requires numeric attribute values, we transformed all categorical data to numeric equivalents. *Yes* and *no* values for attributes *magazine promotion, watch promotion,* and *life insurance promotion* where replaced with *1* and *0*. For attribute *sex,* values *male and female* were also replaced with *1* and *0*, respectively. Finally, values for categorical attribute *income range* were transformed to the lower end of each range score.

Our example was appropriate for illustrative purposes. However, the general methodology of using linear regression to model problems with observed outcome restricted to two values is seriously flawed. The problem lies in the fact that the value restriction placed on the dependent variable is not observed by the regression equation. That is, because linear regression produces a straight-line function, values of the dependent variable are unbounded in both the positive and negative directions. Therefore for the right-hand side of Equation 10.1 to be consistent with a binary outcome, we must transform the linear regression model. By transforming the linear model so as to restrict values for the output attribute to the [0,1] interval range, the regression equation can be thought of as producing a probability of the occurrence or nonoccurrence of a measured event.

Although several options for transforming the linear regression model exist, we restrict our discussion to the logistic model. The logistic model applies a logarithmic transformation that makes the right-hand side of Equation 10.1 an exponential term in the transformed equation.

Transforming the Linear Regression Model

Logistic regression is a nonlinear regression technique that associates a conditional probability score with each data instance. To understand the transformation performed by the logistic model, we begin by thinking of Equation 10.1 as computing a probability. A probability value of 1 denotes the observation of one class (e.g., *life insurance promotion = yes*). Likewise, a probability of 0 indicates observance of the second class (e.g., *life insurance promotion = no*). Equation 10.4 is a modified form of Equation 10.1 where the left-hand side of the equation is written as a **conditional probability**.

$$p(y = 1 \mid \mathbf{x}) = a_1 x_1 + a_2 x_2 + a_3 x_3 \ldots \ldots a_n x_n + c \qquad (10.4)$$

Equation 10.4 shows $p(y = 1 \mid \mathbf{x})$ as an unbounded value denoting the conditional probability of seeing the class associated with $y = 1$ given the values contained in feature (attribute) vector $\mathbf{x}$. To eliminate the boundary problem seen in the equation, the probability is transformed into an odds ratio. Specifically,

$$\left(\frac{p(y = 1 \mid \mathbf{x})}{1 - p(y = 1 \mid \mathbf{x})} \right) \qquad (10.5)$$

For any feature vector $\mathbf{x}$, the odds indicate how often the class associated with $y = 1$ is seen relative to the frequency in which the class associated with $y = 0$ is observed. The natural log of this odds ratio (known as the **logit**) is then assigned to the right-hand side of Equation 10.1. That is,

$$\ln\left(\frac{p(y = 1 \mid \mathbf{x})}{1 - p(y = 1 \mid \mathbf{x})}\right) = \mathbf{ax} + c \tag{10.6}$$

where,

$$\mathbf{x} = (x_1, x_2, x_3, x_4 \ldots \ldots x_n)$$

$$\mathbf{ax} + c = a_1 x_1 + a_2 x_2 + a_3 x_3 \ldots \ldots a_n x_n + c$$

Finally, we solve Equation 10.6 for $p(y = 1 \mid \mathbf{x})$ to obtain a bounded representation for the probability, which is shown in Equation 10.7.

$$p(y = 1 \mid x) = \frac{e^{\mathbf{ax}+c}}{1 + e^{\mathbf{ax}+c}} \tag{10.7}$$

where

e is the base of natural logarithms often denoted as exp

Equation 10.7 defines the logistic regression model. Figure 10.4 shows that the graph of the equation is an s-shaped curve bounded by the [0,1] interval range. As the exponent term approaches negative infinity, the right-hand side of Equation 10.7 approaches 0. Likewise, as the exponent becomes infinitely large in the positive direction, the right side of the equation approaches 1.

The method used to determine the coefficient values for the exponent term $\mathbf{ax} + c$ in Equation 10.7 is iterative. The purpose of the method is to minimize the sum of logarithms of predicted probabilities. Convergence occurs when the logarithmic summation is close to 0 or when the value does not change from one iteration to the next. Details of the technique are beyond the scope of this book. For the interested reader, a description of the process is available from several sources (Hosmer and Lemeshow, 1989; Long, 1989).

Logistic Regression: An Example

We applied the implementation of the logistic regression model available for use at the Web site *http://members.aol.com/johnp71/logistic.html* to the numeric form of the credit card promotion dataset (CreditCardPromotionNet.xls). We selected *life insurance promotion* as the dependent variable and eliminated attributes *magazine promotion* and *watch promotion* so the model could be used to predict the probability of new customers accepting a life insurance promotional offering. Here is the equation for the exponent term seen in Equation 10.7:

$$\mathbf{ax} + c = 0.0001 Income + 19.827 CreditCardIns - \tag{10.8}$$
$$8.314 Sex - 0.415 Age + 17.691$$

Figure 10.4 • **The logistic regression equation**

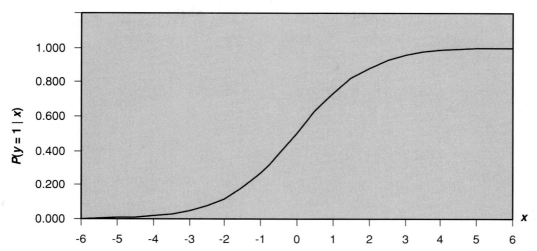

The equation tells us that values for *credit card insurance* and *sex* are most influential in determining a value for the exponent term. Also, *personal income* has very little effect on the value of the exponent.

The training data used to create the logistic model as well as the output computed by the logistic equation is given in Table 10.3. As you can see, all computed values are in the closed interval range [0,1]. Also, all computed output, excepting values for instances 8 and 12, represent correct classifications.

Finally, we can use Equation 10.7 with the exponent term given by Equation 10.8 to compute conditional probability scores for instances representing new credit card customers. To illustrate, consider the new instance:

Income = 35K
Credit Card Insurance = 1
Sex = 0
Age = 39

Applying Equation 10.7, we obtain a computed probability of 0.999. This tells us that the customer represented by the instance is a likely candidate for a new life insurance promotion. However, changing the value of *credit card insurance* from 1 to 0 and *sex* from 0 to 1 results in a probability score of 0.035. Therefore a 39-year-old male credit card customer who makes $35,000 per year and does not have credit card insurance is a poor choice for a new life insurance promotion.

Table 10.3 • **Logistic Regression: Dependent Variable = Life Insurance Promotion**

Instance	Income	Credit Card Insurance	Sex	Age	Life Insurance Promotion	Computed Probability
1	40K	0	1	45	0	0.007
2	30K	0	0	40	1	0.987
3	40K	0	1	42	0	0.024
4	30K	1	1	43	1	1.000
5	50K	0	0	38	1	0.999
6	20K	0	0	55	0	0.049
7	30K	1	1	35	1	1.000
8	20K	0	1	27	0	0.584
9	30K	0	1	43	0	0.005
10	30K	0	0	41	1	0.981
11	40K	0	0	43	1	0.985
12	20K	0	1	29	1	0.380
13	50K	0	0	39	1	0.999
14	40K	0	1	55	0	0.000
15	20K	1	0	19	1	1.000

10.3 Bayes Classifier

Bayes classifier offers a simple yet powerful supervised classification technique. The model assumes all input attributes to be of equal importance and independent of one another. Even though these assumptions are likely to be false, Bayes classifier still works quite well in practice. The classifier is based on **Bayes theorem,** which is stated as:

$$P(H \mid E) = \frac{P(E \mid H) \times P(H)}{P(E)} \qquad (10.9)$$

where H is a hypothesis to be tested and E is the evidence associated with the hypothesis. From a classification viewpoint, the hypothesis is the dependent variable and represents the predicted class. The evidence is determined by values of the input attributes. $P(E \mid H)$ is the conditional probability that H is true given evidence E. $P(H)$ is an **a priori probability,** which denotes the probability of the hypothesis before the presentation of any evidence. Conditional and a priori probabilities are easily computed from the training data. The classifier is best understood with an example.

Bayes Classifier: An Example

Consider the data in Table 10.4, which is a subset of the credit card promotion database defined in Chapter 2. For our example, we use *sex* as the output attribute whose value is to be predicted. Table 10.5 lists the distribution (counts and ratios) of the output attribute values for each input attribute. To demonstrate, Table 10.5 tells us that four males took advantage of the magazine promotion and that these four males represent two-thirds of the total male population. As a second example, Table 10.5 indicates that three of the four female dataset instances purchased the magazine promotion.

Let's use the data in Table 10.5 together with Bayes classifier to perform a new classification. Consider the following new instance to be classified:

> *Magazine Promotion* = *Yes*
> *Watch Promotion* = *Yes*
> *Life Insurance Promotion* = *No*
> *Credit Card Insurance* = *No*
> *Sex* = ?

We have two hypotheses to be tested. One hypothesis states the credit card holder is male. The second hypothesis sees the instance as a female card holder. In order to determine which hypothesis is correct, we apply Bayes classifier to compute a probability

Table 10.4 • **Data for Bayes Classifier**

Magazine Promotion	Watch Promotion	Life Insurance Promotion	Credit Card Insurance	Sex
Yes	No	No	No	Male
Yes	Yes	Yes	Yes	Female
No	No	No	No	Male
Yes	Yes	Yes	Yes	Male
Yes	No	Yes	No	Female
No	No	No	No	Female
Yes	Yes	Yes	Yes	Male
No	No	No	No	Male
Yes	No	No	No	Male
Yes	Yes	Yes	No	Female

Table 10.5 • **Counts and Probabilities for Attribute *Sex***

Sex	Magazine Promotion		Watch Promotion		Life Insurance Promotion		Credit Card Insurance	
	Male	Female	Male	Female	Male	Female	Male	Female
Yes	4	3	2	2	2	3	2	1
No	2	1	4	2	4	1	4	3
Ratio: yes/total	4/6	3/4	2/6	2/4	2/6	3/4	2/6	1/4
Ratio: no/total	2/6	1/4	4/6	2/4	4/6	1/4	4/6	3/4

for each hypothesis. The general equation for computing the probability that the individual is a male customer is:

$$P(sex = male \mid E) = \frac{P(E \mid sex = male)\,P(sex = male)}{P(E)} \qquad (10.10)$$

Let's start with the conditional probability $P(E \mid sex = male)$. This probability is computed by multiplying the conditional probability values for each piece of evidence. This is possible if we make the assumption that the evidence is independent. The overall conditional probability is the product of the following four conditional probabilities:

$P(magazine\ promotion = yes \mid sex = male) = 4/6$
$P(watch\ promotion = yes \mid sex = male) = 2/6$
$P(life\ insurance\ promotion = no \mid sex = male) = 4/6$
$P(credit\ card\ insurance = no \mid sex = male) = 4/6$

These values are easily obtained as they can be read directly from Table 10.5. Therefore the conditional probability for *sex = male* is computed as:

$$P(E \mid sex = male) = (4/6)\,(2/6)\,(4/6)\,(4/6)$$
$$= 8/81$$

The a priori probability, denoted in Equation 10.10 as $P(sex = male)$, is the probability of a male customer without knowing the promotional offering history of the instance. In this case, the a priori probability is simply the fraction of the total population that is male. As there are six males and four females, the a priori probability for *sex = male* is 3/5. Given these two values, the numerator expression for Equation 10.10 becomes:

$$(8/81)\,(3/5) \approx 0.0593$$

We now have,

$P(sex = male \mid E) \approx 0.0593 \, / \, P(E)$

Next, we compute the value for $P(sex = female \mid E)$ using the formula:

$$P(sex = female \mid E) = \frac{P(E \mid sex = female) \, P(sex = female)}{P(E)} \qquad (10.11)$$

We first compute the conditional probability with values obtained directly from Table 10.5. Specifically,

P(magazine promotion = yes | sex = female) = 3/4
P(watch promotion = yes | sex = female) = 2/4
P(life insurance promotion = no | sex = female) = 1/4
P(credit card insurance = no | sex = female) = 3/4

The overall conditional probability is:

P(E | sex = female) = (3/4) (2/4) (1/4) (3/4)
                      = 9/128

As there are four females, the a priori probability for *P(sex = female)* is 2/5. Therefore the numerator expression for Equation 10.11 becomes:

(9/128) (2/5) ≈ 0.0281

We now have

$P(sex = female \mid E) \approx 0.0281 \, / \, P(E)$

Finally, because *P(E)* represents the probability of the evidence whether *sex = male* or *sex = female*, the value is the same for both computations. This being the case, we need not concern ourselves with this value. Therefore because 0.0593 > 0.0281, Bayes classifier tells us the instance is most likely a male credit card customer.

Zero-Valued Attribute Counts

A significant problem with the Bayes' technique is when one of the counts for an attribute value is 0. For example, suppose the number of females with a value of *no* for *credit card insurance* is 0. In this case, the numerator expression for $P(sex = female \mid E)$ will be 0. This means that the values for all other attributes are irrelevant because any multiplication by 0 gives an overall 0 probability value.

To solve this problem, we add a small constant, *k,* to the numerator and denominator of each computed ratio. Therefore each ratio of the form *n /d* becomes

$$\frac{n + (k)(p)}{d + k} \qquad (10.12)$$

where

k is a value between 0 and 1 (usually 1)

p is chosen as an equal fractional part of the total number of possible values for the attribute. If an attribute has two possible values, p will be 0.5.

Let's use this technique to recompute the conditional probability $P(E \mid sex = female)$ for our previous example. With $k = 1$ and $p = 0.5$, the conditional probability of the evidence given $sex = female$ computes to:

$$\frac{(3 + 0.5) \times (2 + 0.5) \times (1 + 0.5) \times (3 + 0.5)}{5 \times 5 \times 5 \times 5} \approx 0.0176$$

Missing Data

Fortunately, missing data items are not a problem for Bayes classifier. To demonstrate, consider the following instance to be classified by the model defined in Table 10.5.

Magazine Promotion = Yes
Watch Promotion = Unknown
Life Insurance Promotion = No
Credit Card Insurance = No
Sex = ?

As the value of *watch promotion* is unknown, we can simply ignore this attribute in our conditional probability computations. By doing so, we have:

P(E | sex = male) = (4/6) (4/6) (4/6) = 8/27
P(E | sex = female) = (3/4) (1/4) (3/4) = 9/64
P(sex = male | E) ≈ 0.1778 / P(E)
P(sex = female | E) ≈ 0.05625 / P(E)

As you can see, the effect is to give a probability value of 1.0 to the *watch promotion* attribute. This will result in a larger value for both conditional probabilities. However, this is not a problem, because both probability values are equally affected.

Numeric Data

Numeric data can be dealt with in a similar manner provided that the probability density function representing the distribution of the data is known. If a particular numerical attribute is normally distributed, we use the standard probability density function shown in Equation 10.13.

$$f(x) = 1/(\sigma\sqrt{2\pi})e^{-(x-\mu)^2/(2\sigma^2)} \qquad (10.13)$$

where

e = the *exponential function*
μ = the class *mean* for the given numerical attribute
σ = the class *standard deviation* for the attribute
x = the attribute value

Although this equation looks quite complicated, it is very easy to apply. To demonstrate, consider the data in Table 10.6. This table displays the data in Table 10.4 with an added column containing numerical attribute *age*.

Let's use this new information to compute the conditional probabilities for the *male* and *female* classes for the following instance.

Magazine Promotion = Yes
Watch Promotion = Yes
Life Insurance Promotion = No
Credit Card Insurance = No
Age = 45
Sex = ?

Table 10.6 ● **Addition of Attribute *Age* to the Bayes Classifier Dataset**

Magazine Promotion	Watch Promotion	Life Insurance Promotion	Credit Card Insurance	Age	Sex
Yes	No	No	No	45	Male
Yes	Yes	Yes	Yes	40	Female
No	No	No	No	42	Male
Yes	Yes	Yes	Yes	30	Male
Yes	No	Yes	No	38	Female
No	No	No	No	55	Female
Yes	Yes	Yes	Yes	35	Male
No	No	No	No	27	Male
Yes	No	No	No	43	Male
Yes	Yes	Yes	No	41	Female

For the overall conditional probabilities we have:

$$P(E \mid sex = male) = (4/6)\,(2/6)\,(4/6)\,(4/6)\,[P(age = 45 \mid sex = male)]$$
$$P(E \mid sex = female) = (3/4)\,(2/4)\,(1/4)\,(3/4)\,[P(age = 45 \mid sex = female)]$$

To determine the conditional probability for *age* given *sex* = *male,* we assume *age* to be normally distributed and apply the probability density function. We use the data in Table 10.5 to find the mean and standard deviation scores. For the class *sex* = *male* we have: $\sigma = 7.69$, $\mu = 37.00$, and $x = 45$. Therefore the probability that *age* = *45* given *sex* = *male* is computed as:

$$P(age = 45 \mid sex = male) = 1/(\sqrt{2\pi}\,7.69)\,e^{-(45-37.00)^2/[2(7.69)^2]}$$

Making the computation, we have:

$$P(age = 45 \mid sex = male) \approx 0.030$$

To determine the conditional probability for *age* given *sex* = *female,* we substitute $\sigma = 7.77$, $\mu = 43.50$, and $x = 45$. Specifically,

$$P(age = 45 \mid sex = female) = 1/(\sqrt{2\pi}\,7.77)\,e^{-(45-43.50)^2/[2(7.77)^2]}$$

Making the computation, we have:

$$P(age = 45 \mid sex = female) \approx 0.050$$

We can now determine the overall conditional probability values:

$$P(E \mid sex = male) = (4/6)\,(2/6)\,(4/6)\,(4/6)\,(0.030) \approx .003$$
$$P(E \mid sex = female) = (3/4)\,(2/4)(1/4)\,(3/4)\,(0.050) \approx .004$$

Finally, applying Equation 10.9 we have:

$$P(sex = male \mid E) \approx (.003)\,(0.60)\,/\,P(E) \approx .0018\,/\,P(E)$$
$$P(sex = female \mid E) \approx (.004)\,(0.40)\,/\,P(E) \approx .0016\,/\,P(E)$$

Once again, we ignore $P(E)$ and conclude that the instance belongs to the *male* class.

10.4 Clustering Algorithms

In this section we describe three unsupervised learner techniques. Each method offers a unique approach for clustering data into disjoint partitions. Although all three techniques are generally considered to be statistical, only the third method actually makes limiting assumptions about the nature of the data.

Agglomerative Clustering 凝聚聚类

Agglomerative clustering is a favorite unsupervised clustering technique. Unlike the K-Means algorithm, which requires the user to specify the number of clusters to be formed, agglomerative clustering begins by assuming that each data instance represents its own cluster. The steps of the algorithm are as follows:

1. Begin by placing each data instance into a separate partition.

2. Until all instances are part of a single cluster:
   a. Determine the two most similar clusters.
   b. Merge the clusters chosen in part a into a single cluster.

3. Choose a clustering formed by one of the step 2 iterations as a final result.

   Let's see how agglomerative clustering can be applied to the credit card promotion database!

Agglomerative Clustering: An Example

Table 10.7 shows five instances from the credit card promotion database described in Chapter 2. Table 10.8 offers the instance similarity scores computed for the first iteration of algorithm step 2(a). An instance-to-instance similarity score is computed by first counting the total number of attribute-value matches between two instances. The total number of attribute comparisons then divides this total, giving the similarity measure. For example, comparing I_1 with I_3, we have four matches and five compares. This gives us the 0.80 value seen in row I_3, column I_1 of Table 10.8.

Table 10.7 ● Five Instances from the Credit Card Promotion Database

Instance	Income Range	Magazine Promotion	Watch Promotion	Life Insurance Promotion	Sex
I_1	40–50K	Yes	No	No	Male
I_2	25–35K	Yes	Yes	Yes	Female
I_3	40–50K	No	No	No	Male
I_4	25–35K	Yes	Yes	Yes	Male
I_5	50–60K	Yes	No	Yes	Female

Table 10.8 • **Agglomerative Clustering: First Iteration**

	I_1	I_2	I_3	I_4	I_5
I_1	1.00				
I_2	0.20	1.00			
I_3	0.80	0.00	1.00		
I_4	0.40	0.80	0.20	1.00	
I_5	0.40	0.60	0.20	0.40	1.00

Step 2(b) requires a merger of the two most similar clusters formed in the first iteration. As table combinations $I_3 - I_1$ and $I_4 - I_2$ each show the highest similarity score, we can choose to merge I_1 with I_3 or I_2 with I_4. We choose to merge I_1 with I_3. Therefore after the first iteration of step 2(b), we have three single-instance clusters (I_2, I_4, I_5) and one cluster having two instances (I_1 and I_3).

Next, we need a method to compute cluster-to-cluster similarity scores. Several possibilities exist. For our example, we use the average similarity of all instances involved in a single table computation. That is, to compute a score for merging the cluster containing I_1 and I_3 with the cluster having I_4, we divide 7 attribute-value matches by 15 compares, giving a similarity score of 0.47. This similarity score is seen in row I_4 column $I_1 I_3$ of Table 10.9. Note that the table gives all similarity scores for the second iteration of the algorithm.

Table 10.9 tells us that the next iteration of the algorithm will merge I_4 with I_2. Therefore after the third iteration of step 2, we have three clusters. One cluster containing I_4 and I_2, a second cluster having I_1 and I_3, and the final cluster with I_5 as its only member. The merging of individual clusters continues until all instances are part of a single cluster.

The final step, requiring the choice of a final clustering, is the most difficult. Several statistical as well as heuristic measures can be applied. The following are three simple heuristic techniques that work well in a majority of situations. Specifically,

1. Invoke the similarity measure used to form the clusters and compare the average within-cluster similarity to the overall similarity of all instances in the dataset. The overall or domain similarity is simply the score seen with the final iteration of the algorithm. In general, if the average of the individual cluster similarity scores shows a higher value than the domain similarity, we have positive evidence that the clustering is useful. As several clusterings of the algorithm may show the desired quality, this technique is best used to eliminate clusterings rather than to choose a final result.

Table 10.9 • Agglomerative Clustering: Second Iteration

	$I_1 I_3$	I_2	I_4	I_5
$I_1 I_3$	0.80			
I_2	0.33	1.00		
I_4	0.47	(0.80)	1.00	
I_5	0.47	0.60	0.40	1.00

2. As a second approach, we compare the similarity within each cluster to the similarity between each cluster. For example, given three clusters, A, B, and C, we analyze cluster A by computing three scores. One score is the within–class similarity of the instances in cluster A. The second score is obtained by computing the similarity score seen when all the instances of cluster A are combined with the instances of B. The third score is the similarity value obtained by grouping the instances of cluster C with those of cluster A. We expect to see the highest scores for within–class similarity computations. As with the first technique, several clusterings of the algorithm may show the desired quality. Therefore the technique is best used to eliminate clusterings rather than to choose a final result.

3. One useful measure to be used in conjunction with the previous techniques is to examine the rule sets generated by each saved clustering. For example, let's assume 10 iterations of the algorithm are initially performed. Next, suppose 5 of the 10 clusterings are eliminated by using one of the previous techniques. To apply the current method, we present each clustering to a rule generator and examine the rules created from the individual clusters. The clustering showing a best set of defining rules is chosen as the final result.

Provided that certain assumptions can be made about the data, a statistical analysis may also be applied to help determine which of the clusterings is a best result. One common statistical test used to select a best partitioning is the **Bayesian Information Criterion** also known as the **BIC.** The BIC requires that the clusters be normally distributed. The BIC gives the odds for one model against another model assuming that neither model is initially favored (Dasgupta and Raftery, 1998).

General Considerations

Agglomerative clustering creates a hierarchy of clusterings by iteratively merging pairs of clusters. Although we have limited our discussion here, several procedures for computing cluster similarity scores and merging clusters exist. Also, when data are real-valued, defining a measure of instance similarity can be a challenge. One common approach is to use simple Euclidean distance.

A widespread application of agglomerative clustering is its use as a prelude to other clustering techniques. For example, the first iteration of the K-Means algorithm requires a choice for initial cluster means. In the usual case, the choice is made in a random or arbitrary manner. However, the initial selection can have a marked effect on goodness of the final clustering. Therefore to increase our chance of obtaining a best final clustering, we first apply agglomerative clustering to create the same number of clusters as that chosen for the K-Means algorithm. Next, we compute the cluster means resulting from the agglomerative technique and use the mean scores as the initial choice for the first K-Means clustering (Mukherjee et al., 1998).

Conceptual Clustering

Conceptual clustering is an unsupervised clustering technique that incorporates **incremental learning** to form a hierarchy of concepts. The **concept hierarchy** takes the form of a tree structure where the root node represents the highest level of concept generalization. Therefore the root node contains summary information for all domain instances. Of particular interest are the **basic-level nodes** of the tree. The basic-level nodes are interesting in terms of human appeal and understanding. An appropriate measure of cluster quality forms these basic-level nodes at the first or second level of the concept tree. The following is a standard conceptual clustering algorithm:

1. Create a cluster with the first instance as its only member.

2. For each remaining instance, take one of two actions at each level of the tree:
    a. Place the new instance into an existing cluster.
    b. Create a new concept cluster having the presented instance as its only member.

The algorithm clearly shows the incremental nature of the clustering process. That is, each instance is presented to the existing concept hierarchy in a sequential manner. Next, at each level of the hierarchy, an evaluation function is used to make a decision about whether to include the instance in an existing cluster or to create a new cluster with the new instance as its only member. In the next section we describe the evaluation function used by a well-known probability-based conceptual clustering system.

Measuring Category Utility

COBWEB (Fisher, 1987) is a conceptual clustering model that stores knowledge in a concept hierarchy. COBWEB accepts instances in attribute-value format where attribute values must be categorical. COBWEB's evaluation function has been shown to consistently determine psychologically preferred (basic) levels in human classification hierarchies. The evaluation function is a generalization of a measure known as **category utility.** The category utility function measures the gain in the "expected number" of correct attribute-value predictions for a specific object if it were placed within a given category.

The formula for category utility includes three probabilities. One measure is the conditional probability of attribute A_i having value V_{ij} given membership in class C_k, denoted as $P(A_i = V_{ij} \mid C_k)$. This is the formal definition of attribute-value predictability introduced in Chapter 4. Recall that if the value of $P(A_i = V_{ij} \mid C_k) = 1$, we can be certain that each instance of class C_k will always have V_{ij} as the value for attribute A_i. Attribute A_i having value V_{ij} is said to be a necessary condition for defining class C_k. The second probability, $P(C_k \mid A_i = V_{ij})$ is the conditional probability that an instance is in class C_k given that attribute A_i has value V_{ij}. This is the definition of attribute-value predictiveness described in Chapter 4. If the value of $P(C_k \mid A_i = V_{ij})$ is 1, we know that if A_i has value V_{ij}, the class containing this attribute value pair must be C_k. Attribute A_i having value V_{ij} is said to be a sufficient condition for defining class C_k.

These probability measures are combined and summed across all values of $i, j,$ and k to describe a heuristic measure of partition quality. Specifically,

$$\sum_K \sum_i \sum_j P(A_i = V_{ij}) \, P(C_K \mid A_i = V_{ij}) \, P(A_i = V_{ij} \mid C_K) \qquad (10.14)$$

The probability $P(A_i = V_{ij})$ allows attribute values that are seen frequently to play a more important part in measuring partition quality. Using the expression for partition quality, category utility is defined by the formula:

$$\frac{\sum_{k=1}^{K} P(C_K) \sum_i \sum_j P(A_i = V_{ij} \mid C_k)^2 - \sum_i \sum_j P(A_i = V_{ij})^2}{K} \qquad (10.15)$$

The first numerator term is the previously described partition-quality expression stated in an alternative form through the application of Bayes rule. The second term represents the probability of correctly guessing attribute values without any category knowledge. The division by K (total number of classes) allows COBWEB to consider variations in the total number of formed clusters.

Conceptual Clustering: An Example

To illustrate the process used by COBWEB to build a concept hierarchy, consider the hierarchy shown in Figure 10.5 created by COBWEB when presented with the instances in Table 10.10. Let's suppose we have a new instance to be placed in the hierarchy. The instance enters the hierarchy at root node N, and N's statistics are updated to reflect the addition of the new instance. As the instance enters the second level of

Figure 10.5 • **A COBWEB-created hierarchy**

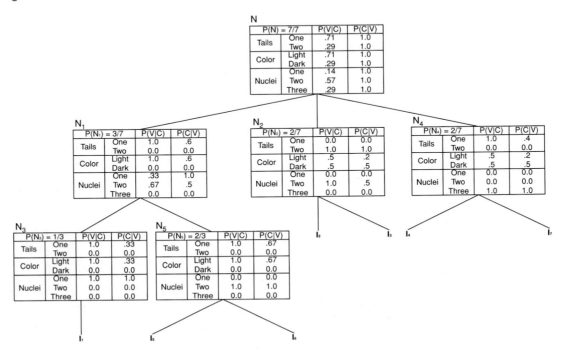

the hierarchy, COBWEB's evaluation function chooses one of four actions. If the new instance is similar enough to one of N_1, N_2, or N_4, the instance is incorporated into the preferred node and the instance proceeds to the second level of the hierarchy through the chosen path. As a second choice, the evaluation function can decide that the new instance is unique enough to merit the creation of a new first-level concept node. This being the case, the instance becomes a first-level concept node and the classification process terminates.

COBWEB allows two other choices. In one case, the system considers merging the two best-scoring nodes into a single node. The last possibility actually removes the best-scoring node from the hierarchy. These final two choices are to help modify nonoptimal hierarchies that can result from skewed instance presentation. If either choice is made, the merge or delete operation is processed and the new instance is once again presented for classification to the modified hierarchy. This procedure continues at each level of the concept tree until the new instance becomes a terminal node.

As a final point, notice that all predictiveness and predictability scores are computed with respect to the parent node. For example, the predictiveness score of 1.0 for *nuclei* = *two* found in N_5 reflects the fact that all instances incorporated into N_1 with *nuclei* = *two* have followed the path from N_1 to N_5.

Table 10.10 • **Data for Conceptual Clustering**

	Tails	Color	Nuclei
I_1	One	Light	One
I_2	Two	Light	Two
I_3	Two	Dark	Two
I_4	One	Dark	Three
I_5	One	Light	Two
I_6	One	Light	Two
I_7	One	Light	Three

General Considerations

Although we have limited our discussion to COBWEB, several other conceptual clustering systems have been developed. CLASSIT (Gennari, Langley, and Fisher, 1989) is a conceptual clustering system that uses an extension of COBWEB's basic algorithm to build a concept hierarchy and classify instances. The two models are very similar with the exception that CLASSIT's evaluation function is an equivalent transformation of COBWEB's category utility for real-valued attributes. Therefore individual concept nodes store attribute mean and standard deviation scores rather than attribute value probabilities.

Like COBWEB, CLASSIT is particularly appealing as its evaluation function has been shown to consistently determine psychologically preferred levels in human classification hierarchies. In addition, both COBWEB and CLASSIT lend themselves well to explaining their behavior because each tree node contains a complete concept description at some level of abstraction.

Conceptual clustering systems also have several shortcomings. A major problem with conceptual clustering systems is that instance ordering can have a marked impact on the results of the clustering. A nonrepresentative ordering of the instances can lead to a less than optimal result. Clustering systems such as COBWEB and CLASSIT use special operations to merge and split clusters in an attempt to overcome this problem. However, the results of these techniques have not been shown to be successful in all cases.

Expectation Maximization

The EM (expectation-maximization) algorithm (Dempster, Laird, and Rubin, 1977) is a statistical technique that makes use of the finite Gaussian mixtures model. A **mixture** is a set of n probability distributions where each distribution represents a cluster. The mixtures model assigns each individual data instance a probability (rather than a specific cluster) that it would have a certain set of attribute values given it was a member of a specified cluster. The mixtures model assumes all attributes to be independent random variables.

The EM algorithm is similar to the K-Means procedure in that a set of parameters are recomputed until a desired convergence value is achieved. In the simplest case, $n = 2$, the probability distributions are assumed to be normal, and data instances consist of a single real-valued attribute. Although the algorithm can be applied to datasets having any number of real-valued attributes, we limit our discussion here to this simplest case and provide a general example in the next section. Using the two-class, one-attribute scenario, the job of the algorithm is to determine the value of five parameters. Specifically,

- The mean and standard deviation for cluster 1

- The mean and standard deviation for cluster 2

- The sampling probability P for cluster 1 (the probability for cluster 2 is $1 - P$)

The general procedure used by EM is as follows:

1. Guess initial values for the five parameters

2. Until a specified termination criterion is achieved:

   a. Use the probability density function for normal distributions (Equation 10.13) to compute the cluster probability for each instance. In the two-cluster case, we have two probability distribution formulas, each with differing mean and standard deviation values.

   b. Use the probability scores assigned to each instance in step 2(a) to reestimate the five parameters.

The algorithm terminates when a formula that measures cluster quality no longer shows significant increases. One measure of cluster quality is the likelihood that the data came from the dataset determined by the clustering. Higher likelihood scores represent more optimal clusterings.

The EM Algorithm: An Example

EM allows us to choose the number of clusters to be formed or we can tell EM to determine a best number of clusters. Table 10.11 shows the results of an application of the EM algorithm where we instructed EM to form three clusters for the gamma-ray burst dataset described in Chapter 4. Recall that the dataset contains a total of six real-valued attributes. We limited the experiment to the three most predictive attributes

Table 10.11 ● **An EM Clustering of Gamma-Ray Burst Data**

	Cluster 0	**Cluster 1**	**Cluster 2**
# Instances	518	340	321
Log Fluence			
Mean	−5.6670	−4.8131	−6.3657
SD	0.4088	0.5301	0.5812
Log HR321			
Mean	0.0538	0.2949	0.5478
SD	0.3018	0.1939	0.2766
Log T90			
Mean	1.2709	1.7159	−0.3794
SD	0.4906	0.3793	0.4825

(Mukherjee et al., 1998). The chosen attributes are given in the table as *Log Fluence* (burst brightness), *Log Hr321* (burst hardness), and *Log T90* (burst length). The table clearly shows that EM formed three distinct gamma ray burst clusters. Cluster 0 contains bursts of intermediate length and brightness. Cluster 1 has the longest bursts, and cluster 2 contains the shortest and hardest bursts. In addition to the summary data shown in Table 10.11, EM offers a final likelihood score and tells us the cluster number associated with each data instance.

General Considerations

EM implements a statistical model that is guaranteed to converge to a maximum likelihood score. However, the maximum may not be global. For this reason, several applications of the algorithm may be necessary to achieve a best result. As initial mean and standard deviation scores selected by the algorithm affect the final result, an alternative technique such as agglomerative clustering is often initially applied. EM then uses the mean and standard deviation values for the clusters determined by the preliminary technique as initial parameter settings.

A lack of explanation about what has been discovered is a problem with EM as it is with many clustering systems. For this reason, our suggested methodology of using a supervised model to analyze the results of an unsupervised clustering is often appropriate.

10.5   Heuristics or Statistics?

Data mining has its foundations in the fields of statistics and a specialized area within Artificial Intelligence (AI) known as machine learning. Each field has its own set of rules and techniques for inductive problem solving. A fundamental difference between a statistical technique and a machine learning technique is in the assumptions or lack thereof about the nature of the data to be processed. As a general rule, a statistical technique assumes an underlying distribution for the data. A frequent assumption is that the data are normally distributed. The soundness of a statistical technique when applied to a particular dataset is dependent upon whether the underlying assumption is valid. On the other hand, machine learning techniques do not make assumptions about the data to be processed. Beyond this, there is much disagreement about the differences between statistical and machine learning techniques.

One way of viewing the issue is to group inductive techniques into three general categories. We can then compare categorical features to better understand similarities and differences between the techniques. Here is one way to categorize inductive problem-solving methods:

- Query and visualization techniques
- Machine learning techniques
- Statistical techniques

Let's examine each category in more detail.

Query and Visualization Techniques

Query and visualization techniques generally fall into one of three groups:

- Query tools
- OLAP tools
- Visualization tools

The main difference between query/OLAP techniques and data mining techniques (statistical or nonstatistical) is that the former are excellent tools for reporting about data but are unable to find *hidden patterns* in data. To use these techniques we must first know what we are looking for.

Visualization tools represent data graphically. Useful visualizations include hierarchical structures such as decision trees, bar and pie charts, two- and three-dimensional histograms, maps, surface plot diagrams, as well as many others. Data visualization is often applied after a data mining process to help us understand what has been discovered. Software packages such as Microsoft Excel and SPSS have several visualization tools to help interpret the output of a data mining session.

Machine Learning and Statistical Techniques

The distinction between machine learning techniques and statistical techniques is not clear. Many machine learning methods can be thought of as statistical techniques because they use at least some component of statistical inference to create models of datasets. This is particularly true with neural networks. However five points of comparison do seem to distinguish the two methods:

1. Statistical techniques typically assume an underlying distribution for the data whereas machine learning techniques do not.

2. Machine learning techniques tend to have a human flavor to their knowledge structure. Machine learning methods such as decision trees and production rules contain knowledge that is easy for us to interpret. Neural networks are actually based on a simple model of the human brain. The output of many statistical techniques is a mathematical structure, such as an equation whose meaning may be difficult to interpret.

3. Machine learning techniques are better able to deal with missing and noisy data. Neural networks are particularly good at building models in very noisy environments. Statistical techniques usually require the elimination of data instances containing noise.

4. Most machine learning techniques are able to explain their behavior whereas statistical techniques are not. Neural networks are an exception to the rule in that they cannot state what has been learned in a form understood by humans.

5. Statistical techniques can deal with small- and modest-sized datasets but have trouble with large-sized data. This is true because large datasets are more likely to contain noise. Also, many statistical methods attempt to model data in a linear fashion. As a dataset increases in size, the possibility of an accurate linear model becomes unlikely.

One misconception is that model speed is a distinguishing factor between statistical and machine learning methods. Statistical methods are thought to be more computationally intense than machine learning methods. Computational complexity depends entirely on the specific technique, not on whether or not the technique is statistical. Probably the most serious misconception is that statistical tests cannot be used to determine significance of outcome for a data mining session unless the data mining technique is statistical. In fact, we have seen that statistical tests can usually be applied to help analyze the results of a data mining session regardless of whether the applied model was built with a statistical or machine learning technique.

10.6 Chapter Summary

Data mining techniques come in many shapes and forms. A favorite statistical technique for estimation and prediction problems is linear regression. Linear regression attempts to model the variation in a dependent variable as a linear combination of one or more independent variables. Linear regression is an appropriate data mining strategy when the relationship between the dependent and independent variables is nearly linear. Microsoft Excel's LINEST function provides an easy mechanism for performing multiple linear regression.

Linear regression is a poor choice when the outcome is binary. The problem lies in the fact that the value restriction placed on the dependent variable is not observed by the regression equation. That is, because linear regression produces a straight-line function, values of the dependent variable are unbounded in both the positive and negative directions. For the two-outcome case, logistic regression is a better choice. Logistic regression is a nonlinear regression technique that associates a conditional probability value with each data instance.

Bayes classifier offers a simple yet powerful supervised classification technique. The model assumes all input attributes to be of equal importance and independent of one another. Even though these assumptions are likely to be false, Bayes classifier still works quite well in practice. Bayes classifier can be applied to datasets containing both categorical and numeric data. Also, unlike many statistical classifiers, Bayes classifier can be applied to datasets containing a wealth of missing items.

Agglomerative clustering is a favorite unsupervised clustering technique. Agglomerative clustering begins by assuming each data instance represents its own cluster. Each iteration of the algorithm merges the most similar pair of clusters. The final iteration sees all dataset items contained in a single cluster. Several options for computing instance and cluster similarity scores and cluster merging procedures exist. Also, when the data to be clustered is real-valued, defining a measure of instance similarity can be a challenge. One common approach is to use simple Euclidean distance. A widespread application of agglomerative clustering is its use as a prelude to other clustering techniques.

Conceptual clustering is an unsupervised technique that incorporates incremental learning to form a hierarchy of concepts. The concept hierarchy takes the form of a tree structure where the root node represents the highest level of concept generalization. Conceptual clustering systems are particularly appealing because the trees they form have been shown to consistently determine psychologically preferred levels in human classification hierarchies. Also, conceptual clustering systems lend themselves well to explaining their behavior. A major problem with conceptual clustering systems is that instance ordering can have a marked impact on the results of the clustering. A nonrepresentative ordering of data instances can lead to a less than optimal clustering.

The EM (expectation-maximization) algorithm is a statistical technique that makes use of the finite Gaussian mixtures model. The mixtures model assigns each individual data instance a probability that it would have a certain set of attribute values given it was a member of a specified cluster. The model assumes all attributes to be independent random variables. The EM algorithm is similar to the K-Means procedure in that a set of parameters are recomputed until a desired convergence value is achieved. A lack of explanation about what has been discovered is a problem with EM as it is with many clustering systems. Applying a supervised model to analyze the results of an unsupervised clustering is one technique to help explain the results of an EM clustering.

10.7   Key Terms

A priori probability. The probability a hypothesis is true lacking evidence to support or reject the hypothesis.

Agglomerative clustering. An unsupervised technique where each data instance initially represents its own cluster. Successive iterations of the algorithm merge pairs of highly similar clusters until all instances become members of a single cluster. In the last step, a decision is made about which clustering is a best final result.

Basic-level nodes. The nodes in a concept hierarchy that represent concepts easily identified by humans.

Bayes classifier. A supervised learning approach that classifies new instances by using Bayes theorem.

Bayes theorem. The probability of a hypothesis given some evidence is equal to the probability of the evidence given the hypothesis, times the probability of the hypothesis, divided by the probability of the evidence.

Bayesian Information Criterion (BIC). The BIC gives the posterior odds for one data mining model against another model assuming neither model is favored initially.

Category utility. An unsupervised evaluation function that measures the gain in the "expected number" of correct attribute-value predictions for a specific object if it were placed within a given category or cluster.

Coefficient of determination. For a regression analysis, the correlation between actual and estimated values for the dependent variable.

Concept hierarchy. A tree structure where each node of the tree represents a concept at some level of abstraction. Nodes toward the top of the tree are the most general. Leaf nodes represent individual data instances.

Conceptual clustering. An incremental unsupervised clustering method that creates a concept hierarchy from a set of input instances.

Conditional probability. The conditional probability of evidence E given hypothesis H denoted by $P(E \mid H)$, is the probability E is true given H is true.

Incremental learning. A form of learning that is supported in an unsupervised environment where instances are presented sequentially. As each new instance is seen, the learning model is modified to reflect the addition of the new instance.

Linear regression. A statistical technique that models the variation in a numeric dependent variable as a linear combination of one or several independent variables.

Logistic regression. A nonlinear regression technique for problems having a binary outcome. A created regression equation limits the values of the output attribute to values between 0 and 1. This allows output values to represent a probability of class membership.

Logit. The natural logarithm of the odds ratio $p(y = 1 \mid \mathbf{x}) / [\, 1 - p(y = 1 \mid \mathbf{x})]$. $p(y = 1 \mid \mathbf{x})$ is the conditional probability that the value of the linear regression equation determined by feature vector $\mathbf{x}$ is 1.

Mixture. A set of n probability distributions where each distribution represents a cluster.

Model tree. A decision tree where each leaf node contains a linear regression equation.

Regression. The process of developing an expression that predicts a numeric output value.

Regression tree. A decision tree where leaf nodes contain averaged numeric values.

Simple linear regression. A regression equation with a single independent variable.

Slope-intercept form. A linear equation of the form $y = ax + b$ where a is the slope of the line and b is the y-intercept.

10.8 Exercises

Review Questions

1. Differentiate between the following:
    a. Simple and multiple linear regression
    b. Linear and logistic regression
    c. Regression tree and model tree
    d. A priori and conditional probability

2. Review the algorithm given in Chapter 4 used by ESX to perform unsupervised clustering. Compare the ESX algorithm with the algorithm for concep-

tual clustering described in this chapter. How do the algorithms differ? How are they the same?

3. Compare and contrast conceptual and agglomerative clustering. Make a list of similarities and differences between the two approaches.

Data Mining Questions

LAB 1. This exercise uses the LINEST function and the cardiology patient dataset.

a. Open the CardiologyNumerical.xls data file located in the samples directory.

b. Copy the data into a new spreadsheet and delete the second and third rows.

c. Delete all columns excepting the columns for *angina, slope, thal,* and *class*.

d. Apply the LINEST function to create a linear regression model with dependent variable *class* using the first 200 data instances.

e. Pick two or three instances not used for training and manually apply the regression equation created by the LINEST function. Does the equation correctly classify the instances?

LAB 2. Visit the Web site *http://members.aol.com/johnp71/logistic.html* and perform a logistic regression using the data selected in the previous question. Pick two or three instances not used for training and manually apply the logistic equation. Does the equation correctly classify the instances?

3. Use ESX to cluster the gamma ray burst dataset into three clusters. Write a description summarizing the characteristics of each of the three clusters. Compare the summary statistics seen in Table 10.10 with your results. How are the clusterings similar? How do they differ?

Computational Questions

1. Consider the data below. The data represents approximate January 1 and June 1 adjusted closing stock prices for the NYSE company EMC Corporation during the years 1996 through 2001.

January 1996	$2.34	June 1996	$2.26
January 1997	$4.63	June 1997	$4.77
January 1998	$7.97	June 1998	$10.96
January 1999	$26.64	June 1999	$26.91
January 2000	$52.48	June 2000	$75.30
January 2001	$74.37	June 2001	$31.45

LAB Denotes exercise appropriate for a laboratory setting.

a. Plot the points using a two-dimensional coordinate system. Plot *price* on the *x*-axis and *year* on the *y*-axis. Does the relationship appear linear?

b. Determine a simple linear regression equation to predict EMC's future stock price. Use the equations in Section 10.3 to manually develop the regression equation or apply Excel's LINEST function.

c. Apply the equation developed in part b to determine the price of EMC stock for January 2002. The actual price of EMC stock on January 1, 2002 was approximately $14.00. How accurate was your prediction? What do you conclude?

2. Repeat the previous exercise using the logistic regression implementation at the Web site *http://members.aol.com/johnp71/logistic.html*.

3. Use the data contained in Table 10.4 to fill in the counts and probabilities in the following table. The output attribute is *life insurance promotion*.

	Magazine Promotion		Watch Promotion	Credit Insurance		Sex	
Life Insurance Promotion	Yes	No	Yes	Yes	No	Male	Female
Yes							
No							
Ratio: yes/total							
Ratio: no/total							

a. Use the completed table together with Bayes classifier to determine the value of *life insurance promotion* for the following instance:

Magazine Promotion = Yes
Watch Promotion = Yes
Credit Card Insurance = No
Sex = Female
Life Insurance Promotion = ?

b. Repeat part a, but assume that the gender of the customer is unknown.

c. Repeat part a, but use Equation 10.12 with $k = 1$ and $p = 0.5$ to determine the value of *life insurance promotion*.

4. Create tables to complete the agglomerative clustering example described in Section 10.4. Choose one of the techniques presented in Section 10.4 to pick a best clustering. As an alternative, develop your own method to make the choice. Explain why your choice represents a best clustering.

5. Consider the new instance I_8 with the attribute values listed below to be added to the concept hierarchy in Figure 10.5.

    Tails = Two
    Color = Dark
    Nuclei = Two

    a. Show the updated probability values for the root node once the instance has been entered into the hierarchy.

    b. Add the new instance to node n_2 and show the updated probability values for all affected nodes.

    c. Rather than having the instance become part of node n_2, assume the instance creates a new first-level node. Add the new node to the hierarchy and show the updated probability values for all affected nodes.

Chapter 11

Specialized Techniques

Chapter Objectives

▶ Know how to perform a time-series analysis.

▶ Know how data mining can be used to discover hidden patterns in data recorded about the clickstream activity of Web site visitors.

▶ Know how data mining is used to automate Web site evaluation and adaptation.

▶ Understand how data mining is employed to present Web users with information that interests them without requiring them to ask for it directly.

▶ Understand that textual data mining concerns itself with extracting useful patterns from unstructured text.

▶ Understand how and when bagging, boosting, and instance typicality can be used to improve the performance of supervised learner models.

In this chapter we overview several specialized data mining techniques. In Section 11.1 we introduce time-series analysis and show how neural networks and linear regression are used to solve time-series problems. In Section 11.2 we show how data mining is used for Web site evaluation, personalization, and adaptation. Section 11.3 offers a brief overview of textual data mining. Section 11.4 presents three methods that, in some cases, can improve the classification correctness of supervised learner models. The first two methods use a multimodel approach to improve performance. The third method attempts to build improved learner models by selecting a best set of training instances.

11.1 Time-Series Analysis

Oftentimes, the data we wish to analyze contains a time dimension. Prediction applications with one or more time-dependent attributes are called **time-series problems.** Time-series analysis usually involves predicting numeric outcomes, such as the future price of an individual stock or the closing price of a stock index. Three additional applications suitable for time-series analysis include:

- Tracking individual customers over time to determine if they are likely to terminate the use of their credit card

- Predicting the likelihood of automotive engine failure

- Predicting the weekly rushing yards of an NFL running back

Much of the work with time-dependent data analysis has been statistical and limited to predicting the future value of a single variable. However, we can use both sta-

The Stock Index Dataset

The stock index dataset contains a time-series representation of average weekly closing prices for the Nasdaq and Dow Jones Industrial Average indices for the first 49 weeks of the year 2000. The dataset is interesting because it represents real data that can be used to develop and test time-series models for predicting stock market trends. See Appendix B for a complete description of the attributes in the dataset as well as more information about how to expand the original data. The dataset is found in the iDA samples directory under the title NasdaqDow.xls. ■

Table 11.1 • **Weekly Average Closing Prices for the Nasdaq and Dow Jones Industrial Average**

Week	Nasdaq Average	Dow Average	Nasdaq-1 Average	Dow-1 Average	Nasdaq-2 Average	Dow-2 Average
200003	4176.75	11413.28	3968.47	11587.96	3847.25	11224.10
200004	4052.01	10967.60	4176.75	11413.28	3968.47	11587.96
200005	4104.28	10992.38	4052.01	10967.60	4176.75	11413.28
200006	4398.72	10726.28	4104.28	10992.38	4052.01	10967.60
200007	4445.53	10506.68	4398.72	10726.28	4104.28	10992.38
200008	4535.15	10121.31	4445.53	10506.68	4398.72	10726.28
200009	4745.58	10167.38	4535.15	10121.31	4445.53	10506.68
200010	4949.09	9952.52	4745.58	10167.38	4535.15	10121.31
200011	4742.40	10223.11	4949.09	9952.52	4745.58	10167.38
200012	4818.01	10937.36	4742.40	10223.11	4949.09	9952.52

tistical and nonstatistical data mining tools for time-series analysis on one or several variables. Fortunately, we are able to apply the same techniques we use for other data mining applications to solve time-series problems. Our ability to succeed is determined to a large extent by the availability of relevant attributes and instances, as well as by the difficulty of the problem at hand.

An Example with Linear Regression

Table 11.1 shows a time-series representation of average weekly closing prices for the Nasdaq and Dow Jones Industrial Average. The first row of the table displays the average closing price on the Nasdaq and Dow for the third (Nasdaq, Dow), second (Nasdaq-1, Dow-1), and first (Nasdaq-2, Dow-2) weeks of January 2000. Specifically, the average Nasdaq closing price for the third week was 4176.75. In week 2, the average closing price was 3968.47, and week 1 showed an average close of 3847.25. Note that *Week* relates to the columns labeled *Nasdaq Average* and *Dow Average*. That is the first row value of 200003 tells us that the Nasdaq average close for week 3 of the year 2000 was 4176.75. Corresponding values for the Dow Jones Average are interpreted in a similar manner.

The table is built to accommodate time-series analysis with a time lag of two. An individual data instance contains a current week average close for each index as well as average closing prices for the two previous weeks. In this way, all data instances have a built-in time dimension. Our choice for a time lag is arbitrary. In general, choosing a best time lag is a matter of experimentation.

Once we have structured a time dimension into the data, our next step is to build a model for predicting future outcome. For the data in Table 11.1, our goal is to predict the Nasdaq and Dow Jones Average closing values for week 200013. To accomplish this, we add a new entry representing week 13 to the table. The row entry for week 13 is:

| 200013 | ? | ? | 4818.01 | 10937.36 | 4742.40 | 10223.11 |

The entry shows that we are looking at two prediction problems. One problem is to predict the Nasdaq Average close for week 13. The second problem is to predict the Dow Jones Average close for the same week.

To make our experiments more interesting, we expanded this dataset through week 49 of the year 2000. The expanded dataset is found in the iDA samples directory under the name NasdaqDow.xls. The description box titled *The Stock Index Dataset,* as well as a summary in Appendix B, offers additional details about this dataset.

For our first experiment we applied linear regression to the expanded data. We assigned the Nasdaq Average close as the output attribute and used weeks 3 through 48 for training. The resulting regression equation is given below. Notice that the equation does not contain attributes representing Dow Jones average closing prices.

$$Nasdaq\ Average = 1.279(Nasdaq - 1\ Average) - 0.330(Nasdaq - 2\ Average) + 179.297$$

The regression equation showed a mean absolute training data error of 146.85. This result is not encouraging if we intend to use the equation to determine when to buy or sell stocks tracking the Nasdaq index. In any case, we used the equation to predict the Nasdaq Average close for week 49. The equation gave an average Nasdaq closing price of 2707.89 for week 49. This value was approximately 92 points above the actual close of 2615.75.

For the second experiment, we employed the same data to formulate a linear regression equation to predict the Dow Jones Average close for week 49. The resulting regression equation is shown as:

$$Dow\ Average = 0.932(Dow - 1\ Average) - 0.303(Dow - 2\ Average) + 3967.093$$

The mean absolute error for the training data was 160.72, which, once again, is not an encouraging result. However, when applied to week 49, the predicted Dow Jones Average close was within 13 points of the actual average weekly close. As you can see, just as the Nasdaq equation did not contain Dow Jones attributes, the equation for the Dow Jones average close does not contain attributes representing Nasdaq closing prices.

Table 11.2 • Actual and Predicted Nasdaq and Dow Closing Prices

Week	Nasdaq Average Close			Dow Average Close		
	Actual	**Predicted**	**Error**	**Actual**	**Predicted**	**Error**
45	3258.61	3408.19	−149.58	10854.73	10954.14	−99.41
46	3065.91	3477.37	−411.46	10638.36	10883.32	−244.96
47	2851.70	3544.05	−692.35	10456.68	10793.97	−337.30
48	2713.12	3602.48	−889.36	10494.16	10731.85	−237.69
49	2615.75	3651.73	−1035.98	10560.95	10701.07	−140.12

For our final experiment with linear regression, we attempted to predict the Nasdaq and Dow average closing prices five weeks into the future. First, we used the data through week 44 to create linear regression equations for predicting closing values for week 45. Next, we added the predicted values to the original training data. We then proceeded to use the modified training set to predict values for week 46. We repeated this process until we had charted future average closing prices through week 49.

Table 11.2 shows the results of this experiment. The table data indicate a sharp decrease in predictive accuracy for Nasdaq average closing prices but a relatively stable error rate for the Dow Jones Average. It is apparent that a nonlinear model for predicting Nasdaq closing averages is likely to be a better choice.

A Neural Network Example

The results of the experiments using linear regression modeling suggest that a nonlinear model may be better suited for predicting Nasdaq weekly average closing prices. To test the hypothesis that a nonlinear model will offer better predictive accuracy for the stock index data, we conducted six experiments with the iDA backpropagation neural network software. We used weeks 3 through 48 to train a neural network and applied the network model to predict the week 49 Nasdaq average closing price.

Table 11.3 presents the outcome of the six experiments. Notice that there are two experiments for each value shown in the *epochs* column. One experiment uses a neural network model built with input attributes representing Nasdaq average closings. The second experiment also incorporates Dow Jones attributes for network training. Recall that the actual week 49 average Nasdaq close was 2615. Notice that, unlike the linear regression model, including the Dow Jones input attributes generally improves predictive accuracy. Although the outcome is inconclusive, the results merit further experimentation. Several end-of-chapter exercises suggest additional experiments with this dataset.

Table 11.3 • **Week 49 Predicted Nasdaq Average Weekly Closing Prices**

		Training Data Limited to Nasdaq Attributes			Data Includes Dow Jones Attributes	
Epochs	RMS	Predicted Value	Prediction Error	RMS	Predicted Value	Prediction Error
10000	0.084	3359	744	0.035	2693	22
20000	0.045	2598	−17	0.033	2652	37
30000	0.032	2672	57	0.033	2712	97

Categorical Attribute Prediction

We can adapt our data to perform time-series analysis using data mining tools limited to categorical output. To accomplish this, we must first transform the output attribute and restate our goal. Let's consider an example.

Table 11.4 displays the data from Table 11.1 with the addition of two columns. The Nasdaq Gain/Loss column indicates whether the average for the current week is a gain or loss when compared to the previous week's average. For example, the first table record shows *gain* in the Nasdaq Gain/Loss column, as 4176.75 is greater than 3968.47. The Dow Gain/Loss column shows the same information for the Dow Jones Industrial Average. When we present the table data to a supervised classifier for training using the *Nasdaq gain/loss* attribute for output, a prediction model containing two classes will be formed. We can use the created model to predict future outcome in terms of a likely gain or loss. That is, using the data from Table 11.4 for training, our goal is to determine whether the Nasdaq is likely to show an average closing price gain or loss for week 13. The test instance has the form:

200013   ?   ?   4818.01   10937.36   4742.40   10223.11   Unknown   ?

As you can see, the instance to be classified has four missing values. The values shown by a "?" must be treated by the learner model as missing data items. The result of the classification will be a value of "gain" or "loss" for the field specified as *unknown*. Notice that we are not able to extend the model beyond week 13 because actual week 13 closing prices cannot be predicted.

When the attribute to be predicted is categorical, we lose most of the precision found with numeric output. To help overcome this problem, we may consider further subdividing values for the output attribute. That is, rather than limiting Table 11.4 to

Table 11.4 • Average Weekly Closings /Categorical Output

Week	Nasdaq Average Close	Dow Average Close	Nasdaq-1 Average Close	Dow-1 Average Close	Nasdaq-2 Average Close	Dow-2 Average Close	Nasdaq Gain/ Loss	Dow Gain/ Loss
200003	4176.75	11413.28	3968.47	11587.96	3847.25	11224.10	Gain	Loss
200004	4052.01	10967.60	4176.75	11413.28	3968.47	11587.96	Loss	Loss
200005	4104.28	10992.38	4052.01	10967.6	4176.75	11413.28	Gain	Gain
200006	4398.72	10726.28	4104.28	10992.38	4052.01	10967.60	Gain	Loss
200007	4445.53	10506.68	4398.72	10726.28	4104.28	10992.38	Gain	Loss
200008	4535.15	10121.31	4445.53	10506.68	4398.72	10726.28	Gain	Loss
200009	4745.58	10167.38	4535.15	10121.31	4445.53	10506.68	Gain	Gain
200010	4949.09	9952.516	4745.58	10167.38	4535.15	10121.31	Gain	Loss
200011	4742.40	10223.11	4949.09	9952.516	4745.58	10167.38	Loss	Gain
200012	4818.01	10937.36	4742.40	10223.11	4949.09	9952.516	Loss	Gain

having two output attribute values (gain/loss), we transform the original numeric data into several categorical intervals. For example, we could have three subclasses for each gain or loss possibility: one subclass for gains less than 5%, a second subclass for gains between 5 and 10%, and a third subclass for gains greater than 10%. Subclasses for losses can be created in a similar manner. The end result is a six-class rather than a two-class structure.

Lastly, we may choose to leave the two-class structure intact and apply logistic regression to our problem. By doing so, we are able to associate a probability of class membership with each new prediction.

General Considerations

Time plays a key role in many real-world problems. The following is a partial list of general considerations for building models for time-series applications:

- Once a model has been created, continue to test and modify the model as new data become available.

- If models built with the data in its current form are not acceptable, try one or more data transformations.

Common transformations include using time-series differences or percent change values. To illustrate, suppose we wish to represent the data in Table 11.1 as a set of difference values. To compute the Nasdaq column table entry for week 200003 we subtract 3968.47 from 4176.75 and obtain 208.28. For Nasdaq-1 we subtract 3847.25 from 3968.47, which gives 121.22. Making similar computations for the Dow Jones attributes, the first row of the revised table becomes:

| 200003 | 208.28 | −174.68 | 121.22 | 363.86 | 0.00 | 0.00 |

- Exercise caution when predicting future outcome with training data containing several fields with predicted rather than actual results.

- Try a nonlinear model if a linear model shows less than optimal results.

- Use unsupervised clustering to determine if values of the input attributes allow the output attribute to cluster into meaningful categories. If this is not the case, the input attributes should be transformed or replaced as necessary.

11.2   Mining the Web

Companies relying on e-commerce for all or part of their business share a common goal—optimizing their Web site design so as to maximize sales. For example, a Web site that sells marketable products profits most by simultaneously displaying products customers are likely to buy together. On the other hand, a Web site requiring potential customers to spend an unwarranted amount of time to find their choice of products is likely to fail.

The success of a Web site ultimately depends on how it is viewed by the user community. Three major factors help determine how users perceive a Web site: the products or services offered by the site, individual Web page design, and overall site design (Spiliopoulou, 2000). Web page design and site design are related; however, the latter refers more directly to the intuitive nature of the indexing structure of a Web site.

Data mining can be deployed to help with at least three tasks that improve how users perceive and interact with a Web site. Data mining can be used to:

- Evaluate a Web site to determine if the intent of the Web designer matches the desires of the user (Spiliopoulou, 2000)

- Personalize the products and pages displayed to a particular user or set of users (Mobasher, Cooley, and Srivastava, 2000)

- Automatically adapt the indexing structure of a Web site to better meet the changing needs of its users (Perkowitz and Etzioni, 2000)

Before examining each of these possibilities in more detail, we first take a look at some of the issues seen with Web-based data mining.

Web-Based Mining: General Issues

Web-based data mining presents a whole new set of unique challenges not seen with other data mining applications. Let's examine a few of these issues through the eyes of the KDD process model.

Identifying the Goal

Recall that the first step of the KDD process requires us to establish one or more goals. Here is a partial list of plausible goals for a Web-based mining project.

- Decrease the average number of pages visited by a customer before a purchase transaction

- Increase the average number of pages viewed per user session

- Increase Web server efficiency

- Increase average visitor retention rates

- Decrease the total number of returns on purchased items

- Personalize Web pages for customers

- Determine those products for sale at a Web site that tend to be purchased or viewed together

Regardless of our goals, over 80% of the time spent on a Web-based mining project involves steps 2, 3, and 4 of the KDD process model. We detail these steps under the general category of data preparation.

Preparing the Data

The data available to us as a result of one or more Web-based user sessions is stored in Web server log files. A typical server log file houses information describing the **click-stream** sequences followed by users as they investigate Web pages and follow page links.

Server log files most often provide information in what is known as **extended common log file format.** The fields associated with the extended common log format are, in order: host address, date/time, request, status, bytes, referring page, and browser type. The description box titled *User Access Log Entries* shows three extended log file entries recorded from the Web site *http://grb.mnsu.edu*. The Web site offers a user-friendly interface for performing data mining experiments with gamma-ray burst data. Notice that each entry represents a different host location, and all three entries show *grb* in the referring page field.

For data mining, we are interested in those common log file fields that allow us to determine the sequence of clickstreams followed by each user as they navigate a specific Web site. Therefore the job of the data preparation process is to extract relevant data from the Web sever logs and create a file suitable for data mining.

Figure 11.1 shows that the file created by the data preparation process is known as a **session file.** A session file contains from a few to several thousand records each representing an instance of a user session. A user **session** is simply a set of pageviews requested by a single user from a single Web server. A single **pageview** is made up of one or more page files each forming a single display window in a Web browser. Each pageview is tagged with a unique uniform resource identifier (URI) for purposes of identification during the data mining process.

Creating the session file is a difficult task for several reasons. First, to create the individual server sessions, we must be able to identify each user among the several users listed in a log file. Host addresses are of limited help because multiple users may be accessing a site from the same host. When the host address is combined with the referring page, we can more easily distinguish one user session from another. However, we are best able to differentiate between users if sites are allowed to use cookies. A **cookie** is a data file placed on a user's computer that contains session information. Unfortunately, we cannot rely on the potential information available in cookies as many users are reluctant to give Web sites the authority to place cookies on their machines.

User Access Log Entries

80.202.8.93 - - [16/Apr/2002:22:43:28 -0600] "GET /grbts/images/msu-new-color.gif HTTP/1.1" 200 5006 "http://grb.mnsu.edu/doc/index.html" "Mozilla/4.0 (compatible; MSIE 5.0; Windows 2000) Opera 6.01 [nb]"

207.172.11.232 — [16/Apr/2002:23:14:19 -0600] "GET /images/cofc-logo.gif HTTP/1.0" 200 6710 "http://grb.mnsu.edu/" "Mozilla/4.0 (compatible; MSIE 6.0; Windows NT 5.1)"

134.29.41.219 - - [17/Apr/2002:19:23:30 -0600] "GET /resin-doc/images/resin_powered.gif HTTP/1.1" 200 571 "http://grb.mnsu.edu/" "Mozilla/4.0 (compatible; MSIE 6.0; Windows 98; Q3312461)"

Figure 11.1 ● **A generic Web usage model**

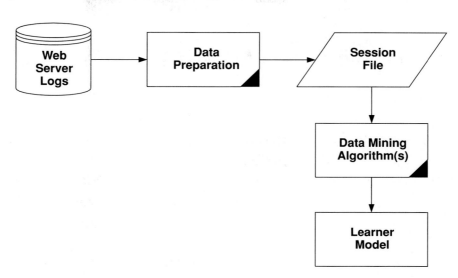

Problems with creating the session file do not end with difficulties in distinguishing users. A second problem is the fact that a single user page request oftentimes generates multiple log file entries from several types of servers. Many of these servers are image or ad servers. As we are not interested in entries created by application, image, and ad servers, we must have a technique to identify unwanted log entries so they do not become part of the session file. Several other potential problems with creating session files are summarized by Edelstein (2001).

Finally, one or more data transformations in the form of adding new variables to session records may be necessary. If repeat customer records are available, information about the amount of money previously spent, average purchase amounts, as well as time of most recent transaction may prove useful.

Mining the Data

Once the session file is created, the session data is presented for data mining. The algorithms applied to the data may be traditional techniques such as association rule generators or clustering methods. However, depending on the goals of a data mining project, algorithms specifically designed for determining sequences of Web page visits (see the second part of this section) may be a better choice.

Interpreting and Evaluating Results

The instances of a session file represent the pageview behavior of a single user during one session. Here we offer a simple example that shows how to interpret the results of a hypothetical Web-based data mining session using an association rule technique.

Consider the four hypothetical session instances where each P_i represents a pageview:

$$I_1: \quad P_5 \rightarrow P_4 \rightarrow P_{10} \rightarrow P_3 \rightarrow P_{15} \rightarrow P_2 \rightarrow P_1$$
$$I_2: \quad P_2 \rightarrow P_4 \rightarrow P_{10} \rightarrow P_8 \rightarrow P_{15} \rightarrow P_4 \rightarrow P_{15} \rightarrow P_1$$
$$I_3: \quad P_4 \rightarrow P_3 \rightarrow P_7 \rightarrow P_{11} \rightarrow P_{14} \rightarrow P_8 \rightarrow P_2 \rightarrow P_{10}$$
$$I_4: \quad P_1 \rightarrow P_3 \rightarrow P_{10} \rightarrow P_{11} \rightarrow P_4 \rightarrow P_{15} \rightarrow P_9$$

Suppose an association rule generator outputs the following rule from our hypothetical session data:

IF $\rightarrow P_4$ & P_{10}
THEN P_{15} {3/4}

The rule tells us that there are three instances where P_4, P_{10}, and P_{15} appear together in a single session record. Also, a total of four session instances have P_4 and P_{10} appearing in the same session. Therefore we are 75% confident that each time a user references P_4 and P_{10}, the user also references P_{15}. Provided that direct links do not exist between the three pageviews, this result may warrant modifying the Web site indexing structure by placing one or more direct links between the pages. As a second possibility, if the precondition of the rule matches the activity of a current user of the system, P_{15} can be added to a list of recommended pageviews to be automatically presented to the user. In this way, the pages viewed by the user can be personalized to their likely interests.

Unsupervised clustering can also be employed to form clusters of similar session file instances. A variety of clustering algorithms and similarity measures can be used. One plausible strategy is to use agglomerative clustering where instance similarity is computed by dividing the total number of pageviews each pair of instances have in common by the total number of pageviews contained within the instances. To illustrate this method, consider the following session instances:

$$I_1: \quad P_5 \rightarrow P_4 \rightarrow P_{10} \rightarrow P_3 \rightarrow P_{15} \rightarrow P_2 \rightarrow P_1$$
$$I_2: \quad P_2 \rightarrow P_4 \rightarrow P_{10} \rightarrow P_8 \rightarrow P_{15} \rightarrow P_4 \rightarrow P_{15} \rightarrow P_1$$

As instances I_1 and I_2 share five of eight total pageviews, the computed $I_1 I_2$ similarity is 0.625. In the third part of this section we show one way to use the clusters formed by similar sessions to personalize the pages viewed by Web site users.

In addition to discovering patterns in Web data, it is often desirable to obtain summary statistics about the activities taking place at a Web site. Several commercial and free downloadable Web server log analyzers are available that offer log file summaries of Web site activity. The output of most log analyzers is an aggregation of gathered log file data displayed in a graphical format. A typical log analyzer produces statistics such as how often a Web site is visited, how many individuals fill a market basket but fail to complete a transaction, and which Web site products are the best and worst sellers. Here are the Web addresses of two free log analyzers for you to try:

- AWStats: *http://awstats.sourceforge.net/*
- Analog: *http://www.analog.cx*

Taking Action

Several possibilities exist for taking action based on the results of a Web-based data mining project. Here is a short list of candidate actions:

- Implement a strategy based on created user profiles to personalize the Web pages viewed by site visitors

- Adapt the indexing structure of a Web site to better reflect the paths followed by typical users

- Set up online advertising promotions for registered Web site customers

- Send e-mail to promote products of likely interest to a select group of registered customers

- Modify the content of a Web site by grouping products likely to be purchased together, removing products of little interest, and expanding the offerings of high-demand products

Lastly, as the interests of users visiting a Web site are in a constant state of change, the effectiveness of the actions taken must be closely monitored and modified as necessary.

Data Mining for Web Site Evaluation

Web site evaluation is concerned with determining whether the actual use of a site matches the intentions of its designer. If the paths traveled by a majority of site visitors are not those expected by the designer, the site is likely to be seen as difficult to navigate. If this is the case, the Web designer must consider changing the architecture of the Web site to more clearly fit the needs of its users.

Data mining can help with site evaluation by determining the frequent patterns and routes traveled by the user population. However, unlike many Web site data mining applications, Web site evaluation is not only concerned about clusterings of pageviews, but also with the sequential ordering of pageviews. In this way, the Web designer can determine if the path structure of the Web site is indeed a best representation of the navigational habits of its users.

Because the data mining problem becomes one of sequence identification, a special class of data mining algorithms known as **sequence miners** are often used for Web site evaluation. Sequence miners are able to discover frequently accessed pages that occur in the same order. Spiliopoulou (2000) describes WUM, a generalized Web log miner that can perform sequence mining tasks but also allows Web designers to express queries in an SQL-like format in order to determine navigational patterns between individual pages. To see an example of how WUM works, visit *http://wum.wiwi.hu-berlin.de.*

Data Mining for Personalization

The goal of **personalization** is to present Web users with what interests them without requiring them to ask for it directly. Personalization can be manually implemented or performed automatically with the help of data mining methods. Manual techniques force users to register at a Web site as well as answer questions or fill out check boxes. As user bias is a factor, manual techniques are not likely to provide Web sites with a true picture of expected user actions. By using data mining to automate personalization, the subjectivity of user response is replaced by actual user behavior.

Figure 11.2 shows the general steps for automated personalization. The process involves creating usage profiles from stored session data. The most difficult part of the procedure is moving from the clusters formed by the data mining process to the usage profiles. Profiling is easier if users are required to register in order to use the services provided by a Web site. In this case, actual user browsing behavior can be supplemented with compiled demographic data.

Mobasher (2000) describes the technique used by WebPersonalizer for creating usage profiles. WebPersonalizer uses two profiling techniques. One technique employs association rules for directly creating usage profiles. A second method creates usage profiles by generalizing clusters. For each cluster, only those pageviews that satisfy a minimum score become part of the usage profile. The score is a ratio computed by dividing the total number of times a pageview appears in a cluster across all session instances by the total number of session instances within the cluster. Pageviews meeting the minimum criterion become part of the usage profile representing the cluster. In addition, each pageview is assigned a weight to reflect its frequency of occurrence across all session instances. This weight is used to compute pageview recommendation scores for individual users. For each user, only those pageviews having a recommendation score above a minimum threshold value are candidates for presentation.

Figure 11.2 ● **Creating usage profiles from session data**

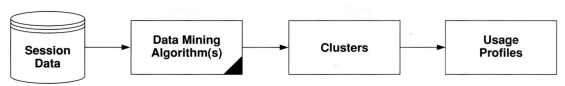

Figure 11.3 ● **Hypertext link recommendations from usage profiles**

Lastly, Figure 11.3 shows that the recommendation engine for WebPersonalizer takes as input the set of created usage profiles and matches current user navigational activity with the stored profiles. The recommendation engine outputs recommended hypertext links to be displayed to the user. For e-commerce applications, the majority of recommended pageviews will be links to products and advertising. To learn more about WebPersonalizer, visit the Web site *http://maya.cs.depaul.edu/~mobasher/personalization/*.

Data Mining for Web Site Adaptation

Web masters make initial decisions about how a new Web site is to be organized. Their decisions are strongly influenced by how they believe the new site will be accessed by its users. However, the chances of a Web designer anticipating a majority of actual user needs is quite slim. Even if an initial design is adequate for most users, over time the needs of users change. Once useful index links become unused and new patterns of Web usage emerge. Therefore for a Web site to remain competitive, it becomes necessary for the indexing structure of the site to change over time. New page links must be added and little-used links deleted. The necessary changes can be manually applied; however, a better approach is to use data mining to automate the process. Web sites that are able to semiautomatically improve their internal structure as well as their methods of presentation by learning from visitor access patterns are known as **adaptive Web sites.**

The internal structure of a Web site has at its core a set of index pages. An **index page** is a Web page having links to a set of pages detailing a particular topic. Therefore the problem of automatically improving the internal structure of a Web site becomes one of index page synthesis. Perkowitz and Etzioni (2000) provide a formal definition of the **index synthesis problem:**

> *Given a Web site and a visitor access log, create new index pages containing collections of links to related but currently unlinked pages. (p. 155)*

Perkowitz and Etzioni (2000) describe IndexFinder, an automated page synthesis system that uses a clustering algorithm to generate candidate index pages for an existing Web site. IndexFinder also creates a rule-based description of each candidate page. The Web master must decide whether to accept or reject the candidate pages. If a new index page is accepted, IndexFinder creates a final page form and automatically adds the page to the Web site. The Web master gives the page a title and determines where in the site the page will reside.

11.3 Mining Textual Data

Textual data mining involves extracting useful patterns from free text. As textual data is unstructured, an initial investigation of such a task seems to be nearly impossible. However, textual data mining is possible because we are only trying to categorize textual data, not completely understand its contents.

A common problem that can be solved using textual data mining is to determine whether or not a document is about a specific topic. This problem can be considered a binary classification problem with the output of a classifier limited to a *yes* or *no* response. For example, we may wish to examine daily articles in several newspapers that deal in one way or another with the stock market. Here is a textual mining algorithm that could be used for the problem:

1. **Train.** Create an attribute dictionary where the attributes represent words from articles dealing with stock market topics. Choose only those words that occur a minimum number of times.

2. **Filter.** Remove common words known to be useless in differentiating articles of one type from another.

3. **Classify.** Check each new document to be classified for the presence and frequency of the chosen attributes. If a certain document contains a predetermined minimum number of references to the chosen attributes, classify the document as a member of the class of articles dealing with stock market topics.

More difficult textual mining problems involve the analysis of free-form text as it is found in e-mail documents, recorded telephone transcripts, and the like. The nature of such messages requires that the textual mining system deal with ambiguities as well as spelling and grammar errors. In the case of transcript analysis, it is easy to understand the desire to be able to analyze telephone transcript documents to better understand customers likely to make purchases or to continue with a provided service. Some success has been achieved in this area by performing a quantitative as well as a qualitative data analysis. The quantitative analysis looks at directly measurable items such as the length of calls and call time of day frequency distributions. The qualitative analysis concerns itself with document content for the purpose of classifying individual transcripts.

As written text has become our most common form of information exchange, textual data mining will continue to play an increasingly important role in our society. In addition, the expansion of the World Wide Web makes the prospects for textual data mining unlimited. You can download evaluation copies of several text-mining products by visiting *www.kdnuggets.com* and clicking on *software*.

11.4 Improving Performance

When we make decisions, we usually rely on the help of others. In the same way, it makes intuitive sense to formulate classification decisions by combining the output of several data mining models. Unfortunately, attempts at employing a multiple-model approach to classification have been met with mixed results. This can be explained in part by the fact that most models misclassify the same instances. However, some success has been seen with a multiple-model approach where each model is built by applying the same data mining algorithm. In the first two parts of this section we describe two techniques that make use of the same data mining algorithm to construct multiple-model classifiers.

After our discussion of multiple-model classifiers, we describe a technique based on training instance selection for improving performance. All three approaches described here work best with unstable data mining algorithms. Recall that unstable algorithms show significant changes in model structure when slight changes are made to the training data. Many standard data mining algorithms have been shown to display this characteristic.

Bagging

Bagging (bootstrap aggregation) is a supervised learning approach developed by Leo Breiman (1996) that allows several models to have an equal vote in the classification of new instances. The same mining tool is most often employed to create the multiple models to be used. The models vary in that different training instances are selected from the same pool to build each model. Here's how the approach works:

1. Randomly sample several training datasets of equal size from the domain of training instances. Instances are sampled with replacement. This allows each instance to be present in several training sets.

2. Apply the data mining algorithm to build a classification model for each training dataset. N sets of training data result in N classification models.

3. To classify unknown instance I, present I to each classifier. Each classifier is allowed one vote. The instance is placed in the class achieving the most votes.

Bagging can also be applied to estimation problems where predictions are numeric values. To determine the value of an unknown instance, the estimated output is given as the average of all individual classifier estimations.

Boosting

Boosting, introduced by Freund and Schapire (1996), is more complex. **Boosting** is like bagging in that several models are used to vote in the classification of new instances. However, there are two main differences between bagging and boosting. Specifically,

*   Each new model is built based upon the results of previous models. The latest model concentrates on correctly classifying those instances incorrectly classified by prior models. This is usually accomplished by assigning weights to individual instances. At the start of training, all instances are assigned the same weight. After the latest model is built, those instances classified correctly by the model have their weights decreased. Instances incorrectly classified have their weights increased.

*   Once all models have been built, each model is assigned a weight based on its performance on the training data. Because of this, better-performing models are allowed to contribute more during the classification of unknown instances.

As you can see, boosting builds models that complement one another in their ability to classify the training data. An obvious problem exists if the data mining algorithm cannot classify weighted training data. The following is one way to overcome this problem:

1. Assign equal weights to all training data and build the first classification model.

2. Increase the weights of incorrectly classified instances and have the weights of correctly classified instances decreased.

3. Create a new training dataset by sampling instances with replacement from the previous training data. Select instances having higher weight values more

frequently than instances with lower weight values. In this way, even though the data mining algorithm cannot use instance weights per say, the most difficult to classify instances will receive increased exposure to subsequent models.

4. Repeat the previous step for each new model.

As incorrectly classified instances are sampled more frequently, the weight values still play their part in the model building process. However, the data mining algorithm does not actually use the weight values during the model building process.

Instance Typicality

In Chapter 4 we defined the typicality of instance *I* as the average similarity of *I* to the other members of its class. We noted that highly typical data instances within a class are called class prototypes and that instances with low typicality scores represent candidate outliers. In this section we show how instance typicality can be applied to help develop supervised learner models.

We conducted research on the topic of training instance selection using several data mining algorithms (Roiger and Cornell, 1996). Our experiments showed that by selecting representative training data from a pool of available instances and limiting the inclusion of atypical instances, test set classification accuracy can be significantly improved. Our work with instance typicality is of an introductory nature. However, we include a discussion here because typicality scores are automatically computed for training set instances each time ESX performs a data mining session. We hope our discussion motivates you to perform your own experiments with instance typicality. In the next section we report the results of two experiments that apply bagging, boosting, and instance typicality to the cardiology patient data described in Chapter 2.

Experiments with Bagging, Boosting, and Typicality

We conducted two experiments using the cardiology patient data to determine the effects bagging, boosting, and typicality have on test set classification correctness for two supervised learning techniques. For our experiments, we applied bagging, boosting, and typicality to Weka's implementations of C4.5 and Bayes classifier. We chose these models to contrast the effects of the three techniques on an unstable algorithm (C4.5) as compared to a stable algorithm (Bayes classifier).

The typicality measure defined with ESX was adopted to assign a typicality score to each instance of the mixed form of the cardiology patient dataset. For the first experiment, we wanted to test the degree to which classification correctness was affected by creating models trained with most typical as compared to least typical cardiology patient data instances. For the experiment, we randomly selected 153 of the 303 data instances for training. Using the training data, we constructed two training sets, one containing the 40 most typical instances from each class (*healthy* and *sick*) and a second set of least typical instances. We then used the training set containing the 40 most typical data instances together with C4.5 to build three classifiers. One classifier was constructed using C4.5, a second classifier was built using C4.5 with bagging. The third classifier employed C4.5 and boosting. The same procedure was applied to the training set with the atypical data instances, giving us a total of six classifier models. The six models were each used to classify the 150 test set cardiology patient data instances. The results of the experiment are given in Table 11.5.

As you can see, Table 11.5 shows large classification correctness differences in test set performance with models created with typical as compared to atypical training data. In addition, bagging and boosting did not show improved classification correctness scores when applied to either dataset. This could be due in part to the small number of training instances used for the experiments. We followed this same procedure with Bayes classifier and obtained similar results (not displayed).

For the second experiment, we made a random selection of 153 training instances to build three decision tree classifiers and three Bayesian classifiers. Specifically, the 153 instances were used to build a decision tree classifier, a multiple-model decision tree classifier using bagging, and a multiple-model decision tree classifier using boosting. The same process was applied to create three Bayes classifier models. Two additional models were built using a training set based on typicality. To construct the typicality-based training set, all 153 training instances were ordered by their typicality score. Following this, every other instance was chosen for the training set. All eight models were applied to the entire set of cardiology patient data. The classification correctness scores are shown in Table 11.6. Although statistically significant differences were not seen between the models, it is interesting to note that the models built with bagging, boosting, and typicality outperformed the decision tree model but did not outperform Bayes classifier. The results of these experiments are by no means conclusive. However, they do provide a model for further exploration of the effects that bagging, boosting, and instance typicality have on classification correctness

---

Table 11.5 • **Test Set Accuracy Scores for Typical and Atypical Training Data**

	Decision Tree	**Bagging**	**Boosting**
Most Typical	76.57%	76.89%	76.56%
Least Typical	49.84%	49.17%	48.84%

Table 11.6 • **Classification Correctness: Bagging, Boosting, and Typicality**

	Single Model	Bagging	Boosting	Typicality
Decision Tree	82.83%	86.47%	88.45%	85.81%
Bayes Classifier	87.79%	86.14%	84.82%	85.81%

Typicality: General Considerations

Here is a list of general considerations for typicality-based learning:

- To compute a typicality score, an instance must be compared to all other domain instances. This is computationally prohibitive for large datasets.

- Typicality scores need only be computed once for any set of nonvolatile data. Once computed, typicality scores can be used to select subsets of representative training instances from the entire dataset. In this way, accurate models can be built from smaller-sized samples. This is particularly appealing with large sets of data.

- Typicality represents an internal measure of instance quality and can be incorporated without modifications to the structural nature of any data mining model.

- Typicality can be applied to models showing both categorical and numeric output.

- Typicality can be employed to select a best set of examples for use by instance-based learners such as the k-nearest neighbor classifier.

As there is a lack of documented research on the effects of typicality on classification correctness, further experimentation is required to determine the future role instance typicality will play in building supervised learner models.

11.5 Chapter Summary

Time-series analysis concerns itself with data containing a time dimension and usually involves predicting numerical outcomes. Time-series analysis is useful because it allows us to use time as a variable for predicting the future. Both linear and nonlinear techniques can be applied to solve time-series problems. If a linear model shows less than optimal results, a nonlinear model is often a better choice. Caution must be exercised when predicting future outcome with training data containing several fields having predicted rather than actual results.

The success of a Web site ultimately depends on how it is perceived by the user community. Data mining can be applied to help determine perceptions users have about the Web sites they visit. However, Web-based data mining presents a new set of problems not seen with other data mining applications. The data available to us as a result of one or more Web-based user sessions are stored in Web server log files. The content of a typical log file houses information describing clickstream sequences followed by users as they investigate Web pages and follow page links. The greatest challenge of Web-based data mining is seen with taking sever log files and extracting the information needed to create useful data mining models.

Textual data mining involves the extraction of patterns from free text. A basic algorithm for mining data in text format involves creating an attribute dictionary of frequently occurring words, filtering common words known to be of little value, and using the modified dictionary to classify new documents of unknown content. The expansion of the World Wide Web provides a bright future for textual data mining applications.

Multiple-model methods such as bagging and boosting can sometimes improve model performance. Instance typicality can also be applied to help improve classification correctness for supervised learner models.

11.6   Key Terms

Adaptive Web site. A Web site having the ability to semiautomatically improve its internal structure as well as its methods of presentation by learning from visitor access patterns.

Bagging. A supervised learning approach that allows several models to have an equal vote in the classification of new instances.

Boosting. A supervised learning approach that allows several models to take part in the classification of new instances. Each model has an associated weight that is applied toward new instance classification.

Clickstream. A sequence of links followed by a user as the user investigates Web pages and follows page links.

Cookie. A data file placed on a user's computer that contains session information.

Extended common log file format. A format frequently used to store Web server log file information.

Index page. A Web page having links to a set of pages detailing a particular topic.

Index synthesis problem. Given a Web site and a visitor access log, the problem of creating new index pages containing collections of links to related but currently unlinked pages.

Pageview. One or more page files that form a single display window in a Web browser.

Personalization. The act of presenting Web users with information that interests them without requiring them to ask for it directly.

Sequence miner. A special data mining algorithm able to discover frequently accessed Web pages that occur in the same order.

Session. A set of pageviews requested by a single user to a single Web server.

Session file. A file that contains from a few to several thousand session instances.

Time-series problem. A prediction problem with one or more time-dependent attributes.

11.7 Exercises

Review Questions

1. Visit one or more Web sites that contain products or information that interests you. Answer the following questions for each site you visit.

   a. How easy was it to find the information you were looking for?

   b. How much information was provided to you that was of little or no interest?

   c. How many ads were you exposed to? Did the ads have anything to do with what you were looking for?

2. List the similarities and differences between bagging and boosting. State a scenario where a multiple model built with bagging is likely to outperform a model built by applying boosting. State a situation where boosting is likely to outperform bagging.

3. Suppose the typicality scores computed for the instances of a dataset show little variation. Is it likely that bagging or boosting will increase test set classification correctness? Explain your answer. Now, suppose the typicality scores for a second dataset show a large degree of variation. Is it likely that either bagging or boosting will increase classification accuracy? Why or why not?

4. Are bagging or boosting appropriate for time-series problems? Why or why not?

5. Can you see any similarities between bagging and instance typicality?

6. Suggest a data transformation on the attributes of the stock index dataset that will allow data mining algorithms that process only categorical data to be applied to perform time-series analysis.

7. Outline an index page structure for a Web site designed to answer user questions about automotive repair. State several typical paths that a novice user may follow in an attempt to find answers to their automotive repair questions.

Data Mining Questions

LAB 1. Open the file NasdaqDow.xls located in the samples directory. Copy the data to a new spreadsheet file and use Excel's LINEST function together with weeks 3 through 48 to create a linear regression equation to predict Nasdaq weekly average closing prices. Does the regression equation contain one or more of the Dow Jones attributes? Use the regression equation to predict the Nasdaq average closing price for week 49. How does the predicted average close compare to the actual closing price of 2615?

2. Use weeks 3 through 48 of the data provided in NasdaqDow.xls together with the Excel's LINEST function to create a linear regression equation to predict weekly Dow Jones average closing prices. Use the regression equation to predict the Dow Jones average closing price for week 49.

LAB 3. Use your iDA backpropagation neural network software and repeat Data Mining Question #1.

4. Use your iDA backpropagation neural network together with weeks 3 through 44 of the NasdaqDow database to predict the Nasdaq average closing for week 45. Use at least 20,000 training epochs. Next, add the week 45 prediction to your training data and build a neural network to predict the week 46 average Nasdaq closing price. Repeat this process through week 49. How does the week 49 predicted value compare to the actual Nasdaq average close of 2615?

5. Complete the table conversion shown in Table 11.4 through week 49. Use ESX and supervised learning to create a classification model with weeks 3 through 48 as training data. Does ESX correctly predict the Nasdaq Gain/Loss for week 49?

6. Repeat the previous exercise using logistic regression. Be sure to replace gain and loss values with 1s and 0s as appropriate.

7. Here is an exercise for a real sports fan. Develop a time-series model to determine how well a professional football running back will perform in any given week. The problem can be treated as a time-series application by having attributes that relate a given week's performance in terms of the performance of previous weeks. Select an appropriate time lag and choose those attributes you believe to be most predictive of future performance. You may wish to consider attributes such as total yards rushing year to date, average yards rushing per game, and average number of carries per game. You may also want to consider performance measures for the opposing team.

8. Perform a time-series analysis for your favorite stock. Go to yahoo.com to get monthly prices for the stock. Set up a time-series analysis using monthly closing prices for the past five years.

LAB Denotes exercise appropriate for a laboratory setting.

Appendix **A**

The iDA Software

A.1   Software Installation

The instructions for installing the iDA software are given in Chapter 4 and repeated here.

Installing iDA

The software should install correctly with all current versions of MS Excel. However, if you are using MS Office 2000 or Office XP, the macro security level of your implementation may be set at *high*. If this is the case, the software will not install. To check and possibly reset the security level, do the following:

- Open Excel and select *Tools*.

- Mouse to *Macro* then select *Security*.

- If the security setting is *high,* change the setting to *medium* and click *OK*.

- Exit Excel and close all other applications.

The following are the steps for installing iDA:

- Insert the CD that comes with the text into your CD drive.

- Mouse to *Start* and left-click on *Run*.

- Specify your CD drive and type *installiDA.exe*. For example, if your CD drive is D, type: *d:\installiDA.exe*.

- Press *Enter*.

- Select *Next,* read the license agreement, and select *Agree*.

- Select *Finish,* then *OK*.

- Answer *Yes* if asked "Would you like to enable macros?"

- Upon completion, a ReadMe file will appear on your screen. Once you close the file, the installation is complete.

A successful installation adds an iDA dropdown menu item to the Excel spreadsheet environment.

If iDA will not install and your computer is on a network, check your computer to determine if a directory that follows the path c:\Program Files\Microsoft Office\...\Library\ESX has been created. If this directory does not exist, your user privileges likely need to be upgraded by your system administrator before the software can be installed.

Installing Java

Your iDA Neural Network software is written in the Java programming language. Java is an interpreted rather than a compiled language. Because of this, a Java interpreter must be resident on your machine for the neural network software to function. The CD that comes with your book contains a program that will install Java version 1.4 on your computer. To install Java on your system, simply double-click on the *j2sdk_1_4_0-win* icon contained on your install CD and follow the instructions. If the installation is not successful, copy the install program to your desktop and attempt the installation a second time. Alternatively, visit www.javasoft.com and click on *Products & APIs* to download and install the latest version of Java.

Reinstalling iDA

The install program does not check for a preexisting iDA installation and does not automatically uninstall any prior version. Therefore if you are installing a new version of iDA and currently have iDA installed on your system, be sure to run the uninstall program located in the iDA directory. Also, if the samples directory is not deleted during the uninstall, manually delete the directory prior to installing a new version of iDA.

A.2   Uninstalling iDA

To uninstall iDA:

1.   Use Windows Explorer to locate the iDA directory.

2.   Double-click on the red *Uninstall* icon.

3.   Answer *Yes* when asked if you want the application removed from your system.

If one or more files contained within the samples directory have been modified, the uninstall program will not remove the samples folder. However, you can manually remove the samples folder by right-clicking on the folder and clicking on delete. If you are reinstalling the software and do not manually remove a modified samples directory prior to reinstallation, the install program will *not* overwrite the existing samples directory files with the original files.

Finally, an uninstall does not remove the iDA dropdown menu item from your Excel spreadsheet. You need not remove the dropdown menu item before reinstalling the software. However, if you will not be using iDA in the future and wish to remove the iDA dropdown menu item, you can do so as follows:

1. Start Excel.

2. Click the *Tools | Add-Ins* menu item.

3. Uncheck the *Ida* item from the selection box.

4. Exit Excel.

A.3 Software Limitations

The commercial version of iDA is bound by the size of a single Excel spreadsheet, which allows a maximum of 65,536 rows and 256 columns. The iDA input format uses the first three rows of a spreadsheet to house information about individual attributes. Therefore a maximum of 65,533 data instances in attribute-value format can be mined.

As each Excel column holds a single attribute, the maximum number of attributes allowed is 256. The maximum size of an attribute name or attribute value is 250 characters. Also, RuleMaker will not generate rules for more than 20 classes. Although not required, it is best to close all other applications when you are using the iDA software suite of tools. This is especially true for applications containing more than a few hundred data instances.

The student version of iDA allows a maximum of 7000 data instances (7003 rows) and is valid for 180 days after initial installation. The student version does not allow iDA backpropagation neural networks to be saved.

A.4 General Guidelines for Software Usage

Your iDA software has been thoroughly tested on the datasets in the samples directory. Here we provide a few helpful rules to avoid problems mining these or other dataset files:

- Keep the original samples directory files intact. Always copy the contents of a samples directory file to a new workbook and use the data in the new workbook for your data mining experiments.

- As much as possible, limit the number of active processes on your system while a data mining session is executing. For best results, close all other active processes prior to initializing a data mining session.

- MS Excel 2000 and XP users should make sure that any file to be mined has the macro security set at *medium* or *low*.

- When using ESX to perform an unsupervised clustering on a large dataset, use the quick mine feature in order to obtain a best similarity setting.

- Use the quick mine feature with large datasets having several attributes. By doing so, you can quickly determine which attributes should be flagged as unused or display-only for later mining sessions.

A.5   Troubleshooting

This section presents four common problems and their potential remedies.

Cannot Initiate a Data Mining Session

If a data mining session does not initiate, single-click in any spreadsheet cell containing data and try again. If this does not work, copy the spreadsheet data to a new workbook and initiate a new data mining session.

Error Message Says There Is a Column Containing Data but There Is No Attribute Name

Any error that implies that data are contained outside the column limits of the spreadsheet is easily remedied. Simply highlight the area of the spreadsheet that contains the actual data and data declarations. Copy and paste the highlighted area into a new workbook.

Running a Data Mining Session Causes an Illegal Operation Error or Excel Closes

If Excel closes or throws an illegal operation error while running a data mining session, the problem is a data formatting error. The iDA preprocessor is designed to catch most formatting errors. However, it is possible for the preprocessor to miss an unusual data file error. The result of the uncaptured error will likely result in an illegal operation message or termination of the mining session.

To locate the error, first make sure an illegal attribute name is not causing the problem. The likely possibility is that one or more carriage return characters exist in one or more attribute names. One simple way to check for an illegal attribute name is to copy the first five lines of the spreadsheet to a new workbook. Make sure that the fourth and fifth lines contain legal attribute values. Next, initiate a data mining session. If the problem occurs a second time, retype the first three lines of the spreadsheet and try again.

If an illegal attribute name is not causing the problem, the error is most likely one or more illegal values for a numeric attribute. You can test this by declaring all real-valued attributes as categorical-unused. Then, initiate a data mining session. If the session completes, you know that one or several of the numeric attributes contain undetected illegal values. To locate the error, perform several mining sessions, each time reintroducing one or more numeric attributes until the error is observed. In this way, you should be able to locate any attribute(s) having illegal values.

As a final option, try copying a subset of the data to a new workbook. A good strategy is to copy the first half of the dataset to a new workbook and initiate a mining session. If the session completes, you will know the problem exists in the second half of the dataset. You can repeat this process to zero in on the instance or instances causing the problem.

Summary Statistics Are Given for Real-Valued Attributes Declared as Unused

Mean and standard deviation scores for real-valued attributes declared as unused show up in all output summary reports. Be assured that real-valued attributes flagged as unused do not take part in the model building process. To prevent an unused real-valued attribute from appearing in the output reports, declare the unused attribute as categorical.

A.6   Software Support

As time permits, the developers of iDA do respond to a limited number of software issues seen by noncommercial users. Problems dealing with software installation and possible software bugs are two such problems that are addressed by the iDA support personnel. If you are having a software problem that you cannot resolve, you can contact iDA support via e-mail at *info@infoacumen.com*. Alternatively, visit the Web site *www.infoacumen.com* and click on *Contact us* to e-mail software support. Finally, although your software license expires 180 days from your initial install, you are entitled to any upgrades of the student software during the time when your license is in effect. Visit the Infoacumen Web site periodically to download the latest student version of the software.

Appendix **B**

Datasets for Data Mining

In this appendix we provide summary descriptions of the datasets that accompany your iDA software suite of data mining tools. The datasets are stored as Excel files within the iDA samples directory. We also provide several Web sites containing interesting datasets available for free download.

B.1 The iDA Dataset Package

Ten datasets are included with your iDA software package. The following is a description of each dataset.

File names:	**CardiologyCategorical.xls**
	CardiologyNumerical.xls
Domain:	**Medical**
Data source:	Dr. Detrano, VA Medical Center, Long Beach, CA
Web site:	The original data is given at the first Web site listed. A modified form of the dataset can be found at the second listed site.
	http://www1.ics.uci.edu/pub/machine-learning-databases/heart-disease/cleveland.data
	http://www1.ics.uci.edu/pub/machine-learning-databases/heart-disease/cleve.mod
Description:	The dataset consists of 303 instances. Of these instances, 165 hold information about patients who are free of heart disease. The remaining 138 instances contain information about patients who have had a heart attack.
Attributes:	The original dataset contains 13 real-valued (numeric) attributes and a 14th attribute indicating whether or not the patient has a heart condition. The dataset was later modified by Gennari (Gennari and Fisher, 1989). He changed seven of the real-valued attributes to categorical (discrete) equivalents for the purpose of testing data mining tools able to function in domains containing mixed data types. The original data is in CardiologyNumerical.xls. The mixed form of the dataset is in CardiologyCategorical.xls.

File names:	**CreditCardPromotion.xls**
	CreditCardPromotionNet.xls
Domain:	**Credit Card Promotional Offerings**
Description:	This is a hypothetical dataset containing information about credit card holders who have accepted or rejected various promotional

offerings. The dataset is used to illustrate many of the data mining techniques discussed in the text.

Attributes: Each instance contains seven attributes providing information about each customer's age, income, gender, whether the customer has credit card insurance, and whether the customer took advantage of various credit card promotional offerings. The data in the file CreditCardPromotionNet.xls is a numerical transformation of the original dataset.

File name:	**CreditScreening.xls**
Domain:	**Credit Card Applications**
Data source:	The data source is confidential. Dr. Ross Quinlan submitted the data to the listed Web site
Web site:	**http://www1.ics.uci.edu/~mlearn/MLRepository.html**
FTP download:	**ftp://ftp.ics.uci.edu/pub/machine-learning-databases/credit-screening/**
Description:	The file contains data about credit card applications. All attribute names and values have been changed to meaningless symbols to protect confidentiality of the data. The dataset offers a mix of categorical and continuous attributes. The data also has a few missing values. These values are given as blank cells in the Excel spreadsheet.
Attributes:	Each instance contains 15 input attributes and one output attribute. The input attributes have been given arbitrary names. The output attribute is specified as *class.* If the value of *class* is +, the individual received credit card approval. A value of − for the *class* attribute indicates a rejected application.

File name:	**DeerHunter.xls**
Domain:	**Wildlife Management**
Data source:	Dr. John Whitehead, Professor of Economics at East Carolina University
Web site:	The dataset, as well as similar datasets for bass and trout anglers, can be found at **http://personal.ecu.edu/whiteheadj/data/ns/**. Dr. Whitehead also provides a nice introduction to logistic regression at **http://www.csb.uncwil.edu/people/whiteheadj/logit/**.
Description:	The dataset contains information about 6059 individual deer hunters who were asked whether they would have taken any hunting trips during 1991 if the total cost of their trips was a specified amount more than what they had paid for the current

year. Although each instance contains only one increase amount, there are a total of 10 possible dollar increase values ranging from as little as $9 to as much as $953. The original data are part of a survey conducted by the U.S. Fish and Wildlife Service. We obtained a cleaned form of the datafile from Dr. John Whitehead.

Attributes: The cleaned dataset contains 20 input attributes and one output attribute indicating whether the hunter responded positively to the aforementioned question. Attribute explanations are provided in the Excel file containing the data. The attribute *wtname* is a survey weighting variable and should not be used.

File name: **grb4u.xls**
Domain: **Astronomy**
Data source: Fourth Catalog of the Burst and Transient Source Experiment (BATSE) on board the Compton Gamma Ray Observatory
Description: Gamma ray bursts are brief gamma ray flashes whose origins are outside of our solar system. More than 1000 such events have been recorded. The gamma ray burst data in this dataset is taken from the BATSE 4B catalog. The bursts were observed by BATSE aboard NASA's Compton Gamma Ray Observatory between April 1991 and March 1993.
Web site: **http://www.batse.msfc.nasa.gov/batse/grb/catalog/**
Attributes: Although many attributes have been measured for these bursts, the dataset is limited to seven attributes. Attribute *burst* gives the burst number, *T90* and *50* measure burst duration (burst length), *P256* and *fluence* measure burst brightness, and *HR321* and *HR32* measure burst hardness. For additional information about these attributes, visit the BATSE Web site.

File name: **NasdaqDow.xls**
Domain: **Finance**
Data source: The Web sites give the Nasdaq and Dow Jones closing prices in downloadable spreadsheet format. You are given options for start and end dates as well as whether the information is to be summarized by day, week, or month.
Web site: **http://chart.yahoo.com/d?s=^IXIC**
http://chart.yahoo.com/d?s=^DJI
Description: The data is a time-series representation of average weekly closings for the Nasdaq and the Dow Jones Industrial Average. The

first table entry shows the average weekly close for the Nasdaq as 4176.753 for week 3 of the year 2000.

Attributes: *Week* gives the year and week of the year. The third week of the year 2000 is represented by 200003. *Nasdaq Av. Close* and *Dow Av. Close* represent respective average closing prices for the current week. *Nasdaq Av. Close −1* and *Dow Av. Close −1* are average closing prices for the previous week. Likewise, *Nasdaq Av. Close −2* and *Dow Av. Close −2* are average closing prices for two weeks prior to the current week.

File name: **SpineData.xls**
Domain: **Medical**
Data source: A metropolitan area spine clinic
Description: The dataset contains information about patients who have had back surgery.
Attributes: The dataset contains 31 attributes. Several attributes relate to the current health status of the patient. Other attributes offer information about general patient characteristics (sex, height, weight, etc.).

File names: **sonar.xls** (supervised)
sonaru.xls (unsupervised)
Domain: **LandSat Image Data**
Data source: Civco (1991)
Description: The dataset contains pixels representing a digitized satellite image of a portion of the earth's surface. The training and test data consist of 300 pixels for which ground truth has been established. These data have been classified into 15 categories: Urban, Agriculture 1, Agriculture 2, Turf/Grass, Southern Deciduous, Northern Deciduous, Coniferous, Shallow Water, Deep Water, Marsh, Shrub Swamp, Wooded Swamp, Dark Barren, Barren 1, and Barren 2. Each category contains approximately 20 instances.
Attributes: Each pixel is represented by six numeric values consisting of the multispectral reflectance values in six bands of the electromagnetic spectrum: blue (0.45–0.52 m), green (0.52–0.60 m), red (0.63 –.069 m), near infrared (0.76–0.90 m), and two middle infrared (1.55–1.75 and 2.08–2.35 m).

File name: **Titanic.xls**

Domain:	**Large–Scale Tragedy**
Data source:	Dawson (1995)
Web site:	**http://www.amstat.org/publications/jse/ jse_data_archive.html**
Description:	The dataset contains 2201 instances. Each instance describes attributes of an individual passenger or crew member aboard the Titanic.
Attributes:	The input attributes include the class, sex, and age of the individual. The output attribute indicates whether the passenger or crew member survived.

File name:	**UsTemperatures.xls**
Domain:	**Weather**
Data source:	Peixoto (1990)
Web site:	**http://lib.stat.cmu.edu/DASL/Datafiles/**
Description:	The dataset offers the normal average January minimum temperature in degrees Fahrenheit for 56 U.S. cities. The data were collected from 1931 through 1960. The daily minimum temperatures in January were computed by adding daily temperatures and dividing by 31. Then, the averages for each year were averaged over the 30-year period.
Attributes:	Each instance has one attribute containing the city and state abbreviation, one attribute holding the average January minimum temperature in degrees Fahrenheit from 1931 to 1960, one attribute giving the latitude of the city in degrees north from the equator, and one attribute stating the longitude in degrees west of the prime meridian.

B.2   Web Sites Containing Datasets for Mining

A wealth of datasets for data mining can be found on the Internet. With a little help from the sites listed in this section, you can have fun exploring the Web for interesting data. The majority of data files listed at the Web sites are not in iDAV format. In fact, you will find that many of the datasets consist of three files. One file containing the data, a second file holding the names of the attributes associated with the data, and a third file describing the data. It will be your job to convert the data to iDAV format. Also, missing attribute values are usually represented in the datasets with a question mark. Be sure to replace any question mark characters that represent missing data items with blank spaces.

DASL

DASL (pronounced "dazzle") is a Web site offering well over 100 datasets for illustrating basic statistical methods. Several of the datasets are appropriate for data mining. Many datasets contain as few as two attributes and have less than 100 instances. The data is conveniently tab delimited. The Web address for DASL is **http://lib. stat.cmu.edu/DASL/Datafiles/**.

StatLib, a statistical data and software distribution site is the parent directory for the DASL Web site. Statlib links to several additional datasets of interest. The Web site for StatLib is **http://lib.stat.cmu.edu/**.

MLnet Online Information Service

Mlnet Online Information Service (MLnet OiS) is a repository of useful information about data mining and knowledge discovery, knowledge acquisition, and case-based reasoning. The Web address for the Mlnet library is **http://www.mlnet.org/**.

The link **http://www.mlnet.org/cgi-bin/mlnetois.pl/?File=datasets.html** offers a list of downloadable datasets for data mining. Several interesting data files are available, including datasets about database marketing, clickstream analysis, and textual data mining.

Several free and commercial data mining software tools are available at **http://www.mlnet.org/cgi-bin/mlnetois.pl/?File=software.html**.

KDNuggets

KDNuggets is the leading information repository for data mining and knowledge discovery. The site includes information on data mining—companies, software, publications, courses, datasets, and more. The home page of the Kdnuggets Web site is **http://www.kdnuggets.com**. The following Kdnuggets site provides links to popular datasets from several domains: **http://www.kdnuggets.com/datasets/index.html**.

UCI Machine Learning Repository

The UCI Machine Learning Repository contains a wealth of data from several domains. The UCI home page address is **http://www1.ics.uci.edu/~mlearn/MLRepository.html**. The FTP archive site for downloading the datasets in the UCI library is **ftp://ftp.ics.uci.edu/pub/machine-learning-databases/**. The following address offers a summary description of each of the downloadable datasets: **http://www1.ics.uci.edu/~mlearn/MLSummary.html**.

JSE Data Archive

The *Journal of Statistics Education* is an international journal on teaching and learning about statistics. The journal's Web site is **http://www.amstat.org/publications/jse/toc.html**. The Web site supports a data archive containing several interesting data mining applications. The address for the data archive is **http://www.amstat.org/publications/jse/jse_data_archive.html**.

Bibliography

Agrawal, R., Imielinski, T., and Swami, A. (1993). Mining Association Rules Between Sets of Items in Large Databases. In P. Buneman and S. Jajordia, eds., *Proceedings of the ACM Sigmoid International Conference on Management of Data*, New York: ACM.

Baltazar, H. (1997). Tracking Telephone Fraud Fast. *Computerworld,* 31, 11, 75.

Baltazar, H. (2000). NBA Coaches' Latest Weapon: Data Mining. *PC Week,* March 6, 69.

Brachman, R. J., Khabaza, T., Kloesgen, W., Pieatetsky-Shapiro, G., and Simoudis, E. (1996). Mining Business Databases. *Communications of the ACM,* 39, 11, 42–48.

Breiman, L. (1996). Bagging Predictors. *Machine Learning,* 24, 2, 123–140.

Breiman, L., Friedman, J., Olshen, R., and Stone, C. (1984). *Classification and Regression Trees.* Monterey, CA: Wadsworth International Group.

Buchanan, B., Sutherland, G., and Feigenbaum, E. (1969). Heuristic DENDRAL: A Program for Generating Explanatory Hypotheses in Organic Chemistry. In B. Meltzer, D. Michie, and M. Swann, eds. *Machine Intelligence* (vol. 4). Edinburgh, Scotland: Edinburgh University Press, 209-254.

Case, S., Azarmi, N., Thint, M., and Ohtani, T. (2001). Enhancing E-Communities with Agent-Based Systems. *Computer,* July, 64–69.

Chester, M. (1993). *Neural Networks—A Tutorial.* Upper Saddle River, NJ: PTR Prentice Hall.

Civco, D. L. (1991). Landsat TM Land Use and Land Cover Mapping Using an Artificial Neural Network. In *Proceedings of the 1991 Annual Meeting of the American Society for Photogrammetry and Remote Sensing.* Baltimore, MD., 3, 66–77.

Cox, E. (2000). Free-Form Text Data Mining Integrating Fuzzy Systems, Self-Organizing Neural Nets and Rule-Based Knowledge Bases. *PC AI,* September–October, 22–26.

Dasgupta, A., and Raftery, A. E. (1998). Detecting Features in Spatial Point Processes with Clutter via Model-based Clustering. *Journal of the American Statistical Association,* 93, 441, 294–302.

Dawson, R. (1995). The "Unusual Episode" Data Revisited. *Journal of Statistics Education*, 3, 3.

Dempster, A. P., Laird, N. M., and Rubin, D. B. (1977). Maximum-Likelihood from Incomplete Data via the EM Algorithm (with Discussion). *Journal of the Royal Statistical Society*, Series B, 39, 1, 1–38.

Dixon, W. J. (1983). *Introduction to Statistical Analysis,* 4th ed. New York: McGraw-Hill.

Duda, R., Gaschnig, J., and Hart, P. (1979). Model Design in the PROSPECTOR Consultant System for Mineral Exploration. In D. Michie, ed., *Expert Systems in the Microelectronic Age.* Edinburgh, Scotland: Edinburgh University Press, 153–167.

Durfee, E. H. (2001). Scaling Up Agent Coordination Strategies. *Computer*, July, 39–46.

Dwinnell, W. (1999). Text Mining Dealing with Unstructured Data. *PC AI,* May–June, 20–23.

Edelstein, H. A. (2001). Pan for Gold in the Clickstream. *Information Week*, March 12.

Fayyad, U., Haussler, D., and Stolorz, P. (1996). Mining Scientific Data. *Communications of the ACM,* 39, 11, 51–57.

Fisher, D. (1987). Knowledge Acquisition via Incremental Conceptual Clustering. *Machine Learning,* 2, 2, 139–172.

Freund, Y., and Schapire, R. E. (1996). Experiments with a new boosting algorithm. In Saitta, L., ed., *Proc. Thirteenth International Conference on Machine Learning.* San Francisco, CA: Morgan Kaufmann, 148–156.

Gardner, S. R. (1998). Building the Data Warehouse. *Communications of the ACM,* 41, 9, 52–60.

Gennari, J. H., Langley, P., and Fisher, D. (1989). Models of Incremental Concept Formation. *Artificial Intelligence*, 40, (1-3), 11–61.

Giarratano, J., and Riley, G. (1989). *Expert Systems: Principles and Programming.* New York: PWS-Kent.

Gill, H. S., and Rao, P. C. (1996). *The Official Guide to Data Warehousing.* Indianapolis, IN: Que Publishing.

Giovinazzo, W. A. (2000). *Object-Oriented Data Warehouse Design (Building a Star Schema).* Upper Saddle River, NJ: Prentice Hall.

Granstein, L. (1999). Looking for Patterns. *Wall Street Journal,* June 21.

Haag, S., Cummings, M., and McCubbrey, D. (2002). *Management Information Systems for the Information Age,* 3rd ed. Boston: McGraw-Hill.

Holland, J. H. (1986). Escaping Brittleness: The Possibilities of General Purpose Learning Algorithms Applied to Parallel Rule-Based Systems. In R. S. Michalski, J. G. Carbonell, and T. M. Mitchell, eds. *Machine Learning: An Artificial Intelligence Approach* (vol. 2). San Mateo, CA: Morgan Kaufmann, 593-623.

Hosmer, D. W., and Lemeshow, S. (1989). *Applied Logistic Regression.* New York: John Wiley & Sons.

Huntsberger, D.V. (1967). *Elements of Statistical Inference.* Boston, MA: Allyn and Bacon.

Inmon, W. (1996). *Building the Data Warehouse.* New York: John Wiley & Sons.

Jain, A. K., Mao, J., and Mohiuddin, K. M. (1996). Artificial Neural Networks: A Tutorial. *Computer,* March, 31–44.

Kass, G.V. (1980). An exploratory technique for investigating large quantities of categorical data. *Applied Statistics,* 29, 119–127.

Kimball, R., Reeves, L., Ross, M., and Thornthwaite, W. (1998). *The Data Warehouse Lifecycle Toolkit: Expert Methods for Designing, Developing, and Deploying Data Warehouses.* New York: John Wiley & Sons.

Kohonen, T. (1982). Clustering, Taxonomy, and Topological Maps of Patterns. In M. Lang, ed. *Proceedings of the Sixth International Conference on Pattern Recognition,* Silver Spring, MD: IEEE Computer Society Press, 114–125.

Lashkari, Y., Metral, M., and Maes, P. (1994). Collaborative Interface Agents. In *Proceedings of the Twelfth National Conference on Artificial Intelligence,* Menlo Park, CA: American Association of Artificial Intelligence, 444–450.

Lewis, M. (1998). Designing for Human–Agent Interaction. *AI Magazine,* 19, 2, 67–78.

Lloyd, S. P. (1982). Least Squares Quantization in PCM. *IEEE Transactions on Information Theory,* 28, 2, 129–137.

Long, S. L. (1989). *Regression Models for Categorical and Limited Dependent Variables.* Thousand Oaks, CA: Sage Publications Inc.

Maclin, R., and Opitz, D. (1997). An Empirical Evaluation of Bagging and Boosting, *Fourteenth National Conference on Artificial Intelligence,* Providence, RI: AAAI Press.

Maiers, J., and Sherif, Y. S. (1985). Application of Fuzzy Set Theory. *IEEE Transactions on Systems, Man, and Cybernetics,* SMC-15, 1, 41–48.

Mamdani, E. H., and Asssilian, S. (1975). An Experiment in Linguistic Synthesis with a Fuzzy Logic Controller. *International Journal of Man-Machine Studies,* 7, 1, 1–13.

Manganaris, S. (2000). Estimating Intrinsic Customer Value. *DB2 Magazine,* 5, 3, 44–50.

McCarthy, V. (1997). Strike It Rich! *Datamation,* 43, 2, 44–50.

McCulloch, W. S., and Pitts, W. (1943). A Logical Calculus of the Ideas Imminent in Nervous Activity. *Bulletin of Mathematical Biophysics,* 5, 115–137.

Mena, J. (2000). Bringing Them Back. *Intelligent Enterprise,* 3, 11, 39–42.

Merril, D. M., and Tennyson, R. D. (1977). *Teaching Concepts: An Instructional Design Guide.* Englewood Cliffs, NJ: Educational Technology Publications.

Mitchell, T. M. (1997). Does Machine Learning Really Work? *AI Magazine,* 18, 3, 11–20.

Mobasher, B., Cooley, R., and Srivastava, J. (2000). Automatic Personalization Based on Web Usage Mining. *Communications of the ACM,* 43, 8, 142–151.

Mukherjee, S., Feigelson, E. D., Babu, G. J., Murtagh, F., Fraley, C., and Rafter, A. (1998). Three Types of Gamma Ray Bursts. *Astrophysical Journal,* 508, 1, 314–327.

Payne, T., and Edwards, P. (1997). Interface Agents that Learn: An Investigation of Learning Issues in a Mail Agent Interface. *Applied Artificial Intelligence,* 11, 1, 1–32.

Peixoto, J. L. (1990). A property of well-formulated polynomial regression models. *American Statistician,* 44, 26–30.

Perkowitz, M., and Etzioni, O. (2000). Adaptive Web Sites. *Communications of the ACM,* 43, 8, 152–158.

Quinlan, J. R. (1994). Comparing Connectionist and Symbolic Learning Methods. In Hanson, S. J., G. A. Drastall, and R. L. Rivest, eds., *Computational Learning Theory and Natural Learning Systems*, Cambridge, MA: MIT Press, 445–456.

Quinlan, J. R. (1986). Induction of Decision Trees. *Machine Learning,* 1, 1, 81–106.

Quinlan, J. R. (1993). *Programs for Machine Learning.* San Mateo, CA: Morgan Kaufmann.

Rich, E., and Knight, K. (1991). *Artificial Intelligence,* 2nd ed. New York: McGraw-Hill.

Roiger, R. J., and Cornell, L. D. (1996). Selecting Training Instances for Supervised Classification. In *Proceedings ISAI/IFIS, IEEE-TAB Products Group*, November, 150–155.

Roiger, R. J., and Cornell, L. D. (1992). An Induction-Based Model for Classification of Landsat Data. *International Archives of Photogrammetry and Remote Sensing*, 29, 3, 651–655.

Senator, T. E., Goldbert, H. G., Wooten, J., Cottini, M. A., Khan, A. F. U., Klinger, C. D., Llamas, W. M., Marrone, M. P., and Wong, R. W. H. (1995). The Financial Crimes Enforcement Network AI System (FAIS): Identifying Potential Money Laundering from Reports of Large Cash Transactions. *AI Magazine*, 16, 4, 21–39.

Shannon, C. E. (1950). Programming a Computer for Playing Chess. *Philosophical Magazine,* 41, 4, 256–275.

Shavlik, J., Mooney, J., and Towell, G. (1990). Symbolic and Neural Learning Algorithms: An Experimental Comparison (Revised). Tech. Rept. No. 955, Computer Sciences Department, University of Wisconsin, Madison, WI.

Shortliffe, E. H. (1976). *MYCIN: Computer-Based Medical Consultations.* New York: Elsevier Press.

Spiliopoulou, M. (2000). Web Usage Mining for Web Site Evaluation. *Communications of the ACM ,* 43, 8, 127–134.

Summers, E. (1990). ES: A Public Domain Expert System. *BYTE,* October, 289.

Sycara, K. P. (1998). The Many Faces of Agents. *AI Magazine,* 19, 2, 11–12.

Turing, A. M. (1950). Computing Machinery and Intelligence. *Mind* 59, 433–460.

Vafaie, H., and DeJong, K. (1992). Genetic Algorithms as a Tool for Feature Selection in Machine Learning. In *Proc. International Conference on Tools with Artificial Intelligence.* Arlington, VA. IEEE Computer Society Press, 200–205.

Weiss, S. M., and Indurkhya, N. (1998). *Predictive Data Mining: A Practical Guide.* San Francisco, CA: Morgan Kaufmann.

Widrow, B., Rumelhart, D. E., and Lehr, M. A. (1994). Neural Networks: Applications in Industry, Business and Science. *Communications of the ACM,* 37, 3, 93–105.

Widrow, B., and Lehr, M. A. (1995). Perceptrons, Adalines, and Backpropagation. In M. A. Arbib, ed., *The Handbook of Brain Theory and Neural Networks.* Cambridge, MA: MIT Press, 719–724.

Winston, P. H. (1992). *Artificial Intelligence,* 3rd ed. Reading, MA: Addison-Wesley.

Witten, I. H., and Frank, E. (2000). *Data Mining: Practical Machine Learning Tools and Techniques with Java Implementations.* San Francisco, CA: Morgan Kaufmann.

Zadeh, L. (1965). Fuzzy Sets. *Information and Control* 8, 3, 338–353.

Index

COMMERCIAL SOFTWARE UPGRADE OFFER: $1,495

BENEFITS INCLUDE:

- Faster data mining execution time;
- Enhanced report generation capabilities;
- Unrestricted lifetime single user license;
- Process up to 65,533 instances (rows);
- Neural networks can be saved and applied to unknown data;
- Re-rule feature which allows creating multiple rule sets with ease;
- Detailed on-line User's Guide.

Normally, iData Analyzer is sold as part of a package which includes an implementation and support component. The minimum charge for this package is $4,995. As a purchaser of Data Mining, A Tutorial-Based Approach, you are entitled to upgrade the publisher's edition of the software that accompanies this text for only $1,495. To purchase the commercial upgrade, simply fill out the form at *www.infoacumen.com/order*. This upgrade allows for the unrestricted use of iData Analyzer for your commercial applications

Information Acumen Corp.
13570 Grove Dr., #155
Maple Grove, MN 55311-4400
www.infoacumen.com
info@infoacumen.com